CHILD PHONOLOGY

Volume 1
Production

This is a volume in

PERSPECTIVES IN

NEUROLINGUISTICS, NEUROPSYCHOLOGY, AND PSYCHOLINGUISTICS

A Series of Monographs and Treatises

A complete list of titles in this series appears at the end of this volume.

CHILD PHONOLOGY

Volume 1
Production

Edited by

GRACE H. YENI-KOMSHIAN

Department of Speech and Hearing Sciences
University of Maryland
College Park, Maryland

JAMES F. KAVANAGH

Center for Research for Mothers and Children
National Institute of Child Health and Human Development
National Institutes of Health
Bethesda, Maryland

CHARLES A. FERGUSON

Department of Linguistics
Stanford University
Stanford, California

ACADEMIC PRESS 1980
A Subsidiary of Harcourt Brace Jovanovich, Publishers
New York London Toronto Sydney San Francisco

Proceedings of a conference in a series entitled *Communicating by Language*, sponsored by the National Institute of Child Health and Human Development.

ACADEMIC PRESS, INC.
111 Fifth Avenue, New York, New York 10003

United Kingdom Edition published by
ACADEMIC PRESS, INC. (LONDON) LTD.
24/28 Oval Road, London NW1 7DX

Library of Congress Cataloging in Publication Data
Main entry under title:

Child phonology.

(Perspectives in neurolinguistics and psycho-
linguistics)
Proceedings of a conference convened by the
National Institute of Child Health and Human
Development, May 28–31, 1978, at the National
Institutes of Health, Bethesda, Md.
Includes bibliographies and index.
CONTENTS: v. 1. Production.
1. Language acquisition––Congresses. 2.
Grammar, Comparative and general––Phonology––
Congresses. I. Yeni–Komshian, Grace H.
II. Kavanagh, James F. III. Ferguson, Charles
Albert, Date. IV. United States. National
Institute of Child Health and Human Development.
[DNLM: 1. Speech––In infancy and childhood––
Congresses. 2. Phonetics––Congresses. 3.
Language development––Congresses.
WS105.5.C* C537 1978]
P118.C46   401'.9   80–981
ISBN 0–12–770601–1 (vol. 1)

PRINTED IN THE UNITED STATES OF AMERICA

80 81 82 83   9 8 7 6 5 4 3 2 1

CONTENTS

Chapter 4

Auditory versus Articulatory Phonological Processes and Their Development in Children

H. STEPHEN STRAIGHT

Chapter 5

Stages of Speech Development in the First Year of Life

RACHEL E. STARK

Chapter 6

The Emergence of the Sounds of Speech in Infancy

D. K. OLLER

LIST OF CONTRIBUTORS

Numbers in parentheses indicate the pages on which the authors' contributions begin.

GEORGE D. ALLEN (227), Dental Research Center, University of North Carolina, Chapel Hill, North Carolina 27514

KAY ATKINSON-KING (277), McLean,Virginia

LYNDA CHRISTENSEN (169), Department of Speech and Hearing, California State University, Hayward, California 94542

HAROLD CLUMECK (257),* Department of Linguistics, Stanford University, Stanford, California 94305

CHARLES A. FERGUSON (1), Department of Linguistics, Stanford University, Stanford, California 94305

SARAH HAWKINS (227),† Dental Research Center, University of North Carolina, Chapel Hill, North Carolina 27514

DAVID INGRAM (169), Department of Linguistics, University of British Columbia, Vancouver, B.C. Canada V6T 1W5

JAMES F. KAVANAGH, Center for Research for Mothers and Children, National Institute of Child Health and Mental Development, National Institutes of Health, Bethesda, Maryland 20205

* Present Address: Department of Speech and Language Pathology, Northwestern University, Evanston, Illinois 60201

† Present Address: Department of Communication Disorders, Emerson College, Boston, Massachusetts 02116

PHILIP LIEBERMAN (113), Department of Linguistics, Brown University, Providence, Rhode Island 02912

JOHN L. LOCKE (193), Department of Hearing and Speech Sciences, University of Maryland, College Park, Maryland 20742

MARLYS A. MACKEN (143), Department of Linguistics, Stanford University, Stanford, California 94305

PETER F. MacNEILAGE (9), Departments of Linguistics and Psychology, University of Texas at Austin, Austin, Texas 78712

LISE MENN (23), Psychology Service, Boston Veterans Administration Hospital, Boston, Massachusetts 02132

PAULA MENYUK (211), Applied Psycholinguistics Program, Boston University, Boston, Massachusetts 02215

D. KIMBROUGH OLLER (93), Mailman Center for Child Development, University of Miami, Miami, Florida 33101

RACHEL E. STARK (73), The John F. Kennedy Institute and Johns Hopkins University School of Medicine, Baltimore, Maryland 21205

H. STEPHEN STRAIGHT (43), Department of Anthropology and Program in Linguistics, State University of New York at Binghamton, Binghamton, New York 13901

SHARON VEACH (169), Department of Linguistics, Stanford University, Stanford, California 94305

BRENDAN WEBSTER (169), Idlewild Children's Center, Los Gatos, California 95030

GRACE H. YENI-KOMSHIAN (1), Department of Hearing and Speech Sciences, University of Maryland, College Park, Maryland 20742

PREFACE

The importance of the study of child phonology for the sciences dealing with speech sounds is only slowly being recognized, and the field is a relatively new area of systematic investigation. Typical of a new field, this one clearly shows its multidisciplinary origins. Researchers in this field come from different disciplines, and their professional identities and research methods differ correspondingly. During the past 10 years there has been active research in child phonology, and the findings are penetrating established areas in linguistics, psychology, and speech science. Acknowledging the need for an interdisciplinary conference, the National Institute of Child Health and Human Development (NICHD) convened a conference on child phonology at the National Institutes of Health in Bethesda, Maryland, May 28–31, 1978, the seventh in the NICHD series on "Communicating by Language." The series has led to such publications as *The Genesis of Language* and *Language by Ear and by Eye*.

All the participants in the conference have a strong interest in phonology—the study of human speech sounds. Except for a few, all have conducted research on some aspect of child phonology. Some participants, better known for their work in adult phonology, were invited to explore how certain aspects of phonology in adults relate to child phonology. Each participant was invited to prepare a paper addressing a specific topic in one of the following areas: speech production, speech perception, and the relationship between perception and production. The papers were prepared prior to the meeting and following the conference the participants were provided with time to revise their papers. This two-volume work is based on the revised papers, however a few of the original papers were omitted and one was added.

The main focus of Volume 1 is on production and in Volume 2 it is on perception. Both volumes contain chapters on aspects of the relationship between perception and production. The two volumes may be viewed as a unitary publication on child phonology in which theoretical and methodological issues are discussed, including a fairly detailed presentation of recent research findings. Since a variety of disciplines are represented, the publication provides different perspectives on how children acquire the phonology of their language(s). Normal acquisition is emphasized, although some aspects of deviation are also addressed. Each volume contains a glossary of terms that also contains a table of phonetic symbols.

We would like to thank Victoria Fromkin, Jerry Punch, and Suzanne Bennett for their advice on technical problems in phonology, and we gratefully acknowledge the help of Daphene Cave, Linda Hale, and Janet Thomson for preparing the manuscript for publication.

CONTENTS OF VOLUME 2

Chapter 1

AN INTRODUCTION TO SPEECH PRODUCTION IN THE CHILD

CHARLES A. FERGUSON AND GRACE H. YENI-KOMSHIAN

The use of language is one of the most distinctive characteristics of the human species, and human language behavior has fascinated many investigators from a wide array of different scientific, scholarly, and philosophical interests. One part of human language behavior, which is to a considerable extent autonomous (i.e., it can be analyzed separately from all the rest), is the pronunciation; the speech sounds themselves as articulated and perceived by human beings in their use of language. The study of pronunciation—*phonetics,* as it is commonly called—is a well-developed field of research making use of a great variety of methods of investigation and has produced an impressive body of knowledge. A somewhat narrower view for the study of speech sounds focuses on linguistically relevant sound differences, sound types, and the rules or processes operating among them; this is usually called *phonology.* Unfortunately, our technical terminology has no term that unambiguously includes all systematic study of human speech sounds, whether traditionally regarded as phonetics, phonology, or something else. We are using the word phonology here as a cover term for this purpose to suggest that what we are interested in are speech sounds as they function in human language rather than speech sounds as samples of acoustic phenomena or of human physiology without reference to language.

Ten years ago it would have been hard to predict the explosion of child phonology research that has taken place. New questions to ask, new hy-

CHILD PHONOLOGY
VOLUME 1: PRODUCTION

potheses, and new technologies have led to surprising bursts of activity, the most obvious being the extensive work on infant speech discrimination that was set off by the well-known report of Eimas *et al.* (1971) and the spate of phonological analyses of children's speech output between about 1:6–4 years of age that appeared after the English translation of Jakobson's *Kindersprache* (1968). It is a good time to pause and take stock of child phonology, and it is our hope that this volume and the accompanying volume on *Perception* will lead to the clarification of major issues and the identification of promising lines of research, whether in continuation of present efforts or in new directions.[1]

Phonological analysis of child speech production during the last 10 years started with theory about adult language and applied it to children. The phonological production research, concerned with the structure of whole phonological systems, falls into three fairly distinct phases, related to successive dominant phonological theories: structuralist, generative, and post-generative. As recently as 10 years ago, most research was in the structuralist tradition of phonological analysis and was directly influenced by Jakobson's views on a universal order of phonological development and a set of universal "laws of irreversible solidarity" that underlie the acquisition or loss of phonology in individuals, as well as diachronic phonological change in languages. Most phonologists at the time, however, were not interested in either acquisition or dissolution, and the phonological theorists of the preceding decades (except for Jakobson) had made no claims about child phonology. But at that very time, generative phonology, the new theoretical model, was rapidly winning the day, at least in the United States, and the new theory was explicitly related to child language development. The classic treatment of generative phonology, Chomsky and Halle's *The Sound Pattern of English* (1968, although it had circulated in earlier versions for several years) referred to language acquisition in a number of places, and most of the linguistic research on child language during the period from 1968 to 1973 was in the generative framework. At the present time, a variety of phonological theories are vying for dominance, most of them representing attempts to repair inadequacies in the classic generative model. A number of these theories are tied to child phonology, either because they assume that

---

[1] The very active field of child phonology research has no good basic book that can be counted upon to present a comprehensive treatment of the major issues and the present state of knowledge. The five books that may be regarded as candidates all suffer from serious defects: Winitz, 1969; Olmsted, 1971; Smith, 1973; Ingram, 1976; and Blache, 1978. Of these, Winitz contains much of value but is riddled with contradictions and misinterpretations of psycholinguistic research. Olmsted presents only one theoretical perspective and is based almost completely on a single cross-sectional study. Smith is highly sophisticated in linguistic analysis but is based entirely on one longitudinal study of a single child, his son. Ingram offers a useful summary of normal development but is principally directed to the analysis of "deviant" phonologies. Finally, Blache is conceived as an elucidation of Jakobson's views; it ignores most post-Jakobson work in phonology and is highly selective in its choice of child phonology studies.

learnability by children is the basic determinant of phonological structure, or because they accept data from child language development research as important evidence for the validation of phonological theory.

During the structuralist period, the predominant form of linguistically oriented child phonology research was the diary study, in which the development of one or two children was followed over a period of months or years, and the usual foci of interest were the order of acquisition of phonemes or oppositions and the nature of the substitutions of child sounds for adult phonemes. The studies of this period generally assumed that the child's phonology was systematically related to the adult phonology but, in important respects, constituted a system of its own that changed phonetically and phonologically over time in much the same way that languages change historically (Ferguson, 1968). The most detailed and informative study from this period is Leopold's four-volume work on his daughter Hildegard (Leopold, 1939–1947); Volume 2 is devoted to phonological development and still serves as a mine of data for theorists to exploit. Leopold's material is arranged for access by word, by adult target sounds, or by the child's sounds; he lists patterns of substitution, discusses order of acquisition, and examines the child's development from the perspectives of a broad range of European and American psychological, pedagogical, and linguistic literature. Leopold had done most of his data collection and had completed his first volume before *Kindersprache* appeared, but for the remainder of his work he took Jakobson as the prime theoretician for phonological development. It is worth noting that those child phonologists who accepted the main outline of the Jakobson framework suggested specific modifications in it on the basis of their data. For example, Leopold (1953) and Velten (1943) allowed more flexibility in the early sequence of consonant acquisition than was included in Jakobson's model.

During the generative period, a new kind of study emerged; the psycholinguistic "experiment," in which data are collected from one or more children and analyzed with some aspect of phonological theory in mind. In these studies, the experimenter usually is looking for evidence that the theory (or a particular aspect of the theory) is right, in contrast to other theories or possible theories. A typical example is the study by Kazazis (1969) that attempted to support the validity of the abstract underlying representations posited by phonologists for Modern Greek. Interest in simple description, apart from theory testing or theory formulation, declined and the papers that aroused the most interest were those such as Kornfeld (1971) that explored issues of generative theory, or Stampe (1969) that argued for a new model of phonology. The most impressive study in the Chomsky–Halle framework, however, was Smith's (1973) detailed, sophisticated diary study of his son's phonological development, which seems likely to remain a landmark. Like Leopold's study, it continues to serve as a source of data for others, and its theoretical arguments are required reading for child phonologists. The principal points of Smith's position are these: The child does not have a system of its own, and its phonology can be analyzed usefully only in relation to the adult system. The child has, at an early age, full perceptual mastery of the adult phonological oppositions and has lexical representations equivalent to the adult surface forms. The child's pronunciation falls short of the adult's because of lack of mastery of the necessary articulatory processes. The child's phonological system includes a set of ordered *realization rules* that apply to the underlying representations to yield the pronunciation. A major part of the child's phonological development consists of steady improvement in these rules, which are held to have psychological reality. No claims are made about the earliest stages of development, and no suggestions are offered as to how the child's representations develop at a later period to attain the abstract level that generative phonology posits for the adult representations.

Several important issues generally were ignored in the literature on phonological analysis of child speech, among them the relation of perception to production, the development from babbling to speech, and the clues that deviant phonological development could offer for the understanding of normal phonology. Phonological analysts either disregarded perception completely or offered perceptual data more or less as anecdotal evidence of children's having more abstract representations than their productions would indicate. Babbling was ignored chiefly because of the powerful influence of Jakobson, who had asserted the existence of a decisive and significant discontinuity between babbling and speech, the former being play and practice without linguistic structure, typically exhibiting a wide range of sounds compared to the reduced but highly structured beginnings of "true speech." Delayed or otherwise deviant child phonology was not examined by phonologists for the same reasons that linguists have not shown much interest in abnormal phonological phenomena in general, apart from some attention to aphasia. All these issues have been explored in more recent work, and they are treated at some length in this volume.

The present period of postgenerative child phonology study is marked by a great variety of topics and approaches. One of the most common types is the descriptive study of particular phenomena that are related to theoretical points in phonology but are not represented as arguments for a general theory. Sample topics are voice onset time (VOT) (e.g., Gilbert, 1975), phonotactic constraints (e.g., Greenlee, 1974 on consonant clusters), and tones (Li and Thompson, 1977). Current studies do not hesitate to make central use of concepts that are marginal to classical generative theory or are even incompatible with it, such as the syllable (Branigan, 1976), the word (Ferguson and Farwell, 1975), or the prosody (Vihman, 1978).

Although the total number of phonological analysts working primarily with children's speech production is still rather small, their output is considerable, and a significant number of linguists, normally concerned with other aspects of language, make profitable forays into child phonology. The study of one's own child is still a common example of this; it may be a simple, one-shot analysis of an interesting phenomenon, such as Priestly (1977), or a detailed longitudinal study, such as Labov and Labov (1978). Priestly's paper gave just one more example of an idiosyncratic strategy for handling words of more than one syllable (a generalized output of CVjVC), yet the data were so persuasive, the strategy so unusual, and the description so thorough and insightful, that it has become the standard reference for this phenomenon. The Labovs' (1978) paper gave an astonishingly detailed analysis of the complete speech output of their daughter for a 5-month period when the overwhelming majority of her utterances were either *cat* or *mama* (over 5000 occurrences of each in the corpus). This well-documented study is replete with spectrograms, phone trees, charts, and tables, and shows how one child gradually acquired a miniphonology, only to dismantle it and start over again in the third year. Diary studies, however, are not the only contribution the nonspecialist linguist makes to our understanding of phonological development. A fine example of another kind of study is the recent investigation of the syllable by Soviet linguists (Vinarskaja *et al.* 1977). These scholars were concerned by the very varied theoretical models of syllable division in current linguistics, experimental phonetics, and neurophysiology, and they turned to child language for evidence. After eliciting over 4500 responses from 59 children 2–10 years of age, they concluded that Russian children make use of quite varied models of syllable division and speculated that this great variability (even in the same child) might be related to the failure of linguists to agree on a single model of the syllable. Intended as evidence for linguistic models in general, the study provided welcome information on child phonology and developmental trends in an area that is rarely explored.

Finally, a new type of study has emerged: the attempt to struggle with the incompatibilities between formal theory and the rapidly accumulating data (e.g., Braine, 1974; Drachmann, 1976; Kiparsky and Menn, 1978). These articles differ from many of the earlier ones in that they tend to use the child data to revise or extend linguistic theory rather than simply to provide confirmation of a theory. By the authors' admission, they are not completely successful; however, the struggles are advancing our understanding of child phonology.

The chapters in this volume are at least as varied as the kind of studies just listed, and there are chapters on issues that have not been mentioned above. One common theme in almost all the chapters is a reaction, to a greater or lesser extent, to the ideas put forth by Jakobson. The authors have added new data, modified the ideas and, in many instances have challenged or significantly reinterpreted Jakobson's original formulations. There is no mistaking the tendency, however, for investigators to begin to present their own findings without direct reference to Jakobson. The field of child phonology is becoming more sophisticated and more rigorous. Above all, it is becoming broader in scope, richer in content, and is developing rapidly.

A successor conference on child phonology 10 years hence, we can be fairly certain, will regard this one as limited and unsure of itself, but we can hope that many of the solid themes of that conference will have been adumbrated in these chapters.

The following three chapters present distinctly different theoretical overviews. The chapter by MacNeilage contains a discussion of certain aspects of the control of speech production by adults and children from the point of view of physiological and acoustic phonetics. In contrast, Menn's chapter is a critical evaluation of phonological theory in relation to child phonology from the point of view of linguistics. The question of the nature of the relationship between speech production and speech perception is discussed by Straight in his chapter, and he argues for the separation of the mechanisms involved in production and perception.

The next two chapters are concerned with a detailed analysis of vocalization types produced during the first year of life. Although Stark's and Oller's chapters differ in the details of the categories of vocalization types and the number of stages they have delineated, both authors stress the interdependency of the stages and the continuity between babbling and early speech.

The next five chapters discuss various aspects of the development of segmental phonemes. Lieberman's chapter is on an acoustic analysis of the vowels produced by young children; Macken's chapter is on the acquisition of initial stop consonants in children raised in different language environments; and the chapter by Ingram, Christensen, Veach, and Webster is on the developmental course of the production of fricatives and affricates in English speaking children. Discussions of production errors at the segmental level are presented by Locke in his chapter on the prediction of child speech errors from an analysis of infant vocalizations and adult speech perception; and Menyuk stresses the importance of specifying the linguistic and situational contexts in which a child's speech production and perception is examined.

The last two chapters deal with suprasegmental aspects of child phonology, an area that has not been studied extensively. Allen and Hawkins inform the reader on phonological rhythm, its definition and development; and Clumeck's chapter on the acquisition of tone includes a review of the relevant literature for various tone languages and focuses on his own work on the acquisition of Mandarin Chinese.

The technical terms and phonetic notations used in this volume and the accompanying volume on *Perception* are defined in the Glossary and the table of phonetic symbols prepared by Atkinson-King.

References

Blache, S.E. (1978) *The Acquisition of Distinctive Features*, University Park Press, Baltimore.
Braine, M.D.S. (1974) "On What Might Constitute Learnable Phonology," *Language*, 50. 270–299.

Branigan, G. (1976) "Syllabic Structure and the Acquisition of Consonants: The Great Conspiracy in Word Formation," *Journal of Psycholinguistic Research*, 5, 117–133.

Chomsky, N., and Halle, M. (1968) *The Sound Pattern of English*, Harper & Row, New York.

Drachmann, G. (1973) "On the Notion 'Phonological Rule'," *Ohio State University Working Papers in Linguistics*, 15, 134–145.

Eimas, P.D., Siqueland, E.R., Jusczyk, P., and Vigorito, J. (1971) "Speech Perception in Infants," *Science*, 171, 303–306.

Ferguson, C.A. (1968) "Contrastive Analysis and Language Development," *Georgetown University Monograph Series on Languages and Linguistics*, 21, 101–112.

Ferguson, C.A., and Farwell, C.B. (1975) "Words and Sounds in Early Language Acquisition, *Language*, 51, 419–439.

Gilbert, J.H.V. (1975) "A Voice Onset Time Analysis of Apical Stop Production," *Journal of Child Language*, 4, 103–110.

Greenlee, M. (1974) "Interacting Processes in the Child's Acquisition of Stop–Liquid Clusters," *Papers and Reports in Child Language Development* (Linguistics, Stanford University) 7, 85–100.

Ingram, D. (1976) *Phonological Disability in Children*, Elsevier, New York.

Jakobson, R. (1968) *Child Language, Aphasia, and Phonological Universals*, Mouton, The Hague. (English translation of *Kindersprache, Aphasie and Allgemeine Lautgesetze*, Uppsala, 1941).

Kazazis, K. (1969) "Possible Evidence for (Near-) Underlying Forms in the Speech of a Child," *Papers of the 5th Regional Meeting, Chicago Linguistic Society*.

Kiparsky, P., and Menn, L. (1978) "The Acquisition of Phonology," in J. McNamara, ed., *Language and Thought*, Academic Press, New York.

Kornfeld, J.R. (1971) "Theoretical Issues in Child Phonology," *Papers of the 7th Regional Meeting, Chicago Linguistic Society*, 454–468.

Labov, W., and Labov, T. (1978) "The Phonetics of *Cat* and *Mama*," *Language*, 54, 816–852.

Leopold, W.F. (1939–1947) *Speech Development of a Bilingual Child: A Linguist's Record* (4 Vols.), Northwestern University Press, Chicago.

Leopold, W.F. (1953) "Patterning in Children's Language Learning," *Language Learning*, 5, 1–14.

Li, C.N., and Thompson, S.A. (1977) "The Acquisition of Tone in Mandarin-Speaking Children," *Journal of Child Language*, 4, 185–199.

Olmsted, D.L. (1971) *Out of the Mouth of Babes*. Mouton, The Hague.

Priestly, T.M.S. (1977) "One Idiosyncratic Strategy in the Acquisition of Phonology," *Journal of Child Language*, 4, 45–65.

Smith, N.V. (1973) *The Acquisition of Phonology: A Case Study*, Cambridge University Press, London.

Stampe, D. (1969) "The Acquisition of Phonetic Representation," *Papers of the Fifth Regional Meeting, Chicago Linguistic Society*, 443–455.

Velten, H.V. (1943) "The Growth of Lexical and Phonemic Patterns in Infant Language," *Language*, 19, 281–292.

Vihman, M. (1978) "Consonant Harmony: Its Scope and Function in Child Language," in J.H. Greenberg *et al.*, eds., *Universals of Human Language*, Stanford University Press, Stanford, Calif.

Vinarskaja, E.N., Lepskaja, N.I., and Bogomazov, G.N. (1977) "Rules of Syllable Division and Models of the Syllable (on the Basis of Material from Child Speech)," in *Problems of Theoretical and Experimental Linguistics*, Moscow University Press, Moscow. pp. 5–20 (in Russian).

Winitz, H. (1969) *Articulatory Acquisition and Behavior*, Appleton-Century-Crofts, New York.

Chapter 2

THE CONTROL OF SPEECH PRODUCTION

PETER F. MacNEILAGE

The primary purpose of this chapter is to give some indication of the present state of knowledge concerning the control of speech production by adults. In a final section, the question of acquisition of control by children will be briefly addressed.

Much of the recent work on the control of speech production in adults has been devoted to the search for simple yet general explanations of three aspects of control: (a) the control of individual movements or gestures associated with particular segments; (b) the coordination of these gestures; and (c) the timing of sequences of gestures. I will briefly consider these three aspects in turn.

The Control of Individual Gestures

The first hypothesis on this matter to receive wide attention was the view of the Haskins Laboratories group that, with a few exceptions, each individual phoneme was produced by a single set of invariant (context independent) "motor commands (Liberman *et al.*, 1967)." Thus control signals were considered to be entirely open loop and for the most part related in a one-to-one way with linguistically defined units—the phonemes. The well-

CHILD PHONOLOGY
VOLUME 1: PRODUCTION

known allophonic variation of the representation of phonemes, in various contexts and with changes in stress and speaking rate, was considered to be due "to mechanical and neuromuscular limitations of the production apparatus and temporal overlap in commands [MacNeilage, 1972, p. 40]." This view has been found to be untenable by numerous studies showing that the motor commands reaching the muscle (as recorded by electromyogram, EMG) for a given phoneme are context dependent (MacNeilage, 1972). And, in retrospect, it is easy to see that they must be, given that the phoneme-related movements must have different origins dependent upon the identity of the previous phoneme. For example, tongue movements for an alveolar stop must differ according to tongue position for the previous vowel.

Another group of theorists focused on the fact that the *results* of gestures associated with a given phoneme (i.e., the positions achieved by them) remained relatively invariant in different contexts and suggested, therefore, that gestures were controlled in terms of the specification of invariant goals or targets. I suggested in 1970 that these goals or targets could be points specified within an internalized space coordinate system of the kind that Lashley (1951) considered to underlie all movement control (MacNeilage, 1970). One indirect argument for this view is that *visual*–motor coordination is certainly guided by an abstract conception of space, and, therefore, the *auditory*–motor coordination of speech may be also. In addition, control of the speech apparatus in the absence of an auditory component, as in the acts of mastication, and in perception of oral stereognosis, would seem to require an abstract spatial analysis mechanism.

Informal evidence of the controlling role of goal or target specification during speech can be obtained by observing a speaker speaking with clenched teeth. Under this condition, acoustic output seems to be minimally impaired, suggesting that goals are successfully approximated, even though extensive compensatory articulation is probably required. More formal evidence comes from Lindblom and his colleagues who have twice performed an experiment in which subjects were required to produce vowels with bite blocks up to 25 mm in size between the teeth (Lindblom, Lubker, and Gay, 1978; Lindblom and Sundberg, 1971). They found that, immediately after bite-block insertion, subjects achieved the correct formant frequencies in the first pitch period of the subsequent vowel. A subsequent midsagittal X ray of these subjects during vowel production, with a bite block inserted, showed close approximations to normal *vocal-tract shapes*. This result suggests that, even under the bite-block condition, articulators may be successfully controlled by invariant spatial goals or targets. However, in an experiment in which Folkins and Abbs (1975) unpredictably impeded jaw-elevation movements associated with closure for a bilabial stop, the *upper* lip responded with compensatory lowering, resulting in bilabial closure at a different (lower) point in space than was normally observed. Such a finding suggests that the specification of goals or targets may not be in terms of absolute space, in this case, but in terms of some other end such as articulator contact or intraoral pressure buildup. In addition, goals specified in terms of pressure would seem to be plausible in the respiratory system, where relatively constant subglottal pressure is preserved during speech, using widely varying patterns of muscular forces (Hixon *et al.*, 1976).

The results of the Folkins and Abbs (1975) study were important not only in terms of the nature of the compensation but in showing that compensation began to occur as soon as 30 msec after the disturbance was introduced. This showed that the system is capable of *on-line* compensation. This ability was also shown in a study by Hughes and Abbs (1976), in which the lips and the mandible were observed to operate reciprocally during a single production to ensure a relatively invariant end point to lip-closure movements. The nature and limits of this on-line compensatory ability of the production-control system are only beginning to be explored.

In recent years, a number of writers have emphasized the possible role of *auditory* targets in speech-gesture control (e.g., Ladefoged *et al.*, 1972; Nooteboom, 1970). Informal evidence for the necessity of auditory targets, in some sense of the term, is quite conclusive. The auditory information provided by our language community is the only source of goals for our acquisition of speech production. A given auditory goal sometimes is achieved in a single subject by more than one spatial configuration of the speech apparatus. For example, single intervocalic [p] is produced in English with vocal-fold abduction (Lisker *et al.*, 1969). But cluster-initial intervocalic [p] as in "upbringing" is produced in some subjects by vocal-fold adduction (glottal stop; Westbury, personal communication). Thus the auditory goal remains invariant, in this case, at the expense of variation in spatial configurations. Further evidence for the relation between internalized auditory standards and movement control comes from an experiment by Riordan (1977). She reported that, if rounding gestures of the lips are mechanically prevented, compensatory larynx lowering to achieve the lengthening of the vocal tract necessary to produce the formant frequencies of rounded vowels occurs. This result shows that the control mechanism is capable of going beyond shape constancy to achieve auditory constancy.

The kinds of targets discussed so far are *static* targets. But, when I produce the diphthong /au/, there is no evidence that any static auditory or spatial target is being aimed at. In the period during which formant frequencies are relatively unaffected by preceding and following segments, the second formant for /au/ is in continuous motion. The perceptual importance of the dynamic properties of formant transitions, even for vowels, leads us to believe that some specification of dynamic properties must underlie the talker's production of them. Of course, close specification of the dynamics of speech movements is always made by the talker in an utterance, whether or not it has any obvious perceptual consequences. Thus the issue to be raised here, to which we will return later, is the relation between static and dynamic aspects of the operation of the system.

In conclusion, it must be conceded that we still know very little about the control of individual gestures. What we have done so far is little more than to point to aspects or consequences of gestures that possess invariance, and suggest that the goal of the control system must be to achieve that invariance. How such invariances are achieved remains quite unclear.

One thing that needs to be emphasized about much of the experimental evidence cited so far is the amazing compensatory ability of the speech-production system in normal adults. It would be a mistake simply to use this ability as a source of evidence on how the production system is constructed. Compensation is the normal mode of operation of the system. Typically, we do not talk while sitting otherwise motionless in front of a microphone, but in the context of intermittent changes in what can be loosely called the postural configuration of the speech apparatus. We talk equally well standing up or lying down, and, as Hixon *et al.* (1976) have shown, we can preserve comparable subglottal pressure levels under the two conditions, even though the effect of gravity, particularly on the abdominal contents, requires two quite different motor-control patterns for the two different postures. A lecturer can "speak across" sizable up–down movements of the head if he is reading text, and across sizable lateral head movements if he is using a blackboard. Lateral head movements are typical in a small group of speakers. I could go on and on citing the changes we choose to impose on ourselves while speaking. It is possible that, to some extent, these changes are simply superimposed on the ongoing speech control and produce acoustic perturbations that the perceptual system can surmount. But I believe many of them require off-line feedforward compensatory strategies in the production-control mechanism. The fact that the mechanism has *chosen* to solve this problem is one of the most central facts we have in attempting to constrain a speech-production-control model. It certainly constrains us to reject models in which the means of speech-production control have a simple and fixed relation to either underlying linguistically defined units on the one hand, or observable ends of the production process on the other.

The Coordination of Gestures

The main concept associated with this issue is that of coarticulation. The term *coarticulation* denotes an overlap in the production of gestures for successive segments of an utterance. Overlap in *adjacent* segments is, of course, inevitable as the speech-production apparatus cannot move instantaneously from one configuration to another. Coarticulation effects on *non-adjacent* segments have been of most interest because of the hope that the precise temporal scope of these effects would provide us with an understanding of the roles of various linguistically defined units in the later stages of the speech-production process. Two directions of coarticulation are relevant here; right-to-left or anticipatory, and left-to-right or perseveratory effects.

First, just as we have found that the motor control of the surface manifestation of phonemes (segments or allophones) was not invariant in terms of the precise form of the gestures composing it, we also find that it is not invariant in terms of temporal aspects of coarticulation. All the gestures for a segment do not always begin together, and they do not always begin a fixed time before they have their greatest effect. For example, Benguerel and Cowen (1974) found that lip rounding for a front-rounded vowel in French may begin 5–6 segments before the tongue-body gestures for that vowel begin to affect tongue position. Furthermore, the actual time relation between the beginning of rounding and the beginning of the tongue-body gestures varied with context, mainly due to variability in the amount of right-to-left coarticulation of rounding. Thus, in this case as in many others, one gesture associated with a segment can be independently variable with respect to the others. This provides a temptation to regard the rounding gesture as a distinctive feature and to treat coarticulation as the spreading of the feature to neighboring segments that do not take a minus value for that feature. Data from Benguerel and Cowan (1974) are not consistent with this hypothesis. They observed that anticipatory rounding often began, during an *unrounded* vowel, seven segments before the rounded vowel. Other counterexamples to this feature-spreading view have also have been noted (Kent and Minifie, 1977).

Coarticulation has often been found to cross syllable boundaries whether boundaries are defined conventionally, or in terms of the end of each vowel as suggested by Kozhevnikov and Chistovich (1965), though occasional counterexamples to this phenomenon have been claimed. A number of examples of coarticulation crossing word boundaries in continuous speech have been observed. The only clear counterexample that I know of has some interesting theoretical implications. Ghazelli (1977) has made a cinefluorographic study of coarticulation, in Arabic, of the secondary articulation, called "pharyngealization." Pharyngealization is a movement of the tongue toward the superior-posterior pharynx. Ghazelli observed that coarticulation of pharyngealization does not cross word boundaries in either a right-to-left or a left-to-right direction, though it can extend for as many as seven segments in either direction. Furthermore, it *always* coarticulates back to the immediately previous word boundary and (except for being impeded, to various degrees across dialects, by a high front vowel) always coarticulates ahead to the next word boundary. Such a result may best be thought of as not involving coarticulation in the sense of a relatively low-level co-ordination of segments, but, instead, of involving minimal pairs, in terms of a pharyngealization feature, at the lexical-item level.

The most general conclusion to be derived from studies of coarticulation is that coarticulation does not necessarily respect any hypothetical unit boundary in continuous speech. This conclusion seems to be equally true for right-to-left and for left-to-right effects.Even formulations of rules governing the scope of coarticulation, in terms of the mechanical compatibility of the coarticulatory gesture and gestures for other segments, are not uniformly successful. Coarticulatory tongue fronting has been reported in segments requiring tongue backing (Kent and Moll, 1972), and coarticulatory jaw lowering has been reported in segments requiring jaw elevation (Sussman *et al.*, 1973). The only variable that always seems to restrict coarticulation successfully, apart from pauses, is what Kent and Minifie (1977) have called "immediate successional impact" defined in acoustic terms. They cite the example of the word "snooze," in which vowel rounding can and does exhibit right-to-left coarticulation without changing the immediate successional impact of [s] or [n], but nasalization cannot coarticulate with [s] without changing the acoustic impact of the segment. Thus they argue that "the basic temporal plan for motor control of articulation is determined by the transitions that have immediate successional impact [p. 131]." They cite some evidence that the onsets of coarticulated gestures without immediate successional impact are synchronized with onsets of other gestures. This seems to be a promising hypothesis, though it still requires an objective, universally applicable definition of immediate successional impact, presumably in perceptual terms.

The Timing of Sequences of Gestures

It has been generally agreed that the temporal control of speech production is the result of the interaction of two major components; (*a*) a specification of basic properties of segments including targets, perhaps intrinsic segment durations, and maybe coarticulation rules; and, (*b*) a superimposed timing component that systematically shapes observed segment durations and sometimes target attainment as a function of a number of variables. I want to consider briefly three of these variables: utterance length; stress, in languages in which it has durational consequences; and tempo, or speaking rate. For the most part, I will simply be presenting results that depart from what I will call the most straightforward expectation, and that need explanation.

The most straightforward way in which a timing program could interact with a set of base values for segments, in terms of duration, would be an equal decrease in duration of each segment proportional to the amount of change in the values of the three variables; utterance length, stress, and speaking rate. This is the way segments on a phonograph record would respond to changes in revolutions per minute (rpm) of the turntable. Obtained results differ from this outcome in a number of ways.

First consider utterance length. In an impressive series of experiments on Swedish (discussed collectively in Lindblom, et al., 1977), Lindblom and his colleagues found that segments were shorter in duration in longer utterances. Utterance was defined in three ways; (a) number of segments in a syllable; (b) number of syllables in a word; and (c) phrase length. Results differed from the most straightforward outcome in a number of ways. Segments showed incompressibility in that they did not shorten beyond a certain minimum value. Amount of shortening was greater for vowels than it was for consonants. Utterance-final syllables were always much longer than others, as they are in English, and shortening depended in an asymmetrical way on amount of preceding and following context. The effect of number of following syllables was greater than that of number of preceding syllables. Lindblom et al. (1977) presented the hypothesis that asymmetrical shortening effects may be side effects of the operation of a limited capacity short-term memory store underlying speech production. Although many aspects of Lindblom's results have been observed in other languages, it is not yet known whether the existence of all effects described is universal or even widespread.

Segment durations are shorter in unstressed syllables than they are in stressed syllables in a number of languages. Again the vowel is more affected than the consonant. Vowel targets are undershot in unstressed syllables, and this is at least partly a result of active reorganization of muscle activity rather than an inertial effect due to the smaller amount of time available for movement. If there are underlying targets for vowels, they may be changed in unstressed syllables with respect to their values for stressed syllables; undershoot of the stressed vowel target may simply be "tolerated" in the unstressed case.

There seem to be two types of results in studies of speaking rate. The subject of Lindblom's initial study (1963) and some of Kuehn's (1973) subjects behaved as they would for unstressed vowels and showed undershoot of target values at increased speaking rates. The remainder of Kuehn's subjects and the subjects in a study by Gay (1977) did not show undershoot; and in Kuehn's study, in which movements were measured, articulator velocities were higher at the faster rate. It seems conceivable that which of these results is observed depends on the subject's tacit assumptions about the need to speak precisely or to communicate clearly in the experimental situation.

Phonology and Speech Production

In accordance with the concern with phonology in this monograph, some specific comments should perhaps be made about the relation between phonology and control of speech production. It is obvious that there has been, for the most part, no straightforward correspondence between phonological concepts such as phoneme, distinctive feature, syllable, word, and the main findings and hypotheses discussed here. At the single-gesture level, the motor-command hypothesis of a one-to-one relation between the phoneme and the motor-system's output was rejected, and postural requirements were considered to prevent any simple relation between underlying units and output. The possible utility of biologically defined surrogates of phonological units, namely, goals or targets, was considered without a decisive outcome. The question of whether these surrogates should complement or replace abstract underlying phonological units such as the phoneme or feature has been a neglected issue in the field.

A main finding in the discussion of coarticulation has been the independence of coarticulation from any phonologically defined boundary. In the consideration of timing, vowel–consonant differences have emerged strongly but not in terms of any property that has been explicated in phonological theory. Central concerns have been biological and cognitive issues such as the status of targets in unstressed syllables, the role of short-term memory underlying production, and the possibility of alternative strategies for the control of speaking rate.

An Alternative View

Perhaps the solution to, or at least a new perspective on, many of the problems I have considered will come from an alternative view of the speech-production process, according to which all of the views I have expressed so far are misguided. The view arises from what has come to be known as action theory, which has as its aim a general theory of coordinated movement. (Perhaps a better term at present would be action metatheory, as it consists primarily of ideas about the form that a theory of action should take.) Action theory was originated primarily by the Russian physiologist Bernstein (1967) and has been developed in this country particularly by Greene (1972), Turvey (1977), and, with respect to speech, by Fowler (1977, Fowler et al., 1978). The theory calls for a radical reformulation of the theory of speech production. Current speech-production theories that assume underlying units and elaborate processes governing the surface manifestation of these units are dubbed "translation theories [Fowler et al., 1978, p. 387]." These theories are considered to be unnecessary as the linguistic units are, in some sense, directly and invariantly represented in the output and do not exist independently of that representation. Temporal and spatial aspects of control are regarded as being integral to each other and, therefore, are not to be considered separately. The two components of current models (the basic segmental specification and timing schemes) are thus also considered integral to each other, and timing is described as intrinsic rather than as extrinsic. This means that the timing-determined properties of the output arise naturally from its intrinsic organization.

The central concept of action theory is that of "coordinative structure." A coordinative structure (Turvey, *et al.*, 1978) is defined as "a set of muscles, often spanning many joints, that is constrained to act as a unit [p. 563]." These structures are considered to be established by biasings of reflex circuits referred to as "tunings." Some properties of coordinative structures are modulable; "For example, rate of walking and gait are modulable properties of the muscle systems that determine walking [Fowler,.1977, p. 206]." The constraints arising from the coordinative structures are considered to determine directly what effects the modulable properties will have on movement. For example, I assume speaking rate would be a modulable property of the coordinative structures governing speech production, and thus its effects would arise directly from those structures rather than from being imposed on them from an external source. An act such as utterance

> is believed to be governed by functionally embedding (as opposed to temporally concatenating) coordinative structures. Each nesting level delimits a broader equivalence class of movements than the finer grain level nested within. . . . The more coarse grained nesting levels are established by altering the relationships among smaller coordinative structures, and at the same time they act as constraints on the lower ones [Fowler *et al.*, 1978, p. 28].

For example, in Fowler's (1977) analysis, the most coarse-grained coordinative structure embodies an entire utterance, and at the other extreme four coordinative structures are proposed for vowels.

A good candidate for one of the most coarse-grained coordinative structures could be one that is responsible for maintaining a relatively constant level of subglottal pressure during a single expiratory phase. One coordinative structure for vowels is considered closely analogous to the state underlying the voluntary assumption of a certain fixed joint angle at the elbow, by a human subject, and the maintenance of that angle in the face of various loads (Asatryan and Fel'dman, 1965). The subject is considered to adopt an arbitrary "zero-state" of the joint–muscle system, thus creating a system with spring–mass properties. The production of /ɛ/ is considered to be achieved partly by the imposition of a "zero-state of the extrinsic tongue system [Fowler, *et al.*, 1978, p. 71]" that will produce tongue elevation following /æ/, but tongue depression following /i/.

It is obviously not possible to do justice to this new theoretical orientation in the space available here. The theory is provocative in its attempt to place speech production in a general biological perspective, and in its implication that speech production is by no means special. Nevertheless, it is my overall impression that the relation between traditional theories of speech production and action theory has so far only been loosely defined, and that the value of the analogies made between speech and other coordinated-movement sequences needs to be carefully scrutinized. The specific consequences of action theory for speech production have not yet been well established. For example, are changes in vowels with stress and speaking rate consistent in form with some specific coordinative structures with specific modulable properties? Is what is descriptively labeled as "undershoot," a result of changes in the coordinative structures or in the effects of modulable properties? How does the theory handle the case mentioned earlier of two opposite movement *outcomes* (abduction and adduction) in the achievement of voicelessness for /p/? Do short-term memory constraints influence the operation of coordinative structures?

It is to be hoped that these and many other problems will be fruitfully addressed as the implications of action theory for speech become clearer, and the interface between action theory and traditional ideas about speech-production control becomes more clearly defined.

Acquisition of Speech-Production Control

As Ferguson and Yeni-Komshian have pointed out in the introductory chapter of this volume, there are two main areas of study of child speech: (a) the experimental study of speech perception; and (b) intensive case studies of individual children, using phonetic transcription, and the construction of phonological-rule systems from the observed sound patterns. There has been virtually no study of the phonetics of speech production analogous to that described in this chapter for adults. This is partly due to methodological problems. The child's cooperation in producing long inventories of careful utterances in the presence of transducers is limited, and experimenters eschew the use of invasive techniques on children. But there is another reason: The extremely influential theory of language acquisition put forward by Jakobson (1941) diverted interest from phonetic aspects of child speech production by the assertion that these aspects were irrelevant to the acquisition of speech. As is well known, Jakobson proposed that learning to speak consisted of learning a set of linguistic contrasts between sounds. This he regarded as "a purely linguistic matter" and different, for example from sound use in babbling, which was for him a question "of external phonetics, predominantly articulatory in nature [p. 27]." In the past few years, not only has Jakobson's contrast-based theory been called into question (Ferguson and Garnica, 1973; Kiparsky and Menn, 1977) but a number of lines of evidence have suggested a powerful role of speech-production control capabilities (Jakobson's external articulatory phonetics) in the shape and development of early speech. Oller *et al.* (1976) and others (e.g., Cruttenden, 1970; Menyuk, 1968) have shown an extremely close relation between the sounds and sound sequences of babbling, even the earliest babbling (6–8 months) and the sounds and sequences used in the first words. As to sounds, aspirated stops, fricatives, and liquids are rare in babbling and in first words, while unaspirated stops, nasals, and glides are frequent in both. As to sequences (or phonotactic constraints), consonant clusters and final consonants (especially voiced final consonants) are rare in babbling and in first words, while initial consonants are common in both. Oller *et al.* conclude: "After examining our data on babbling it is possible to predict quite accurately the nature of the most commonly reported substitutions and deletions which occur in meaningful child speech [1976, p. 9]."

It is extremely probable that the rigid constraints on the form of early babbling just described are primarily production-based in nature and do not arise primarily from selectivity in perception of adult segmental sound forms and adult phonotactic patterns. Consequently, in terms of the framework used earlier to describe adult speech production, preferences among individual sounds reflect facts about *control* of single gestures, and phonotactic preferences reflect facts about *control* of coarticulation, though in a somewhat broad sense that would include phonatory and respiratory influences. In addition, there are at least two other well-known facts about child speech that seem to be directly relevant to the question of control of coarticulation. These are the presence of assimilations (e.g., doggy → [gɔgi]) and the preferences for reduplicated forms (biscuit → [be: be:] [Waterson, 1971]). Kiparsky and Menn (1977) point out that such rules "increase the redundancy of the articulatory instructions in the word [p. 59]." Presumably *coarticulatory* instructions share in this increase in redundancy.

There has been virtually no work done on the timing of speech production in young children. However, a study by Smith (1978) suggests that, even by the age of 3, the relative durations of different segments (e.g., in stops differing in place of articulation, stressed versus unstressed syllables, final versus nonfinal syllables) are, for the most part, virtually identical to those of adults, although segments in general are about 30% longer than those of adults. These results suggest somewhat surprisingly that by age 3 a child has learned most of the adult timing rules.

Study of children's compensatory ability might prove to be a useful probe of the extent to which their speech-production control approximates that of adults, in that it may not be as well developed as other aspects of the child's speech control might lead one to expect. No formal studies have been reported on this question.

Finally, one aspect of child speech seems particularly amenable to an action theory approach. Chapters 5 and 6 by Stark and Oller in this volume add to an increasing body of evidence that the child's first words follow a long and, for the most part, orderly series of stages of prelinguistic vocalization that are quite stereotyped in nature, and occur in the absence of model vocalizations of others. These vocalizations would seem to be pure manifestations of mechanisms of the biology of movement, and their understanding, either in terms of their mechanisms or their role as precursors to speech production, would presumably place useful constraints on theories of speech-movement control.

References

Asatryan, D., and Fel'dman, A. (1965) "Functional Tuning of the Nervous System with Control of Movement or Maintenance of a Steady Posture—I. Mechanographic Analyses of the Work of the Joint on Execution of a Postural Task," *Biophysics*, 10, 925–935.

Benguerel, A.-P., and Cowan, H.A. (1974) "Coarticulation of Upper Lip Protrusion in French," *Phonetica*, 30, 41–55.

Bernstein, N. (1967) *The Coordination and Regulation of Movements*, Pergamon Press, London.

Cruttenden, A. (1970) "A Phonetic Study of Babbling," *British Journal of Disorders of Communication*, 5, 110–118.

Ferguson, C.A., and Garnica, O.K. (1975) "Theories of Phonological Development," in E.H. Lenneberg and E. Lenneberg, eds., *Foundations of Language Development: A Multidisciplinary Approach* (Vol. 1), Academic Press, New York, pp. 153–180.

Folkins, J.W., and Abbs, J.H. (1975) "Lip and Jaw Motor Control during Speech Responses to Resistive Loading of the Jaw," *Journal of Speech and Hearing Research*, 18, 207–220.

Fowler, C. (1977) "Timing Control in Speech Production," Unpublished Doctoral Dissertation, University of Connecticut.

Fowler, C.A., Rubin, P., Remez, R.E., and Turvey, M.T. (1978) "Implications for Speech Production of a General Theory of Action," in B. Butterworth, ed., *Language Production*, Academic Press, New York.

Gay, T. (1977) "The Effect of Speaking Rate on Vowel Formant Movements," *Haskins Laboratories Status Report* SR 51–52, 101–118.

Ghazelli, S. (1977) "Back Consonants and Backing Coarticulation in Arabic," Unpublished Doctoral Dissertation, University of Texas at Austin.

Greene, P.H. (1972) "Problems of Organization of Motor Systems," in R. Rosen and F. Snell, *Progress in Theoretical Biology* (Vol. 2), Academic Press, New York, pp. 304–322.

Hixon, T.J., Mead, J., and Goldman, M.D. (1976) "Dynamics of the Chest Wall during Speech Production: Function of the Thorax, Rib Cage, Diaphragm, and Abdomen," *Journal of Speech and Hearing Research*, 19, 297–356.

Hughes, O.M., and Abbs, J.H. (1976) "Labial–Mandibular Coordination in the Production of Speech: Implications for the Operation of Motor Equivalence," *Phonetica*, 33, 199–221.

Jakobson, R. (1968) *Kindersprache, Aphasie, und Allgemeine Lautegesetze*, Almqvist and Wicksell, Uppsala, 1941. Reprinted as *Child Language, Aphasia, and Phonological Universals*, Mouton, The Hague.

Kent, R.D., and Minifie, F.D. (1977) "Coarticulation in Recent Speech Production Models," *Journal of Phonetics*, 5, 115–134.

Kent, R.D., and Moll, K.L. (1972) "Tongue Body Articulation during Vowel and Diphthong Gestures," *Folia Phoniatrica*, 24, 286–300.

Kiparsky, P., and Menn, L. (1977) "On the Acquisition of Phonology," in J. Macnamara, ed., *Language Learning and Thought*, Academic Press, New York.

Kozhevnikov, V.A., and Chistovich, L., eds., (1965) "Speech: Articulation and Perception," Washington Clearing House for Federal, Scientific, and Technical Information, *JPRS*, 30, 543.

Kuehn, D.P. (1973) "A Cinefluorographic Investigation of Articulatory Velocities," Unpublished Doctoral Dissertation, University of Iowa.

Ladefoged, P., DeClerk, J., Lindau, M., and Papcun, G.A. (1972) "An Auditory–Motor Theory of Speech Production," *UCLA Working Papers in Phonetics*, 22, 48–75.

Lashley, K.S. (1951) "The Problem of Serial Order in Behavior," in L.A. Jeffress, ed., *Cerebral Mechanism in Behavior, The Hixon Symposium*, Wiley, New York.

Liberman, A.M., Cooper, F.S., Shankweiler, D.P., and Studdert-Kennedy, M. (1967) "Perception of the Speech Code," *Psychological Review*, 74, 431–461.

Lindblom, B.E.F. (1963) "Spectrographic Study of Vowel Reduction," *Journal of the Acoustical Society of America*, 35, 1773–1781.

Lindblom, B., Lubker, J., and Gay, T. (1979) "Formant Frequencies of some Fixed-Mandible Vowels and a Model of Speech Motor Programming by Predictive Simulation," *Journal of Phonetics*, 1, 147–161.

Lindblom, B., Lyberg, B., and Holmgren, K. (1977) "Durational Patterns of Swedish Phonology: Do they Reflect Short-term Memory Processes?" (Unpublished manuscript).

Lindblom, B.E.F., and Sundberg, J. (1971) "Neurophysiological Representation of Speech Sounds," Paper presented at the Fifteenth World Congress of Logopedics and Phoniatrics. Buenos Aires, Argentina, August.

Lisker, L., Abramson, A.S., Cooper, F.S., and Schvey, M.H. (1969) "Transillumination of the Glottis in Running Speech," *Journal of the Acoustical Society of America*, 45, 1544–1546.

MacNeilage, P.F. (1970) "Motor Control of Serial Ordering of Speech," *Psychological Review*, 77, 182–196.

MacNeilage, P.F. (1972) "Speech Physiology," in J.H. Gilbert, ed., *Speech and Cortical Functioning*, Academic Press, New York, pp. 1–72.

Menyuk, P. (1968) "The Role of Distinctive Features in Children's Acquisition of Phonology," *Journal of Speech and Hearing Research*, 11, 138–146.

Nooteboom, S. (1970) "The Target Theory of Speech Production," *IPO Annual Progress Report*, 5, 51–55.

Oller, D.K., Wieman, L.A., Doyle, W.J., and Ross, C. (1976) "Infant Babbling and Speech," *Journal of Child Language*, 3, 1–11.

Riordan, C.J. (1977) "Control of Vocal-tract Length in Speech," *Journal of the Acoustical Society of America*, 62, 998–1002.

Smith, B.L. (1978) "Temporal Aspects of Speech Production: A Developmental Perspective," *Journal of Phonetics*, 6, 37–68.

Sussman, H.M., MacNeilage, P.F., and Hanson, R.J. (1973) "Labial and Mandibular Mechanics during the Production of Bilabial Stop Consonants," *Journal of Speech and Hearing Research* 16, 397–420.

Turvey, M. (1977) "Preliminaries to a Theory of Action with Reference to Vision," in R. Shaw and J. Bransford, eds., *Perceiving, Acting and Knowing: Toward an Ecological Psychology*, Erlbaum, Hillsdale, N.J.

Turvey, M.T., Shaw, R.E., and Mace, W. (1978) "Issues in the Theory of Action," in J. Requin, ed., *Attention and Performance VII*, Erlbaum, Hillsdale, N.J.

Waterson, N. (1971) "Child Phonology: A Prosodic View," *Journal of Linguistics*, 7, 179–211.

Chapter 3

PHONOLOGICAL THEORY AND CHILD PHONOLOGY

LISE MENN

Beware Procrustes bearing Occam's razor

Introduction

This chapter attempts a philosophical consideration of the theory of child phonology, philosophical that is, in the sense of examining the evolution of theory and knowledge

A historical account in science usually is a tale of progress in which the pioneers are left respectfully unexamined; if one does look at them critically, after all, it is difficult to avoid doing them injustice, since their work has been improved upon. In this chapter, I will attempt to remedy this inherent bias toward the contemporary by setting up a very general perspective in which to view our field.

Child phonology is a young field. We occasionally consult sources of data perhaps 100 years old. However, we tend to go back no further than Leopold's great work published in the 1930s and the 1940s. Child phonology, as a field whose theory is supposed to be part of a general theory of phonology, begins with Jakobson's *Kindersprache, Aphasia, and Allgemeine Lautgesetze* (1941). His elegant vision of the successive acquisition of phonemic contrasts became the standard account, cited everywhere, especially after the publication of Keiler's translation of *Kindersprache* in 1968.

CHILD PHONOLOGY
VOLUME 1: PRODUCTION

The 1960s also saw the emergence of generative phonology as the dominant phonological theory in this country, with 1968, when *The Sound Pattern of English* was published, again as a landmark date (Chomsky and Halle, 1968).

Let us begin to evaluate what has happened since 1968 by considering the general nature of the interaction of linked psychological fields that stand in the relationship of "central" or "general" fields of study to developmental study; from this we can obtain some of the perspective that is needed to understand the evolving relationship between phonological theory and child phonology from about 1968 to the present.

"Center" and "Periphery"

First, it is more than adult egocentrism that is behind the general equating of the center of psychological fields with the study of adults and the relegation of developmental studies to that periphery which is otherwise occupied by hyphenated interdisciplines. It also seems that we prefer to deal first with steady states and quantized phenomena. Adults, we assume, are stable.

There are some significant exceptions to this adult-centered structure: Educational psychology and Piagetian genetic epistemology have had no adult counterparts, at least until recently, and, in certain eras, a developmental field and its corresponding adult field may have had so little contact with one another that they may be considered autonomous. But when the central field concerns the adult, as is clearly the case in child phonology, initial attempts to construct a theory for children start from the theory of adult behavior.

Let us consider the general problem of extending a theory to cover a related area. We can schematize the sequence of events in three stages: First, a straightforward extension stage, which we might think of as an initial approximation; second, a stage of discovering the ways in which this approximation fails to deal with the new area felicitously; third, the creation of a new theory that is either specialized for the new area or able to handle both areas on a more general level.

The initial approximation can take into account only those phenomena in the new area that can be described as similar to phenomena in the older area. Phenomena in the new area that are not paralleled in the established theory must be neglected temporarily, unless they can be seen as "special cases." After the initial approximation has been worked out in detail, its inadequacies can be studied.

Thus, when this chapter points out some of the problems with the initial approximation to a theory of child phonology, it is not for the purpose of passing judgment on pioneering work. Rather, we have two goals: (*a*) to achieve a historical understanding of what has happened in our field; and (*b*) to encourage continued careful examination of the concepts that we work with, to make sure that simplifications which were appropriate for an initial approximation do not become built-in assumptions.

Let us discuss, in general, how initial approximations of theories may be made and consider Jakobson's work in the light of this discussion. Next, we shall consider the emergence of the comparison stage and the forces which tended to retard that emergence; we shall conclude by congratulating ourselves on having begun to mature into the stage of the creation of new theoretical concepts.

How do people go about reasoning from the known to the unknown before they have much data to work with? When we have few data points and need an initial theory, one procedure is to assume that the unknown world is as similar to the known as is possible: We might style this the "parallel projection" procedure. Another procedure is to fix the unknown between two areas considered to be known and to hypothesize the unknown to be the simplest interpolation between these two knowns. A vivid way to illustrate these modes of reasoning is to start with pure examples of each one, and to take these examples from settings well removed from our own. A good source of such remote examples for studying the operation of skilled reasoning on sparse data seems to be medieval cosmology, and a charming introduction to that field is C. S. Lewis' book *The Discarded Image* (Lewis, 1904). From it, let us consider the following examples of the modes of reasoning with which we are concerned.

The reader may recall the term "Antipodes." The classical and medieval earth (at least as envisioned by scholars) was spherical and divided into five zones; from north to south, these were the Arctic, the North Temperate, the Torrid, the South Temperate or Antipodes (opposite our feet), and the Antarctic (opposite the Arctic). The Torrid Zone was usually considered to be too hot even to cross, let alone to live in. The nature of the whole southern hemisphere was thus necessarily derived by pure deduction, and we can see that it was done by parallel projection: The southern hemisphere was construed as a mirror image of our own. Lewis renders for us the writings of one Macrobius, who lived about the beginning of the fourth century A.D.: "It is reasonable to suppose that the southern temperate zone is, like ours, inhabited, 'but we never have had, and shall never have, the possibility of discovering by whom' [p. 61]."

We may illustrate pure interpolation by considering the classical theory of Daemons (Lewis, 1904, pp. 40–43). Source works begin with Plato and continue through many authors, including Apuleius (A.D. 125). Daemons are spirits whose function is to mediate between the human and the divine. Their existence is derived by Plato's "principle of the triad," which states: "It is impossible that two things only should be joined together without a third

[Lewis, 1904, p. 40]." As daemons are intermediate between the human and the divine, strict interpolation between these two end points is explicitly applied to derive all their properties, such as life span, dwelling place, and degree of corporeality.

The third major way of making a theoretical foray into the unknown is by extrapolation from a sequence of known points, as the ancients deduced the supposedly unbearable heat of the Torrid Zone. However, the limiting factor in the early period of theory-building in child phonology was the scarcity of "known points" for the child, so that extrapolation was not involved in theorizing and will not be considered further.

Returning from the Middle Ages: I think we may agree that the ideal relationship between central and developmental portions of a field would be one in which the investigators in each portion could make use of the data from the entire field and would construct model children who were capable of developing into adults and, conversely, model adults who could have developed from children. In practice we fall short of this ideal. At best, center and development sometimes exchange useful information. Roger Brown (personal communication) discusses an example of such an exchange from social psychology: Winterbottom (1953) did research showing that achievement motivation in sons is strongly predicted by their mothers' expectations for them. This was utilized by McClellan (1975) who formulated and found evidence to support the hypothesis that rate of development of an emerging nation could be predicted from the prominence of "protestant ethic" themes to be found in that nation's typical official educational literature for children.

All too often, however, perhaps due to the relatively greater prestige of the central topic, investigators from the center pay little attention to the developmental field: They develop the initial acquisition model by interpolation or parallel projection and then rest content with this initial approximation. Either they ignore the data being gathered, or they overinterpret it. For example, generative syntax has paid amazingly little attention to the evidence from acquisition studies on the way semantics and syntax interact, or to the evidence for successive re-analyses of syntax as the child matures. Brown, again, points out (personal communication) that this situation has a close parallel in psychoanalytic theory: There too, the hypothetical child plays a major role, since the neurotic personality is explained as due to fixation at supposed early stages of development. Independent observational evidence for these early stages, however, is at least as problematic as evidence for a syntactically oriented Language Acquisition Device.

Nevertheless, one of the innovations of generative grammar, including generative phonology, is its explicit philosophical commitment to attend to language acquisition. For example, in Chomsky and Halle (1968) we find the statement: "The search for essential linguistic universals is, in effect, the study of the a priori *faculté de language* that makes language acquisition possible under the given conditions of time and access to data [p. 4].'' In other words, a cardinal fact about language is that it is possible to learn to talk, and from this fact we should be able to derive important properties of language. The general situation, then, is the following: An initial developmental theory is formulated by parallel projection and interpolation on a basis of the adult theory.

However, a theory devised to account economically for an adult behavior cannot generally account for the acquisition of that behavior. The relation between child and adult is, among other things, the relation between skilled and unskilled performer. If the adult produces no unskilled acts, the central theory is unlikely to have a way of modeling the production of unskilled acts. And if it cannot model unskilled acts, it cannot model the child's acts. Therefore, the child cannot be modeled merely as one who possesses a subset of the capacities of the adult. Both parallel projection and interpolation, being admirably economical, must fail.

After all, one must move beyond the initial hypotheses and accomodate to new data, or one's theory will remain fixated at an early stage of development. If the center ignores this fact, the developmental investigators must develop their own theory, independent of the center or they will find themselves assimilating their data to the Procrustean bed of central theory. Unfortunately, there are significant sociological forces on the side of Procrustes. If many new concepts are required to handle developmental data, the people at the center are likely to see such data as irrelevant to their enterprise, and/ or be unwilling to invest the necessary time in learning the developmental material. Developmentalists are thus under pressure to maximize the similarity between their constructs and those used by the center, and tend to follow central theory rather slavishly, especially when their field is young and data are not plentiful.

Other kinds of difficulties arise when workers from the center do turn to the developmental field for input. The basic problem for both groups of investigators is to determine whether or not a central construct applies directly to the child, or whether certain patterns of child behavior that appear to correspond to certain adult patterns must, in fact, be explained by quite different constructs: in sum, whether or not a tempting projection from the center is legitimate.

Within this epistemological and sociological framework, let us review how the initial step from ''central'' phonological theory to child phonology was taken.

The First Phase: Roman Jakobson

Kindersprache was published in 1941 in Sweden, where the author's long flight from the Nazis had taken him. He had no reason to believe that this last accessible refuge would remain safe; his book is almost certainly more speculative and daring than it would otherwise have been.

World War II and the delays of translation meant that the full work was little studied in this country until 1968, although it was well known in Europe and less detailed versions had been published earlier. Simplified versions of the acquisition theory were included in works in English written during the interim, notably Jakobson, Fant, and Halle (1955) and Jakobson and Halle (1965). These, however, were missing many of the subtleties, exceptions, cautions, and details present in *Kindersprache*. In these works the reader finds an elegant theory grandly integrated with general linguistics and presented with force and assurance. There seems to have been no competing account that could be called a theory, and the preceding descriptive accounts were few in number.

Velten and Leopold became acquainted with *Kindersprache* shortly after its publication. They found its broad outlines valid and stimulating, admired it greatly, but, speaking from their excellent data bases, each offered some reservations and modifications. In one striking example of such a reservation, Leopold (1953) states clearly that, in the case he studied, babbling overlapped with speech for many months, flatly contradicting Jakobson's notion of a "silent period."

Such reservations, however, were not generally noticed; instead, an overwhelmed *ipse dixit* response to Jakobson's work was found in every general mainstream language-acquisition text, from McNeill's chapter in Mussen (1970) to the phonology section of Dale (1976). Cautions in a general work are not seen until Clark and Clark (1977). (Ingram's [1976] text has a critical discussion, but that work is specifically on phonology.) Consequently, those who had difficulties accepting Jakobson felt that they ought to do a great deal of fieldwork before they could publish counterarguments; one might suggest that the entire cautious and meticulous modern tradition of child phonology fieldwork was forged by this necessity. Referring to the framework set up in the introduction, we have Jakobson as a scientist from the center who made a highly economical initial extension from his structuralist phonology to child phonology. In retrospect, we can analyze his extension as having a strong interpolative component. The extremes are the child who makes no contrasts on the one end and the adult who maintains many on the other; the interpolation consists of the postulation of the successive sequence of contrasts, and some intermediate data points are taken into account in deriving the order in which those contrasts are supposedly acquired. The rest of the extension consists of the straightforward transfer of concepts and terminology (contrast, phoneme, minimal pair) and so falls under the heading of parallel projection. Jakobson proceeded from the infant to the adult in the most economical way, and was concerned only with accounting for the development of the behaviors of interest to structuralist phonology: the development of contrast. Though phonetics was discussed, it was not of theoretical concern: Jakobson was not trying to account for all of the acquisition of phonology, but only to show that one major aspect of it could be derived from his sweeping general theory. We must note that his general theory was not based on his acquisition theory, and does not logically depend on it. Unlike generative theory, Jakobson's general theory does not claim that it ought to depend on acquisition either. His account of phonological acquisition, like his account of aphasia, was primarily intended as an illustration of the power of the general theory.

First Phase Continued: Generative Phonology

Because of coincidences of timing and notation, it is sometimes thought that the development of generative phonology was necessary before the systematic relations between child and adult word could be studied. Logically, at least, this is not so; Jakobson could have done it easily if he had cared to. The conceptual tool required is the notion of rules relating forms used by one speaker to forms used by another speaker, and this type of rule, under the name "sound law," is the oldest type of phonological rule studied in the Western tradition, first in historical change and then in dialect studies. Such rules were also formulated in terms of natural classes (labials, fricatives, etc.) where possible, which is equivalent to the use of a feature notation. Anyone who understood the notion of conditioned sound change—any good neogrammarian—could, with enough data, have dealt insightfully with Hildegard Leopold, Joan Velten, Daniel Mann, or Amahl Smith. For example, Ferguson (1968) used a contrastive analysis framework to describe several children's language in relation to adult language. Rewrite rules are not needed until one reaches the crucial point where the child's underlying form must be dealt with as different from the adult surface form. And in fact, this problem was not dealt with, even for some years after the introduction of generative formalism.

This seems to me to be the reason why there is so little lag between the development of generative phonology and the use of its formalism for child language work: Linguists with structuralist training could see the value of the notation for child language and use it creatively even if they were not trained generativists; if they were, so much the better. Clearly the outstanding practitioner of this period was N.V. Smith; he also had the fortune to deal with a data set whose principal phenomena were very well suited to an ordered-rule account (Smith, 1973).

Others, for example Ingram (1974a) and Stampe (1969), also seized upon ordered rules; so did I, but I originally followed a different model, one developed by L.G. Jones (1967) dealing directly but rather cumbersomely with surface-structure constraints on phonology.

One might, then, describe child phonology circa 1973 as having a mainstream (generative) theory consisting of Jakobsonian acquisition of phonemic contrasts and an ordered-rule account of the relationship between adult words and their child counterparts.

This theory was still completely dominated by the phonological center; the categories that we dealt with (phone, phoneme, contrast, rule, underlying form, lexicon) were borrowed whole. In retrospect, most of us were, at least in our published work, operating mostly by parallel projection from the adult theory, and were consciously concerned about showing similarities between the adult and the child. Part of that concern came from a desire to show that we were making valid use of the tools that were developed by the center, but part of it came from a desire to show that child phonology was *real* phonology, to establish it as legitimate and potentially relevant.

The only theory-oriented work of this period that does not fall under this description is Stampe (1969). Stampe, like Jakobson, is not principally a child phonologist; his concern was with the enrichment of central phonological theory, and he attempted to use data from child phonology to that end. His approach to the rules of child phonology consciously paralleled Jakobson's approach to the acquisition of phonemic contrast, and was equally interpolative: the speechless child again at one pole, and the articulate adult at the other. A discussion of some aspects of his theory will be given in a later section.

The Comparison Phase

Around 1973, various investigators began to discuss in the literature those weaknesses of the center-derived theory that their individual data bases or individual sensitivities had brought to light. One such weakness has been principally probed, over the years, by the Stanford group; noted by Moskowitz (1970), focused on by Ferguson and Farwell (1975), and considered in other papers: the adequacy of describing a child as "acquiring contrasts" or even as "acquiring phoneme." Because the categories of "contrast" and "phoneme" (or something like them) are valid for the analysis of adult language does not mean that they are necessarily valid for child language.

Most of the difficulty with these terms is encountered in the early months of speech, leading some workers (Nakazima, 1972) to use terms like "prephonemic stage." But no general adequate account exists of how children end up with phonemes—there is as yet no replacement for Jakobson. When there is one, it will have to deal with the following problems:

1. Distinguishing between the acquisition of the motor ability to hit a phonetic target accurately and the more "cognitive" acquisition of the in-

formation that two phones contrast phonologically. It seems at present that a child may sometimes acquire the ability to hit phonetic targets accurately before acquiring the ability to maintain phonological contrast between them; conversely he or she may sometimes give behavioral evidence of understanding that two phonemes contrast before being able to hit the respective targets accurately (see Macken and Barton 1977).

2. Describing how a phone in one position in a syllable comes to be identified with its counterparts in other parts of a syllable.

3. Handling other aspects, articulatory and acoustic, of allophony, even at the purely phonetic level.

4. Dealing with the possibility that the phone, as an element that is by definition comparable from one word to the next, is not a viable unit in the first months of speech: That instead, at least for some children, sound-sequence-plus-meaning (lexical entry) is a minimal unit. There is a comparable marginal phenomenon in adult language—a few words, for example, words denoting animal sounds, often exist outside the general system; it may be that unanalyzed word-length units are central phenomena in early child language (Ferguson and Farwell, 1975).

5. Dealing with the possibility that the segment is not an optimal unit in early child speech, but that longer, prosodic units may be needed in some cases, either in addition or instead (Menn 1977a, b; Waterson 1971).

Another weakness in the initial phase account of child phonology is one that Ingram and I have been particularly concerned with over the years (Ingram, 1974, 1975, 1976; Menn, 1971, 1976, 1977a, b). Child speech, from the possibly prephonemic early stage and on through perhaps the first nine months of speaking, is subject to severe output constraints, stronger than anything found in adult phonology. Output constraints are, however, found playing some important roles in adult phonology—vowel harmony is the classic example, and syllable-structure constraints are a standing area of concern. Rewrite-rule notation can handle such phenomena (Langendoen, 1968), but only by brute force (Clements, 1976), not perspicuously. This problem has been a cause of ferment in generative phonology: phonotactic derivations (Jones, 1967), redundancy rules (Stanley, 1967), related morpheme structure conditions (Chomsky and Halle, 1968), parts of natural phonology (Stampe, 1973), autosegmental phonology (Clements, 1976; Goldsmith, 1976) and conspiracy theory (Kisseberth, 1970) have all arisen to deal with it. This is the area in which generative phonology was seriously deficient with respect to British (Firthian) prosodic phonology (see Palmer, 1970), and where Waterson's (1971) prosodic approach to child phonology yielded important insights: For example, that the child might be seeking out whole-word patterns in the adult language that were similar to whole-word patterns, that the child had learned to produce. Autosegmental generative phonology may be able to handle prosodic phenomena properly, but it is still evolving.

Most of these attempts by central theorists to deal with output constraints have been eagerly seized on by one or more child phonologist, because of the prominence of vowel and consonant harmony and other word-
structure constraints in early child speech. As was mentioned earlier, I tried
the Jones (1967) model; Ingram used Stanley's (1967), which proved a better
choice, and most of us then followed Ingram (1974a). Smith (1973), whose
analysis of Amahl begins after the most severe harmony constraints were
no longer present, used Kisseberth's (1970) conspiracy theory, which is less
direct than the others; in recent papers (1977a,b), I have used autosegmental
phonology. Stampe's work has been used extensively by Ingram, and also
by Edwards (1974). In each of these cases, the center supplied material used
by our field, and in a few cases (Stampe, 1973; Jones, 1967), child phonology
was of explicit interest to the formulator.

The third weakness of child phonology *circa* 1973 is of a more insidious
nature. The formal resemblance between the rules written to relate child
output to adult-model word and the rules written to relate adult surface-
forms to their underlying forms made it all too easy for us to forget that the
"underlying form" in child phonology is not equivalent to the underlying
form in phonological theory. The underlying form in phonological theory is
a well-defined construct designed primarily to capture morphophonemic interrelationships. It is not a "perceived" form or an object that should be
thought of as a sequence of sounds or even as a sequence of categories of
sounds; it is a highly encoded representation of a pattern, and cannot be
interpreted outside of a complete phonology of the language.

The underlying form in early child phonology, in contrast, is taken to
be the child's shallow encoding of the adult spoken form. Debate of a high
quality continues as to how accurate the child's representation of the adult
form is (Macken, in press; Smith, 1973; Waterson, 1971), and whether or
not it may sometimes be based on a different set of features from the adult
phonemic representation (Chaney, 1978; Kornfeld, 1974; Menyuk, 1971),
and there is much interest in how soon the child realizes that certain phones
are in free variation with one another (perhaps only in certain environments).

But this underlying form is barely more abstract than the systematic
phonetic level of generative phonology, certainly no deeper than an autonomous phonemic representation, nor should it be. The child just learning
to talk, or at least the child just learning to speak English, knows nothing
of allomorphy. The simple "one morph, one meaning," principle is surely
followed until proven inadequate: Children use Occam's razor too (cf. the
excellent discussion in Braine, 1974).

We must describe the eventual acquisition of morphophonemic patterning as the construction of underlying forms; for evidence concerning the
sorts of abstraction processes children go through, see MacWhinney (1978)
and the whole acquisition-of-morphology literature from Berko (1958) on
(Drachman and Malikouti-Drachman, 1973 on Greek; Dresel, 1978 on Hausa;

articles in Ferguson and Slobin, 1973 on Russian and Latvian are to be noted). But all of the familiar rules of child phonology, except the few that purport to be about the child's encoding of the adult phonetic sequence, are at least intended to correspond functionally to a minuscule proportion of the rules of general phonology: to the low-level rules, the detail rules that determine pronunciation. Such rules are barely touched on *The Sound Pattern of English* and are considered seriously only in sociolinguistics and in such recent works as Kahn (1976) and, of course, by Stampe (1969, 1973) and his students. Most rules of English-learning child phonology concern pronunciation; none concern morphophonemics. Indeed, for practical purposes of description, we write rules that ignore the problems of inferring the child's encoding of the word altogether: We write surface-to-surface rules directly relating the adult surface to the child's output; 'truck' "becomes" [gak], 'shoe' "becomes" [tsu].

Arguments from Child to Adult

Two very different groups of central theorists have recently had recourse to the child in arguments. We have observed that problems arise in going back and forth from child to adult when similarly labeled theoretical constructs prove to be "about" different phenomena. The difficulties with Stampe's work seem to arise at this level. It is not possible in a short general chapter to review Stampe's (more recently, Donegan and Stampe, 1968) work and do justice to the subtlety of the problem he has been working on. Stampe desires to improve generative phonology's computation of the "cost" of rules by incorporation of considerations of how hard it would be for a child to learn those rules. This is a reasonable objective; indeed it would seem to be a necessary step in bringing the proposed constraint "language must be learnable" into contact with the writing of grammars. However, we have yet to determine empirically and generally what makes one phonological rule easier to learn than another. Furthermore, there are many uncertainties within generative grammar as to what content the rules describing a particular language pattern should have—for example, whether or not morphological information should be incorporated freely when writing phonological rules.

This means that we are a long way from knowing how to compute the learnability of a rule. For rules that are agreed to be morphological, Slobin's (1971) principles give us very effective guidelines for what rules should be the easiest. But we have no comparable set of explicit principles for rating the learnability of "purely" phonological rules, such as English vowel neutralizations in unstressed syllables, or deaspiration of voiceless stops in #sC clusters, or syllable-final obstruent devicing in German. In fact, the formulation of a tentative set of such principles is clearly a research priority for theoretical child phonology.

Stampe deals with one of the variables that will surely be involved with the learnability of a rule, namely, its psychophysiological "naturalness." But he deals with only one variable, and he simply assumes that natural rules are easier to learn, no matter what step in a derivation they represent. Stampe proposes that the rules that we know as child phonology rules, and that have the effect of reducing the number of contrasts maintained in a child's output, are "innate," applied automatically, and in unordered fashion by the child in his or her attempts to match the adult-model word. The process of learning to master adult phonology is modeled as a matter of learning to overcome the effects of these rules by suppressing or reducing them.[1]

Stampe's child who says [kǽi] for 'candy' has, according to him, applied the innate rules or "natural processes" of assimilation of /d/ to /n/, degemination of the resulting /nn/, flapping of the /n/, flap deletion, and desyllabification of the final vowel (as well as nasalization of the first vowel). Stampe derives this elaborate sequence by comparing the child's rendition of the word candy with the adult fast-speech version, which may be almost as degraded at maximum speed and casualness. (The investigation of fast-speech processes is presently riddled with introspection, and complex instrumental techniques will be needed before these processes can be understood.) Suppose we accept for the sake of argument that, for an adult, the gradation from a crisply produced [kʰaendiy] to a hypercasual [kǽni] can be represented as the application of more and more fast-speech rules to some sort of a phonemic representation.

Now: Is there truly an analogue between the child saying [kǽi] and the adult saying [kǽni]? Stampe notes the same input to a rule system, similar sorts of output, similar auditory and acoustic apparatus, and says yes, enough of an analogue to unify the phenomena under a single theory. The difference between the child and the adult is that, for the child, the rules are obligatory, but, for the adult, they are optional; this represents the child's articulatory clumsiness. Here we see interpolation and parallel projection at work again. Stampe is consciously Jakobsonian in his economical approach to a theory of child phonology.

---

[1] Stampe derives an output form kǽi from an "underlying form" /kændi/ by the steps (omitting nasalization)

nd → nn	kændi → kænni
degemination	kænni → kæni
flapping	kæni → kæî
flap deletion	kæni → kæî
desyllabification	kæî → kæi̯

/nd/ is not deleted in a single rule, but undergoes four separate weakening processes.

What is wrong here? Some problems have been discussed elsewhere (Kiparsky and Menn, 1977; Menn, 1976a); some of these could be remedied by minor modifications of the theory. And certainly we want to preserve the commonsense quality of the claim that childish and casual pronunciations of a word are both less precisely controlled than an adult citation-form production. What I want to question is the claim that the same "processes" are operating in the two cases.

Note this term "process." As it is used, it is a richer, more substantive term than "rule." A rule is a mere correspondence at most; it can be completely abstract. But a process is taken to be something the articulators do or undergo. Flapping a coronal is a modification of the tongue's action when an occlusion is made lightly and rapidly; vowel nasalization in English comes from raising the velum in anticipation of the production of a following nasal consonant, and so on. A process does not merely have an abstract input and an articulatory output; it has an *articulatory input*, unrealized but potential. Putting it another way, the *input* to a process is an articulatory target; the *process* is undershooting or overshooting that target with respect to one or more articulatory parameters (e.g., position, degree of closure, vocal cord position) often due to coarticulatory factors; the *output* is an articulation different from the target articulation. This notion makes excellent sense when one is modeling fast speech (within the limitations of a standard rule system).

But what about the child? Suppose a certain child produces no intervocalic coronals at all, and says [kǽi] in attempting to match the sound of the word candy. Can we say that the processes of nasal assimilation, degemination, flapping, and flap deletion have applied? Not unless we postulate that the /nd/ cluster exists as an articulatory target (as well as an acoustic target) to the child. But if the child in question never makes intervocalic coronal contact, how can we speak of degemination (shortening of contact), or of flapping (making contact during ballistic tongue movement)? The child simply has failed to make contact: He or she has not learned to get the blade of the tongue up to the anterior part of the palate and down again while continuing to phonate.

These considerations do not tell against all of Stampe's postulated processes. Some of them do make sense for the child. If the child is trying to reach an articulatory target and shows signs of knowing how to make some features of that target, and the hypothesized process is a plausible by-product of attempting to match those features, then it seems legitimate to speak of a process applying. But if there is no indication that the child has the articulatory target as such, if, instead, the child simply seems to be settling for an acoustic approximation to the sound, then the notion of process must be weakened until it is no stronger than the notion of rule, if one says that processes have applied in the case. In Menn 1977a,b, I proposed that the child's "tonguetiedness," that overwhelming reality which Stampe and Jakobson both tried to capture with their respective formal structures, could be handled more felicitously if one represented the heavy articulatory limitations of the child by the formal device of output constraints, as I mentioned earlier in this chapter. The child's gradual mastery of articulation then is formalized as a relaxation of those constraints. One could say that the *constraints* are largely innately determined but that the *rules*—some natural, some not—that the child uses to relate adult sounds to his own limited repertoire of productions are devised or discovered through trial and error (for counterarguments to this position, see Smith, 1978).

The other group of arguments from child to adult that I want to discuss are less important to child phonology because they are so crude in their conception of language acquisition that child phonologists are unlikely to be attracted to them. However, because these claims are taken seriously by many central phonologists, we have a responsibility to argue against them at some point. I refer to the controversy over the admissibility of extrinsic language-particular rule ordering (Derwing, 1973; Koutsoudas, Sanders, and Noll, 1971).

These works are built primarily on the claim that extrinsic arbitrary rule ordering cannot be present in adult language because, if it were, it would not be possible for children to learn the language. This claim attracts some people for whom a mystique of abstruseness clings to the ordered rule and, in particular, those who seem to be victims of the fallacy that the native speaker learns rules somewhat the way a student might.

If this were the case, one could indeed argue that the addition of extrinsic arbitrary rule ordering represents a great increase in the complexity of a grammar as compared to a grammar in which rules can only be used in certain pre-set naturally determined orders. Bear in mind that some rule orders are more complex than others, and that, as we have noted, there are unsettled arguments about what might make a set of rules harder or easier to learn—for example, certain points are at issue between e.g. Kisseberth (1970, 1973) and Kiparsky (1971, 1972) that concern the permissible degree of abstractness of underlying forms. Empirical resolution for this argument will depend on the development of fine tests of speakers' knowledge and on the question of what overgeneralizations are made by children as they learn the language: In this controversy, child phonology has the normal role of providing evidence.

But in the work of Derwing (1973), for example, the arguments simply proceed from the assumption that rule ordering is unlearnable. What does such a claim mean?

One goes about writing rules by looking at the patterns in output and then trying to formulate an account of those patterns. Rules themselves are never in evidence, only patterns. If someone holds that writing ordered rules is a priori illegitimate as a way of describing phonological patterns, no exhibition of patterns that are nicely described by ordered rules and clumsily described without them will be taken as counterevidence. It is of little added moment whether it is a child or an adult who is using these patterns. Counterargument, then, is not a matter of adducing child phonology data, but of demystifying ordered rules, which one can do by showing how such rules represent certain types of phonological patterns and considering how such patterns can be learned.

Ordered rules are an economical formal device used to capture a property that is frequently found in natural language: The exceptions to a pattern may themselves form a (less general) pattern. Such nested patterns are easy to exemplify. Take the set of irregular verbs in English, all of which are exceptions to the regular rules for forming past tense and past participle. Among these, a considerable subset form the past participle in *-en*: *taken*, *given*, and so on. We know that this pattern is psychologically accessible to speakers, because children are reported to overgeneralize it.

Irregular verbs must be lexically marked as such, but after that, rule ordering is one of several formal devices that can be used to express the difference between "one-of-a-kind" strong verbs such as *stand–stood–stood* and the members of the group that take *-en*.

There can be no valid argument about the claim that speakers can or cannot use a particular formal device, because such a claim does not make sense. Linguists use formal devices; speakers have access to patterns, have partial access to patterns, or do not have access to patterns. Linguists may argue about whether a particular device is a good way to encode the knowledge of patterns that speakers seem to have, and about whether speakers have access to certain patterns of language. But the claim that ordered rules are unlearnable makes no sense. The only way to make sense out of it is to translate it into the claim that minor patterns cannot be recognized. And this, as an empirical claim, is false: Some minor patterns can be recognized and some cannot.

Another example of rule ordering being used to represent a pattern that seems to be quite accessible to speakers is taken from Catalan and provided by G.N. Clements (personal communication). It will illustrate how rule ordering serves to encode a pattern holding the set of exceptions to a rule together. In general, in Catalan, final /n/ and final /nt/ are not found. (There are a few lexical exceptions.) Consider the following pairs of masculine and feminine adjective forms; notice that the masculine forms in the second set have final /n/.

M	F		M	F	
/fi/	/finə/	delicate	/bəlen/	/bəlentə/	brave
/plɛ/	/plena/	full	/kunten/	/kuntentə/	happy
/sa/	/sanə/	healthy	/san/	/santə/	saintly

In descriptive terms, the adjectives that have a final /n/ in the masculine are exactly those that have an /n/ cluster in the feminine. The generative–phonological way of encoding this generalization is to set up underlying forms for the masculine that are the same as the feminine minus the final /ə/, and then to apply the rules n → ∅ | _# and t → ∅ | n_# in that order. This captures the patterning among the exceptions precisely. But to say that a speaker "knows" these ordered rules is *not* to say that the speaker learns two separate rules and learns to apply them in this order. I have no data on the acquisition of Catalan, but if it proceeds as in other languages, the child probably first learns a small set of these pairs correctly by rote; then overgeneralizes the fact that the masculine and feminine are usually related by /ə/-drop, probably producing such incorrect masculines as /sant/ and /fin/ or else also overapplies the phonological rules, giving incorrect masculine /bale/, /kunte/ and correct /fi/, /plɛ/; then learns not to drop the /n/ in /balen/, /kunten/ etc., as a list of exceptions and finally learns the pattern that holds among the exceptions.

Now, some patterns are clearer than others; some minor generalizations are so obscure that only the historical linguist can recognize them (Lightner, 1971; Maher, 1969), and the ability to apprehend the lesser phonological patterns undoubtedly varies across speakers (Wilbur and Menn, 1974, 1975). There is room for a good deal of argument as to what should constitute evidence that a speaker has learned a pattern and as to how particular patterns of varying generality should be represented in a grammar (Braine, 1974; Wilbur and Menn, 1974, 1975). But to claim that (arbitrary) ordered rules in themselves are unlearnable is, in my opinion, to commit a sort of category error; it seems to involve conceiving the learning of rules as being separable from, or different from, the apprehension of patterns, and, as I said, to involve conceiving the learning of a complex set of rules by the child as being similar to the memorization of such rules by a student.

The Third Phase

Inevitably, as we move closer to consideration of the present time, it becomes harder to see our work in perspective. Part of the recent history consists of attempting to amend the weaknesses of the adult-derived theory outlined in the previous section: We are working on problems with the notion "phoneme," problems with handling output constraints, and problems arising from failure to completely understand what the natures of "underlying form" and "rule" are in child phonology. But part also consists of framing new questions and problems in our own terms: We have rich sources of data now, so much that we need computer-assisted search procedures to utilize it properly, and we have learned to adapt instrumental techniques to our needs. A philosophical account of child phonology and phonological theory in the last two or three years must wait until the impact of these changes can be assessed.

Acknowledgments

I am grateful to Roger Brown for providing me with more examples than I have been able to use of the types of relationships between central and developmental psychological fields; to Paul Kiparsky for extensive discussions of Roman Jakobson; to Nick Clements for the Catalan material, and to Robin Ault for editorial advice.

References

Bar-Adon, A., and Leopold, W,F., eds. (1971) *Child Language: A Book of Readings*, Prentice-Hall, Englewood Cliffs, N.J.

Berko, J. (1958) "The Child's Learning of English Morphology," *Word*, 14, 150–177.

Braine, M.D.S. (1974) "On What Might Constitute Learnable Phonology," *Language* 50, 270–299.

Chaney, C. (1978) "Production and Identification of /j, w, r, l/ in Normal and Articulation Impaired Children," Doctoral Dissertation, Boston University.

Chomsky, N., and Halle, M. (1968) *The Sound Pattern of English*, Harper & Row, New York.

Clark, H.H., and Clark, E.V. (1977) *Psychology and Language*, Harcourt Brace Jovanovich, New York.

Clements, G.N. (1976) "Vowel Harmony in Non-linear Generative Phonology," Manuscript, Linguistics Department, Harvard University.

Dale, P.S. (1976) *Language Development: Structure and Function* (2nd ed.), Holt, Rinehart and Winston, New York.

Derwing, B.L. (1973) *Transformational Grammar as a Theory of Language Acquisition*. Cambridge University Press, Cambridge.

Dingwall, W.O. (1971) *Survey of Linguistic Science*, University of Maryland, College Park, Md.

Donegan, P.J., and Stampe, D. (1978) "The Study of Natural Phonology," Manuscript.

Drachman, G., and Malikouti-Drachman, A. (1973)"Studies in the Acquisition of Greek as a Native Language 1," *Ohio University Working Papers in Linguistics*, 15, 99–114.

Dresel, L.H. (1977) "Palatalization in Hausa Child Language," Paper read at the Fifty-second Annual Meeting, Linguistic Society of America, December.

Edwards, M.L. (1974) "Perception and Production in Child Phonology: "The Testing of Four Hypotheses," *Journal of Child Language*, 1, 205–220.

Ferguson, C.A. (1969) "Contrastive Analysis and Language Development," *Georgetown University Monograph Series on Language and Linguistics*, 21, 101–112.

Ferguson, C.A., and Slobin, D.I., eds. (1973) *Studies of Child Language Development*, Holt, Rinehart and Winston, New York.

Ferguson, C.A., and Farwell, C.B. (1975) "Words and Sounds in Early Language Acquisition," *Language*. 51, 419–439.

Goldsmith, J. (1976) "Autosegmental Phonology," (mimeo), MIT Doctoral Dissertation, circulated through Indiana University Linguistics Club.

Ingram, D. (1973) "Phonological Analysis of a Developmentally Aphasic Child," (mimeo), Institute for Childhood Aphasia, Stanford University.

Ingram, D. (1974) "Phonological Rules in Young Children," *Journal of Child Language*, 1, 49–64. (a)

Ingram, D. (1974) "Fronting in Child Phonology," *Journal of Child Language*, 1, 233–241. (b)

Ingram, D. (1976) "Current Issues in Child Phonology," in O.M. Morehead and A.E. Morehead, eds., *Normal and Deficient Child Language*, University Park Press, Baltimore, Md., pp. 3–27. (a)

Ingram, D. (1976) *Phonological Disability in Children*, Elsevier, New York. (b)

Jakobson, R. (1968) *Child Language, Aphasia and Phonological Universals*, Trans. A. Keiler, Mouton, The Hague.

Jakobson, R., Fant, G., and Halle, M. (1955, reissued, 1963) *Preliminaries to Speech Analysis*, MIT Press, Cambridge, Mass.

Jakobson, R., and Halle, M. (1965) *Fundamentals of Language*, Mouton, The Hague.

Jones, L. G. (1967) "English Phonotactic Structure and First-Language Acquisition," *Lingua*, 19, 1–59.

Kahn, D. (1976) "Syllable-based Generalizations in English Phonology," MIT Doctoral Dissertation, circulated by Indiana University Linguistics Club.

Kiparsky, P. (1971) "Historical Linguistics," in W.O. Dingwall, ed., *Survey of Linguistic Science*, University of Maryland, College Park, Md., pp. 576–649.

Kiparsky, P. (1972) "Explanation in Phonology," in S. Peters, ed., *Goals of Linguistic Theory*, Prentice Hall, Englewood Cliffs, N.J., pp. 189–225.

Kiparsky, P., and Menn, L. (1977) "On the Acquisition of Phonology," in J. Macnamara, ed., *Language Learning and Thought*, Academic Press, New York, pp. 47–78.

Kisseberth, C.W. (1973) "The Interaction of Phonological Rules and the Polarity of Language," (mimeo), Indiana University Linguistics Club.

Kisseberth, C.W. (1970) "The Functional Unity of Phonological Rules," *Linguistic Inquiry*, 1, 291–306.

Kornfeld, J.R., and Goehl, H. (1974) "A New Twist to an Old Observation: Kids Know More Than They Say," *Papers from the Parasession on Natural Phonology*, Chicago Linguistic Society.

Koutsoudas, A., Sanders, J., and Noll, G. (1971) "On the Application of Phonological Rules," (mimeo), Indiana University Linguistics Club.

Langendoen, D.T. (1968) *The London School of Linguistics*, MIT Press, Cambridge, Mass.

Leopold, W.F. (1939–1949) *Speech Development of a Bilingual Child*, Northwestern University Press, Evanston, Ill.

Leopold, W.F. (1953) "Patterning in Children's Language Learning," *Language Learning*, 5, 1–14, Reprinted in A. Bar-Adon and N.F. Leopold, eds., *Child Language: A Book of Readings*, Prentice-Hall, Englewood Cliffs, N.J., pp. 134–141.

Lewis, C.S. (1964) *The Discarded Image: An Introduction to Medieval and Renaissance Literature*, Cambridge University Press, Cambridge.

Lightner, T. (1971) "Generative Phonology," in W.O. Dingwall, ed., *Survey of Linguistic Science*, University of Maryland, College Park, Md., pp. 498–574.

Macken, M.A. (in press) "The Child's Lexical Representation: Evidence from the 'Puzzle-Puddle-Pickle' Phenomenon," *Journal of Linguistics*. [also in Stanford University *Papers and Reports on Child Language Development*. 16, 26–41.]

Macken, M.A., and Barton, D. (1977) "A Longitudinal Study of the Acquisition of the Voicing Contrast in American–English Word–Initial Stops, as Measured by VOT," Stanford University *Papers and Reports on Child Language Development*, (Linguistics, Stanford University) 14, 74–120 Revised version to appear in *Journal of Child Language*.

MacWhinney, B. (1978) "The Acquisition of Morphophonology," *Monographs of the Society for Research in Child Development*, 43 (1–2), serial no. 74.

Maher, J.P. (1969) "The Paradox of Creation and Tradition in Grammar: Sound Pattern of a Palimpsest," *Language Sciences*, 7, 15–24.

McClellan, D. (1975) *The Achieving Society*, Halstead Press, New York.

McNeill, D. (1970) "The Development of Language," in P. Mussen, ed., *Carmichael's Manual of Child Psychology* (Vol. 1), Wiley, New York.

Menn, L. (1971) "Phontactic Rules in Beginning Speech," *Lingua*, 26, 225–251.

Menn, L. (1976) "Pattern, Control, and Contrast in Beginning Speech: A Case Study in the Development of Word Form and Word Function," Unpublished Doctoral Dissertation, University of Illinois. (a)

Menn, L. (1976) "Evidence for an Interactionist–Discovery Theory of Child Phonology," *Papers and Reports on Child Language Development*, (Linguistics, Stanford University) 12, 169–177. (b)

Menn, L. (1977) "An Autosegmental Approach to Child Phonology—First Explorations, in G.N. Clements, ed., *Harvard Studies in Phonology I*, Linguistics Department, Harvard University, 315–334. (a)

Menn, L. (1977) "Phonological Units in Beginning Speech," To appear in A. Bell, and J.B. Hooper, eds., *Syllables and Segments*, North Holland, Amsterdam. (b)

Menyuk, P. (1971) "Clusters as Single Underlying Consonants: Evidence from Children's Production," *Proceedings*, Seventh International Congress of Phonetic Sciences, Montreal.

Morehead, D.M., and Morehead, A.E., eds. (1976) *Normal and Deficient Child Language*, University Park Press, Baltimore, Md.

Moskowitz, A. (1970) "The Two-year-old Stage in the Acquisition of English Phonology," *Language*, 46, 426–441. Reprinted in C.A. Ferguson and P.I. Slobin, eds., *Studies in Child Language Development*, Holt, Rinehart and Winston, New York.

Mussen, P., ed., (1970) *Carmichael's Manual of Child Psychology* (Vol. I), Wiley, New York.

Nakazima, S. (1972) "A Comparative Study of the Speech Development of Japanese and American Children (Part Four—The Beginning of the Phonemicization Process)," *Studia Phonologica VI*, 1–37, University of Kyoto.

Palmer, F.R., ed. (1970) *Prosodic Analysis*, Oxford University Press, London.

Peters, S. (1972) *Goals of Linguistic Theory*, Prentice-Hall, Englewood Cliffs, N.J.

Slobin, D.I. (1971) "Developmental Psycholinguistics," in W.O. Dingwall, ed., *Survey of Linguistic Science*, University of Maryland, College Park, Maryland, pp. 298–410.

Smith, N.V. (1973) *The Acquisition of Phonology: A Case Study*, Cambridge University Press, Cambridge.

Smith, N.V. (1978) "Lexical Representation in the Acquisition of Phonology," Revised version of Forum lecture, Linguistic Institute, University of Illinois at Urbana-Champaign.

Stampe, D. (1969) "The Acquisition of Phonetic Representattion," *Papers from the Fifth Regional Meeting*, Chicago Linguistic Society, 443–454.

Stampe, D. (1973) "A Dissertation on Natural Phonology," Doctoral Dissertation, University of Chicago.

Stanley, R. (1967) "Redundancy Rules in Phonology," *Language*, 43, pp. 393–435.

Velten, H.V. (1943) "The Growth of Phonemic and Lexical Patterns in Infant Language," *Language*, 19, 440–444. Reprinted in A. Bar-Adon and W.F. Leopold, eds., *Child Language: A Book of Readings*, Prentice-Hall, Englewood Cliffs, N.J., pp. 82–90.

Waterson, N. (1970) "Some Speech Forms cf an English Child: A Phonological Study," *Transactions of the Philological Society*, 1–24.

Waterson, N. (1971) "Child Phonology: A Prosodic View," *Journal of Linguistics*, 7, 179–221.

Wilbur, R.B., and Menn, L. (1974) "The Roles of Rules in Generative Phonology," Paper read at the Summer Meeting of the Linguistic Society of America, August.

Wilbur, R.B., and Menn, L. (1975) "Psychological Reality, Linguistic Theory, and the Internal Structure of the Lexicon," *San Jose State University Occasional Papers in Linguistics*.

Wilbur, R.B. (in press) "Theoretical Phonology and Child Phonology: Argumentation and Implications," in Goyveart, ed., *Phonology in the 1970's*. Story-Scientia, Ghent.

Winterbottom, M.R. (1953) "The Relation of Childhood Training in Independence to Achievement Motivation," Doctoral Dissertation, University of Michigan.

Chapter 4

AUDITORY VERSUS ARTICULATORY PHONOLOGICAL PROCESSES AND THEIR DEVELOPMENT IN CHILDREN

H. STEPHEN STRAIGHT

The relationship between the perception and the production of speech has been viewed in a number of different and conflicting ways by various theorists (see Strange and Broen, Volume 2, for a discussion of some of these contrasts). The view to be presented here, however, constitutes a rather radical shift away from the historically familiar and currently popular views. For one thing, it will challenge the long-standing and widely held assumption that there is some form of phonological representation that is common to perception and production. Several of the authors in these two volumes also challenge this assumption, but most people seem to believe that it is merely sensible, obvious, or parsimonious to assume that phonological knowledge is in some respects psychologically neutral regarding what you know about a given linguistic form that enables you to perceive it and what you know that enables you to produce it. But I think that that assumption is wrong (i.e., not sensible, see Straight, 1977c; far from obvious, see Straight, 1977b; and even unparsimonious, see Straight, 1977a). The view offered here will also, therefore, dispute all claims that one of the two modes of performance, whether perception or production, is in fact the basis for both modes, with the other merely employing some additional heuristic or other paraphernalia to specify a relationship between its operations and the operations of the primary mode. Analysis occurs by analysis and syn-

CHILD PHONOLOGY
VOLUME 1: PRODUCTION

thesis by synthesis: That is my thesis in a nutshell (Cole, 1977, provides a clear statement of, and one kind of argument for, the first half of this thesis; Blumstein, Volume 2, presents evidence that auditory phonetic analysis may not depend upon knowledge of the motoric aspects of phonetic output; and MacNeilage, Chapter 2, this volume, refutes—in passing—the idea that auditory phonetic representation could play a central role in the explanation of ongoing speech production).

An understanding of the nature of auditory and articulatory phonological processes, I will argue, demands the establishment of two distinct processing components, each with its own units of information and physiological mechanisms for the manipulation of these units. I call this the "processual" theory (see Straight, 1971, 1977b; Vandamme, 1972, 1977). Previous theories of the workings of the speech mechanism have sought to achieve structural integration of these two kinds of processes by means of such theoretical entities as "distinctive phonetic (or phonological) features," "phonemes," "morpheme structure rules," and so forth. The basic units in such entities have been claimed to be definable in simultaneously auditory and articulatory terms. That such a simplifying assumption has brought deep and far-ranging insights into phonology over the years is undeniable. But I think that this success is an index, not of the validity of the assumption, but of the high degree of mutual accommodation between auditory and articulatory processing that is achieved through their constant interaction during speaking and listening.

Surely these claims demand to be defended with empirical evidence, and such empirical evidence will be outlined later in this chapter. First, however, let me expand a bit upon what I have just referred to as the dominant "simplifying assumption" in current phonological theory (cf. Ferguson and Garnica, 1975). This seemingly harmless assumption consists simply of the assertion that phonological representations—the features that define them and the rules that relate them—are neutral between speaking and listening. Many linguists would certainly argue that this processual neutrality assumption, which is ubiquitous in linguistic theory, is a necessary idealization rather than an arbitrary simplification. They might go on to agree that the separation of comprehension mechanisms from production mechanisms is feasible, and perhaps even necessary, for a theory of actual perception and production (cf. Bever, 1975). But they would undoubtedly insist that a theory of the knowledge that underlies these input and output mechanisms can and should focus upon the deep commonalities between them. A theory that treats these commonalities as superficial (even epiphenomenal) by-products of concrete interactions between the mechanisms will appear thoroughly paradoxical to some. And when it goes on, as it will, to insist that these structural commonalities have no specific representation in the speaker–listener's knowledge, then anyone who believes that one's knowledge of a language consists of all the true generalizations about that language will exhibit strong negative reactions.

Negative reactions notwithstanding, the major upshot of the line of reasoning that Fernand Vandamme, of the University of Ghent, and I have been developing over the past 10 years—first independently and now in concert (see Straight, 1971, 1977b; Vandamme, 1972, 1977)—is simply that a theory of language knowledge must be bifurcated into a theory of comprehension know-how and a theory of production know-how. The subsidiary upshot that I will be addressing here is the conclusion that the debate over "motor theory" versus "perception theory" in the phonological literature has simply failed to recognize that we need to develop fully functional models of both receptive and expressive performance rather than try to pit them against each other.

Phonology: A Tendentious Historical Overview

The idea that linguistic theory, and hence phonological theory, is neutral regarding the actual processes whereby language and speech are interpreted and created has become deeply ingrained in most people's view of the division of labor among the disciplines engaged in scientific work on language. In fact, the difference between linguistics and psycholinguistics is now almost universally defined as the difference between abstract, processually neutral investigations of what language is, and concrete, processually focused investigations of how language is comprehended, produced, and acquired. Many commentators have noted that psycholinguistics has gone through a rapid evolution over the past 10 years, away from its initial parasitic connection to linguistics (e.g., Maclay, 1973; Reber, 1973; Wanner, 1977). The formal, axiomatic approach characteristic of much of the linguistic research of the past 25 years has simply not produced testable hypotheses to confirm the notion that set-theoretic models of language have any plausibility as psychological mechanisms (see Straight, 1979).

Nevertheless, the idea that linguistic, and hence phonological, theory has (or ought to have) some direct psychological content, whether in terms of the units, the features, the rules, or the levels of analysis it employs, remains very much "in the air." Indeed, this idea has been in the air since the beginning of modern linguistics three-quarters of a century ago under the inspiration of Ferdinand de Saussure and other philologically trained scholars. Saussure himself made the specific psychological basis of structural linguistic theory very overt in his most careful theoretical statements, as reconstructed from student notes on his lectures at the University of Geneva in the 5 years before the First World War:

> In order to separate from the whole of speech [langage] the part that belongs to language [langue], we must examine the individual act from which the speaking-circuit [circuit de la parole] can be reconstructed. . . .

How does the social crystallization of language [langue] come about? Which parts of the circuit are involved? For all parts probably do not participate equally in it.

The nonpsychological part can be rejected from the outset.

Neither is the psychological part of the circuit wholly responsible: the executive side is missing, for execution is never carried out by the collectivity. Execution is always individual, and the individual is always its master: I shall call the executive side *speaking* [parole].

Through the functioning of the receptive and co-ordinating faculties, impressions that are perceptibly the same for all are made on the minds of speakers. . . .

To summarize, . . . Language [langue] . . . can be localized in the limited segment of the speaking-circuit where an auditory image [image auditive] becomes associated with a concept. . . . It is such a distinct thing that a man deprived of the use of speaking retains it provided that he understands the vocal signs that he hears [1916/1959, pp. 11–15].

We see from this extract that Saussure rejected articulatory description as the basis for phonology, thereby flying in the face of a long history of attentiveness to, and his own use of, fundamentally articulatory variables in the explanation of sound change as well as in the elementary description of speech. His principled insistence upon the acoustic–auditory–receptive–associative focus of structural–linguistic investigation, and also on the inherently psychological content of linguistic description, introduced a fundamentally nonneutral psychological element into the body of guiding principles for linguistics. Even greater emphasis upon the perceptual basis of linguistics was present in Sapir's (1921) treatise on *Language*:

Language is primarily an auditory system of symbols. In so far as it is articulated it is also a motor system, but the motor aspect of speech is clearly secondary to the auditory. In normal individuals the impulse to speech first takes effect in the sphere of auditory imagery and is then transmitted to the motor nerves that control the organs of speech. The motor processes and the accompanying motor feelings are not, however, the end, the final resting point. They are merely a means and a control leading to auditory perception in both speaker and hearer [pp. 17–18].

Note that Sapir had gone one step farther than Saussure by suggesting that perceptual processes were not only descriptively primary but also (neuro)psychologically primary: even the "impulse to speech" is in the first instance an "auditory image."

The idea of a perceptual basis for language expression remains rather inexplicit in Sapir's other work, but his notion of the primacy of the perceptual mode bears an ancestral resemblance to the more current notion that to know a language is to have access to a system of perceptual and cognitive contrasts among phonological, morphological, syntactic, and lexical entities that can be described in a manner that will function in accounts of both language comprehension and language production (cf. Eliasson, 1975). According to this widely held current doctrine, the structural elements and rules of phonology (and syntax) describe knowledge that is employed both in the recognition and in the creation of utterances. Each of the phonetic (and syntactic and semantic) features that specify the sounds (and meanings) of words and phrases is associated with both the interpretation and the production of these objects. However, the fact that most current phonological (and syntactic) models include various kinds of transformations that convert abstract and unpronounceable objects into increasingly concrete and pronounceable ones is, we are told, not a claim that one has to be able to say something to understand it (Chafe, 1971). This would quickly reduce to the absurd claim that receptive experience with a language is not a necessary condition for acquiring it. In any case, a properly worked out theory of performance, we are assured, will in time show how such apparently production-oriented rules function in both perception and production.

Notice that the only similarity between this point of view and Sapir's is that linguistic description is relevant to both perception and production. The basis for this alleged relevance has, however, been completely reversed. Sapir posited an auditory, perceptual basis, with speech production parasitic upon auditory perception, but current theories mostly imply an articulatory, motoric basis, with speech perception assumed to be explicable with reference to the same phonological rules that define the derivation of overt articulatory output from underlying representations. And neither the Sapirian nor the more recent account takes seriously the original Saussurean insistence that linguistic theory is based solely in perception.

Wells, who was very sensitive to Saussure's dicta (Wells, 1947a), put the case for the perceptual orientation in phonology admirably clearly over 30 years ago (I am grateful to C.F. Hockett for having called this passage to my attention):

> A purely phonemic transcription, by definition, records all and only the significant distinctions that can be heard. If two utterances or parts of utterances sound perfectly alike to native speakers of the language to which they belong, their phonemic transcription is identical, even if they differ in grammar or lexicon.
>
> The rationale of this stipulation is clear. Phonemics takes the point of view of the hearer [Wells, 1947b, pp. 270–271].

I will not rehearse here the problems and inconsistencies that arise if one accepts this principle as the basis for the postulation of underlying forms for the production of speech. I will, however, assert that the overthrow of so-called "taxonomic" phonemics by so-called "systematic" phonemics succeeded as it did largely because of these problems and inconsistencies. The systematic phonemic approach insists that, although a potential phonetic contrast between two items might be neutralized in some contexts by the operation of very general articulatory phonological processes, the items should nontheless be given distinct phonological representations in both neutralizing and nonneutralizing contexts (Chomsky, 1964). The opposition between taxonomic and systematic phonemics, though it often masquerades as a "paradigm clash" of Kuhnian proportions (Kuhn, 1962), thus derives primarily from a contrast between auditory and articulatory phonetics as the basis for phonology. Unfortunately, this contrast is greatly obscured by the use of articulatory phonetic descriptions by taxonomic theorists and the use of "simultaneous articulatory–acoustic" phonetic descriptions by systematic theorists.

The connections between perception and taxonomic phonemics and between production and systematic phonemics are further obscured by their shared allegiance to the processual neutrality doctrine, whereby the phonological representation of a word forms the basis for both its identification and its pronunciation. It is becoming clear, however, that no theory is capable of attaining such a goal, so the debate between champions of these two approaches is destined to be both futile and eternal.

The notion that the perception mechanisms and the production mechanisms for language and speech are separable has been appearing off and on in recent years (cf. Vandamme, 1972). The evidence for an important dichotomy between these two as distinct realms of language processing is now both varied and persuasive (Straight, 1976, 1977c). It runs from semantics to sociolinguistics, from diachronic studies to neuroanatomy, from syntax to phonology. Ironically, however, the very people who present the best evidence for a functional and structural distinction between comprehension and production processes (e.g., the neuropsychologist H.A. Whitaker, 1971; the phonologist G. Drachman, 1973; the psycholinguist T.G. Bever, 1970; the developmental psycholinguist L. Bloom, 1974; the phonetician P. Ladefoged, 1971; the historical linguist P. Kiparsky, 1972) all argue at the same time for preservation of the competence–performance dichotomy, which they see, though in varying degrees, as necessitating a processually neutral model of the language user's linguistic knowledge. And still the contrast between articulation-oriented accounts (e.g., Griffen, 1976) and audition-oriented accounts (e.g., Leben and Robinson, 1977) of phonology goes largely unidentified and completely unelaborated, and the associated fruitless debates go on and on.

Child Phonology and the Perception–Production Split

Research on child phonology has been disproportionately focused upon children's vocalizations rather than on their perceptual discriminations. Only in the last 7 years have corrective measures been taken, beginning with the work of Graham and House (1971), of Garnica (1971), of Edwards (1974) and continuing with the work of Zlatin and Koenigsknecht (1975, 1976), of

Barton (1976), Macken and Barton (1977), and other people represented in this volume. Increasingly, the perceptual capacities of children and interaction between those capacities and their productions are being subjected to truly informed analysis. Nevertheless, it is still frequently the case that the very term "acquisition" is used to refer primarily to the emergence of language or speech in the output mode, just as the bias in phonological theory itself is to look primarily at patterns of articulatory activity rather than at patterns of speech understanding (but see van den Broecke, 1976, and the works cited there). The basic assumption of both general and developmental phonologists is put forward very clearly in an article by Smith (1978, p. 37):

> The sound systems of all languages consist of a set of discrete phonemes that are invariant units lacking durational values [and a wide variety of other phonetic details—HSS]. During the process of speech production, phonemes are acted upon by elaborate sets of rules and are converted into phonetic units which do manifest durational values and temporal variability [and other such detailed specifications—HSS].

It is this sort of assumption that inspires the observation that each person has a "unique phonology [Ferguson, 1977, p. 289]." Such a conclusion is fully justified by the evidence of individual differences in pronunciation, but the range of individual variability in word-recognition skills remains unexplored and might in fact be expected to exhibit very little variability within a highly interacting speech community, even in the face of considerable social, regional, and registral variation in pronunciation. Accounting for the wide range of fully interpretable input that is available to the typical language user may well constitute the methodologically richest and theoretically most revolutionary goal of linguistic theory in the coming years. And the study of child phonology shows signs of leading the way in this new direction, as does the whole field of developmental psycholinguistics.

In some recent summary comments on children's developing phonological skills, Menyuk (1977) compares the work of Garnica with earlier work and concludes,

> it is not clear that the sequence of observation of distinctions in production matches that in perception. . . . [In] the Garnica study, . . . there were individual variations in the sequence of acquisition of perceptual distinctions among members of [the stop and fricative] sets and there were clear differences in the data obtained in this study and studies of productive distinctions. For example, although perception of the /w/ versus /y/ distinction appears to be an earlier distinction than the labial versus nonlabial distinction in perception, the inverse occurs in production. Even at a later time in development, at age 3 to 4 rather than 1 to 2 years, the order of correctness of perceptual distinction made between members of speech sound sets (fricatives, + voice, and − voice stops and liquids) in a minimal pairs test (for example, *white, write, light*) does not stand in a one-to-one relation to the order of correctness of productive distinction (Menyuk, 1972a) [p. 40].

In an earlier survey of this sort of work, Menyuk (1974) used such evidence to support a radically new way of conceiving of the nature of phonology:

> The sequence of development of the perception of feature distinctions does not quite match the sequence of development of the production of feature distinctions (Menyuk, 1972b).
>
> One could . . . argue that at this stage the two processes [i.e., perception and production] are developing independently and are tied to different kinds of perceptual [sic] categorization—words with semantic properties and phonological features for perception, and semantic features and syllabic units for production (Menyuk, 1973). The process of integration of the perception and production of the speech signal at the segmental level takes place over a long period of time. The evidence for this is not only behavior which indicates that children appear to perceive segmental differences before they can produce them, but also the fact that delayed auditory feedback of the speech produced does not appear to act as a disruption of ongoing speech behavior until about 2:6–3:0 years of age (Yeni-Komshian, Chase, & Mobley, 1967). Before this age infants seem to monitor or listen to the delayed signal, as if it were any speech stimulus rather than a signal related to their own production [p. 220–221].

It is essentially this position that I will elaborate here, though I will have to add to this an account of echoic ability, which is the clear and necessary exception to the general rule that children's productions are not under the control of their perceptions (cf. Ferguson, Peizer, and Weeks, 1973, especially pp. 55–57, for a similar but far less insistent argument for separate sets of underlying representations for speech perception and production). I will be defending this view both for child phonology and for adult phonology, even though Menyuk herself has apparently retreated from the strongest interpretation of what she said in the previous passage (Menyuk and Menn, 1979).

Auditory versus Articulatory Phonetics

Central to the argument that is being made here is the claim that auditory phonetics and articulatory phonetics are not only distinct but, in some important respects, independent of each other.

A number of researchers have challenged the idea that the acoustic cues for the differentiation of phonetic stimuli are associated in a one-to-one manner with the articulatory parameters whereby the production of these same differentiated phonetic elements is programmed. This "distinctive articulatory–acoustic feature" idea has been around for quite a while (Jakobson, Fant, and Halle, 1951; Jakobson and Halle, 1956). And it has formed the theoretical bedrock for the overwhelming majority of work on adult and child phonology in the past quarter century. It was by means of the development of these articulatory–acoustic features that the transition from audiocentric (taxonomic) to articulocentric (systematic) phonological theory could be brought about without any overt attention to the shift in phonological directionality that accompanied the replacement of the old, "concrete" phoneme by the new, "abstract" one (though it might be argued that the other much-touted contrasts between the two approaches simply overshadowed this perception–production contrast). However, both Lieberman (1970) and Ladefoged (1971) have provided detailed phonetic evidence that various features that have been employed in fact make differential appeals to audition or to articulation in their definition.

The crucial point is that some features simply do not lend themselves to anything other than auditory definitions, with the articulatory realization varying according to the particular phonetic context, whereas other features can only be defined univocally in articulatory terms, with a range or even a disjunction of properties—some of which may overlap the properties of other, distinct features—characterizing their acoustic effects. Examples of primarily auditory features are voice onset, stop, gravity, and sibilance; examples of primarily articulatory features are glottalicness, articulatory place, and backness (see Ladefoged, 1971, pp. 91–94). For each of the former, there exist relatively invariant acoustic correlates but no invariant neuromuscular ones (see MacNeilage, Chapter 2, this volume), whereas for each of the latter, there exist relatively invariant neuromuscular correlates but no invariant acoustic ones (Studdert-Kennedy, 1976).

A more complex example is the nasality feature, which appears at first to exemplify a single neuromuscular correlate—raised versus lowered velum—paired with a single acoustic correlate—increased formant density. However, recent research has revealed that the muscular commands to the velum covary with the position of the tongue, and that without this variation in articulation the differences in formant density between some oral–nasal pairs of vowels would not be perceptually distinct, because high oral vowels have high formant densities even without nasalization (Tzeutschler, 1977). This kind of complex interaction of factors will probably prove to be the norm as more becomes known about the actual auditory and articulatory variables that underlie the various putative features of structural phonology.

The ready acceptance of processually neutral theories of phonology results from their ability to "account" for people's capacities (a) to identify acoustically distinct inputs with each other; and (b) to produce articulatorily distinct outputs that have identical auditory effects and are identified as the same sound. The details of how listeners might manage to equate acoustically nonisomorphic signals are assumed to be either very simple—the result of "acquired similarity" exposure learning—or very complex—the result of analysis by synthesis. But the fact that they do so identify them is assumed to be inherent in the interpretive mechanism itself rather than being an experimental artifact based upon, for example, a cycling through the articulatory processing mechanism *after* the sounds have been recognized, categorized, and interpreted in strictly auditory terms (cf. Strange and Broen,

Volume 2). Processually neutral theories thus merely assume, on the basis of no clear evidence, that sound-perception and sound-production mechanisms share some sort of phonological representation.

Similarly, then, an account of how speakers might manage to produce articulatorily distinct gestures as realizations of a particular feature in different contexts is assumed to be constructible on the basis of highly abstract and involved phonological rules, though some phoneticians might argue that auditory feedback was sometimes also an important controlling variable (cf. Ladefoged, 1967). But the possibility that these varying gestures may be governed by distinct underlying representations is dismissed as unparsimonious and empiricist (Liberman and Studdert-Kennedy, 1977). In fact, much theoretical work has revolved around the putative distinctions among audition, articulation, and phonetics. The assumption is made that phonetics provides a single set of "units" that function as end points of speech perception and the starting points of speech production (Fodor, 1975, p. 166).

Rejection of these misguided, or at least unwarranted, appeals to parsimony and abstractness in linguistic theory (cf. Straight, 1977a) leads to a reassessment of the notion of linguistic phonetics. Instead of grouping acoustic and physiological factors together, a processual theory establishes two distinct realms of linguistic phonetics. The receptive realm is based on analysis of the auditory cues and data-reduction processes whereby sounds are recognized, with close attention to such things as confusability and categorical perceptibility, which provide vital information concerning the perceptual variables that are being attended to by listeners. The executive realm is based on analysis of the articulatory programs whereby sounds are produced, with close attention to such things as variable and generalizable assimilation and neutralization, which are indicative of articulatory processes intervening between deep and superficial realizations. That these two realms are distinct from each other in ways that make it valuable to separate them in fine-grained phonological analysis has often been recognized. Parker (1977), for example, has recently explored the historical evidence concerning the loss of final stops in English words ending in the nasal + stop clusters − mb and − ng, such as thumb and ring. He made a very persuasive case for the notion that the loss of vowel-initial case endings led, by natural articulatory tendencies, to the loss of audible release on the final stops in such words, thus making the stops themselves imperceptible. Their imperceptibility then led to their extinction, for, although they were still being produced, new learners of the language could not perceive them and therefore had no grounds for establishing articulatory programs that would include them.

The receptive realm of phonetics must have a strict auditory basis. It was no fluke that at least two generations of presystematic phonologists were able to learn as much as they did about the sound pattern of language while harboring such an audiocentric bias: The patterns of perception are

just as real as the patterns of production. However, the receptive and executive realms must live in peaceful coexistence rather than become unified.
There are profound underlying differences between the auditory and the
articulatory features of speech. These show up, for example, in the differences between rapid and careful speech, where a contrast that is absent in
rapid speech suddenly appears when the speaker shifts to careful speech—
as in my pronunciation of the first syllables of the words *fanatic* and *phonetic*. The fact that such a perceptible distinction can emerge in careful
speech, or in specific morphological environments, correctly implies that
it may often be present, though imperceptible, in other situations. Spectrographic and myographic analyses support the generative phonologist's analyses, in which articulatory phonological processes often merely weaken
rather than eliminate underlying distinctions (Chomsky and Halle, 1968).

There is, to be sure, considerable pressure upon these two mechanisms,
audition and articulation, to accommodate themselves to each other by developing matched sets of inventories and one-to-one relationships between
the articulatory and the auditory elements of speech, but even in those rare
cases where the match is nearly perfect, there is no excuse for calling these
inventories and elements the "same" psychological entities: Isomorphism
is not identity. Even in the *semantic* analysis of lexical items there is evidence that our understanding of an "item" when we hear it may be at var-
iance with the meaning that we can infer for that item from our own use of
it. This conclusion is particularly clear in the study of child language (Thomson and Chapman, 1975). Passive and active vocabularies are made up of
two different sets of entities, despite their accommodations.

Furthermore, there are inherent limits upon the degree to which such
accommodation can be accomplished, particularly in the phonological realm.
The nasality example given earlier shows one way that such limits may be
imposed. There are also inherent coarticulatory programming tendencies
toward assimilation and neutralization in speech production. These conspire
with the inherent noisiness and redundancy of communicative interaction
to lead listeners to accept less than the perfect realization of auditory distinctions. And there are inherent auditory-processing tendencies toward
categorical perception and confusability in speech perception. These conspire with the inherent variability of speech input and of the information-
processing limits of the auditory apparatus to force speakers to keep the
number, complexity, and subtlety of phonetic cues that need to be attended
to within certain bounds. The result is an inherently dynamic and (micro-
and macro-) historical relationship between perception and production,
wherein conflicts and incommensurabilities are never completely eliminated
but are always creating changes of one kind or another within each of the
two systems. Let us turn now to an examination of a couple of particularly
interesting examples of the articulatory–auditory dichotomy, one from adult,
and one from child phonology.

Flege (1977) notes that perceptual experiments by Hadding-Koch and Abramson (1964) and Bennett (1968) show that, although spectral quality and relative duration were the dominant cues for the discrimination of German tense–lax and Swedish long–short vowel pairs, respectively, in both languages there are clear instances in which this expected relationship is reversed. That is, there are some circumstances under which the tense–lax distinction in German is cued primarily by duration rather than by quality and some circumstances under which the long–short distinction in Swedish is cued primarily by quality rather than by duration. Flege concludes that a one-to-one relationship between a linguistically relevant phonetic distinction and the perceptual cue that will be employed to recognize the distinction is not needed. This putative contrast between a linguistically relevant distinction and a perceptual cue deserves to be examined more closely, but first let us look at a developmental parallel.

The findings reported in a study by Higgs and Hodson (1978) might prove to be interpretable along the same lines as those of Flege. Higgs and Hodson report that their research corroborates earlier findings (Naeser, 1970) to the effect that very young children produce appropriate long versus short vowel-length distinctions in words ending with voiced versus voiceless obstruents, even though they may never produce any voiced versus voiceless distinction in the final obstruent itself. However, Higgs and Hodson have determined that, even at age 4:6, children are not as good as adults are at using this duration cue as the primary cue for the perception of the distinction between the minimal pairs *rope–robe*, *seat–seed*, *pick–pig*, and *ice–eyes*. On the other hand, they do hear the difference between these items when the voiced–voiceless distinction is present in the final stop. Higgs and Hodson concluded that children can use a different phonetic feature for the perception of a distinction than they use for the production of that very distinction. A closer look at their data, however, reveals that, although their conclusion is conceptually accurate, the empirical evidence for it may be even more complex than they realize.

There are clear differences in confusability among the four pairs of stimuli, and these differences may well be due to the unexamined variable of spectral quality rather than that of duration. The stimuli were carefully selected from painstakingly elicited recorded speech. The chosen stimuli were judged to possess no release feature or other final-segment cue of the voicedness or voicelessness of the final obstruent. They were also judged to be clearly identifiable as one or the other of their respective pair by adult listeners. It was assumed that this must be due to the duration of the vowel, though some other features were examined and discounted.

Omitted from consideration was the possibility that some of the pairs may have differed in the height and complexity of their vowels, with the long vowels being also low or diphthongal in comparison with the short ones.

In my own speech, the difference between *ice* and *eyes* clearly includes vowel height, and therefore also the extent of diphthongality, with *ice* beginning in a midcentral vocoid and *eyes* beginning in a low central one. Significantly, I think, only one of the 86 errors Higgs and Hodson's children made involved this pair, though they attribute this fact to some difficulty in keeping the voicing out of the final sibilant in *eyes*. I am less certain about a vowel-height difference between *pick* and *pig*, but the possibility that the latter is diphthongal is supported by the observation that there appear to be no / − ig/ versus / − Ig/ minimal pairs in English, possibly because the well-known diphthongal cue to perception of the tense–lax distinction is masked before the voiced velar (in fact, this voiced-velar environment selects against all of the tense–lax vowel pairs). Again, only one error consisted in mishearing *pig* as *pick*, though there were several instances of *pick* misheard as *pig*. This last fact is a very general one, by the way: Only one-fifth (.1976) of the total errors made by the children consisted in mishearing a voiced example as voiceless. The clear implication here is that the presence of extended duration, lowering, or diphthongization of a preceding vowel is a better cue for the perception of voicing than their absence is for the perception of voicelessness. And it can also be seen that there are in this case possibilities for alternative sources of auditory cuing (duration, position, and glide, as well as release features) for a single phonetic feature, which was the central point of Flege's (1977) argument as well.

The gratuitous assumption that gets in the way of a deeper interpretation of the results of both of these studies is the same old one (Higgs and Hodson, 1978):

> Because of the limited research done in this area, most of our notions of the young child's perception of the phonological system of the language come from the study of language production. Moskowitz, for example, suggests: "A phoneme can be said to have been acquired when the pattern of phonetic realization of X is consistently distinct from the pattern of phonetic realization of any other phoneme, Y" (Moskowitz, 1975, p. 146). Though few observers of child language would dispute that phonetic patterning of this sort constitutes evidence that the child perceives those portions of the adult system, they disagree with one another about the extent to which the perceptual competence is in *excess* of the production performance [p. 26].

The disagreement referred to here derives primarily from the insistence upon viewing "competence" as neutral with regard to perception and production, with underlying forms and phonological rules constituting the "knowledge" upon which both perception and production are based. The essential basis for phonological knowledge may, we can now see, consist instead of two distinct information-processing mechanisms, one for the perception of auditorily presented stimuli and the other for the production of articulatorily realized responses.

Auditory Phonological Processes

Evidence concerning our abilities to perceive various aspects of the acoustic waveform of speech suggests that the mechanisms in the receptive domain consist of a large, partly language-specific and partly universal set of recognition devices (cf. Blumstein, Volume 2). Each device yields a categorical identification, whether of an acoustic feature or of a simultaneous or sequential configuration of acoustic features. A given acoustic stimulus may succeed in triggering a large number of these devices, each with its own categorical output, even though this may result in conflicting (that is, ambiguous) percepts. The individual devices differ considerably with respect to the type and range of stimuli that can trigger them: some may be highly sensitive to minute details in the signal, such as those devices that permit us to recognize individual voices, whereas others may ignore everything except a single acoustic dimension, such as those that permit us to identify formant density or pitch shift. Furthermore, the phenomenon of "feature adaptation" (cf. Aslin and Pisoni, Volume 2; see Cooper, 1974) indicates that the parameters of sensitivity of these recognition devices are subject to sharpening and limitation by contextual factors, in something like the same way our other sense receptors become fatigued or sensitized. For purposes of strictly "linguistic" perception, all of this auditory processing serves to reduce the input to a set number of phonetic distinctions that are employed for the recognition of words and phrases. These distinctions correspond to some extent to the most strictly defined phonemic elements of pregenerative phonological theory, except insofar as pregenerativists (a) disallowed contextual "tuning" of phonetic parameters; (b) tended to assume that perception was based on segments (see Waterson, 1971, for a corrective to this idea); and (c) allowed articulatory similarity to serve as a unifying property independently of auditory similarity (cf. Wells, 1947b). Furthermore, the idea that such phonemic categories cannot overlap with respect to the stimuli that may trigger them has no merit: Certainly many stimuli are simply ambiguous—they fall in the range of overlap between two or more categories instead of within the exclusive domain of a single category.

Arguments against this sort of analysis-by-analysis model of speech perception (e.g., Fodor, Bever, and Garrett, 1974, pp. 279–313) have always been predicated upon the assumption that introspective judgments such as "both of those words contain a /b/-sound" are based upon information that is immediately present in the percept upon which linguistic interpretation is based. The counterclaim that is being made here is that such judgments result from perception–production interaction that is relevant to the judgment but not to the percept, which might in fact contain no common element in cases of widely disparate realizations of /b/, despite their common articulatory basis.

Articulatory Phonological Processes

For the adult speaker, the deepest underlying basis for speech production is undoubtedly something close to the systematic phonemic representations of generative phonology. Even if we were to disallow the most abstract examples of the genre on the grounds that they do not in fact represent productive patterns of alternation (such as the vowel-shift rules of Chomsky and Halle, 1968; see Moskowitz, 1973), we would be left with some undeniable cases of conversions and detailed specifications that yield a number of auditorily distinct forms for a "single" item. These crucial cases can, moreover, be readily explained on the basis of relatively invariant articulatory specifications whose precise motor realizations and auditory effects can be drastically modified by natural coarticulation processes. Following Reimold's (1974) insightful discussion of the nature of the underlying "psychophonetic" units of speech production, we may tentatively identify these as complexes of three different kinds of articulatory targets: "tactile targets (which are anticipated tactile sensations), auditory targets (which are anticipated stimulations of the auditory nerve), and motor targets (which are anticipated sensations relating mainly to muscle length) [p. 243]." (Never mind that Reimold adheres to, but neither defends nor provides evidence for, the claim that these bundles of targets serve as the basis for both production and perception.) This account needs only to be supplemented by something like Fairbanks's (1954) idea of speech production as a "servo-system" to be a fully functional framework for articulatory phonological modeling (comparable, I believe, to the position sketched by MacNeilage, Chapter 2, this volume).

Special attention should be given to the ways in which this description of articulatory phonology differs from the description of auditory phonology. The sensations that serve as the basis for the articulatory target that guides speech production include expectations for particular tactile and kinesthetic feedback that can have no correlate in speech perception. This much of the perception–production dichotomy seems secure. But what of the auditory feedback expectations that many phoneticians have believed to play an important role in the regulation of tongue position for vowels, where tactile feedback is largely unavailable and kinesthetic feedback largely insufficient (e.g., Ladefoged, 1967)? Could these, at least, represent a unity of perceptual and productional units, just as Sapir suggested? To some extent, yes, perhaps: But it seems that the auditory target that might guide production would have to be far more specific and constraining than is the auditory representation that underlies perception (cf. MacNeilage, Chapter 2, this volume). The range of sensitivity and tunability that characterizes our abilities to recognize speech accurately despite noise, dialect differences, speaker idiosyncrasies, and so on, requires a set of flexible categories for vowel perception unlike the set needed to account for our demonstrably very stable idiolectal vowel-production patterns. The phenomenon of mutual phonetic accommodation, whereby speakers and listeners tend to converge upon a shared phonetic system during the course of a conversation, indicates clearly that one's own articulatory targets are subject to displacement as a result of perceptual input (the auditory subtargets first, presumably, but then also the tactile and kinesthetic, as an accommodating speaker achieves a match with another's speech patterns). Furthermore, the auditory targets that con-tribute to the regulation of speech production are quite abstract in many cases, and also subject to change in the course of the speech act. For ex-ample, the kinesthetic features of an underlying vowel may undergo assim-ilative conversion from back to front of the oral cavity, and so the auditory target will also be shifted.

Auditory versus Articulatory Phonology in Children

The evidence for a basic dichotomy between auditory and articulatory phonological processes in child language comes from a number of different sources, some of which have already been mentioned. The notion that per-ception of phonological distinctions is dependent upon the development of articulatory skills would scarcely require refutation if it were not for the analysis-by-synthesis theories of speech perception, which have sometimes been linked with this wildly unsubstantiated claim (Liberman and Studdert-Kennedy, 1977). Clear evidence that children perceive phonological dis-tinctions that they do not produce has been amply demonstrated. Barton's (1976) dissertation is a prominent example in a series of studies that have set out to test very young children's speech-perception capacities, improving upon the methodology (see Barton, 1975) used by Schvachkin (1948/1973) and developed by Garnica (1971) and Edwards (1974).

Barton, whose theoretical orientation is essentially that of Smith (1973), concluded that both experimental and observational evidence supports the claims that the deficiencies in children's earliest phonological output are not caused by deficiencies in their perceptual capacities. Nor are there differ-ences, according to Barton, between the distinctions a child perceives and the distinctions present in the underlying forms the child employs in initiating speech. Instead, the child's deficient articulatory-processing mechanism in-troduces distortions of various kinds in the course of converting these un-derlying forms into motor output. The underlying forms themselves are acoustically based distinctive feature complexes of the familiar generative phonological variety, except that—in early childhood—they are much closer to the adult systematic phonetic (surface) forms than to the systematic pho-nemic (deep) forms of adult speech (cf. Chomsky and Halle, 1968). However, none of the evidence that Barton presents for this theoretical position selects in its favor over a position in which the underlying forms for speech production are different in composition from the representations employed in speech perception. The processual neutrality of phonological forms is, as usual, merely assumed rather than demonstrated.

Furthermore, even if we accept Barton's claim that children can, in fact, perceive virtually all of the surface phonemic distinctions of adult speech by the time they begin speaking themselves, we are left with a number of items of evidence against the idea that these accurate perceptual representations constitute the basis for children's articulations. And Barton himself presents quite a number of examples of this evidence. First, there are the forms that Moskowitz (1975) has referred to as "phonological idioms," words that children produce more accurately than their productional infelicities in other words would allow you to predict. The classic instance of this is Hildegard Leopold's correct pronunciation of the word *pretty* at a time when she produced other words containing this initial consonant cluster without the liquid /r/ (Leopold, 1947). Other investigators have compiled examples of such articulatorily precocious forms (e.g., Ferguson and Farwell, 1975; N. Smith, 1973). However, children, in contrast to adults, exhibit a high degree of variability from word to word in the degree of specificity of their articulatory targets. Barton (1976) observed that at the same time that some words may be produced consistently with initial /p/ or /b/, other words may be produced with gestures that vary greatly, even randomly, along the /p/–/b/ continuum. Nevertheless, it is clear that even 3-year-olds can control highly complex and accurate articulatory routines even before their perceptual mechanisms have achieved full sensitivity to the auditory parameters affected by these articulatory maneuvers (Barton, 1976; Higgs and Hodson, 1978; Naeser, 1970; B. Smith, 1978).

Granted that such examples provide striking naturalistic evidence that children can perceive distinctions that are not generally present in their productions (and produce distinctions that are not generally recognized in their perceptions), they also provide a problem for those who would argue, as Barton and Smith do (along with Stampe, 1969, 1972), that perceptual representations serve as the input to the articulatory–phonological–processing mechanism. For if this were the case, what in the world could serve as the input to this mechanism to yield, for example, /prIti/ for *pretty* but /pamIs/ for *promise*? The answer Barton (among others) gives to this sort of question is a bit inexplicit, but it seems to boil down to the claim that phonological idioms are "exceptions" to the phonological realization rules that otherwise apply to underlying forms to yield output lacking the "idiomatic" material. The possibility that the production forms might differ from the perception forms in the nonidiomatic cases is simply never recognized and therefore never eliminated.

Another source of difficulty for the processual-neutrality claim is the fact that children are often able to perceive their own recorded speech accurately even when they are not producing the same distinctions adults do, but that they lose this ability as their own output improves (N. Smith, 1973). This phenomenon would appear to demand that children have a developing perceptual representation for their own speech that may sometimes be distinct from the one they use for perceiving adult speech, and, if this is so, why not use this distorted auditory form as the auditory target-monitoring component in the child's articulatory routine for speech? Changes in the child's articulatory potential could then be explained in terms of gradual improvement in the match between the auditory representation of input forms and the auditory representations of the correlated output forms, as new imitation correspondences emerge through perceptuomotor maturation. The occasional idiomatic form could then be explained on the basis of a routine arrived at through trial-and-error manipulation of output, manipulation that was not governed by any stable imitation-strategy correspondence.

The hypothesis just presented receives further support from the evidence that phonological improvements are not always "across-the-board," but are instead sometimes only gradually "diffused" through the child's lexicon, morpheme by morpheme (Ferguson and Farwell, 1975; Hsieh, 1972). If it were true that the representations that underlie a child's production of speech are the representations that also determine their perception of others' speech, accurately perceived forms would necessarily improve in pronunciation in an across-the-board manner: As soon as the child acquired the capacity to block a particular distorting process, all forms that were subject to that distortion (except previously established idioms) would improve. And even if the improvement were not absolutely consistent at first, exceptions would have to occur in an essentially random manner with all lexical items involved and definitely not in a word-by-word progression. Notice, however, that the across-the-board and diffusion patterns of change can easily coexist in a processual model. One need only assume that children's underlying productional forms could in some cases be quite different from adults', with no distorting processes needed to make them perceptually distinct from adults' output, whereas in other perceptually similar cases their underlying forms could be quite close to adults', with distortions introduced during the production process. Words in the latter category would therefore be subject to across-the-board change as *processes* became more adult-like, whereas words in the former category would change only one-by-one on the basis of a change in the underlying articulatory program for each word. Such changes in underlying forms would presumably result from recognition that they did not sound like the adult input but could be made to do so through application of a newly developed or even momentary perceptuomotor imitation routine. If the child were being particularly attentive to its own output, a newly established imitation routine could serve as the basis for a diffusion through the lexicon so rapid that close observation would be needed to distinguish this process from an across-the-board change.

An anecdotal example of such a difficult case was obligingly provided to me by my 6-year-old daughter. She had persisted for a very long time in pronouncing /s/ and /š/ both as [ṣ] (a dentalized laminal fricative). But she had just recently begun to distinguish the two articulatorily (as she had long been doing auditorily). My 8-year-old inquired as to what we were going to talk about in Bethesda and I told him that we would be trying to figure out how children learn to understand speech and to produce it. His sister then piped up with approximately the following:

> You mean like how I learned to say 'shoe'. I used to say '[suw]' for 'shoe' and [looking at each item as she named it] '[sɚt] for 'shirt' and '[sak]' for 'shock'— [realizing her mistake] No! [much laughter from her and everyone else in the car] I mean, '[sak]' for 'sock'. I said *that* one right!

Of course, she had not said that one right back then either, but she was right in thinking that her old [ṣ] had sounded more like adult /s/ than adult /š/. And her articulatory programs for words containing these sounds were quite definitely undergoing change in the adult direction, but this change, as the anecdote shows, was very much under the influence of her own, independent knowledge of how each word ought to *sound*. Such interaction between developing articulatory and auditory knowledge can be used to explain not only the cases of across-the-board and diffusive change but also cases of idiomatic change and fleeting improvement in pronunciation: Children, like adults, monitor and correct their own productions only occasionally and incompletely.

Many of the natural phonological processes identified by generative phonologists could, on this account, be seen to operate in much the way they say they do. That is, they serve to distort a perceived adult form in a certain manner in the child's attempt to reproduce it. However, in some cases, this distorted output itself, its inaccurate articulatory shape and its acoustic form, constitutes the basis for the child's subsequent nonimitative productions, whereas in other cases, the distorting process is synchronically applied to an underlying form that is in fact, in some deep articulatory sense, closer to the adult form than its surface realization reveals.

Conspiracies and Echoic Responses as Results and Vehicles of the Interaction between Auditory and Articulatory Phonology

Study of the interaction between the speech-perception and speech-production mechanisms promises to provide the greatest source of insight into the nature and development of each of these mechanisms. There are two basic objects of investigation in this area: conspiracies and echoic responses. The latter were discussed briefly at the end of the previous section and will be looked at more closely in this section. But first let us look at conspiracies.

Fodor (1975) expressed bemused consternation over the phenomenon of linguistic conspiracies:

> There seem to be convergences between the outputs of linguistic rules which, so far as one can tell, have nothing *but* the convergences in common; as though the rules were conspiring, by many different means, to bring about desired ends. . . . What is one to make of this?
>
> I don't know. I so much don't know that I don't even feel confident about what the explanatory options are [p. 305].

Fodor's discussion of what he does think might count as explanatory options is, predictably, biased by his conviction that the grammar (i.e., the linguistic rules) of a language is something quite distinct from the production and perception processes that occur in performance. Lacking his scruples, we will find ourselves accepting options he dismissed out of hand.

To focus discussion, consider a simple but representative instance of a phonological conspiracy. The language is Bengali and the source is Ferguson (1977):

> Within the verb system all verb stems have an automatic vowel alternation such that you only need to posit five underlying vowels. There are seven vowel qualities, but you do not need to talk about seven vowels in analyzing Bengali verb stems. But those seven surface vowel qualities are identified by any Bengali with the seven distinctively different vowels in the nonverbs of the language, which are all over the place and do not alternate so neatly. . . . Somehow we have to get both those facts strongly and importantly in any phonological description of Bengali. It is not accidental or superficial that there are only five stem-differentiating vowels in the verb system and seven vowels elsewhere, and that the seven surface vowels of verbs are phonetically identical with the seven vowels that contrast elsewhere. The interlocking systems must somehow be captured in a way that I cannot feel any current phonological theory does [p. 291].

Processual phonology to the rescue! (I think.) The separation of underlying articulatory representations, and the rules that relate them to output, from the auditory categories whereby speech perception takes place provides a clear basis for accounting for this 5–7 conspiracy: To produce fewer than seven distinctive vowel qualities in the output of Bengali verb stems would be to underutilize the phonetic resources of the language and probably to complicate an otherwise exceptionless pattern of phonological conditioning (Ferguson does claim that the alternations can be subsumed under phonological rules; I am assuming he means rules that apply to something more than simply the verb stems). But to produce more than seven vowels would be to complicate the system of perceptual distinctions that would have to be attended to. It remains, on this account, to account for the seven-minus-two inventory of underlying vowels in verb stems, and my ignorance emboldens me to surmise that some historical facts or even some lexical-simplicity principles could be invoked to explain how a five-vowel system, the canonical /i e a o u/, was established and is retained in this subset of the lexicon despite the presence of /ɔ/ and /æ/ in other items.

Branigan (1976) has examined this issue of conspiracies in early child language and has concluded that the pattern of development in speech production between the ages of 16 and 21 months for the child he studied was governed by a set of phonological processes that conspired to limit the child's output to a small set of syllable shapes that were optimally suited to the child's capacity to produce perceptible segmental contrasts. The details of Branigan's analysis hang, as usual, on the unsubstantiated claim that the underlying form for the child's productions was something approximating the adult surface form that the child had received auditorily. Be that as it may, Branigan's observations complement those of other investigators to the effect that children are sensitive to the fact that their output will have to serve as auditory input.

Ingram (1975; also see Drachman, 1973), for example, has argued convincingly that the reason that children's productions do not exhibit the degree of homonymy that would be predicted from acquaintance with the severe limitations in their productive repertoire is that "the child . . . is constantly comparing his productions and making changes in those that do not maintain a surface contrast [p. 288]." This maintenance of contrasts often requires the establishment of special contrasts and conspiratorial processes that succeed in keeping homonymous pairs apart but do not generalize to forms that have no potentially homonymous mates. And, most importantly, Ingram shows that the contrasts and processes thus introduced "cannot always be . . . directly traced back to features of the adult model. Apparently unnatural or at least unmotivated processes in children's speech can be explained once the need to preserve surface contrast is considered [p. 288]." The conclusion that children do, contrary to the usual generative grammar assumption, develop phonemic systems that are distinct from those of their adult model, even at the deepest level of representation, is incontrovertible. And the contradiction between this conclusion and the equally incontrovertible conclusion that children are, by and large, responsive to the *adult* distinctions in their perception of speech (Barton, 1976) can only be resolved, I believe, by positing a distinction between the representational bases for speech perception and those for speech production.

Turning now to the topic of imitation, we can see that the model proposed here readily provides an account of this otherwise rather mysterious phenomenon. Our production of words is, after all, determined in some very common and direct sense simply by our having heard them. Contrary to the perverse but vain hope of the prototypical, and probably mythical, behaviorist, people do not wait for us to produce some intelligible sound so that they can reward it suitably to enhance its likelihood of recurrence. Instead, we can make a pretty good stab at reproducing words we hear by means of imitation, and the sense of virtue we feel in having done so successfully is all the reward we need.

Let me begin by showing the ways in which this phenomenon is made mysterious in current accounts. Remember that, even in the most "natural" generative phonological account of the process of phonology acquisition, the "adult surface form" serves as the input to the child's ongoing articulatory programming routines. But if this were the case, not only would we be faced with the mysteries brought to light by Ingram's demonstration of child-specific idiosyncratic contrasts and conspiratorial processes, but also we would be led to wonder what sort of mechanism could possibly account for children's gradual improvement of the match between their own and adult's pronunciation. Once homonymy has been eliminated, there would appear to be little pressure on children to bring their output into line with adults', and yet they consistently do. The only processually neutral alternative to the generative assumption is that it is the features of the *child's* output that serve as the basis for the perception of adult input (which would require a prosodic analysis à la Waterson, 1971). But this alternative is incompatible with the solid evidence that children perceive distinctions that do not appear in their own productions in any way. And it also makes mysterious the process of self-initiated successive approximation of adult forms (see Branigan, 1976; Weir, 1962).

Clearly the mystery of imitation is intimately linked to the doctrine of processual neutrality, just as the mystery of Christ's conception is linked to the doctrine of his divine paternity. Take the doctrine away and the mystery goes with it, though the plain descriptive problems remain to be solved. The problems that remain to be worked through within the processually dichotomous view of phonology have primarily to do with the ways in which children establish any connections at all between the developing auditory representations that constitute the basis for perception of adult speech and the developing articulatory representations that constitute the basis for their initial and intermediate approximations to adult words (Ferguson *et al.*, 1973).

Beyond rather glib allusions to Piagetian "circular reactions" or the maturation of the arcuate fasciculus (which connects auditory association cortex to vocal-tract motor cortex), I really have nothing to say concerning the psychological and physiological mechanisms that might account for the establishment of echoic response capacities. It is clear, however, that even in the first half-year of life some such connection between auditory input and articulatory output is established. Moreover, quite a lot is known about the *form* of this connection. Specifically, the notion of "substitution rules," which has been around in one form or another from the beginning of child-language studies (see the papers on phonology in Bar-Adon and Leopold, 1971), and which has been honed to a keen edge in the generative phonological work (cf. Menn, Chapter 3, this volume) that I have been so critical of here, lends itself very readily to reinterpretation as the basis for *imitation* processes. On this account, imitation, but not immediate production, consists of the conversion of an auditory input form into an abstract representation that can serve as the basis for articulatory output processing. Such a conversion can be modeled as a set of rules having a particular range of perceptual representations, specified in strictly auditory terms, as their triggering input, and a particular range of articulatory specifications as their output. The relationships that can be expressed between features of auditory input and features of articulatory programming may vary greatly in complexity and in specificity, but in no case will they be so simple and specific as to be univocal, because there must be alternative results to choose among to account for phonological idioms and the establishment of surface contrasts between homonymous pairs. This means that something we might wish to call "articulatory play" may cause substitution rules to vary from moment to moment in the process of trying to get one's output to match the input or to exhibit auditory distinctiveness. But since it is the arrived-at articulatory specification that will be retained, if anything is, as the basis for nonimitative production, there is no need to insist upon a highly abstract and exception-ridden set of rules as the basis for spontaneous speech production, as there is in current generative phonological accounts. On the other hand, the prosodic phonological account of the auditory specificity of early child speech output (Waterson, 1971) can now be reconciled with the evidence that children can perceive distinctions that are not present in their own output: The auditory specificity noted in the prosodic account can be related to the substitution rules that convert adult auditory input into the auditory feedback targets that comprise one aspect of the articulatory program.

Experimental corroboration of this model of imitation has yet to be pursued. However, one recent study of the development of VOT in stop perception and production provides the model some aid and comfort. Zlatin and Koenigsknecht (1976) have found that young children distinguish between voiced–voiceless pairs of words on the basis of quite different VOT values than those that characterize their own productions of those pairs, even though the latter are quite consistently distinct in their own right. This difference between their own productions and their perception processes was so great that when asked to identify the picture named by their own recorded productions, 2-year-old children "did not recognize the first word presented as being associated with the pictures [p. 108]," though with practice they were able to "adapt" their perception to their recorded productions and perform the picture identification task at a fairly high level of success.

This phenomenon of perceiving one's own speech less well than others' strikes me as a possibly crucial phenomenon for the study of phonological deviance. I would like to supplement my discussion of perception and production with one tragic example of developmental deviance that does seem to involve a major perception–production mismatch. I am speaking of Genie, the "modern-day Wild Child" described by Curtiss (1977). Genie seems not to have developed the capacity to relate auditory input to stable articulatory programs. She can mimic input quite well, but these mimicked responses are not retained for use in spontaneous speech:

> Her success with the [rhyming] task implies that Genie had a mental representation (at some level) of the "normal" adult phonetic forms that she was able to use. There is no other way she would have been able to make the kind of comparisons and matches against my pronunciation with such consistency, especially in light of her own highly variable pronunciation of the vowels and consonants involved [p. 59].

> Genie could at will produce a final consonant she had just deleted if an adult imitated her (Genie's) pronunciation of the word. Typically Genie would laugh and say, *Silly*, (with a gesture) at someone's imitation of her distorted pronunciation of a word, and immediately would repronounce the word *with* the final consonant (as well as other phonological content she had previously deleted). It was often as if she simply did not monitor her own output; and when someone monitored it for her (by imitating her), she could modify and "correct" it [p. 67].

> Genie's phonological system appears abnormally variable and unpredictable. Almost all of the rules are optional, and many of the substitutions and deletions distort the phonological structure to a degree which at times makes Genie's speech almost impossible to understand [pp. 90–91].

These phenomena are fully consonant with the idea that Genie might have a completely normal adult auditory representation available for each of the words she could recognize, but that it was by no means invoked as the basis for her own productions except under very unusual circumstances. Curtiss advances my case beyond phonology, by the way, when she concludes that: "The disparity between comprehension and production suggests two independent systems, one underlying comprehension, one underlying production [p. 203]."

Conclusion

Kornfeld's (1971) trenchant discussion of two basic competing hypotheses concerning the origin of the child's system of phonological representation phrases these hypotheses as follows:

> H_0 (the null hypothesis): *The adult system of phonological distinctions determines the child's system.*
> H_A (the alternative hypothesis): *The child perceives and produces in his own system*, which need not bear a simple relationship to that of the adult [p. 454].

The account given here of the nature of auditory and articulatory phonological processes and of their development in children would see such a dichotomy as false. There is no reason why H_0 could not hold, more or less, in regard to the auditory determinants of children's early accuracy in the perception of input, while H_A held, more or less, in regard to the inaccurate imitative and motoric bases of their developing production (and for their perception of their own production). The "more or less" qualifications are what make developmental phonology developmental, and the unresolvable differences (or dialectic) between the bases of perceiving and the bases of producing are what account for linguistic change, linguistic creativity, and some measure of the contrariness of language as an object of scientific investigation.

Acknowledgments

The lack of knowledge of the literature on child and adult speech perception and production that is revealed in this chapter would have been even more egregious if it were not for the bibliographic assistance and other advice that was so graciously supplied to me by the following people, though I am sure that all of them will be surprised at the number of excellent sources and ideas that I did not manage to work into the chapter, and that each of them will find more than enough to disagree with me about concerning what I did put into it: V. Jud, G. Drachman, P. Menyuk, L. Menn, M. Macken, J. Flege, H. Tzeutschler, J. Lovins, F. Gooding, and L. Bloom.

References

Bar-Adon, A., and Leopold, W.F., eds. (1971) *Child Language: A Book of Readings*. Prentice-Hall, Englewood Cliffs, N.J.

Barton, D. (1975) "Statistical Significance in Phonemic Perception Experiments," *Journal of Child Language*, 2, 297–298.

Barton, D. (1976) "The Role of Perception in the Acquisition of Phonology," unpublished Doctoral Dissertation, Department of Phonetics and Linguistics, University College, London.

Bennett, D. (1968) "Spectral Form and Duration as Cues in the Recognition of English and German Vowels," *Language and Speech*, 11, 64–85 (Cited in Flege, 1977).

Bever, T.G. (1970) "The Cognitive Basis for Linguistic Structures," in J.R. Hayes, ed., *Cognition and the Development of Language*, Wiley, New York, pp. 279–362.

Bever, T.G. (1975) "Psychologically Real Grammar Emerges because of its Role in Language Acquisition," in D.P. Dato, ed., *Georgetown University Round Table on Languages and Linguistics 1975*, Georgetown University Press, Washington, D.C., pp. 63–75.

Bloch, B. (1941) "Phonemic Overlapping," *American Speech*, 16, 278–284.

Bloom, L. (1974) "Talking, Understanding, and Thinking," in R.L. Schiefelbusch and L.L. Lloyd, eds., *Language Perspectives: Acquisition, Retardation, and Intervention*, University Park Press, Baltimore, Md., pp. 285–311.

Branigan, G. (1976) "Syllabic Structure and the Acquisition of Consonants: A Great Conspiracy in Word Formation," *Journal of Psycholinguistic Research*, 5, 117–133.

van den Broecke, M.P.R. (1976) *Hierarchies and Rank Order in Distinctive Features*, Van Gorcum, Assen (Cited in Barton, 1976).

Chafe, W.L. (1971) "Directionality and Paraphrase," *Language*, 47, 1–26.

Chomsky, N. (1964) *Current Issues in Linguistic Theory*, Mouton, The Hague.

Chomsky, N. and Halle, M. (1968) *The sound pattern of English*, Harper & Row, New York.

Cole, R.A. (1977) "Invariant Features and Feature Detectors: Some Developmental Implications," in S.J. Segalowitz and F.A. Gruber, eds., *Language Development and Neurological Theory*, Academic Press, New York, pp. 319–345.

Cooper, W.E. (1974) "Adaptation of Phonetic Feature Analyzers for Place of Articulation," *Journal of the Acoustical Society of America*, 56, 617–627. (a)

Cooper, W.E. (1974) "Contingent Feature Analysis in Speech Perception," *Perception and Psychophysics*, 16, 201–204. (b)

Curtiss, S. (1977) *Genie: A Psycholinguistic Study of a Modern "Wild Child,"* Academic Press, New York.

Drachman, G. (1973) "Some Strategies in the Acquisition of Phonology," *Working Papers in Linguistics* (Department of Linguistics, Ohio State University), 15, 83–98.

Edwards, M.L. (1974) "Perception and Production in Child Phonology: The Testing of Four Hypotheses," *Journal of Child Language*, 1, 205–219.

Eliasson, S. (1975) "On the Issue of Directionality," in K.-H. Dahlstedt, ed., *The Nordic Languages and Modern Linguistics 2*, Almqvist & Wiksell, Stockholm, pp. 421–444.

Fairbanks, G. (1954) "A Theory of the Speech Mechanism as a Servo-system," *Journal of Speech and Hearing Disorders*, 19, 133–139.

Ferguson, C.A. (1977) "New Directions in Phonological Theory: Language Acquisition and Universals Research," in R.W. Cole, ed., *Current Issues in Linguistic Theory*, Indiana University Press, Bloomington, pp. 247–299.

Ferguson, C.A., Peizer, D.B., and Weeks, T.E. (1973) "Model-and-Replica Phonological Grammar of a Child's First Words," *Lingua*, 31, 35–65.

Ferguson, C.A., and Farwell, C.B. (1975) "Words and Sounds in Early Language Acquisition: English Initial Consonants in the First Fifty Words, *Language*, 51, 419–439.

Ferguson, C.A., and Garnica, O.K. (1975) "Theories of Phonological Development," in E.H. Lenneberg and E. Lenneberg, eds., *Foundations of Language Development: A Multidisciplinary Approach* (Vol. 1), Academic Press, New York, pp. 153–180.

Flege, J. (1977) "Perceptual Cues and Phonetic Features," Paper read at the annual meeting of the Linguistic Society of America.

Fodor, J.A. (1975) "Comments on Ross's Paper," in J.F. Kavanagh and J.E. Cutting, eds., *The Role of Speech in Language*, MIT Press, Cambridge, Mass., pp. 305–309.

Fodor, J.A., Bever, T.G., and Garrett, M.F. (1974) *The Psychology of Language: An Introduction to Psycholinguistics and Generative Grammar*, McGraw-Hill, New York.

Garnica, O.K. (1971) "The Development of the Perception of Phonetic Differences in Initial Consonants by English Speaking Children: A Pilot Study," in *Papers and Reports on Child Language Development*, (Department of Linguistics, Stanford University) 3, 1–29.

Graham, L.W., and House, A.S. (1971) "Phonological Opposition in Children: A Perceptual Study," *Journal of the Acoustical Society of America*, 49, 559–566.

Griffen, T.D. (1976) "Toward a Nonsegmental Phonology," *Lingua*, 40, 1–20.

Hadding-Koch, K., and Abramson, A. (1964) "Duration versus Spectrum in Swedish Vowels," *Studia Linguistica*, 2, 94–107 (Cited in Flege, 1977).

Higgs, J.A.W. and Hodson, B.W. (1978) "Phonological Perception of Word-final Obstruent Categories," *Journal of Phonetics*, 6, 25–35.

Hsieh, H.-I. (1972) "Lexical Diffusion: Evidence from Child Language Acquisition, *Glossa*, 6, 89–104.

Ingram, D. (1975) "Surface Contrast in Children's Speech," *Journal of Child Language*, 2, 287–292.

Jakobson, R., Fant, C., Gunnar, M., and Halle, M. (1951) *Preliminaries to Speech Analysis: The Distinctive Features and Their Correlates*, MIT. Press, Cambridge, Mass.

Jakobson, R., and Halle, M. (1956) *Fundamentals of Language*, Mouton, The Hague.

Kavanagh, J.F., and Cutting, J.E., eds. (1975) *The Role of Speech in Language*, MIT. Press, Cambridge, Mass.

Kiparsky, P. (1972) "Explanation in Phonology," in S. Peters, ed., *Goals of Linguistic Theory*, Prentice-Hall, Englewood Cliffs, N.J., pp. 189–227.

Kornfeld, J.R. (1971) "Theoretical Issues in Child Phonology," in *Papers from the Seventh Regional Meeting* (Chicago Linguistic Society), pp. 454–468.

Kuhn, T. (1962) *The Structure of Scientific Revolutions*, The University of Chicago Press, Chicago, Ill.

Ladefoged, P. (1967) "Units in the Perception and Production of Speech," in *Three Areas of Experimental Phonetic*, Oxford University Press, London, pp. 143–172.

Ladefoged, P. (1971) *Preliminaries to Linguistic Phonetics*, The University of Chicago Press, Chicago, Ill.

Leben, W.R., and Robinson, O.W. (1977) "'Upside-down' Phonology," *Language*, 53, 1–20.

Leopold, W.F. (1947) *Speech Development of a Bilingual Child: A Linguist's Record* (Vol. 2), *Sound Learning in the First Two Years*, Northwestern University Press, Evanston, Ill.

Liberman, A.M., and Studdert-Kennedy, M. (1977) "Phonetic Perception," in R. Held, H. Leibowitz, and H.-L. Teuber, eds., *Handbook of Sensory Physiology* (Vol. 8), *Perception*, Springer-Verlag, Heidelberg.

Lieberman, P. (1970) "Towards a Unified Phonetic Theory," *Linguistic Inquiry*, 1, 307–322.

Macken, M.A., and Barton, D. (1977) "A Longitudinal Study of the Voicing Contrast in American-English Word-initial Stops, as Measured by VOT," in *Papers and Reports on Child Language Development* (Department of Linguistics, Stanford University), 14.

Maclay, H. (1973) "Linguistics and Psycholinguistics," in B.B. Kachru, ed., *Issues in Linguistics*, University of Illinois Press, Urbana, pp. 569–587.

Menyuk, P. (1971) *The Acquisition and Development of Language*, Prentice-Hall, Englewood Cliffs, N.J.

Menyuk, P. (1972) "Speech Sound Categorization within Sets by Children," in *Quarterly Progress Reports* (Research Laboratory of Electronics, MIT), 105, pp. 119–123. (a)

Menyuk, P. (1972) *The Development of Speech*, Bobbs-Merrill, Indianapolis, Ind. (b)

Menyuk, P. (1973) "Clusters as Single Underlying Consonants: Evidence from Children's Production," in *Proceedings of the VIIth International Congress of the Phonetic Sciences* Mouton, The Hague, pp. 1163–1166.

Menyuk, P. (1974) "Early Development of Receptive Language: From Babbling to Words," in R.L. Schiefelbusch and L.L. Lloyd, eds., *Language Perspectives: Acquisition, Retardation, and Intervention*, University Park Press, Baltimore, Md., pp. 213–236.

Menyuk, P. (1977) *Language and Maturation*, MIT Press, Cambridge, Mass.

Menyuk, P., and Menn, L. (1979) "Early Strategies for the Perception and Production of Words and Sounds," in P. Fletcher and M. Garman, eds., *Studies in Language Acquisition*, Cambridge University Press, Cambridge.

Moore, T.E., ed. (1973) *Cognitive Development and the Acquisition of Language*. Academic Press, New York.

Moskowitz, B.A. (1973) "On the Status of Vowel Shift in English," in T.E. Moore, ed., *Cognitive Development and the Acquisition of Language*. Academic Press, New York, pp. 223–260.

Moskowitz, B.A. (1975) "The Acquisition of Fricatives: A Study in Phonetics and Phonology," *Journal of Phonetics*, 3, 141–150.

Naeser, M.A. (1970) "The American Child's Acquisition of Differential Vowel Duration," In Technical Report No. 144, Wisconsin Research and Development Center for Cognitive Learning, The University of Wisconsin, Madison (Cited in Higgs and Hodson, 1978).

Parker, F. (1977) "Perceptual Cues and Phonological Change," *Journal of Phonetics*, 5, 97–105.

Reber, A.S. (1973) "On Psycho-linguistic Paradigms," *Journal of Psycholinguistic Research*, 2, 289–319.

Reimold, P.M. (1974) "An Alternative to Ladefoged's System of Universal Phonological Parameters," in R.W. Shuy and C.-J.N. Bailey, eds., *Towards Tomorrow's Linguistics*, Georgetown University Press, Washington, D.C., pp. 239–252.

Sapir, E. (1921) *Language: An Introduction to the Study of Speech*, Harcourt Brace, New York.

de Saussure, F. (1916/1959) *Course in General Linguistics*, The Philosophical Library, New York.

Schvachkin, N. Kh. (1948/1973) "The Development of Phonemic Speech Perception in Early Childhood," in C.A. Ferguson and D.I. Slobin, eds., *Studies in Child Language Development*, Holt, Rinehart and Winston, New York, pp. 92–127.

Smith, B.L. (1978) "Temporal Aspects of English Speech Production: A Developmental Study," *Journal of Phonetics*, 6, 37–67.

Smith, N.V. (1973) *The Acquisition of Phonology: A Case Study*, Cambridge University Press, Cambridge.

Stampe, D.L. (1969) "The Acquisition of Phonetic Representation," in *Papers from the Fifth Regional Meeting* (Chicago Linguistic Society), pp. 443–454.

Stampe, D.L. (1972) "A Dissertation on Natural Phonology," unpublished Doctoral Dissertation, Department of Linguistics, The University of Chicago.

Straight, H. S. (1971) "On Representing the Encoding–Decoding Dichotomy in a Theory of Idealized Linguistic Performance," in *Papers from the Seventh Regional Meeting* (Chicago Linguistic Society), pp. 535–542.

Straight, H.S. (1976) "Comprehension versus Production in Linguistic Theory," *Foundations of Language*, 14, 525–540.

Straight, H.S. (1977) "Persistent Fallacies in Psycholinguistic Metatheory and How to Overcome Them," Paper read at the Fourth International Salzburg Linguistics Meeting. To appear in *Salzburger Beiträge zur Linguistik 5*. (a)

Straight, H.S. (1977) "Processual Linguistics: A Post-structural Approach to Language," Contribution distributed to participants in the Working Group on Alternatives to Transformational Grammar: Limitations and Opportunities, Twelfth International Congress of Linguists. (b)

Straight, H.S. (1977) "Psycholinguistics: A Review Essay," *Canadian Journal of Linguistics*, 22, 169–195.

Straight, H.S. (1979) "The Set-theoretic Metaphor versus the Information-processing Metaphor: A Case Study in the Development of Theories in the Behavioral Sciences," in Marc DeMey et al., eds., *Theory of Knowledge and Science Policy*, Communication and Cognition, Ghent, Belgium.

Studdert-Kennedy, M. (1976) "Speech Perception," in N.J. Lass, ed., *Contemporary Issues in Experimental Phonetics*, Academic Press, New York, pp. 243–293.

Thomson, J. and Chapman, R.S. (1975) "Who is 'Daddy'? (Revisited): The Status of Two-year-olds' Overextensions in Production and Comprehension," in *Papers and Reports on Child Language Development* (Department of Linguistics, Stanford University), 10, pp. 59–68.

Tzeutschler, H. (1977) "Perceptual Salience in Nasal Vowels," Paper read at the annual meeting of the Linguistic Society of America.

Vandamme, F.J. (1972) *Simulation of Natural Language: A First Approach*, Mouton, The Hague.

Vandamme, F.L. (1977) "Semantics and Processual Linguistics I: General Outline," Contribution distributed to participants in the Working Group on Alternatives to Transformational Grammar: Limitations and Opportunities, Twelfth International Congress of Linguists.

Wanner, E. (1977) "Review of Fodor, Bever, & Garrett, *The Psychology of Language*," *Journal of Psycholinguistic Research*, 6, 261–270.

Waterson, N. (1971) "Child Phonology: A Prosodic View," *Journal of Linguistics*, 7, 179–211.

Weir, R.H. (1962) *Language in the Crib*, Mouton, The Hague.

Wells, R.S. (1947) "de Saussure's System of Linguistics," *Word*, 3, 1–31. (a)

Wells, R.S. (1947) "Review of Kenneth L. Pike, *The Intonation of American English,*" *Language,* 23, 255–273. (b)

Whitaker, H.A. (1971) *On the Representation of Language in the Human Brain,* Linguistic Research, Edmonton.

Yeni-Komshian, G.H., Chase, R.A., and Mobley, R.L. (1967) "Delayed Auditory Feedback Studies in the Speech of Children between Two and Three Years," in *Annual Report, Neurocommunications Laboratory* (School of Medicine, Johns Hopkins University), pp. 165–188. Also (1968) *Journal of Speech and Hearing Research,* 11, 307–315.

Zlatin, M.A., and Koenigsknecht, R.A. (1975) "Development of the Voicing Contrast: Perception of Stop Consonants," *Journal of Speech and Hearing Research,* 18, 541–553.

Zlatin, M.A., and Koenigsknecht, R.A. (1976) "Development of the Voicing Contrast: A Comparison of Voice Onset Time in Stop Perception and Production," *Journal of Speech and Hearing Research,* 19, 93–111.

Chapter 5

STAGES OF SPEECH DEVELOPMENT IN THE FIRST YEAR OF LIFE[1]

RACHEL E. STARK

Introduction

The development of speech-production skills in infants and young children may be viewed as occurring in a sequence of stages, each one of which is related to its predecessors in a coherent way. The orderly progression appears to have certain universal aspects. Individual differences are found within each stage of development and possibly in the degree of overlap of behaviors deriving from one stage and those that are characteristic of its successors. However, it may be that essentially the same progression is observed in all normal infants and probably, at a slower rate, in many retarded children. In this sense, the development of speech may be like the development of motor skills in general (Peiper, 1963) and of intelligence (Piaget, 1952) in the sensorimotor period.

Throughout the sensorimotor period, the infant's ability to communicate is also evolving. It will, therefore, be important ultimately to study the infant's developing speech-production skills in relation to his communicative use of these skills. Initially, however, it is important to examine this relationship from the point of view of the evolution of one or the other system. In this chapter, a recent approach to the study of stages of development of

[1] This work was supported by NINCDS Grant NS.09628 and by NICHD Grant HD.11970.

speech-production skills will be discussed. This new approach was derived
from the cross-sectional observation of a great many infants and was worked
out in detail in the longitudinal study of two normal female infants. It makes
use of descriptions of auditory and spectrographic features of vocalization.
The approach will be illustrated by descriptions of the vocal behavior of
these infants in the first year of life. It has made possible a more detailed
account than before of the manner in which vocalizations change as the
infant progresses from one stage of development to another. These results
will be employed in proposing a theoretical orientation to guide future analyses of infant vocal development.

Stages of Speech Development

The stages of development of speech production that have been described by a number of investigators working independently (Oller, 1976,
Chapter 6, this volume; Stark, 1979; Zlatin, 1975) have been reviewed elsewhere. They are:

Stage 1. Reflexive vocalization, 0–6 weeks: These vocalizations comprise cry and fussing (discomfort) sounds, and vegetative sounds including
some of a primitive variety that are found in the output of the very young
infant but subsequently disappear.

Stage 2. Cooing and laughter, 6–16 weeks: These sounds are first produced in pleasurable interaction with an adult or older child but may subsequently be elicited in situations that do not involve interaction. At the time
of onset of cooing, the presence of a smiling, nodding face would appear to
be a powerful if not a necessary eliciting stimulus.

Stage 3. Vocal play, 16–30 weeks: This stage has been described as an
expansion stage by Oller (1977) and as an exploratory mapping stage by
Zlatin (1975) who quotes Mattingly (1973) in support of this view. It is characterized by playful use of behaviors such as squealing, growling, yelling
loudly, production of noises by blowing air, food, or saliva through a constriction in the mouth or pharynx, and nasal murmurs. It terminates in a
mixed vocal play referred to as marginal babbling by Oller (1977). In marginal
babbling, long series of segments are found in which consonantal and vocalic
elements both occur but they do not resemble syllables of adult speech in
their durational aspects or other articulatory features. In this later form of
vocal play, consonantal and vocalic elements that were prominent earlier
are combined with one another in novel ways.

Stage 4. Reduplicated babbling, 31–50 weeks, (6–10 months): In this
babbling, canonical forms are found for the first time. The babbling is characterized by a series of consonant–vowel (CV) syllables in which each syllable is perceived as being similar to every other. It resembles speech much

more closely in its timing than the vocal behaviors found in any previous stage.

Stage 5. Nonreduplicated babbling, 10–14 months: This babbling (referred to by Oller as variegated babbling) is characterized by the use of different consonants and vowels within a series, and by the use of vowel (V), vowel–consonant (VC), and consonant–vowel–consonant (CVC) syllables in addition to the CV syllable type found exclusively in reduplicated babbling. In addition, a greater variety of stress pattern and of intonation contour is found in this later babbling. The unstressed syllables, like those of adult speech in the case where the language spoken is unknown, are very hard to capture in transcription. This activity may be that referred to by Gesell and Thompson (1934) as "expressive jargon."

Stage 6. Single-word productions (period of variable duration): These productions in the output of the infant are variously defined. They include (a) protowords, with onset at approximately 10 months, in which phonetically consistent forms are used to refer to primitive experimental groupings (Dore, 1976) as an accompaniment to a regularly occurring set of circumstances (Piaget, 1952), or to gain adult attention and express wishes and demands (Carter, 1974); and (b) words used as symbols and to refer to specific, recurring sets of objects or events.

Although there is agreement about the general nature of these stages and their order of succession, ways of discriminating the onset of each have not yet been clearly specified. The onset of certain stages such as cooing and laughter, and reduplicated babbling, appears to be more clearly marked than the onset of others, such as vocal play and single-word production. Behaviors typical of any given stage may have precursors in a previous stage and may continue into the following one. For example, the cry and vegetative sounds typical of Stage 1 are still found frequently in Stage 2, as well as the new behaviors of cooing and laughing. In such a case, time-series analyses in which frequency of occurrence of a given sound tape is charted over time, may provide the most useful means of defining stage onset. Problems of sampling speech behavior would then have to be dealt with.

Auditory and Spectrographic Features of Vocal Output

Description of Classes of Vocal Behavior in Stages 1 and 2

It has been proposed that the phonemic elements of speech, although not recoverable as invariant physical units from the acoustic speech signal, are made up of bundles of auditory features. These features serve to distinguish one phoneme from another perceptually (Chomsky and Halle, 1968; Jakobson, Fant, and Halle, 1963). The distinctive features have both acoustic and articulatory correlates. They are represented in phonetic transcription by means of the International Phonetic Alphabet. It has frequently been observed, however, that phonetic transcription is not a reliable tool for describing infant speech production (Winitz, 1969). It was hypothesized in the present studies that infant speech output might be made up of feature complexes or associations that differ from those of phonemes and, for this reason, cannot properly be described by means of phonetic transcription.

The vocalization data obtained in the first 15 weeks of life from all infants were first classified as cry, discomfort, vegetative, and comfort (cooing and laugh) sounds. This classification was made on the basis of nonvocal behaviors accompanying vocal output; that is, of facial expression, direction of gaze, movements of the limbs, and posture, as well as on the basis of the mother's behavior toward her infant (Stark et al., 1978). This information was available in a commentary made at the time of the recording on a second channel of an audio tape recorder, and later on videotape. Speech segments were then sampled from each of the above classes in the output of two female infants who were studied longitudinally. These segments were then subjected to detailed auditory and spectrographic analysis. This two-level approach had the advantage of avoiding circularity in describing cry, discomfort, and other sounds. It worked well for the analysis of the first two stages of speech development, in which the relation between vocal and nonvocal behavior appears to be a close one. For those utterances that did not clearly fall into one category or another on the basis of nonvocal behaviors, the vocal behaviors were often judged to have features that were typical of more than one class of sound. The mothers were likely to regard these sounds as ambiguous also.

It was found that many, if not all, of the features of speech that are distinctive in adult languages are present in the vocal output of the very young infant. In addition, features such as ingressive breath direction, vocal fry, and subharmonic break in voicing (Buhr and Keating, 1977; Stark and Nathanson, 1974) that are used distinctively in few if any adult languages appear to be prominent in the output of the very young infant. The prosodic features of variation in intensity and pitch, rhythmic patterning, and phrasing are all present in cry. Vocalic elements are found in all sound types but predominate in cry. Consonantal elements and transitions from a closed to an open vocal tract are found predominantly in vegetative sounds.

The primitive forms in which these features occur differ from the phonetic forms of adult speech in the following ways: (a) in the manner in which the vocalic and consonantal elements succeed one another within larger phraselike units; and (b) in the set of possible feature combinations that may be found in vocalic or in consonantal elements.

Vocalic elements frequently succeed one another within a cry segment (a unit separated from its neighbors by at least 50 msec of silence). These vocalic elements are set off from one another by steplike changes in their feature content. For example, a vocalic element containing vocal fry may abruptly succeed a vocalic element that is voiced normally. The mean steady-state duration of vocalic elements exceeds that of vowel segments of adult speech. The range of vocalic element duration is also much greater than that of vowels in adult speech. The less common consonantal elements of cry may precede or follow vocalic elements. That is, they may occur at the beginning or end of a segment or in midsegment. In the newborn period, the consonantal elements are almost always glottal stops, nasals, or liquids (Stark and Nathanson, 1974). Smooth transitions from consonantal to vocalic elements are absent except in the case of glottal stops where the sound source and the articulatory mechanism are one and the same. The succession of nasal or liquid consonantal elements and vocalic elements, like that of one vocalic element and another, is marked by abrupt change.

Consonantal elements have a much higher frequency of occurrence in vegetative sounds than in cry. The consonantal elements that are found in vegetative sounds are predominantly made up of stops, clicks, friction noises, and trills (described in what follows), and, much less often, of nasals and liquids. They appear to succeed one another in a manner more like that of adult speech than is true of the consonantal elements found in cry. Stops may precede or follow the friction noises and trills. However, smooth CV and VC transitions are found only in voiceless ingressive vegetative sounds.

It is important to stress that complex feature combinations are present in consonantal and vocalic elements in the earliest infant vocal output. However, they do not resemble the feature combinations of adult speech. The ways in which voice quality features may combine with fundamental frequency (pitch) and pitch change, intensity, and duration within a vocalic element, for example, may be quite complex. However, there are restrictions upon the types of feature combinations that may occur. Because the tongue is very large in relation to the size of the oral cavity, it is much more likely, during any maneuver, to make contact with the anterior or posterior part of the palate than in the older infant. As a result, changes in tongue height and position appear to be associated with consonantal production, not with vocalic. In addition, certain consonantal elements are found only in the context of lack of voicing; and the use of certain place features in sound production may be confined to segments characterized by ingressive breath direction, such as the bilabial feature in sucking noises.

Description of Types of Speech Elements in Stages 1 through 3

The feature-analysis system just described is capable of documenting new feature combinations as they emerge in the infant's output. However, from Stage 3 onward, it becomes much more difficult than in Stages 1 and 2 to classify utterances on the basis of accompanying nonvocal behavior.

Thus, the application of the feature-analysis system to classes of vocal be-havior is a less useful approach than in the earlier stages. It is still useful to regard crying, fussing, laughter, and the production of vegetative sounds separately from nonreflexive types of sounds. However, the earlier cate-gories of reflexive sound making are themselves changing and beginning to be used in a more highly controlled manner as the vocal-play sounds and babbling of Stages 3 and 4 develop. In other words, the relationship between features of vocal behavior and the nonvocal behavior context in which sounds are produced is much less compelling than for the vocal behaviors in Stages 1 and 2.

An alternative approach to classification of vocal output followed by the description of classes of vocal behavior is to select a specific type of element or syllable and to study the history of production of that element or syllable across a number of developmental stages. The element type may be identified in terms of its primary features (vocalic versus consonantal, voicing, and breath direction) and of some secondary features also (e.g., vowel quality, manner of consonantal production). The natural history of an element type defined in terms of its primary features, for example, voiced vocalic elements, may then be studied over a number of developmental stages. Changes of the formant structure of these vocalic elements as they are produced at different ages may be investigated (Lieberman, Chapter 7, this volume; Stark *et al.*, 1976). The speech environment may further be described in terms of the features of adjacent elements within a segment or the suprasegmental features of the "phrase" in which that segment is embed-ded. Finally, the social and behavioral contexts in which certain elements or larger segmental units typically occur may be studied. Thus, although the order in which the two levels of behavior, the speech or vocal behavior itself and its nonspeech behavioral context, are studied is reversed, it is still em-inently possible, by using this second approach, to ask questions about the development of speech skills in relation to other aspects of development such as social and cognitive factors.

Consonantal Noises

This second approach was applied to the vocal output of an infant in Stage 3. Infant V. was one of the subjects of the longitudinal study referred to earlier. The element type first selected for longitudinal study in her output was the nonsonorant consonantal element. This element type was selected for study because it is always found in the earliest stages of speech devel-opment, especially in vegetative sounds. Also it was believed that these consonantal elements are primitive precursors of the nonsonorants found in adult spoken languages. For convenience, they will be referred to as con-sonantal noises. This class of element included stops, clicks, friction noises, and trills. Friction noises are produced when a constriction is formed in the vocal tract above the glottis, and air, food, and/or saliva is forced through that constriction. Trills are similarly produced, but, in their case, the constriction is forced open several times in succession, yielding a series of taps of tongue against the palate or against the lips. The quality of the noise depends upon the degree of muscular tension at the constriction, presence or absence of saliva, and rate of flow of air or liquid through the constriction.

A review of the findings from previously reported studies of the Infant V. and a second female infant (Stark, 1978; Stark *et al.*, 1975) indicated that, in Stages 1 and 2, consonantal noises were found predominantly in vegetative and comfort sounds. Consonantal noises had a high frequency of occurrence in the vegetative sounds of the infants in both Stage 1 and Stage 2. They were infrequent in discomfort sounds and in cry sounds. In vegetative sounds of Stages 1 and 2, these consonantal elements were all voiceless; they might be produced on an ingoing (ingressive) or outgoing (egressive) breath. They were produced at the beginning or at the end of a segment. The mean duration of the clicks (ingressives) and friction noises was about 100 msec. Stops almost always preceded friction noises, but their duration could not be measured. The few consonantal noises found in discomfort sounds in Stages 1 and 2 were voiced, egressive, and of similar duration to those identified in vegetative sounds. They occurred at the beginning, midportion, and end of a segment. In comfort sounds in Stage 2, the consonantal noises were both voiced and voiceless. They were all egressive,[2] and were found at the beginning, midportion, and at the end of a segment.

In summary, for both of the female infant subjects studied longitudinally, it was found that the consonantal noises that were present only in vegetative sounds in the first 6 weeks of life were incorporated into the comfort sounds produced after 6–8 weeks of age. Consonantal noises were still found in vegetative sounds from 6 to 12 weeks of age.

It was concluded that in comfort sounds a new combination of features was formed, namely, that of voicing with the consonantal noises—friction noises, stops, and trills previously found only without voicing and exclusively in vegetative sounds. This new combination appeared to reflect increased control over voicing, which could now be elicited in pleasurable situations as well as in discomfort or distress; and also the persistence of the reflexive adjustments within the vocal tract necessary for management of the airway in the young infant that create consonantal constrictions. Many of these reflexes appear to be suppressed after 3 months of age. They may, however, be superimposed upon pleasure voicing early in Stage 2, thus giving rise to consonantal noises. For the two infants combined, the mean duration of the friction noises and trills in comfort sounds, which were sometimes preceded by stops, was approximately 120 msec.

---

[2] We have since observed infants who produce both voiced and voiceless ingressives (clicks) in comfort sounds in Stage 2.

The results of the study of consonantal noises in Stage 3 must still be regarded as preliminary because they reflect the output of one infant only (Infant V). In addition, some of the detailed observations of the context in which the friction noises occurred could be made by only one listener. The findings may be summarized as follows:

1. The most striking finding with respect to Stage 3 in Infant V. is its duration. Reduplicated babbling did not have its onset until 37 weeks of age. In most infants, reduplicated babbling appears at approximately 30–35 weeks. The first examples of comfort sounds also appeared somewhat late in Infant V.'s output (8 weeks of age) and, as indicated above, comfort sounds did not occur very frequently until she was 10 weeks of age. It is possible, therefore, that her early vocal development was somewhat delayed as compared with that of many other infants.

2. The duration of consonantal noises produced in vocal-play sounds in Stage 3 was greater than that of the comfort sounds produced in Stage 2 for this infant. The increase in duration was a gradual one at first, but, in the midportion of Stage 3, mean duration was more than 10 times greater than it was for the noises in comfort sounds produced in weeks 10–15 or in the segments produced at the onset of vocal play. Individual consonantal noises of more than 1.5 sec were observed. From week to week in Stage 3, marked increases and decreases in the duration of consonantal noises were associated with changes in manner of articulation of the noise itself (friction versus trill versus fricative versus click), place of articulation as documented at the time of the recording, voicing, and other features of the overall speech context.

3. At the end of Stage 3, fricatives, affricates, and affricate clicks were produced with a high frequency of occurrence. Voiceless consonantal elements judged to be affricates and true fricatives appeared first. These sounds showed a concentration of energy in the higher frequencies and fewer interruptions in the form of stops or trill taps than before. Furthermore, the constriction appeared to be maintained throughout the consonantal element as in the fricative consonants produced by adults. Many of these noises were immediately preceded by stoplike closure of the vocal tract and could therefore be considered as affricates. Similar sounds were produced shortly afterward in combination with voicing. Affricate clicks appeared with great regularity in Infant V.'s output toward the end of Stage 3. Lingual–alveolar–ridge affricate clicks were observed for several weeks before the appearance of babbled stop–vowel-syllable series in the output of a number of additional infant subjects who were studied more recently by the author. They were also produced by Infant V. before stop–vowel syllables were mastered.

4. When vocalizing, Infant V. appeared to have little ability to release

a consonantal constriction in the vocal tract *under active control* until 36 weeks of age. This control is needed to produce stop–vowel syllables. Where friction noises or trills were followed by a vowel in comfort or vocal-play sounds, Infant V. merely had to increase the buildup of air pressure sufficiently behind the constriction to force it open. The affricate clicks observed toward the end of the vocal-play period, like those observed in vegetative activity in the first 12 months of life, demanded some active separation of tongue from palate. The mechanism for separation was thought to be increased negative pressure at the constriction in the vocal tract above the glottis, which forced the constriction to open. It is possible that the ability to open the vocal tract above the glottis from a closed position during vocal output may not be acquired until the second 6 months of life by many infants.

5. The Infant V. did not begin to acquire control of pitch and intensity until Week 25. It has been reported that some infants begin to play with squeals, growls, and yells earlier in the vocal-play period, others later. The number of weeks spent in play with pitch–intensity and with friction noises also appears to vary from infant to infant. It may be, however, that both play with pitch–intensity and play with consonantal noises must precede the onset of reduplicated babbling. In reduplicated babbling, sufficient control over phonation is needed to coordinate it with repeated opening and closing of the vocal tract above the glottis and to impose at least a simple fundamental frequency contour upon the syllable series produced.

It has been observed that the output of infants in the vocal-play stage, as well as in other stages of vocal development, is highly variable; and that utterance types tend to appear and to reappear in a manner that cannot readily be accounted for. The data presented in this study suggest that infants in these stages may constantly be trying out new combinations and recombinations of sound-making skills as these skills become increasingly accessible to them. Thus, what appears to be the recurrence of an old utterance type may be a modification of previous patterns of vocal output in the form of addition of one or more features, such as addition of voicing or change in place of articulation. Not all of these new feature combinations are found in later speech production. Trills and friction noises of long duration, for example, are not found in any spoken language. As one or more new features are added to a consonantal element type such as friction noise, other features that were previously well established in combination with that consonantal element type, may drop out temporarily. Marked increase in the duration of friction noises, for example, appeared, in Infant V.'s case, to be associated with a temporary disappearance of other consonant-like elements and of vowels from the segment context in which they occurred.

The appearance of true fricatives and affricates before the onset of reduplicated babbling was unexpected. It was believed that series of stop–vowel and nasal consonant–vowel syllables would emerge before fricatives and affricates, even isolated fricatives–affricates. The order of appearance of these classes of output may vary from one infant to another.

Other Element Types

Similar studies might be carried out with respect to nasal consonantal elements, vocalic elements, and glides. It would be of interest, for example, to find out if transitions from nasal consonantal to vocalic elements in the vocal-play period are effected by increasing the air pressure behind the constriction, as appeared to be the case of nonsonorant consonantal noises, or by active opening of that constriction. Pitch change and rate of change in vocalic elements may be measured as well as means and ranges of fundamental frequency. This work has already been initiated by Delack and Fowlow (1975), Laufer and Horii (1977) and Keating and Buhr (1978). The study of formant structure of vocalic elements, begun by Lieberman (1978) and Stark et al., (1976) could be approached in a similar way, that is, by examining auditory features (perceived vowel quality and voice quality) and spectral features in relation to the speech environment. Such studies will make it possible to find out whether or not vowel quality feature combinations approximate those of the language spoken in the adult environment in a more linear fashion over time than do consonantal or suprasegmental feature combinations. The approach also enables aspects of vocalic and consonantal features to be examined in relation to one another in infant speech. It should prove to be a very productive one.

Description of Syllables from Stage 4 Onward

Vocal-play behaviors persist in the infant's output after the onset of reduplicated babbling, although with reduced frequency of occurrence in many cases; consonantal noises, nasal murmurs, high-pitched squeals, and other types of vocal play are later combined with CV syllables in nonreduplicated babbling series in Stage 5. From the onset of Stage 4 onward, however, the CV syllable becomes a unit of interest in its own right. It may be studied over the second 6 months of life in terms of its speech environment, and also of the nonspeech behavioral context in which it is produced. Thus far, only syllable duration and the voicing features of initial stops have been studied. With respect to syllable durations, Oller (1977) has shown that between 7 and 12 months of age, final-syllable lengthening is much less prominent in the CV syllable production of infants than of English-speaking adults. He concludes, somewhat tentatively, that this lengthening may be learned in languages such as English, in which it is a very robust effect outweighing all possible errors of measurement or of interpretation. With respect to voicing, Port and Preston (1974), Moslin (1978), and others have generally found that infants of 6–12 months use both the short-lag and long-lag VOT ranges in producing stop–vowel syllables. Values in the voicing-lead range may also be found, but the modal value is usually a short-lag value. Moslin also suggested that infants may use quite different strategies in production of the voicing feature than do adults or older children. It is not necessarily true, however, that infants are deliberately attempting to produce voiced and voiceless stops. They may merely be working to obtain sound effects of interest to them. Studies in which both auditory judgments and acoustic measurements are made will be necessary to trace the developmental history of CV syllable production in infant speech from reduplicated babbling through first words, in the same manner as for the consonantal noises and other elements found in the first three stages of speech development. It will be most important in these studies to trace the development of pitch contour and rhythmic and stress patterns especially in the nonreduplicated babbling period.

The Ontogeny of Speech

The earliest characteristics of infant speech that have been described may be explained at least partly on the basis of differences in vocal-tract structure and function from infant to adult. The structure of the newborn infant vocal tract is said to resemble that of the nonhuman primate (Lieberman et al., 1972). The tongue is large in relation to the oral cavity; the larynx is high, and the dorsal wall of the oral pharynx slopes at such an angle that the oral pharyngeal space is limited and leaves little room for the posterior part of the tongue to maneuver (Bosma, 1972; Lieberman et al., 1972). The number of recognizably different vowel sounds that may be produced by the newborn infant is correspondingly limited (Irwin and Chen, 1946). To put it very simply, if the tongue is raised, it is likely to contact the lips or the palate. If the tongue moves anteriorly or posteriorly, it is likely to form a constriction, either with the lips in front, or with the soft palate and pharyngeal wall at the back. In all cases, a consonantal element will be perceived. It is only at about 3 months of age, when the angle of the mandible changes rapidly with downward and forward growth of the face that an increased vowel space begins to be available to the infant (George, 1978).

The earliest characteristics of infant speech may also be accounted for on the basis of the nonspeech functioning of the infant vocal tract. At birth, the infant is a compulsive nasal breather, except during cry. Thus, when voice is produced, the mouth tends to be open and the probability of occurrence of consonantal elements is low. The reflexive adjustments of the vocal tract that are associated with protection of the airway, with maintaining its patency, and with food ingestion are produced with the vocal tract closed. These adjustments give rise to a great variety of noises; the clicks, stops, friction noises, and trills referred to previously as consonantal noises. Thus, the newborn infant has two separate sound-making systems; one associated with expression of distress in which vocalic elements predominate and which has rhythmic and stress variation and pitch contours; the other associated with management of nutrients, in which consonantal elements predominate and in which breath-excited formant transitions from vocalic to consonantal elements, or the reverse, may be found at least on ingressive sound production.

The theoretical approach to speech development that is outlined in what follows rests upon the belief that the presence of these two sound-making mechanisms in the human infant is essential to later speech development. It is suggested that the vocalic and suprasegmental features of cry and the consonantal features of vegetative sounds enter into fresh combinations with one another at each of the developmental stages described. At the same time, the infant's ability to control laryngeal and articulatory gestures above the larynx is increasing. It is important in any theory of speech development to show how these two phenomena, the combination and recombination of features, and the increasing control of the speech musculature, interact with one another. These interactions, and also the interaction of vocal and cognitive development, may best be observed in relation to the stages of vocal development already described.

Stage 1

The first combination is found in Stage 1. Although the mouth is usually open during cry, the tongue tends to resume its usual opposition to the soft palate. This tendency is most marked during low-level crying and fussing (discomfort) sounds. The resumption of closure gives rise to the voiced nasal or liquid consonantal elements found in cry and discomfort sounds (Stark and Nathanson, 1974). Thus, these nasals and liquids appear to result from the imposition of vegetative functioning upon cry. It is noteworthy that the low-level fussing in which the closure occurs is often associated with a change in state from lower-level distress to higher-level distress, or the reverse.

Stage 2

In cooing sounds in Stage 2 nasal consonantal elements are also found. In addition, voicing is, for the first time, combined with the nonsonorant consonantal elements that were previously present, without voice, in vegetative activity only. This combination, as was indicated, is thought to result primarily from the newly acquired ability to produce voice in states of pleasure. In pleasurable states, as in low-level fussing, the vocal tract is likely to assume a closed position, a tendency favoring the production of nasal consonantal elements. Under certain circumstances, that is, where the soft palate is elevated in response to reflexive adjustments of the vocal tract, friction noises and trills may be imposed on voicing instead of on nasals. The reflexive mechanisms themselves, however, undergo a change early in Stage 2. Between 6 and 12 weeks of age, the infant forms the habit of playing with the tongue and lips when he is awake, alert, and not in distress. The tongue is protruded and retracted, the lips rounded, the mouth silently opened and closed. Piaget (1952) likens these play movements to the movements of feeding and refers to them as "acquired sucking habits." The infant may make them as he gazes at the mother or tries to take the nipple. They may be associated for the infant with the pleasure of feeding or they may reflect a generalized state of excitement. Meltzoff and Moore (1977) have demonstrated that such movements (without voice) may also be produced in imitation of adults as early as 2 weeks of age. It is in interaction with adults that infants are also most likely to produce their first brief voiced pleasure sounds. After a few weeks, however, pleasure (cooing) sounds in longer series are as likely to be produced when the infant is looking at interesting objects, especially those that move, as when he is looking at faces. So, too, are movements of the tongue and lips. Thus, the frequency of occurrence, both of tongue and lip movement and of voicing, may increase in similar states of the infant or under similar circumstances as he progresses through Stage 2; if so, the probability of their cooccurrence will also be enhanced, and, with it, the likelihood that consonantal noises will continue to be superimposed upon pleasure voicing. Observations suggest that these noises have predominantly a velar place of articulation. If the tongue is moving, it always moves dorsally in retraction or is just beginning to move forward in protrusion. It does not appear to rest between the lips or to extend outside the mouth during voicing. By about 3 months of age, abrupt reflexive adjustments of the tongue, palate, and pharynx are all beginning to be suppressed. In addition, oral tidal respiration is being established and closure of tongue with soft palate is no longer obligatory. Play movements of tongue and lips may persist and lip closure during voicing may now give rise to /m/ like nasal murmurs.

Laughter, which emerges at 16–20 weeks (Gesell and Thompson, 1934), is produced mainly in interaction with adults and older children, at least initially. It manifests a new combination, of segment types rather than of elements, that is, the segments of laughter derive from both cry and cooing sounds. The first segments of the laugh series, which resemble certain portions of a cry episode, are characterized by rapid alternation of voicing with voicelessness. They are followed by a voiced inspiratory segment of a kind also found in cry. This introductory phrase is succeeded by a typical cooing sound, possibly as tension is relieved. After the infant enters the vocal-play period, segments that are characteristic of the infant's output in that period may also be incorporated in laughter; for example, extended squeals, prolonged ingressive voicing, and pharyngeal or velar friction noises.

Stage 3

At about 16 weeks of age, infants begin to manipulate the features of vocalic or consonantal elements in a number of ways. The vocalic features selected are pitch level, pitch change (growling, squealing, use of extreme pitch glides), and loudness. The consonantal features are friction and other noises and nasal murmurs. Both the vocalic and the consonantal elements may be lengthened at some time during the vocal-play stage and may then occupy an entire segment rather than combining with one another within a segment. Glides and ingressive voicing may also be exercised; glottal stops are freely distributed among series of vocalic and of syllabic consonantal segments. Some infants concentrate first upon manipulation of vocalic features; others, like Infant V., concentrate upon consonantal features. Observations suggest that in the first of these groups of infants, the acquired habits of moving tongue and lips (acquired sucking habits) may disappear at the onset of vocal play. Consonantal noises may later be rediscovered by these infants during feeding when they play with semisolid foods in the mouth. In the second group of infants, the acquired habits of lingual and labial movement appear to persist throughout the vocal-play period, but *in association with speech output only*. They are not evident, that is, unless the infant is vocalizing. In either case, the infant takes apart the elements, of which his utterances are formed, selects single elements, produces them over and over, prolongs them, elaborates them, and divides the elaborated versions into new segment types by means of glottal stops and silent intervals. The infant then shortens them again and puts the new segment type or new element back in series with others that are of earlier origin or are more highly practiced.

This disassembly of parts and their reassembly in new series is an essential characteristic of all subsequent development in speech production. In the vocal-play period, these operations are carried out in a manner reminiscent of secondary circular reactions (Piaget, 1952). By repeating certain familiar routines (short squeals of excitement, consonantal noises) over and over and later prolonging segments made up of these features, the infant increases both the frequency and duration of interesting sound effects. He is also discovering a quantitative relation between the degree and duration of tension and effort at the articulators, and the acoustic parameters of his own output. It is true that his output is not truly external to himself as are the obtained effects of visual exploration or movement of the limbs in other secondary circular reactions. Nevertheless, they do represent a new and skillful coordination of the two separate sound-making systems which may previously have impinged upon one another only by virtue of the fortuitous cooccurrence of simpler primary circular reactions.

At the beginning of the vocal-play stage, the element type that is being exercised at any one time is likely to be produced in many different social contexts; in complaining, laughing, playing imitation games, gazing at the environment, and others. At the end of this stage, when forms less exaggerated in duration or pitch are being produced, and when they are being combined with one another in series, vocal-play sounds are much more likely to be associated with the mouthing of objects, including the infant's own fists. They may also come to be associated with visual exploration of the environment more often than with social interaction of any kind (Stark, 1979). At this time, the infant tries to grasp everything of interest that is within reach and to put it in his mouth. As he mouths an object, he may gaze fixedly at some more distant point in the environment. He may also take the object out and turn it around, inspecting its angles and surfaces. Thus, vocal-play sounds, especially their consonantal components, tend to become more closely associated over time with visual and oral exploration of objects, and of the environment in general, than with social interaction.

Stage 4

In Stage 4, the infant suddenly acquires mastery over the more speech-like activity of reduplicated babbling. The essential component to this new skill may be that of opening the vocal tract at some point above the glottis from a closed position under active control; or it may merely be that of timing of the opening gesture as Oller (Chapter 6, this volume) has suggested. For the first time CV transitions are handled efficiently in a continuous series of segments.

The transition from C to V or V to C may be the most essential characteristic of adult speech. It provides parallel transmission of information with respect to both vowel and consonant (Lieberman et al., 1967) and may also have the function of binding the elements of speech together perceptually and of maintaining their order for the listener (Dorman, et al., 1975). As a result of the acquisition of smooth, controlled CV transitions, the segments of infant output now resemble syllables of speech much more closely than they did before. At the onset of Stage 4, reduplicated babbling sounds, in common with the vocal-play sounds emitted at the end of Stage 2, are more likely to be produced in association with exploration of the environment than with social interaction. At the time when the babbling first appears, the infant has begun to wave, shake, and repeatedly strike objects that he has in his hand. If no object is available to him, he may wave, shake, or strike surfaces with his hands or strike one hand with the other. Piaget (1952) observed that the infant is likely to do this when he catches sight of an object that may be shaken but that is at some distance from him or, for some other reason, is not likely to be grasped. He views the activity as one of recognitory assimilation, and he believes that the infant is assimilating the unexpected sight of a familiar object by performing the action of shaking his own hands or legs. Thus, the infant uses a motor concept to assign objects to a class, that is, of objects that may be shaken. The infant is also more likely to emit a reduplicated babble sequence when he holds an object that may be shaken, or when he visually explores his environment, than in any other context. There is, at present, no clear indication in the case of visual exploration as to whether or not the infant is regarding distant objects that may be grasped and moved when he shakes his hands or legs, or when he engages in reduplicated babbling. It is clear only that, at the beginning of Stage 4, infants are not usually looking at a person when they engage in shaking the limbs or in babbling. It may be that a very general association of babbling with the shaking and waving of objects is present, in the same manner as persisting vocal-play sounds appear to have very general association with the mouthing of objects, and the sensing of shapes and surfaces with the mouth. Both sound types may, in this sense, have a recognitory function for the infant.

Mothers and other caretakers frequently imitate the babbling of an infant and try to elicit babbling behavior by producing the infant's CV syllables themselves. If they imitate a babbled sequence immediately after the infant has produced it, the infant may respond by repeating that sequence. It is difficult, however, to initiate exchanges of this kind if the infant is intent upon some other activity. It is only after considerable experience with babbling that the infant will begin to look directly at an adult as he babbles. In some instances, he may seem to do so without communicative intent and to ignore the response of the adult. At other times, however, the infant will enjoy social imitative games and may take the initiative in offering utterances for the adult to imitate. These utterances may be vocal-play or babbled sounds.

Stage 5

The activities of nonreduplicated babbling and production of protowords may overlap to considerable extent. Nonreduplicated babbling is quite likely to be used by the infant when he is playing with objects or looking about him has he pauses from this play, with the objects still in his hands. The sounds of this babbling may or may not appear to be addressed to an adult. More and more, it becomes possible to engage in "conversations" with the infant, either by responding with real words or phrases that closely approximate the babbled sequence, or with nonsense syllables in reply. Phrase-like utterances embedded in the syllable sequences of nonreduplicated babbling may be imitated by the adult. These utterances may keep recurring in the infant's output and become incorporated in play rituals such as those of giving and taking of objects or playing peek-a-boo (Bruner, 1975). Before the end of the first year, the infant may initiate the use of phonetically consistent forms such as "hi" or "ma" in social situations that are constantly recurring, for example, in situations in which he demands or rejects an object or activity (Carter, 1974). The infant's communicative intent in these situations is inferred from his nonverbal behavior, that is, eye contact with an adult, facial expression, and the gestures of pointing, reaching, showing, and pushing away. Many of these protowords are syllable types that have been repeated many times over by the infant in both reduplicated and nonreduplicated babbling. Now, however, they are separated from the babbled sequences and used to express attitudes and wishes. The use of these protodeclaratives and protoimperatives at about 10 months of age is likely to emerge at the same time as behaviors such as recovering a hidden object and indicate the onset of Stage 5 of sensorimotor development, that is, the means-end stage (Bates, 1976). The infant has now learned to coordinate the schemata of producing a syllable type in relation to objects or actions with that of initiating and maintaining social exchanges with an adult. He is also able to use his output to manipulate adults and to obtain their aid in achieving his own ends. Those who have studied the infant's communicative behavior under such circumstances (Carter, 1974; Halliday, 1975) have described the speech output in terms of phonetic transcription only, that is, without employing any kind of acoustic analysis. Phonetic and phonological analyses have also been carried out with respect to words produced in the second year of life after representational thought and symbolic behavior have been acquired in Stage 6 of the sensorimotor period (Ingram, 1974; Leopold, 1947; Moskowitz, 1970; Velten, 1943). However, the ways in which protowords develop and their relation to later symbolic words remain to be studied acoustically.

Conclusions

Clearly, this chapter has focused upon the manner in which the infant's own system develops, not upon his acquisition of an adult system. The infant has been viewed as manipulating the features of output available to him in a variety of ways, as acquiring control of vocal-fold vibration and of movements of the supraglottal articulators and skill in coordinating these movements with one another. This development is seen as one of practicing subroutines and combining them with one another. It is considered to be motivated by the need to exercise abilities and to play rather than by any conscious effort to learn to talk.

It has also been shown that some of the sounds, for example, squealing, voiced ingressives, and long-duration friction noises that infants produce, are very unlike those of adult language. Adult speech production is a very finely tuned and efficient motor activity that does not employ all of the capacity of the speech-production mechanism. The infant does use that capacity to its maximum and explores the limits of the speech-production mechanism in his output in the vocal-play period. As he acquires greater skill, he uses his capabilities more conservatively. Vocal-play sounds may reappear in a modified form in adult paralinguistic systems, that is, as vocal expressions of feeling or mood or as onomatopoeic sounds associated with feeding, with animal noises, or with sound-making objects, but they are not used by the infant of 3–6 months in this manner.

The consonants and vowels preferred by the infant from the onset of reduplicated babbling onward are found in most of the languages of the world (Oller *et al.*, 1975). It is not surprising that the stock of phonemes that the infant is able to produce as he approaches production of meaningful speech should also be common to many languages. The capabilities of infants and young children as well as considerations of ease of production, speed of transmission, and optimum matching of speech production and perception capabilities must exert some influence upon the systems evolved by adults.

It is not clear at exactly what point the infant begins to be influenced in his output by the language he hears. Lewis (1951) pointed out that very early in life the infant shows a remarkable ability to respond vocally to speech addressed to him by an adult. It is not as often stressed that the infant also shows a remarkable tendency, from the second trimester onward, to respond to interesting objects by speaking. Often he pays no attention to adults as he does so. At some point he must, however, attempt to match the speech models in use in his environment. He may begin to do so unconsciously quite early in life, even when he does not use his own output interactively or respond to adult imitation of his sounds with any interest. It is therefore important and worthwhile to view the infant's system in relation to the adult model as well as to examine it as a system in its own right. Both approaches will surely aid us in understanding the development of speech.

References

Bates, E. (1976) "Pragmatics and Sociolinguistics in Child Language," in D. Morehead and E. Morehead, eds., *Normal and Deficient Child Language*, University Park Press, Baltimore, Md.

Bosma, J.F. (1972) "Form and Function in the Infant's Mouth and Pharynx," in J.F. Bosma, ed., *Third Symposium on Oral Sensation and Perception: The Mouth of the Infant*, Charles C. Thomas, Springfield, Ill.

Bosma, J.F. (1975) "Anatomic and Physiologic Development of Speech Apparatus," in D.B. Tower, ed., *Human Communication and its Disorders* (Vol. 3), Raven Press, New York.

Bosma, J.F., Truby, H., and Lind, J. (1965) "Cry Motions of the Newborn Infant," in J. Lind, ed., *Newborn Infant Cry*, Almquist and Wiksells, Uppsala.

Bruner, J. (1975) "The Ontogenesis of Speech Acts," *Journal of Child Language*, 2, 1–21.

Buhr, R., and Keating, P. (1977) "Spectrographic Effects of Register Shift in Speech Production," *Journal of the Acoustical Society of America*, 62, S25.

Carter, A.L. (1974) "The Development of Communication in the Sensorimotor Period: A Case Study," Doctoral Dissertation, University of California, Berkeley.

Chomsky, N., and Halle, M. (1968) *The Sound Pattern of English*, Harper & Row, New York.

Delack, J., and Fowlow, P. (1975) *The Ontogenesis of Differential Vocalizations: Proceedings of the Third International Child Language Symposium*, London, 1975.

Dore, J., Franklin, M.B., Miller, R.T., and Ramer, A.L.H. (1976) "Transitional Phenomena in Early Language Acquisition," *Journal of Child Language*, 3(1), 1–28.

Dorman, N.F., Cutting, J.E., and Raphael, L.J. (1975) "Perception of Temporal Order in Vowel Sequences with and without Formant Transitions," *Journal of Experimental Psychology: Human Perception and Performance*, 104, 121–129.

George, S.L. (1978) "The Relationship between Cranial Base Angle Morphology and Infant Vocalizations," Doctoral Dissertation, University of Connecticut.

Gesell, A., and Thompson, H. (1934) *Infant Behavior, Its Genesis and Growth*, McGraw-Hill, New York.

Halliday, M.A.K. (1975) *Learning How to Mean: Explorations in the Development of Language*, Arnold, London.

Ingram, D. (1974) "Phonological Rules in Young Children," *Journal of Child Language*, 1, 49–64.

Irwin, O.C., and Chen, H.P. (1946) "Development of Speech During Infancy: Curve of Phonemic Types," *Journal of Experimental Psychology: Human Perception and Performance*, 36, 431–436.

Jakobson, R., Fant, G., and Halle, M. (1963) *Preliminaries to Speech Analysis*, MIT Press, Cambridge, Mass.

Keating, P., and Buhr, R. (1978) "Fundamental Frequency in the Speech of Infants and Children," *Journal of the Acoustical Society of America*, 63, 567–571.

Laufer, M.Z., and Horii, Y. (1977) "Fundamental Frequency Characteristics of Infant Nondistress Vocalization during the First Twenty-four Weeks," *Journal of Child Language*, 4, 171–184.

Leopold, W. (1947) *Speech Development of a Bilingual Child: A Linguist's Record, 2: Sound-learning in the First Two Years*. Northwestern University Press, Evanston, Ill.

Lewis, M.M. (1951) *Infant Speech*, Routledge and Kegan Paul, London.

Lieberman, A.M., Cooper, F.S., Shankweiler, D.P., and Studdert-Kennedy, M. (1967) "Perception of the Speech Code," *Psychological Revue*, 74, 631–661.

Lieberman, P., Crelin, E.S., and Klatt, D.H. (1972) "Phonetic Ability and Related Anatomy of the Newborn and Adult Human, Neanderthal Man, and the Chimpanzee," *American Anthropologist*, 84, 287–307.

Lieberman, P., Harris, K.S., Wolff, P., and Russell, L.H. (1971) "Newborn Infant Cry and Nonhuman Primate Vocalization," *Journal of Speech and Hearing Research*, 14, 718–727.

Mattingly, I.G. (1973) "Phonetic Prerequisites for First Language Acquisition," *Status Report on Speech Research*, SR 341–5, Haskins Laboratories.

Meltzoff, A.N., and Moore, M.K. (1977) "Imitation of Facial and Manual Gestures by Human Neonates," *Science*, 198, 75–78.

Moskowitz, A. (1970) "The Two-year-old Stage in the Acquisition of English Phonology," *Language*, 16, 426–441.

Moslin, B. (1978) "The Role of Phonetic Input in Child's Acquisition of Phonological Contrast: A VOT Analysis," Doctoral Dissertation, Brown University.

Oller, D.K. (1976) "Analysis of Infant Vocalizations: A Linguistic and Speech Scientific Perspective," invited miniseminar given at the American Speech and Hearing Association Convention. Houston.

Oller, D.K., Wieman, L.A., Doyle, W.J., and Ross, C. (1975) "Child Speech, Babbling and Phonological Universals," *Journal of Child Language*, 3, 1–11.

Oller, D.K., and Smith, B.L. (1977) "Effect of Final-syllable Position on Vowel Duration in Infant Babbling," *Journal of the Acoustical Society of America*, 62, 994–997.

Peiper, A. (1963) *Cerebral Function in Infancy and Childhood*, Consultants Bureau, New York.

Piaget, J. (1952) *The Origins of Intelligence in Children*, International Universities Press, New York.

Port, D.K., and Preston, M.S. (1974) "Early Apical Stop Production: A Voice Onset Time Analysis," *Journal of Phonetics*, 2, 195–210.

Stark, R.E. (1978) "Features of Infant Sounds: The Emergence of Cooing," *Journal of Child Language*, 5, 379–390.

Stark, R.E. (1980) "Prespeech Segmental Feature Development," in P. Fletcher and M. Garman, eds., *Studies in Language Acquisition*, Cambridge University Press, Cambridge.

Stark, R.E., and Nathanson, S.N. (1974) "Spontaneous Cry in the Newborn Infant; Sounds and Facial Gestures," in J.F. Bosma, ed., *Fourth Symposium on Oral Sensation and Perception: Development in the Fetus and Infant*, United States Government Printing Press, Bethesda, Md.

Stark, R.E., Rose, S.N., and McLagan, M. (1975) "Features of Infant Sounds: the First Eight Weeks of Life," *Journal of Child Language*, 2, 205–221.

Stark, R.E., Heinz, J.M., and Wright-Wilson, C. (1976) "Vowel Utterances of Young Infants," *Journal of the Acoustical Society of America*, 60, 543.

Stark, R.E., Rose, S.N., and Benson, P.J. (1978) "Classification of Infant Vocalization," *British Journal of Communication Disorders*, 13, 41–47.

Velten, H. (1943) "The Growth of Phonemic and Lexical Patterns in Infant Language," *Language*, 19, 281–292.

Winitz, H. (1969) *Articulatory Acquisition and Behavior*, Appleton-Century-Crofts, New York, pp. 2–21.

Zlatin, M. (1975) "Explorative Mapping of the Vocal Tract and Primitive Syllabification in Infancy: The First Six Months," Paper presented at the American Speech and Hearing Association Convention. Washington, D.C.

Chapter 6

THE EMERGENCE OF THE SOUNDS OF SPEECH IN INFANCY

D. K. OLLER

Purpose

Infant vocalizations have long been studied on the assumption that their form might reveal aspects of a developing capacity for speech. Some infant sounds, especially late in the first year of life, are so speechlike as to leave little doubt that they are related to a verbal linguistic capacity. In fact, it is hard to tell, at times, whether infants are producing words or merely babbling. Other infant vocalization types, however, would never be mistaken for words, because their physical form differs too widely from mature linguistic utterances. To reveal relationships between such vocalizations and speech, it is necessary to offer a general definition of "speechiness." The definition must encompass a variety of characteristics of spoken languages, and must provide a basis upon which any infant sound can be described in terms of crucial speech parameters.

The general parameters manipulated in the world's languages will be referred to here as "metaphonological." For example, pitch, phonation type (voice quality), resonance pattern, timing, and amplitude are properly called "metaphonological features." It is in terms of such general dimensions that concrete phonological or phonetic features (plosive, fricative, high vowel, stressed vowel, unstressed vowel, etc.) are defined. The kinds of infant sounds that differ substantially from speech prove awkward or impossible

CHILD PHONOLOGY
VOLUME 1: PRODUCTION

to describe in terms of concrete phonology. The speechiness of such sounds can be effectively assessed only within a metaphonological description. More speechlike sounds of infants can be assessed in both concrete phonological and metaphonological terms.

The purpose of this chapter is to review existing data on infant vocalizations during the first year of life, and then to examine commonly observed vocalization categories in terms of speechiness. By considering both concrete phonological and metaphonological speech parameters, it will be possible to evaluate the sense in which infant vocalizations reflect the systematic emergence of the capacity to produce the sounds of speech.

Scope

The present work will focus on infant vocalizations that have the potential for entirely arbitrary meaningfulness. The focus excludes "reflexive" vocalizations (i.e., sounds that can be elicited by specific sorts of internal or external stimulation, and consequently cannot be said to be arbitrary). Cries, coughs, and hiccups, for example, usually "mean" something nonarbitrary about the physical state of their producer. There are often special facial expressions or gestures that accompany such sounds. Under normal circumstances, reflexive sounds can be said to be involuntary. Because "words" usually consist of an arbitrary pairing of a sound sequence and a meaning, it seems justified, at least temporarily, to focus studies of vocalization development on nonreflexive sounds.[1]

Because a great variety of sounds are produced by infants, it is practically impossible to define stages of phonetic speechiness development unless relative frequency of occurrence of sound types is taken into account. The present discussion focuses on frequent sound types at each stage. Frequent occurrence is taken as an indication that the vocalization type is under control and is not produced accidentally. In general, then, the following discussion will focus on sounds that are produced with apparent control, as evidenced by high frequency of usage, and that have the general phonetic potential for functioning as units in a communication system of arbitrary sound–meaning pairs.

Salient Vocalization Categories of the First Year of Life

Each infant vocalization category to be treated here requires definition, as previous authors have used some of the terms differently. These category

---

[1] This is not to say that there is no relationship between the form of reflexive and nonreflexive vocalizations (see Stark *et al.*, 1975; Stark, Chapter 5, this volume).

definitions are not trivial methodological details. In large measure, the definitions are the meat of the implied theory, and they are intended to be empirically vulnerable. The categories are not, however, intended to be exhaustive. Other systematically manipulated categories have been observed in some infants. In addition, the categories are probably not all universal even in normal infants, though there may be a universal subset. The time scale is somewhat pliable, and the ages suggested are intended to be representative of most, though not all, infants. Vocalizations in these categories are salient in that they occur with relatively high frequency during some stage of development, and they represent the incorporation of some new nonreflexive vocalization characteristic(s) into the infant's controlled repertoire. It should be pointed out that some of these categories may not be the single most frequent vocalization type throughout any stage. However, the categories to be listed have all been shown to be among the two or three predominant types during more restricted time periods within the stage to which they primarily pertain. Beyond their primary stage, the vocalization types drop off in frequency, though sometimes the disappearance seems to be gradual. In addition to their relatively high frequency of occurrence, the categories of vocalizations to be discussed may be salient in that they largely appear to reflect a step-by-step advancement of the child's ability to produce the phonological or metaphonological characteristics of spoken language.

The Phonation Stage (0–1 month)

It has traditionally been observed that during the first and second month, speechlike sounds are relatively rare (cf. Taine, 1877). However, during this time, normal infants do seem to produce some nonreflexive, nondistress sounds. The largest number of these fit into a category I have referred to a quasi-resonant nuclei (QRN). These elements have been categorized by previous authors as vowels, syllabic consonants, and/or "small throaty sounds." Quasi-resonant nuclei include normal phonation (not vocal fry, not breathy voice, etc.), but do not seem to involve any systematic contrast between opening and closure of the vocal tract, and do not make use of the full potential of the vocal cavity to function as a resonating tube. The limited resonance of the elements gives the category its name. Acoustic analysis of the QRN shows it to consist of a broad band of low amplitude resonances primarily below 1200 Hz (Murai, 1963; Nakazima, 1962; Oller, 1976). Auditory phonetic analysis suggests that the QRN ranges from a syllabic nasal to a high, mid, unrounded, nasalized vowel (Doyle, 1976; Oller, 1976). In QRNs, infants seem to phonate with their mouths closed or nearly closed.

A small proportion of fully resonant nuclei (FRN; often referred to as vowels or coos in previous research) occur along with QRNs in nonreflexive vocalization during the first 2 months of life. These may occur haphazardly, and do not seem to evidence the repetitive occurrence that indicates control over resonance characteristics. Verification of this prediction awaits empirical work employing time series analyses of the vocalizations of infants in the first months of life. During the phonation stage, the FRNs and syllabic nasals that occur may be low-frequency-of-occurrence variants of the basic highly frequent, nonreflexive vocalizations of the stage, the QRNs. GOOs, which consist of postalveolar (usually velar) consonant-like elements, often voiced fricatives (note Stark, Chapter 5, this volume, refers to "friction noises"), optionally combined with QRNs, may also be a low-frequency variant of the basic QRN type during the phonation stage.

Even at the height of the succeeding GOO stage, QRNs are still the most frequent utterances in an apparently typical 2-month-old infant (hereafter designated as L.) whose vocalizations were recorded on seven occasions during that month (389 nonreflexive utterances were considered). Other data collected in collaboration with B. L. Smith and W. J. Doyle on five normal infants showed QRNs as the most frequently occurring nonreflexive vocalization type across at least the first 4 months of life.

The GOO Stage (2–3) months)

Not long after infants achieve some level of control over production of QRNs, controlled, repetitive GOOs appear (Doyle, 1976; Fenton, 1925; Leopold, 1947; Zlatin, 1974). In the seven taped samples analyzed for subject L. at age 2 months, the percentage of nonreflexive utterances fitting into the GOO category ranged from 13–49% with a mean of 25%. Irwin's (1947a) widely reported data on velar consonant preferences early in infancy reflect the use of GOOs in infants at this stage and also reflect a tendency for velar closure to be common in many infants even later (beyond the fourth month) in utterances where FRNs are combined with consonant-like closures. Zlatin (1974) has characterized some GOO utterances as showing "primitive syllabification." One should emphasize primitive here, since GOOs appear to be less regular in their timing of openings (QRN) and closures (velar consonant-like elements) than syllables normally are in mature languages. A later vocalization category (canonical babbling) includes regularity of timing much as in mature languages (see what follows). The temporal limitations of GOOs should be kept in mind to avoid the spurious conclusion that infants at this stage have already achieved a full phonetic competence.

The Expansion Stage (4–6 months)

Beginning about the fifth month, there are a number of vocalization types that regularly appear in the normal infant's controlled repertoire. Roughly, this stage corresponds to Zlatin's (1975) stage of "exploratory phonetic behavior,'' and to Stark's (Chapter 5, this volume) "vocal play" period. The vocalization types are not clearly ordered in their appearance although infants do seem to manifest "concentrated periods" (Stark, Chapter 5, this volume; Zlatin Laufer and Horii, 1977) of repetition with individual types. The categories to be described are not exclusive; rather, they represent utterance features, and any utterance may require multiple categorizations.

One of the major occurrences of the expansion stage is widespread repetitive usage of FRNs (Doyle, 1976; Oller, 1976), vowel-like elements that systematically include strong resonances above 1200 Hz. Isolated occurrences of FRNs without closures or other consonant-like elements may not be the most frequent vocalizations at any stage. They accounted for less than 10% of total vocalizations in seven taped samples (380 nonreflexive utterances) of infant L. between 4 and 5 months. However, the sum of utterances that included consonant-like elements adjacent to FRNs and isolated FRNs accounted for a substantial proportion of all utterances at the age of 4–5 months (59% in this single infant).

Raspberry (RSP) vocalizations, consisting of bilabial or labiolingual trills or vibrants, (also referred to as "trills" or "friction noises," cf. Stark, Chapter 5, this volume) are also systematically manipulated during this period (Doyle, 1976; Hoyer and Hoyer, 1924). Although this sometimes occurs during feeding, suggesting the possible interpretation that infants are simply playing with spitting things out of their mouths, RSPs also occur as playful vocalizations in nonfeeding settings. Normal infants do not seem to produce a particularly high proportion of utterances with RSPs over a long period. In a cross-sectional study with B. L. Smith, the average proportion of nonreflexive utterances including RSPs did not exceed 10% during the intervals of 4–5 months (7% of 385 utterances from six normal infants) or 6–7 months (8% of 322 utterances from seven normal infants). However, the longitudinally studied infant L. showed wide variation from sample to sample. In 21 samples from 4–7 months, a range of from 0 to 57% of utterances included RSPs, indicating variability in the infant's vocalization focus from day to day.

Squealing (SQ) is very common during this period (see Doyle, 1976; Stark, Chapter 5, this volume; Zlatin Laufer and Horii, 1977). Often SQ utterances either begin or end in a normal vocal register but, at some point, enter falsetto or a highly tense maximal pitch register. Although SQ may occur in response to tickling, it is clear that infants often employ this sort of vocalization in concentrated periods where no immediate external stimulus has elicited it. The concentrated periods tendency is reflected in wide variation in the frequency of occurrence of SQ from sample to sample (cf. Zlatin Laufer and Horii, 1977). Across the period from 4 to 7 months, 21 samples of infant L. showed a maximum of 44% SQs and a minimum of 0.

Growling (GRL), which seems to be the inverse of SQ, consists of very low-pitch, often creaky-voice vocalizations. Again, whereas GRL may sometimes occur in response to some sort of physical exertion or to social stimulation, infants at this stage also produce GRLs in systematic concentrated periods of playful vocalization (Stark, Chapter 5, this volume; Zlatin Laufer and Horii, 1977). Yelling (YEL), which consists of high amplitude nondistress vocalization, and ingressive–egressive sequences (IES), consisting of alternating vocalization on ingress and egress of the breathing cycle, also occur in concentrated periods during this stage (Oller, 1976; Zlatin, Hixson, and Coggins, 1975; Zlatin Laufer and Horii, 1977).

Marginal babbling (MG), consisting of sequences in which a closure of the vocal tract is opposed with an FRN, also occurs during the expansion stage (Doyle, 1976; Oller, 1976). It must be pointed out that MBs do not have the mature regular-syllable timing characteristics that appear in succeeding stages, and normally do not include the reduplication of later canonical babbling. Impressionistically, MBs include slow or shaky transitions between consonant-like and vowel-like elements. MBs do not seem to occur with extremely high frequency. Subject L.'s MBs represented only about 5% of over 1800 nonreflexive utterances from 4–8 months, with a sample-to-sample range from 0 to 44%.

As has been seen, the usage of the vocalization types of the expansion stage fluctuates radically from day to day. The infant may produce many exemplars of one category on one day and none at all of the same category on the next. Thus, especially during the expansion stage, it appears difficult to obtain a realistic picture of the infant's capacities or activities by using wide-interval sampling, cross-sectional methods, or by using a simple monitoring of total frequency of occurrence of a vocalization type across a period of months.

The Canonical Stage (7–10 months)

The relatively rigid timing characteristics of syllabification in natural languages are introduced into the child's vocalization system at the onset of canonical babbling (BB). BB includes both consonant-like units and FRNs (vowels) in a timing relationship that conforms to mature natural language restrictions. The onset of this stage, which is fairly sudden, is usually seen with reduplicated syllables (hence, a subcategory of BB is called reduplicated babbling, RB), for example, [bababa], [dadada], [mamama] (Gesell and Amatruda, 1941; Leopold, 1947; McCarthy, 1952; Nakazima, 1962; Smith and Oller, in press). Parents often report at this stage that their children have begun to talk even though there may be no evidence of denotative meaning associated with the RBs.

An important negative characteristic of RB is its lack of substantial variation within utterances in terms of consonantal and vocalic units occurring in a sequence. Often infants seem to focus on a particular syllable type to the exclusion of all others during concentrated periods. It is, however, important not to leave the impression that all BBs are reduplicated. In fact, nonreduplicated canonical utterances, especially single consonant babbles (SCB) (e.g., [ba], [ada], [imi]), seem to be about as frequent as reduplicated utterances. In 16 samples (1453 nonreflexive utterances) from 7 to 8 months, subject L. produced an average of 22% reduplicated utterances (sample-to-sample range 0–82%) and an average of 20% nonreduplicated canonical sequences (range 0–47%).

The Variegated Babbling Stage (11–12 months)

During variegated babbling (VAR) the relatively rigid syllabic characteristics of languages continue to appear in many of the infant's utterances, but the restriction against varied consonantal and vocalic types within a multisyllabic string seems to be at least partially overcome (Oller, 1976). In VAR, infants systematically produce utterances with differing consonantal or vocalic elements. In addition, during this stage, infants often produce a category referred to as gibberish (GIB), which seems to be the infant's rendition of phonetic sequences with contrasts of syllabic stress. In GIB, fully canonical syllables occur in the same utterances with low-stressed, often slurred syllables that seem to have QRNs as nuclei.

Metaphonology and Infant Sounds: Speechiness of Infant Vocalizations

There are two related vantage points from which one might try to evaluate the speechiness of the infant sounds described in this chapter. One may list the categories infants produce and ask, "How do these categories relate to speech?" Or one may formulate a set of metaphonological parameters and to ask, "How do the categories of infant sounds manipulate these parameters?" The first method looks toward the mature system from the vantage point of the infant's productions; the second looks toward infant sounds from the vantage point of the mature system. Both methods will be discussed in following sections.

The issue at stake is how to explain the consistencies of infant vocalizations. Why do so many infants produce precisely the categories described? Although some aspects of the vocalization types that seem to occur most commonly may be partially explainable in terms of purely physical (for example, anatomical) or physiological factors, it may be fruitful and enlightening to interpret infant vocalizations and their changes across time in terms of the extent to which they incorporate metaphonological aspects of the languages of the world into the child's repertoire. Because most of the vocalization types discussed seem at first to be substantially different from mature speech, we must look below the surface to see the sense in which these vocalization types represent the fabric of a phonology. To maintain a broad perspective, infant sounds will be considered in the light of metaphonological and concrete phonological features of all mature languages. By comparing infant sounds with universals of linguistic sound systems, we can assess the sense in which infant vocalizations prepare the child to learn any phonology.

Metaphonology and Infant Vocalizations: From the Vantage Point of the Infant's Sounds

QRNs constitute the introduction into the child's vocal repertoire of nonreflexive vocalizations with normal phonation. Because the QRN lacks many features of syllables in natural languages, it cannot be thought of as a full-fledged phonological element. However, as normal phonation is a basic feature of all mature languages, the child's capacity to produce QRNs may represent an important metaphonological accomplishment.

During the GOO stage, infants seem to produce their first controlled consonant-like elements and also their first controlled instances of oppositions between consonant-like and vowel-like quasi-resonant elements. All languages possess consonants and all languages possess oppositions between consonants and vowels. Even though the appearance of GOOs does not indicate that the child has fully mastered consonant and vowel oppositions, it can be interpreted to mean that the infant has begun to produce a basic opposition between closure and opening of the vocal tract during phonation. Closure and opening oppositions contribute an important metaphonological characteristic of languages.

During the expansion stage, the infant seems to manipulate a series of further metaphonological parameters. For example, with the appearance of FRNs, the vocal tract's capacity for resonance is exploited. All languages make use of such resonance in vowel contrasts. SQs and GRLs seem to represent manipulation of the characteristic of vocal pitch. YELs seem to represent manipulation of volume or amplitude of utterance. Both pitch and amplitude are systematically manipulated in all the world's languages. With the appearance of MB, the child seems to be creating a fuller opposition between closure and fully resonant opening of the vocal tract. This occurrence is related to the GOO stage accomplishment although MBs require FRNs in addition to consonant-like closures.

All of these accomplishments of the expansion stage in infant vocalizations represent metaphonological rather than concrete phonological accomplishments. Languages of the world do not merely include fully resonant vowels. They systematically manipulate resonance properties forming vowel contrasts. Furthermore, languages do not simply differentiate between high pitches as in SQ and low pitches as in GRL. They exploit the capacity of the vocal tract to use complex contours of intonation, and they use pitch as a secondary characteristic of stress and tone contrasts in many instances. Furthermore, manipulation of amplitude is far more subtle in languages than would be suggested simply by the appearance of YELs. As with pitch, amplitude variations participate in intonation contrasts, in vocalic contrasts, in stress constrasts in many languages and, to a very large extent, in the basic differentiation of consonantal and vocalic elements. Finally, all languages create oppositions, as in MB, between full closures and fully resonant openings of the vocal tract.

An MB would not, however, constitute an acceptable utterance in a mature language under normal circumstances. What MBs lack is a proper timing relationship between closure and opening. It has been determined in previous research (Liberman *et al.*, 1956; Minifie *et al.* 1977) that the duration of the transition between closure and opening is crucial to the determination of the syllabic nature of a speech sequence. By extending the duration of a transition for a syllable [be] the perception of the sequence can be changed to [we] and with further extension to [ue], indicating that the syllabic perception is dependent upon a vowel transition that does not exceed certain limits of duration. MBs do seem to violate these limits and thus can be characterized as only marginally syllabic. However, with the onset of BBs, infants seem to accomplish well-formed syllabic structure with timing characteristics that do appear to conform to the restrictions of mature natural languages.

In VAR and GIB, normal infants begin to elaborate the basic syllabic structures that have been developed. Concrete phonological contrasts of consonantal and vocalic type, as well as contrasts of stress type, seem to appear with considerable regularity at the end of the first year of life. Since all languages have these sorts of contrasts of closure and opening type, the occurrence of VAR and GIB may reflect an important advancement in the child's phonological capacity.

Table 6.1 summarizes the proposed stages of development, the vocalization categories, and the purported metaphonological achievements of each stage.

Metaphonology and Infant Vocalizations: From the Vantage Point of Mature Speech Systems

Assuming a universal perspective on natural languages, it is possible to isolate several metaphonological parameters that are manipulated in all

TABLE 6.1
Stages of Development in Phonetic Control

Normal infant's age	Characteristic vocalization types		Metaphonological characteristic of mature languages
0–1 month phonation stage	QRN	(Quasi-resonant nucleus)	Normal phonation in nonreflexive vocalizations.
2–3 months GOO stage	GOO	(QRN plus velar or uvular consonant-like element)	Vocalizations with closure: alternation between opening and closure of the vocal tract.
4–6 months expansion stage	FRN	(Fully resonant nuclei)	Use of resonance capacity providing possibility for contrasts of resonance types.
	RSP	(Raspberry)	? Front as opposed to back (GOO) closures? Further manipulation of vocalizations during clousure?
	SQ	(Squeal)	Pitch contrasts
	GRL	(Growl)	
	YEL	(Yell)	Amplitude contrasts
	IES	(Ingressive–egressive sequence)	? Further control of vocal breath stream?
	MB	(Marginal babble)	Alternation of *full* opening and closure of the vocal tract
7–10 months canonical stage	BB	(Canonical babbling)	Syllabic timing constraints on relationship of openings and closures (vocalic transitions)
11–12 months variegated babbling stage	VAR	(Variegated babbling)	Contrasts of consonantal and vocalic type
	GIB	(Gibberish)	Contrasts of stress

linguistic sound systems. Among the obviously crucial and most general parameters are (*a*) pitch and voice quality; (*b*) resonance (spectrum); (*c*) timing; and (*d*) amplitude.

The Pitch and Voice Quality Parameter: Development of the Glottal Sound-Source Capacity

Zlatin Laufer and Horii (1977), investigating fundamental frequency across the first 24 weeks of life, observed a tendency for infants to use concentrated periods of high-pitched SQs and low-pitched GRL's. Other studies (Doyle, 1976; Oller, 1976; Stark, Chapter 5, this volume) have also noticed this widespread tendency. SQs and GRLs may indicate an interest on the infant's part in controlling pitch as an independent parameter. Furthermore, in the study by Zlatin Laufer and Horii (1977), except for the first

4-week interval, infants during the first 24 weeks of life manifested a generally increasing range and standard deviation of fundamental frequencies, suggesting an increasing ability to control a broad range of fundamental frequencies. By the end of the first year, infants showed considerable control over fundamental-frequency contour in GIB and VAR.

The frequent usage of both SQs and GRLs also indicates a mastery of voice quality variations. GRLs are usually tense and creaky whereas SQs include a tense falsetto register. Normal phonation, the unmarked phonation type of all the world's languages, is employed in both QRNs and FRNs starting in the first weeks of life.

The Resonance (Spectral) Parameter: The Control of Supraglottal Cavity Size and Shape

The development of the capacity to control resonance patterns underlies the ability to produce vocalic contrasts. A series of studies has shown that the magnitude of the infant "vowel space" and hence the number of potential vocalic resonance contrasts increases dramatically across the first year of life (Lieberman, Chapter 7, this volume; Lieberman et al., 1976 Pierce, 1974; Stark et al., 1976). QRNs, because their weak resonances are concentrated primarily below 1200 Hz, do not provide the full range of linguistic contrastive possibilities. With the progressive addition of FRNs to the repertoire, the infant's vowel space can be considerably expanded, since FRNs can be widely varied in resonance pattern. About 80% of subject L.'s vocalizations at 2 months included QRNs, whereas only about 10% included FRNs. By 7–8 months, the same child had virtually reversed the pattern, with over 80% of utterances showing FRNs and less than 10% showing QRNs. By the end of a child's first year, FRNs are articulated with substantial variations and the vowel space is near maximum, often encompassing identifiable exemplars of the point vowels, [a], [i] and [u] (even though the acoustic nature of these vowels is still not identical to adult renditions; cf. Lieberman, Chapter 7, this volume). All other vowels in natural languages can be characterized as having intermediate resonance properties among these three limiting vowels.

The Timing Parameter: Syllabicity

Studies of control over patterns of timing in vocalizations during the first year of life have been relatively few. Zlatin Laufer and Horii (1977) have shown a generally increasing duration of nonreflexive vocalizations across the first 24 weeks of life and have observed that infants during this time period seem to systematically manipulate and practice different durations of vocalizations. In addition, data from subject L. showed far greater total durations of GOOs occurring at nearly 5 months (about 1400 msec) as opposed to those occurring at 3 months (about 700 msec). This tendency for utterances of greater duration to occur at later ages may indicate that the infant is achieving vocal breath control, allowing the breathing cycle to be modified at will, as is clearly necessary in speech.

A salient temporal achievement of the first year's vocalizations occurs with the onset of RB. Oller and Smith (1977) studied timing characteristics of infant RB and claimed that duration of CV transitions in RB are quite similar to syllables occurring in mature natural languages. Data from subject L. indicated that previous vocalization types are far more variable in their timing of syllable events. Figure 6.1 presents data on early GOO, MB, precursor MB (a type of MB that occurred in this infant a few days prior to the onset of RB), and, finally, RB as it occurred at about 10 months of age. The last VCV (opening-closure-opening) sequence in each utterance of the sample was considered for analysis as seen in Figure 6.1. The ratio of standard deviation to mean duration of each individual vowel or consonant position offers a measure of stability of segment duration. The ratios were much greater for precanonical utterances (GOO, MB, and precursor MB) than for RB. These data indicate that RB constitutes a form of utterance in which

PRECANONICAL

		V^a	C	V^a
GOOING	$\bar{X}$	275	140	215
(N = 9)	σ	101	102	173
	ratio σ:$\bar{X}$	.37	.73	.81

		...V	C	V
MB (N = 12)	$\bar{X}$	$?^b$	247	274
	σ	$?^b$	278	135
	ratio	$?^b$	1.13	.49

		...V	C	V
PRECURSOR	$\bar{X}$	199	167	312
MB (N = 7)	σ	96	63	283
	ratio	.48	.38	.90

CANONICAL

		...V	C	V
RB (N = 11)	$\bar{X}$	182	150	154
	σ	30	21	56
	ratio	.16	.14	.36

[a] These are, of course, QRNs in Gooing, FRNs in later categories.

[b] No nonfinal vowel is used in these calculations due to extreme variations in measurability of the segments.

FIGURE 6.1 *Timing of speechlike segments in precanonical and canonical vocalizations: duration in milliseconds of last VCV sequence in representative utterances from a single child (subject L.).*

syllabic timing is more consistent from utterance to utterance and more like mature speech than in previous stages of development.

The Amplitude Parameter

The development of full resonance is a crucial step in establishing the infant's capacity for contrasts in amplitude because *both* consonant-like closures and quasi-resonant elements are relatively low in amplitude. All the world's languages employ contrasts between minimally resonant stop consonants and maximally resonant low back vowels, as in the syllables [pa] or [ta]. As the infant develops fully resonant elements *and* consonant-like elements, it becomes possible to employ maximal contrasts between low- and high-amplitude elements. This possibility is exploited in MB, and with the beginning of RB, manipulation of requisite timing relationships between low and high points in an amplitude spectrum comes fully into the child's repertoire.

In addition to using relative amplitude as a parameter along which vowels (or syllable nuclei) are differentiated from consonants (or syllable margins), languages exploit amplitude variations in a number of suprasegmental and paralinguistic ways. The occurrence of concentrated periods of YELs in infants starting in the expansion stage indicates a systematic manipulation of the amplitude parameter in a way that could be put to use in mature suprasegmental and paralinguistic systems.

Theoretical Problems of the Proposed Framework

Although many of the otherwise mysterious characteristics of infant vocalization categories during the first year of life are explainable, at least to some extent, by taking metaphonological parameters into account, there remain aspects of the categories that are not so easily interpreted linguistically. For example, why during the GOO stage are the vast majority of consonant-like elements velar? Why are RSPs (i.e., the friction noises of the expansion stage) usually labial or labiolingual? And why are the earliest nonreflexive utterances quasi-resonant (i.e., why does not the infant simply open his or her mouth when phonating in the first weeks of life)?

To some extent, questions about why infant vocalizations have the particular form they do appear to be answerable in terms of anatomical and physiological development. The velar preference, for example, of early GOOs may be related, in part at least, to the fact that the infant's tongue is relatively large with regard to the size of the vocal cavity at rest. The dorsum of the tongue is situated nearly in contact with the velum and epiglottis making back closure far more likely than dental or alveolar closure if any tongue movement occurs (see Stark, Chapter 5, this volume). McCarthy's (1952) proposal that gravity affects infant sounds can be elaborated to suggest that production of GOOs may be related to the infant's characteristic body position (flat on its back). In this position, the tongue mass might tend to drift downward and result in back articulations.

The nature of RSPs might also be explained in some physiological terms. For example, some special sensitivity of the lips or some special ability for motoric control of the lips may occur at just the time when RSPs appear.

The occurrence of QRNs in the first months might also be attributed in part to physical factors. In fact, it might be claimed that infants produce QRNs due to physical limitations of the vocal tract that make it difficult to open; namely, the cavity is small and the tongue nearly fills it at rest (Crelin, 1969; cf. Stark, Chapter 5, this volume). Moreover, although there is a small oral cavity, there is virtually no pharyngeal cavity at this age (Hast, 1970).

Whereas these anatomical and physiological possibilities are surely worth careful consideration and further investigation, it is important to keep them in perspective. For example, one should not jump to the conclusion that the infant during the phonation stage does not have the anatomical capacity to vocalize with full resonance or to produce vocal contrasts of opening and closure. Lieberman et al. (1971) have reported acoustic analyses of infant cries that possess far fuller resonance characteristics than QRNs. The cries were described as "schwa-like" and as having three strong resonances at about 1.1, 3.3, and 5.5 kHz. Lieberman, et al. were interested in showing that the birth cry was limited in its resonance potential by anatomical factors (i.e., infants may be physically unable to produce the vowels /a/, /i/ and /u/); it is worthy of note, however, that the acoustic pattern of the cry included both a second and a third formant far higher in frequency than normally occurs in QRNs. Furthermore, a small proportion of FRNs do occur even in the phonation stage. It must be concluded that even though nonreflexive phonation during the first months of life does not usually include full resonance, infants at this stage do possess the physical potential to produce full resonance.

Future Research Directions

Much of the formulation presented here is theoretical and, it is hoped, predictive in suggesting a series of patterns that must be verified by future research. The theory asserts that infant sounds represent explorations of the capacity for speech. All the most basic metaphonological parameters seem to be explored. In general, the explorations involve a variety of values on any dimension. For example, pitch is explored at the high end in SQ and at the low end in GRL. However, a noticeable gap appears in the evidence with regard to exploration of overall utterance amplitude. Although high-amplitude utterances *do* occur in YELs, systematic low-amplitude utterances (e.g., whispers) have not been focused on in recent reports. It is possible that our own studies have missed most whispers because we have focused only on utterances with high signal-to-noise ratios. The emerging theory of the relationship of infant vocalizations and speech predicts that whispers, or other systematically employed low-amplitude sounds, should occur as a common category during the first year of life.

The theory asserts that each major vocalization type occurs in repetitive or systematically alternating patterns. Time series and transitional probability analyses will be keys to quantitative specification of this assertion.

Such analyses will also help shed light on variability of category usage from stage to stage. Day to day experience with infants has shown that most of the categories described occur at least in some measure during all of the stages; even some RBs seem to occur long before the onset of the canonical stage.[2] The theory predicts that such premature utterances will not occur day after day during repetitive or systematically alternating sequences until the appropriate stage. During the GOO stage, for example, one would expect to see considerable sequences on a number of different days during which a large proportion (not necessarily the majority) of the utterances could be characterized as GOOs. During the same time period, utterances of the MB category, which indeed may occur, should not occur repetitively and should always be rare in terms of overall frequency of occurrence.

Quantification through time series and transitional probability analyses may help justify the intuition that infants are systematically, consciously, attempting to produce speechlike utterances. It is worth considering the possibility that the infant repeatedly asks him or herself the question, "What am I supposed to sound like?" At each stage of development the vocalizations produced by the child seem to represent finer and finer approximations toward an overall metaphonological pattern that is presented by mature speakers and that the infant seems to be attempting to replicate. Although it has been traditionally believed that systematic vocal imitation does not begin until the middle of the first year or even later, there is reason to believe that the traditional wisdom may have been mistaken. It may be that we have not thought of many of the earliest vocalizations in infants (e.g., during the first 2 months) as being imitative simply because what the infant intends as an approximation to speech seems extremely distant from speech to adults. Meltzoff and Moore (1976) have demonstrated gestural imitation by infants in the first weeks of life. The demonstration depended

---

[2] It has been observed by B.L. Smith (personal communication) and myself that infants may have a very brief period of RB long before the canonical stage. Why RBs drop out and do not return for months is a mystery. Bower (1976) reviewed other cognitive and physical developments that occur briefly and then drop out sometimes for months before reappearing.

upon the use of four, very broad gestural categories (lip protrusion, mouth opening, finger movement, tongue protrusion), allowing considerable variations in the infants' imitations. Experimentally blind observers of a videotape of the infants only (i.e., the observers did not know what gesture the experimenter was modeling) were asked to rank order the infant's actions in terms of how similar they were to the four possible categories. Results showed that infants imitated the gestures. Without the broad categorization of gestures, many infant imitations might be seen as random movements. Employing a broadly similar methodology, Kessen et al. (1979) found imitation of vocal pitch by 3–6-month-old infants.

It may be that the early responsive vocalizations of the first months of life (cf. Anderson et al., 1977; Stern et al., 1975) are imitative in a large proportion of cases. The failure to incorporate all features of modeled utterances may simply mean that the infant has not yet mastered a sufficient number of basic metaphonological characteristics of languages to produce easily identifiable imitative utterances. One would not expect a beginning piano student to play a flawless advanced piece on the first attempt. Yet it is clear that the beginning piano student is attempting to learn to play the piano. Similarly, the infant may from the very beginning be attempting to learn to produce speech—to sound like a person talking.

A possible kind of supporting evidence for the intuition that there is conscious speech-related vocal activity during the first year of life might derive from comparison of a variety of anatomical and physiological developments and purportedly corresponding vocal developments. If the onset of vocal developments seems to be very tightly dependent upon the onset of specific physiological changes, it would seem possible that the infant's activities are not particularly conscious. However, if the anatomical and physiological developments are grossly out of phase with the presumably related vocal achievements, it would seem fair to conclude that the physiological and anatomical developments alone cannot explain vocal systems. Suppose, for example, there is a smooth curve of increase in vocal cavity size across the first year of life, while at the same time there is an abrupt change in the use of FRNs not explainable in any simple anatomical terms. Such a result would suggest that an infant's introduction of FRNs is motivated at least in part by central (nonanatomical) factors. One possibility is that the infant is attempting to produce sounds like those heard in his or her environment.

Recent evidence on infant speech perception seems to suggest that infants are extremely interested in the sounds of speech (Eilers and Minifie, 1973; Eimas et al., 1971; Morse, 1973). On the one hand, such evidence has indicated that infants may be more interested in listening to speech sounds than other kinds of sounds (Butterfield and Siperstein, 1971). In addition, recent work has shown that, at least in some cases, infants seem to modify their perceptual abilities to discriminate specific phonetic contrasts of the language of their environment (Eilers et al., 1979; Streeter, 1976).

Future studies may show that this intense awareness of the sounds of speech has impact upon infant vocalization characteristics. Thus far, cross-linguistic studies of infant babbling seem to be more focused on the gross similarities that occur in infants from a variety of language backgrounds than on possible differences (cf. Atkinson *et al.,* 1970; Nakazima, 1962; Olney and Scholnick, 1976; Preston *et al.,* 1967). In fact, there have been, to my knowledge, no convincing demonstrations of any systematic babbling differences that could be attributed to language experience during the first year of life. Such a lack of demonstration does not necessarily indicate that infants do not attempt to match the kinds of sounds that they hear, nor does it indicate that there are no differences between babbling of infants from different language environments. Languages around the world employ a central core of metaphonological and phonetic types. It is largely these metaphonological and phonetic types that are most common in infant babbling (see, e.g., Oller *et al.,* 1975). We might, therefore, interpret the general similarity of infant babbling across various cultures simply to mean that when infants try to approximate speech, they produce predominantly the universal core elements, no matter what their linguistic environment. Eventually, it may be possible to demonstrate the existence of subtle differences in the vocalizations of infants from different language backgrounds. Such differences would add considerable weight to the suggestion that infants are actively and consciously involved in learning to talk (i.e., to sound like what they perceive talking to be).

Looking Back: The Relationship between Babbling and Speech

A review of data on infant vocalizations seems incomplete without reference to the formerly widely accepted notion that infant babbling bears no phonetic relationship to young child speech (Jakobson, 1941). This view was unfounded empirically throughout the period of its acceptance, and by now it has been thoroughly discredited. A number of studies have shown that commonly occurring phonetic types of the last half of the first year are quite similar to phonetic types of early meaningful speech (cf. Cruttenden, 1970; Lieberman, Chapter 7, this volume; Menyuk, 1968; Vanvik, 1971). Oller *et al.* (1975) analyzed canonical babbling from 10 normal infants 6–13 months of age. The data demonstrated that phonetic tendencies of early speech could be seen in babbling. Both in early speech and in babbling (*a*) singleton consonants outnumber clusters; (*b*) initial consonants outnumber finals; (*c*) initial stops outnumber initial fricatives and affricates; (*d*) initial unaspirated stops outnumber aspirated ones; (*e*) glides outnumber liquids; (*f*) apical consonants outnumber dorsal ones; (*g*) final voiceless obstruents outnumber final voiced ones; and (*h*) final fricatives outnumber final stops.

These data indicate that babbling and speech are related to important ways. The data to not necessarily indicate that *no* discontinuities exist between phonetic features of babbling and speech. The similarities are worth focusing on, however, since they suggest that babbling reflects an emerging capacity for speech. The metaphonological framework invoked in the present chapter offers a further possibility of tracing precursors to speech throughout the first year of life.

References

Anderson, B.J., Vietze, P., and Dokecki, P.R. (1977) "Reciprocity in Vocal Interactions of Mothers and Infants," *Child Development,* 48, 1676–1681.

Atkinson, K.B., McWhinney, B. and Stoel, C. (1970) "An Experiment in the Recognition of Babbling," *Papers and Reports in Child Language Development,* 1, Stanford.

Bower, T.G.R. (1976) "Repetitive Processes in Child Development," *Scientific American,* 235, 38–47.

Butterfield, E., and Siperstein, G.N. (1972) "Influence of Contingent Auditory Stimulation upon Non-nutritional Suckle," in J. Bosma, ed., *Oral Sensation and Perception: The Mouth of the Infant,* Charles C Thomas, Springfield, Ill.

Crelin, E.S. (1969) *Anatomy of the Newborn: An Atlas,* Lea and Febiger, Philadelphia.

Cruttenden, A. (1970) "A Phonetic Study of Babbling," *British Journal of Disorders of Communication,* 5, 110–118.

Doyle, W.J. (1976) "On the Verge of Meaningful Speech," Master's Thesis, University of Washington, Seattle.

Eilers, R.E. and Minifie, F.D. (1975) "Fricative Discrimination in Early Infancy," *Journal of Speech and Hearing Research,* 18, 158–167.

Eilers, R.E., Gavin, W., and Wilson, W. (1979) "Linguistic Experience and Phonemic Perception: A Cross Linguistic Study," *Child Development,* 50, 14–18.

Eimas, P., Siqueland, E., Jusczyk, P., and Vigorito, J. (1971) "Speech Perception in Infants," *Science,* 4, 303–306.

Fenton, J.C. (1925) *A Practical Psychology of Babyhood,* Houghton Mifflin, Boston, New York.

Gesell, A., and Amatruda, C.S. (1941) *Developmental Diagnosis,* P. B. Hoeber, New York.

Hast, M.H. (1970) "The Developmental Anatomy of the Larynx," *Otolaryngology Clinics of North America,* 3, 413–439.

Hoyer, A., and Hoyer, G. (1924) "Uber die Lallsprache eines Kindes," *Zeitschrift fur angewandte Psychologie,* 24, 363–384.

Irwin, O.C. (1974) "Infant Speech: Consonantal Sounds According to Place of Articulation, *Journal of Speech and Hearing Disorders,* 12, 397–401.

Jakobson, R. (1941) *Kindersprache, Aphasie und Allgeimeine Lautgesetze,* Almqvist and Wiksell, Uppsala.

Kessen, W., Levine, J., and Wendrich, K.A., (1979) "The Imitation of Pitch by Infants," *Infant Behavior and Development,* 2, 93–100.

Leopold, W.F. (1947) *Speech Development of a Bilingual Child: A Linguist's Record* (Vol. 2), Sound Learning in the First Two Years, Northwestern University Press, Evanston, Ill.

Liberman, A.M., Delattre, P., Gerstman, L.J., and Cooper, F.S. (1956) "Tempo of Frequency Change as a Cue for Distinguishing Classes of Speech Sounds," *Journal of Experimental Psychology,* 52, 127–137.

Lieberman, P., Buhr, R., Keating, P., Hamby, S.V., and Landahl, K.H., (1976) "Speech Development in Infants—Vowel Production," *Journal of the Acoustical Society of America,* 60, Supplement I, S43. (Abstract)

Lieberman, P., Harris, K.S., Wolff, P., and Russell, L.H. (1971) "Newborn Infant Cry and Non-human Primate Vocalizations," *Journal of Speech and Hearing Research*, 14, 718–727.

McCarthy, D. (1952) "Organismic Interpretation of Infant Vocalizations," *Child Development*, 23, 273–80.

Meltzoff, A. N., and Moore, M. K. (1977) "Imitation of Facial and Manual Gestures by Human Neonates," *Science*, 198, 75–78.

Menyuk, P. (1968) "The Role of Distinctive Features in Children's Acquisition of Phonology," *Journal of Speech and Hearing Research*, 11, 138–46.

Minifie, F., Kuhl, P. K., and Stecher, B. (1977) "Categorical Perception of /b/ and /w/ during Changes in Rate of Utterance," Paper, read at ASA Convention.

Morse, P. (1974) "Infant Speech Perception: A Preliminary Model and Review of the Literature," in R. Schiefelbusch and L. Lloyd, eds., *Language Perspectives: Acquisition, Retardation and Intervention*, University Park Press, Baltimore, Md. pp. 19–53.

Murai, J. (1963) "The Sounds of Infants: their Phonemicization and Symbolization," *Studia Phonologica*, 3, 18–34.

Nakazima, S.A. (1962) "A Comparative Study of the Speech Developments of Japanese and American English in Childhood," *Studia Phonologica*, II, 27–46.

Oller, D.K. (1976) "Infant Vocalizations: A Linguistic and Speech Scientific Perspective," Miniseminar for the American Speech and Hearing Association, Houston.

Oller, D.K., and Smith, B.L. (1977) "Effect of Final-syllable Position on Vowel Duration in Infant Babbling," *Journal of the Acoustical Society of America*, 62, 994–997.

Oller, D.K., Wieman, L.A., Doyle, W., and Ross, C. (1975) "Infant Babbling and Speech," *Journal of Child Language*, 3, 1–11.

Olney, R.L., and Scholnick, E.K. (1976) "Adult Judgments of Age and Linguistic Differences in Infant Vocalization," *Journal of Child Language*, 3, 145–156.

Pierce, J.E. (1974) "A Study of 750 Portland, Oregon Children during the First Year," *Papers and Reports on Child Language Development*, Stanford University, 8, 19–25.

Preston, M.S., Yeni-Komshian, G., and Stark, R.E. (1967) "Voicing in Initial Stop Consonants Produced by Children in the Prelinguistic Period from Different Language Communities," *Johns Hopkins University School of Medicine, Annual Report of Neurocommunications Laboratory*, 2, 305–323.

Smith, B.L., and Oller, D.K. (in press) "A Comparative Study of Pre-meaningful Vocalizations Produced by Normal and Down's Syndrome Infants," *Journal of Speech and Hearing Disorders*.

Stark, R.E., Heinz, J.M., and Wright-Wilson, C. (1976) "Vowel Utterances of Young Infants," *Journal of the Acoustical Society of America*, 60, *Supplement 1*, S42. (Abstract)

Stark, R.E., Rose, S.N., and McLagen, M. (1975) "Features of Infant Sounds: The First Eight Weeks of Life," *Journal of Child Language*, 2, 205–222.

Stern, D.N., Jaffe, J. Beebe, B., and Bennett, S.L. (1975) "Vocalizing in Unison and in Alternation: Two Modes of Communication within the Mother-infant Dyad," *Annals of the New York Academy of Sciences*, 263, 89–100.

Streeter, L.A. (1976) "Language Perception of Two-Month-Old Infants Shows Effects of Both Innate Mechanisms and Experience." *Nature*, 259, 39–41.

Taine, H. (1877) "Acquisition of Language by Children," *Mind*, 2, 252–259.

Vanvik, A. (1971) "The Phonetic-phonemic Development of a Norwegian Child," *Norsk Tidsskrift for Sprogvidenskap*, XXIV, Oslo.

Zlatin, M.A. (1975) "Correspondence between Perceptual Judgments and Acoustic Attributes for Selected Infant Vocal Behaviors during the First 24 Weeks—A Preliminary Study," from *Final Report*, Project No. 3–4014, Grant No. NE–G–OO–3–0077.

Zlatin, M.A. (1975) "Preliminary Descriptive Model of Infant Vocalization during the first 24 Weeks: Primitive Syllabification and Phonetic Exploratory Behavior" Final Report, Project No. 3-4014, Grant NE–G–00–3–0077.

Zlatin, M.A., Hixson, P.K., and Coggins, C.R. (1975) Classification of Early Infant Cry and Non-cry Vocalization," *Final Report*, Project No. 3–4014, Grant No. NE–G–OO–3–0077.

Zlatin Laufer, M.A., and Horii, Y. (1977) "Fundamental Frequency Characteristics of Infant Non-distress Vocalization during the First 24 Weeks," *Journal of Child Language*, 4, 171–184.

Zlatin, M.A. (1974) "Variations on a Theme: [agɤUə]," Paper presented at the American Speech and Hearing Association Convention, Las Vegas.

Chapter 7

ON THE DEVELOPMENT OF VOWEL PRODUCTION IN YOUNG CHILDREN

PHILIP LIEBERMAN

This study forms part of a comprehensive acoustic analysis of the development of speech in normal children from birth through the preschool years. We have systematically recorded and analyzed the utterances of a small group of normal children. Our objective has been to gather quantitative acoustic data that are sufficiently detailed to develop and test hypotheses that bear on the biological bases of language. Although our data base is too small to allow us to state with any reasonable degree of confidence what may constitute the range and limits of normal speech development in children, it has yielded some insights on the variations that may be expected and has refuted traditional theories claiming that all children acquire speech in the same manner.

Procedures

Recording

We started the study by recording, at weekly or 2-week intervals, the utterances of five children whose ages ranged at the start of the project from 16 weeks to 5 years. All of the children were raised in upper middle class, monolingual English-speaking environments in Providence, Rhode Island.

CHILD PHONOLOGY
VOLUME 1: PRODUCTION

As the project went on, we "lost" some of our subjects when it became difficult to schedule recording sessions or when the family moved, and we added three more children. Two of these children were started at 10 and 12 months respectively, to focus on the transition from babbling to word acquisition. The third child was first recorded 1 week after birth. We also have recorded, at intervals, one child raised in a bilingual Polish–English environment, and five children from Korean-speaking environments to acquire data that address specific hypotheses.

The recording sessions typically involve the child and his or her mother interacting in situations that are normal in the context of the child's maturation. In the early months of life, the child may be recorded while eating or bathing; in later stages of development, the mother and child may be "reading" picture books aloud or playing games with various toys. "Older" children have been recorded as they engage in monologues or converse with their parents, other people, or the recording crew. The members of the recording crew and the process of recording are essentially normal aspects of these children's environment; the process of being recorded is usually not a source of tension or a perturbation of normal life. They are as accustomed to tape recorders, microphones, and the recording crew as they are accustomed to telephones, TV sets, and other acquaintances.

We have used Nagra type 4.2 portable tape recorders at a tape speed of 7.5 ips using 1.5 mil Scotch low noise tape. The tape recorders have been used with battery supplies to ensure the least perturbation of the children's home environment. A study of the development of vowel production necessarily depends on having accurate formant-frequency measurements. We adopted a systems approach to meet this problem and tailored our recording techniques to optimize the measurement of formant frequencies from speakers who have extremely high fundamental frequencies. We have emphasized recording breathy-voice excitation, which yields noiselike excitation of the supralaryngeal vocal tract's filter function (Fant, 1960), by using directional AKG D900 microphones positioned close to our children during the early stages of their lives. As the children mature and grow accustomed to the presence of microphones, recording, and so on, we have, in certain cases, used electret condenser microphones attached near the child's mouth.

Analysis

We analyzed the tape recordings made under these conditions, which emphasized breathy excitation, with spectrograms made on a Kay Elemetrics type 6061B Sound Spectrograph using 90-Hz and 600-Hz bandwidth analysis filters. Figure 7.1, for example, shows two spectrograms of the word [dagi] produced by speaker J. B. at age 91 weeks. The lower spectrogram was made with an analyzing bandwidth of 90 Hz; and the upper with a filter bandwidth of 600 Hz. A Kay type 6076C scale expander was used in both cases and calibration signals spaced at 1-kHz intervals were put on both spectrograms.

The use of 90-Hz and 600-Hz bandwidth spectrograms, the scale expander, and calibration signals, which we check against a signal generator, is standard procedure for all our analyses. The increased bandwidth on the 600-Hz analyzing filter makes it possible to estimate formant frequencies for fundamental frequencies up to at least 250 Hz, whereas it is quite difficult to estimate formant frequencies with the usual 300-Hz "wideband" analyzing filter of the sound spectrograph when the fundamental frequency exceeds 150 Hz (Lieberman, 1977). The arrow symbol that appears after .8 sec on the upper spectrogram indicates the point at which the formant frequencies of the vowel [i] were measured for this utterance. We made formant-frequency measurements for vowels at points like that indicated by the arrow where "steady state" conditions occurred. Formant frequencies were not discernable in all utterances even with these techniques. Because the fun-

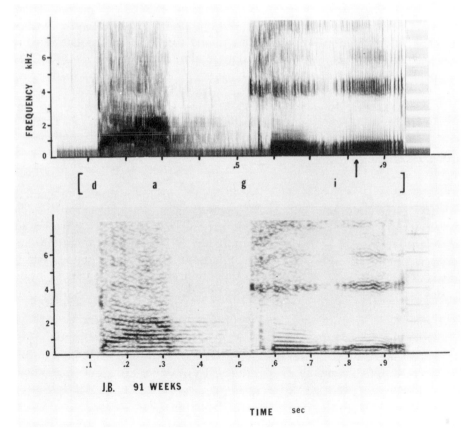

FIGURE 7.1 *Sound spectrograms of word [dagi] produced by speaker J. B. at 91 weeks. The upper spectrogram (a) was made with a 600 Hz bandwidth analyzing filter, the lower (b) with a 90 Hz bandwidth analyzing filter.*

damental frequency of the utterance displayed in Figure 7.1 ranged between 250 and 300 Hz, the formant frequencies could be derived by means of the averaging technique inherent in the use of the 600 Hz bandwidth analyzing filter. The formant frequencies of the vowel [i], which are at approximately .5, 4.2, and 6.0 kHz are measurable, however. Note the "extra" dark "bars" that occurred during the [a], the results of nasalization. The [a] in Figure 7.1 is nasalized and the formants and antiformants of the nasal airway make it difficult to derive the formant frequencies of the [a]. In cases of doubt, which were many, we simply did not use the utterance (i.e., if it was too nasalized, or if the fundamental frequency was too high and there was not sufficient breathy excitation present to resolve the formants). The data that we will discuss in this report are drawn from a corpus of approximately 18,000 spectrograms, of which approximately 50% were discarded for the afare mentioned reasons.

All of the data that will be discussed was derived from sound spectrograms. In a few cases, we checked our measurements by computer-implemented Fourier analysis and linear predictive analysis (Atal and Hanauer, 1971). Measurements of vowel duration and fundamental frequency were also derived from spectrograms. Fundamental frequency was usually derived by measuring higher harmonics of the fundamental frequency. In the case of the comparatively low fundamental frequencies associated with fry-register phonation (Keating and Burh, 1978), the wide bandwidth spectrograms also were used (Lieberman, 1977).

Classification of Vowels

The process of perceptually identifying vowels in the noncry utterances of very young children is not easy. The children in their babbling stage may not be referring to any known objects, actions, or requests, so it is difficult to determine what they are attempting to say, if indeed they are attempting to produce any specific vowel. Despite these difficulties, perceptually based phonetic transcriptions of the sounds that children make in the first 3 months of life are in substantial accord (George, 1978; Irwin, 1948). The transcriptions of phonetically trained listeners responding to the sounds that children make as they grow up in an English-speaking environment note that the "front" vowels of English, excepting [i], occur. It is in the latter stages of babbling that some phoneticians claim to hear children producing the phonetic repertoires of languages other than the one of their immediate linguistic environment (Jakobson, 1940). As we were expending a great deal of effort to derive reliable acoustic data, we assessed our phonetic classifications of the vowels that the children produced.

We used two different procedures to check the consistency and validity of the perceptually based phonetic transcriptions that we made of the childrens' vowels. The first method that we used to assess the transcriptions was applied to the utterances of speaker L. S. who was recorded from the age of 16 weeks onward. All of the tape recordings for this speaker were transcribed by a single phonetically trained investigator (R. B.). We assessed the consistency and validity of these transcriptions (i.e., would other phonetically trained listeners agree with these transcriptions?) by preparing a tape recording that contained 89 "identified" vowels. The sample was drawn from tape recordings that had been made when the child was 16 and 62 weeks old. The child was still in the babbling stage at 62 weeks.

Each stimulus was repeated six times in a random sequence on this tape recording and the recording was then independently transcribed by six different phonetically trained listeners who transcribed every stimulus on the tape. The listeners were able to stop the tape recording, change their transcriptions, go back over sections, and so on. In other words, the six listeners were asked to transcribe the tape as though they were making the primary transcription, the object being to make as accurate a transcription as possible from the tape recording. The overall agreement between the six listeners and the person who originally transcribed the tape recordings was 73%; 76% of the vowel stimuli recorded at 16 weeks and 70% of those recorded at 62 weeks were in agreement with the original transcription. Of the total number of vowels identified, at least four of the six listeners agreed with the original observer. Within this subset of vowels, the overall consistency was 81%.

We also used a second method to transcribe the tape recordings to achieve consistent classifications for sounds that were perceived as vowels of English. The transcriptions of the tape recordings of speakers J. B., F. R., R. C., and G. R. were made by a panel of three phonetically trained listeners who each independently listened to the tape recordings. Only those vowel stimuli for which there was agreement among the three listeners are plotted on the graphs that follow. The overall agreement of these three listeners was 74%, which turned out to be essentially the consistency derived in our test of the consistency of a single phonetically trained listener.

In addition to the vowels that were consistently identified as vowels of English, we recorded many other vowel-like sounds. We also analyzed some of these sounds in connection with that aspect of Jakobson's (1940) theory claiming that, at one stage of development, children raised in English-speaking environments produce non-English vowels in their babbling. We will return to these data later.

Acoustic Data and Observations

We will first present data for one child, L. S., who was babbling throughout the period (16–64 weeks of life) that we shall cover. Child L. S., who is a normal male, was recorded at the intervals noted in Table 7.1. The total number of occurrences of each vowel identified and plotted through Week

TABLE 7.1
The Number of Occurrences of each Individual Vowel per Week

Vowels														Weeks														
	16	17	18	19	21	22	23	24	25	26	29	31	33	35	36	37	38	41	43	45	47	48	51	54	57	60	62	64
i		1				1				2		2		2		1	3	6	1		3		3	8	4	2	5	5
I	3	4		3	1	5	2	3		1	3	2	6		3	2	7	13		2	6	3	17	6	2	5	6	9
e	1	1					1	1	1	2	3		3			1		4	1	1	1		2	9	3	5	1	4
ε	18	20	6	7	2	11	12	22	6	16	8	2	12	17	5	4	7	20	2	8	17	6	14	7	6	16	10	13
æ	13	2	5	4	1	16	6	8		4		2	6	2	2	1	6	7	2	12	10	19	3	14	3	9	5	1
a		3		1		1							2	6	2			3	1	-1	6	5	5	1	3	2	3	1
ʌ	9	9	1	1	1	3		4			1	3	3	2			1	9	1	4	10	13	11	6	4		6	
ɲ												1				1			1									
o																					1	1	2	1	1	3		
ʊ	8	4	6	3	1	3	3	9		3		1		2	2	2	3	4	6	2	4	4	6	7	5	7	7	3
u								1		1														1	2			

64 is also shown on Table 7.1. As the entries in in Table 7.1 show, vowels like [u], [o], [ɲ], and [i] occurred infrequently throughout the data sample and not at all before Week 16. The absence of [i], [u] and [a] from the early vocalizations of children is consistent with the data of George (1978), who notes their complete absence before the age of 12 weeks and infrequent occurrence in the weeks thereafter in a sample of 29 normal children. The most common vowels are [æ] and [ɛ]. In Figures 7.2 and 7.3, the ranges and means of F_1, F_2, and F_3 are plotted for these vowels. Note the high absolute value of these formant frequencies; F_3 is about 5 kHz, which compares with values of about 2.5 kHz for adult males (Peterson and Barney, 1952). In Figures 7.4 and 7.5, F_1, F_2, and F_3 are plotted for the vowels [i] and [a]. Note that F_3 is about 6.5 kHz for [i]; it is about 3 kHz for adult males. There is little change in the average values of the formant frequencies for speaker L. S.'s vowels from Weeks 16 to 64. This is to be expected since there was probably little change in the length of his supralaryngeal vocal tract, as his height changed only 7.5cm (3 in.) through this period; from 62.5 to 70cm (25–28 in.) The length of the supralaryngeal vocal tract is closely correlated with overall growth in this period of life (George, 1978). It thus is very probable that his supralaryngeal vocal tract's overall length did not change very much throughout this period. X rays of our subjects, which would have established the growth pattern of their supralaryngeal vocal tracts would have been useful but could not be made within present ethical guidelines for research.

Speaker L. S.'s vowels cannot be regarded as simple imitations of the formant frequencies of adult speech. They have the correct spectral *patterning*. Note that F_1 and F_2 converge in the midfrequency region for [a] (in Figure 7.5) whereas F_2 and F_3 converge at the high end of the spectrum for [i] (Figure 7.4). However, the absolute values of the formant frequencies are completely outside the range that occurs for adult speech and are consistent with the short length of the child's supralaryngeal vocal tract. Note also the variation in the formant frequencies that was measured for particular vowels. This is especially so for vowels like [i] and [u] that appear infrequently and later than other vowels.

The development of speaker L. S.'s acoustic vowel space can be seen in the graphs that follow. In Figure 7.6, these vowels are plotted at 16 weeks, when there is considerable overlap for all the vowels identified [Iɤ ɛ, æ, ʌ, and ʊ]. In Figure 7.7, the identified vowels recorded in Week 24 are plotted. Note that the formant frequencies of [ʊ] have dropped on the plot, that [æ] has moved rightward (i.e., F_1 has been raised). It would appear that in this time period the vowels produced by L. S. are moving into the acoustic positions that resemble a rudimentary vowel triangle. In Figures 7.8 and 7.9, the vowels identified during Weeks 41 and 62 are plotted. Note that the general trend toward expanding the acoustic vowel space continues, though the trend may not be apparent if we simply compare the vowels recorded

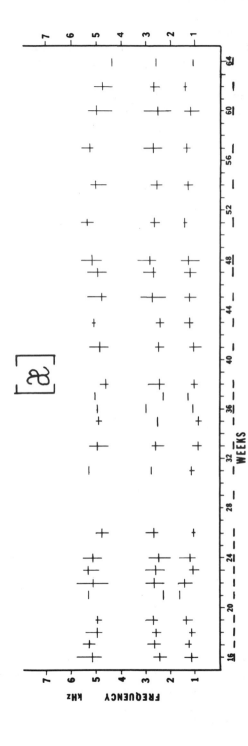

FIGURE 7.2 *Means and ranges of formant frequencies of vowel [æ] of speaker I. S. for tape recordings made at specified weeks. See Table 7.1 for number of tokens for each week.*

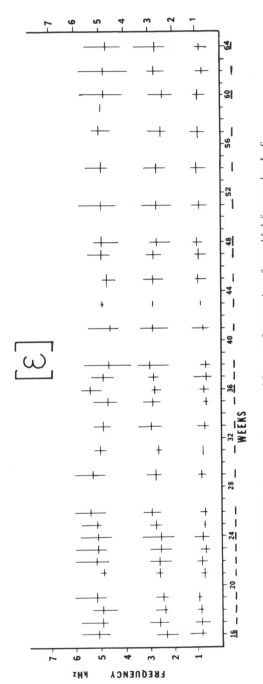

FIGURE 7.3 *Means and ranges of formant frequencies of vowel* [ɛ] *for speaker L. S.*

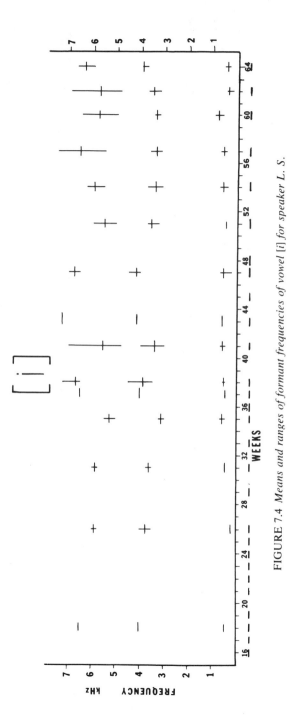

FIGURE 7.4 *Means and ranges of formant frequencies of vowel* [i] *for speaker L. S.*

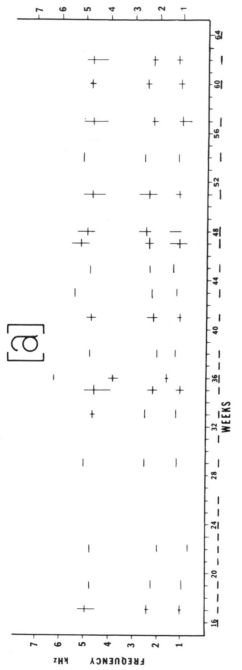

FIGURE 7.5 *Means and ranges of formant frequencies of vowel [a] for speaker L. S.*

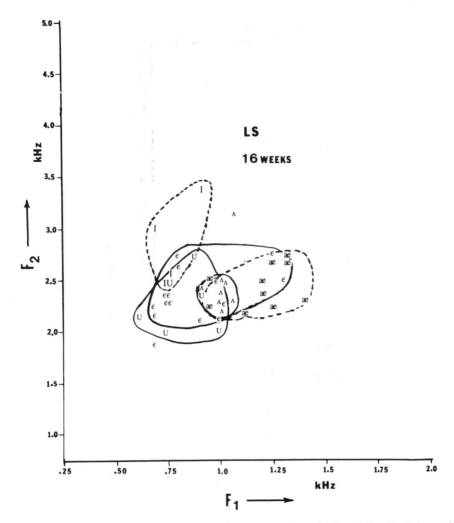

FIGURE 7.6 *Plot of first and second formant frequencies of vowels identified as English vowels for speaker L. S. at 16 weeks. The frequency of the first formant is plotted with respect to the abcissa; the frequency of the second formant is plotted with respect to the ordinate.*

during two single weeks. For some reason, which we do not know, the formant frequencies of the vowels plotted during Week 41 overlap more than those plotted in Weeks 24 and 62. Some of the sounds that we identified as [I in Week 41 have formant-frequency patterns that would make them [i], but their durations are too short (about 80–100 msec). The child is not yet coordinating the formant-frequency pattern and temporal pattern of English vowels. In Week 62 (Figure 7.9), this overlap disappears.

One question that comes to mind is whether or not the formant-frequency patterns of the vowel sounds that we were not able to identify as

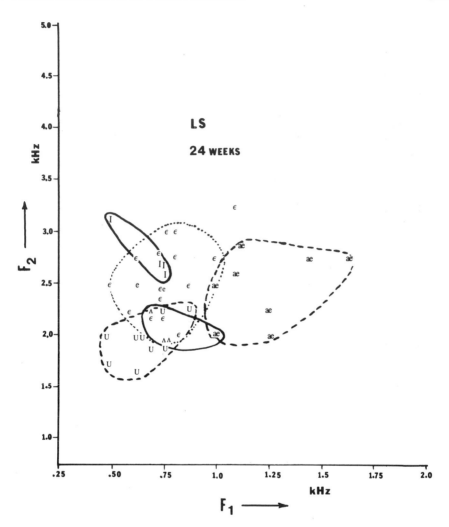

FIGURE 7.7 *Plot of first and second formant frequencies of vowels identified as English vowels for speaker L. S. at 24 weeks.*

vowels of English fall outside the range of the acoustic vowel space of the vowels that we were able to identify. In Figure 7.10, F_1 and F_2 are plotted for all the vowels that we were able to identify during Week 64. Figure 7.10 also shows F_1 and F_2 of all the other vowel stimuli that we were able to measure on spectrograms, though we could not reliably identify them as vowels of English. The identified vowels are noted with the appropriate phonetic symbols; the unidentified vowels are indicated as Xs. A total of 48 unidentified vowels are plotted. The total acoustic vowel space of the unidentified vowels is quite similar to that of the identified vowels. If we were to pool the identified vowels for Weeks 62 and 64 (Figures 7.9 and 7.10),

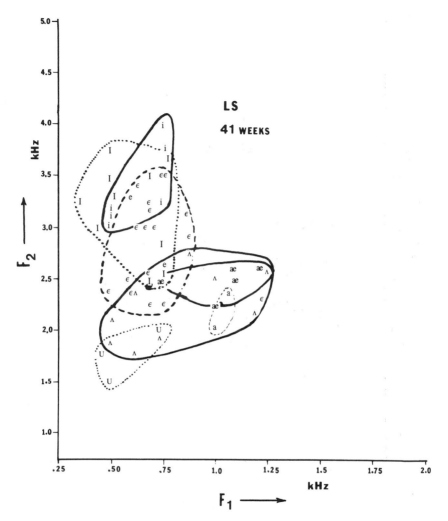

FIGURE 7.8 *Plot of first and second formant frequencies of vowels identified as English vowels for speaker L. S. at 41 weeks.*

there would be virtually no difference except for the cluster of unidentified vowels that occupy the position that should be filled by [u]. These sounds were nasalized (i.e. the spectrograms show the presence of additional nasal formants), which may account for their not being identified as English [u]s. In general, the unidentified vowels were nasalized.

The data in Figures 7.8, 7.9, and 7.10 and in Table 7.1 also demonstrate that it is not possible to assess the phonetic repertoire of a child by simply recording and identifying all his or her utterances during a single recording

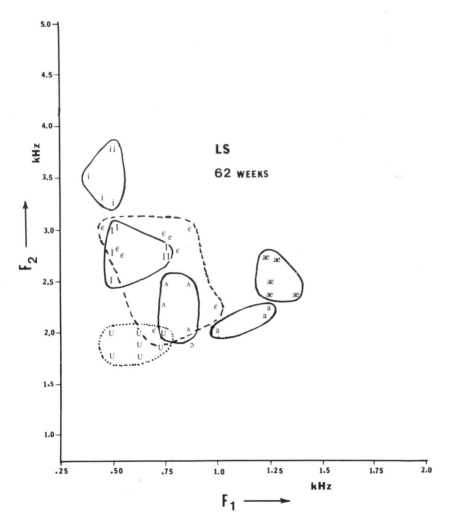

FIGURE 7.9 *Plot of first and second formant frequencies of vowels identified as English vowels for speaker L. S. at 62 weeks.*

session. Even when an hour of "speech" is recorded, tokens of various sounds may be missing.

The trend toward elaboration of the acoustic vowel space that is evident in speaker L. S. can also be seen in Figures 7.11 and 7.12 for speaker R. C. The F_1 and F_2 values for her identified vowels are plotted for Weeks 38 and 69; speaker R. C. was babbling throughout this period. In contrast, the vowels plotted in Figures 7.13 and 7.14 for speaker J. B. for Weeks 66 and 147 are derived from her productions of meaningful words. Our transcrip-

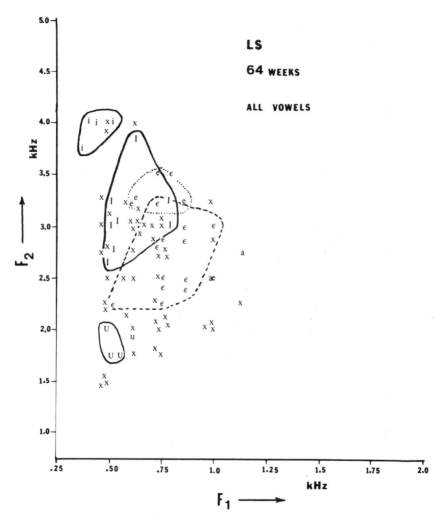

FIGURE 7.10 *Plot of first and second formant frequencies of vowels identified as English vowels for speaker L. S. at 64 weeks plus all other vowel-like sounds whose formant frequencies could be measured. The Xs* indicate these sounds, which were generally nasalized.

tions continued to be phonetic rather than phonemic when children produced meaningful words. Thus we transcribed a sound as an [I] when it occurred in a word where the child should have been producing an [æ]. Note the change in the "shape" of her acoustic vowel space, as well as the fall in the absolute values of the formant frequencies. This trend is most apparent in F_2 for [i].

The same trends are apparent in Figures 7.15 and 7.16 for speaker G. R., a boy, who also was producing meaningful words with the vowels plotted in Weeks 69 and 162. Speaker F. R., a boy, who was producing meaningful

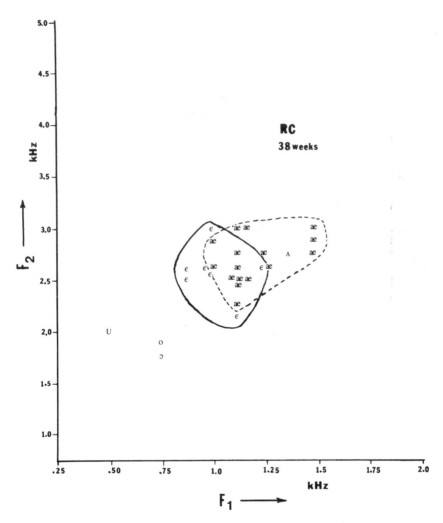

FIGURE 7.11 *Plot of first and second formant frequencies of vowels identified as English vowels for speaker R. C. at 38 weeks.*

sentences throughout the period that we recorded him, demonstrated similar though smaller changes and expansion of his acoustic vowel space. Note the decrease in frequency of F_1 in [i] and [I] between the vowels recorded in Weeks 125 and 169 that are plotted in Figures 7.17 and 7.18. Note also that the formant frequencies of the vowels are moving toward a better fit with the acoustic vowel space typical of adult speakers of American English. When the data on Figures 7.17 and 7.18 are compared with those of Peterson and Barney (1952) for adults and older children it is apparent that speaker F. R. has moved his [I], [ɛ], and [æ] vowels into better alignment along the

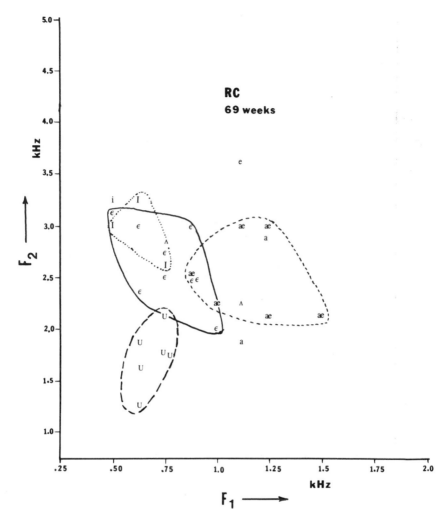

FIGURE 7.12 *Plot of first and second formant frequencies of vowels identified as English vowels for speaker R. C. at 69 weeks.*

"acute" [i]–[a] axis (Jakobson *et al.*, 1952) and [ʌ] and [o] along the "grave" axis. This is also the case for speaker G. R. in Figures 7.15 and 7.16, but the trend is not as obvious, and the interval between the two plots (93 weeks) is longer. The trend towards "perfecting" the acoustic vowel space thus continues from babbling well into the phonologic and syntactic stages of language acquisition.

There is also an improvement in the consistency with which children produce the formant-frequency patterns that specify various vowels in the phonologic stage of language acquisition. In Figures 7.19 and 7.20, formant-

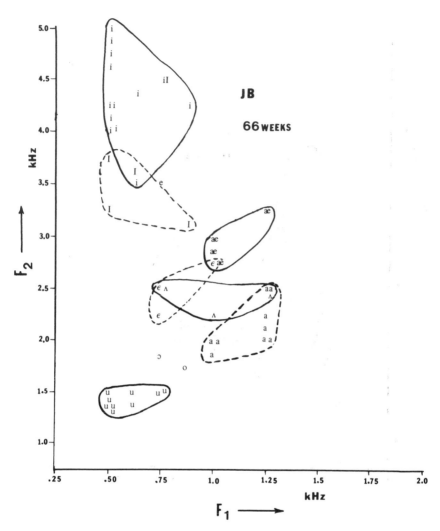

FIGURE 7.13 *Plot of first and second formant frequencies of vowels identified as English vowels for speaker J. B. at 66 weeks. This speaker was producing words.*

frequency data are plotted for the vowel [i] for speaker J. B. from Weeks 66 to 109, and for speaker F. R. from Weeks 125 to 161. Both of these children were using meaningful words. Note the greater range of variation in the formant frequencies in Figure 7.20 for the younger speaker who also frequently made gross errors and failed to produce the appropriate vowel when she tried to utter specific words. There is also a great deal of variation in the durations of her words, which tend to to be much longer than those of "well formed" speech of adults and older children.

Note that the degree of variations between tokens of [i] is lower in

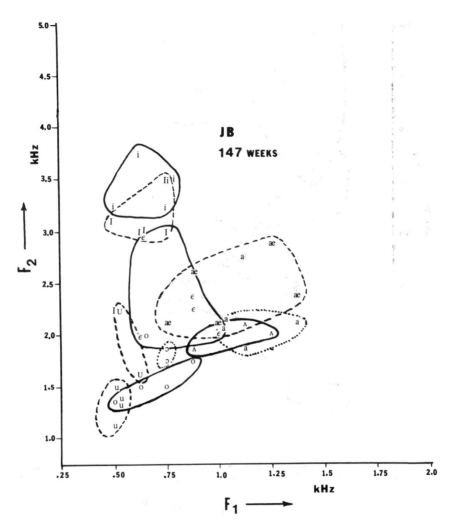

FIGURE 7.14 *Plot of first and second formant frequencies of vowels of speaker J. B. at 147 weeks.*

speaker F. R.'s utterances plotted in Figure 7.20 for Weeks 125–161. Note also that the formant frequencies of speaker F. R. are lower than those of speaker J. B.; he is older and larger than speaker J. B. Formant₃ of [i] is about 4.5 kHz for speaker F. R., whereas it is about 5.5 kHz for speaker J. B. The heights and weights of both these children and thus their supra-laryngeal vocal-tract lengths, did not change markedly over the interval of time that is presented in these plots.

In Figure 7.21, the range of formant frequencies of the vowel [i] for speaker R. C. is plotted for Weeks 57 through 69. Speaker R. C. was in the

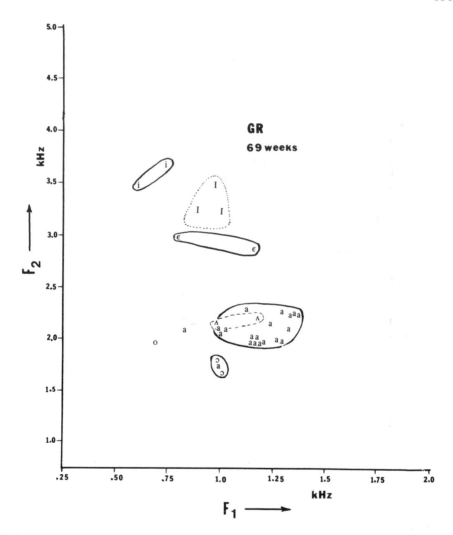

FIGURE 7.15 *Plot of first and second formant frequencies of vowels of speaker G. R. at 69 weeks. This speaker was producing words.*

babbling stage throughout this period, but note that F_3 of her [i]s is about 4.7 kHz, though she is almost two years younger than speaker F. R. (Figure 7.20). It is not possible to present a formula or a table that would specify the formant frequencies that children use at a specific age. Note that there is also less variation in the formant frequencies from week to week than is the case for speaker J. B. (Figure 7.19). Children differ from each other with respect to physical growth and the development of motor skills like those involved in walking. They also differ with respect to the development of speech with respect to other aspects of linguistic ability.

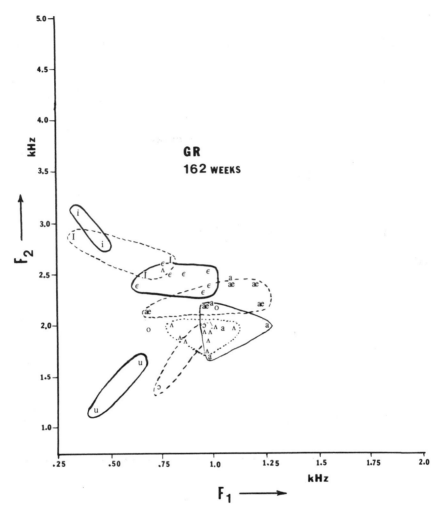

FIGURE 7.16 *Plot of first and second formant frequencies of speaker G. R. at 162 weeks. Note the lower values of formant frequencies and the shape of the vowel "triangle" with respect to Figure 7.15.*

Discussion

The formant-frequency data that we have presented address two issues. The most obvious acoustic distinction between the formant frequencies of the vowels of these young children and the vowels of older children and adults is the higher values of the formant frequencies. The younger and smaller the child, the higher are the formant frequencies for specific vowels. F_3 for speaker L. S. is about 6.5 kHz for [i] at ages 50–60 weeks, 5.5 kHz

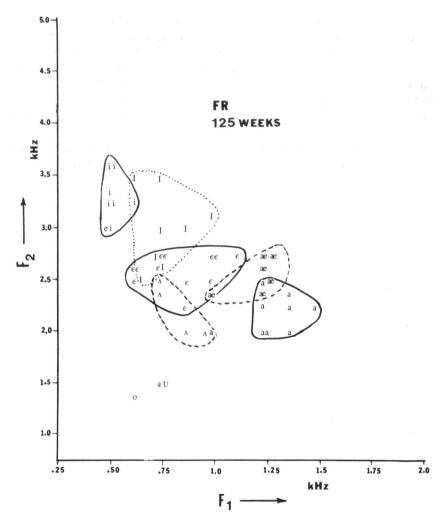

FIGURE 7.17 *Plot of first and second formant frequencies of vowels of speaker F. R. These vowels were produced in short sentences.*

for speaker J. B. from 81 to 96 weeks, and 4.5 kHz for speaker F. R. from 125 to 161 weeks. As the children grow, their formant frequencies fall. There is no evidence that children attempt to mimic the absolute formant frequencies of the adult speech that they hear. This is so even for vowels, where, in theory, the child could shift the formant frequencies toward the lower frequencies of adult speech. Computer modeling studies (e.g., Stevens and House, 1955) demonstrate that a child could, by means of "compensatory" maneuvers (e.g., lip rounding), produce an [I] vowel that has lower formant frequencies than we would expect if we considered the length of

the child's supralaryngeal vocal tract. The acoustic data that we have presented, however, show that the formant frequencies of these vowels ([I, [æ],
[Θ], etc.) are in "proper" relation to those of vowels like [i] and [a], where
the supralaryngeal vocal tract effectively constrains the possible absolute
values of the formant frequencies that would yield the proper spectral relations that define the vowel acoustically (Stevens and House, 1955). This
is quite apparent in the plots for children producing vowels in meaningful
words (e.g., Figures 7.14, 7.16, and 7.18).

The higher values of the formant frequencies for vowels like [i], [u] and
[a] thus follow from the fact that the child can in no way imitate the absolute

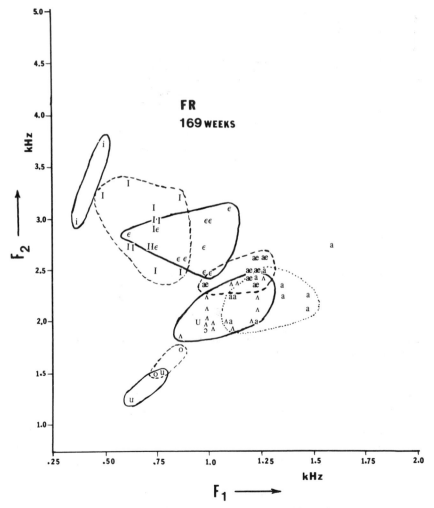

FIGURE 7.18 *Speaker F. R.'s vowels at 169 weeks. Note the better approximation to the
acoustic vowel triangle of adult English vowels with respect to Figure 7.17.*

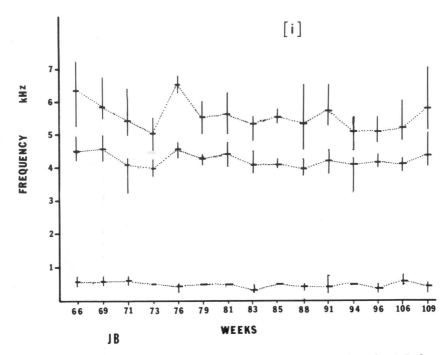

FIGURE 7.19 *Means and ranges of formant frequencies of vowel* [i] *of speaker J. B. for tape recordings made at specified weeks. All of these vowels were produced in words.*

values of the formant frequencies of the vowels that he hears from his or her parents, or from older children. Although some degree of variation is possible in the production of vowels like [I], [ɛ], and [æ], where a speaker with a shorter vocal tract can, in theory, produce a formant-frequency pattern having absolute frequency values that we might expect to find in the acoustic vowel space of a speaker having a longer supralaryngeal vocal tract (Neary, 1976; Stevens and House, 1955); we do not find that either. The children instead produce vowels whose formant frequencies are consistent with their shorter supralaryngeal vocal tracts. This fact can be explained if we hypothesize the presence of a perceptual mechanism that is present in all normal human beings that "normalizes" incoming speech sounds in terms of the presumed length of the speaker's presumed supralaryngeal vocal-tract length and that, likewise, allows the child to "know" that it has produced an equivalent signal as it listens to its own speech. The development of an approximation of the acoustic vowel space of English during the babbling stage of speech by the children argues for the early presence of this perceptual normalization mechanism, indeed for the presence of an innate, species-specific neural mechanism.

Cineradiographic data on the speech production of adult speakers show that there is no set of invariant supralaryngeal vocal-tract shapes that all

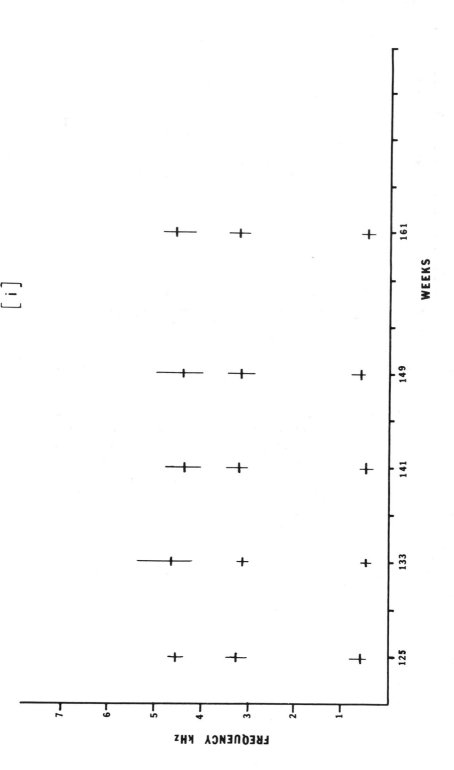

[i]

FR

FIGURE 7.20 Means and ranges of formant frequencies of vowel [i] of speaker J. B. for tape recordings made at specified weeks. All of these vowels were produced in words. Note the lower absolute values of the formant frequencies with respect to Figure 7.20. Also note the lesser variability from week to week.

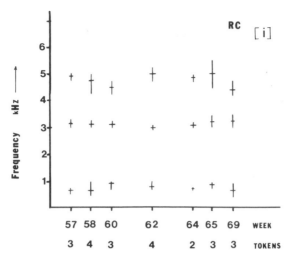

FIGURE 7.21 *Means and ranges of formant frequencies of vowel [i] of speaker R. C. for tape recordings made at specified weeks. Speaker R. C. was still in the babbling stage, but note the lower absolute formant frequencies and lesser variability from week to week with respect to speaker J. B. (Figure 7.20), who was older and producing words.*

speakers of a particular language use to generate the vowels of that language (Ladefoged *et al.,* 1972; Nearey, 1976; Russell, 1928) Different speakers, for example, use different supralaryngeal vocal-tract maneuvers to generate the vowels [I] and [ε]. Therefore, there cannot be a set of innately determined instructions for specific supralaryngeal vocal-tract maneuvers that the child brings into play as it begins to produce the vowels of English. Indeed, the child has no way of determining what specific supralaryngeal vocal-tract shape might underly the production of the formant-frequency pattern that specifies its mother's, father's, or older sibling's production of the vowel [I] (nor can anyone do this, a fact that argues forcefully against a strict "motor theory" of speech perception). The child thus has to imitate the *acoustic* signal that specifies the vowel [I] to produce that sound. The child, however, cannot produce the formant frequencies of the adult speech that it hears; its supralaryngeal vocal tract is too short, but it never attempts to mimic the lower formant frequencies of the incoming adult speech. Children instead produce "equivalent" formant frequency patterns that are scaled to their shorter supralaryngeal vocal-tract length. Moreover, as children grow, the formant frequencies of their vowels continually fall. The only plausible hypothesis that can account for these data is the presence of an innately determined vocal-tract normalization mechanism.

Note that we have not made any claims regarding either the neural implementation or the functional modeling of the normalization mechanism. The normalization could be effected by means of an algorithm like that proposed by Nearey (1976), in which the formant frequencies of the incoming speech sound are divided by a vocal-tract normalizing factor. The listener could derive the normalizing factor from the formant frequencies of vowels like [i] that yield effective indices of the speakers' supralaryngeal vocal tracts (Nearey, 1977) or the burst frequencies and initial invarient formant frequencies of "quantal" consonants (Blumstein et al., 1977; Stevens, 1972). The normalization mechanism, however, might not be implemented by means of the active computational process that we have outlined. Human beings may instead be equipped with arrays of all possible formant-frequency patterns corresponding to all possible supralaryngeal vocal-tract lengths. The listener, on receiving the incoming speech signal and making an estimate of the presumed length of the supralaryngeal vocal tract, would classify the incoming vowels in terms of the appropriate-patterns inventory that would specify the total acoustic vowel space of the speaker producing the incoming speech signal. The effect though, would still be one of vocal-tract normalization.

The process of vowel identification would have to be "plastic" in the sense that different dialects and languages make use of different acoustic partitionings of the acoustic vowel space delimited by the quantal vowels [i], [u], and [a] (Lieberman, 1976, 1977). The plasticity would be manifested in the child's setting up different acoustic partitionings of the available vowel space by means of either different neural acoustic "templates" or property detectors, or neural implementations of appropriate algorithms. The gradual elaboration of the acoustic vowel space and even more gradual "perfection" of the acoustic vowel space that we can see in the formant-frequency data of the children whose vowel production we have followed is consistent with the hypothesis that the normalization device is innate and manifests itself at the start of babbling, and that the process of forming appropriate vowel categories for a specific language is gradual and plastic.

This brings us to the second issue that the formant-frequency data address. There seems to be a gradual and consistent "improvement" in the childrens' productions of the vowels of English from the earliest stages of babbling well into the state (3 years of age) when the children are using meaningful sentences and are conversing with the experimenters. Though we cannot tell whether the children are attempting to produce the vowel sounds that they hear when they babble, there does not appear to be any "abrupt" break or discontinuity in their behavior as they go from the babbling to the phonologic stage of language acquisition. The perfection of the vowel repertoire that is manifest in the better approximation of the child's F_1 versus F_2 acoustic vowel space continues well into the stage (Figure 7.18) when the child is acquiring other aspects of language, at 3 years, such as morphology, syntax, and semantic interpretation. Thus there cannot be a "dedicated" language learning device (in the sense of the word dedicated in computer terminology) that applies itself to one task at a time as various linguists have suggested. The child simultaneously is perfecting phonetic, morphological, and syntactic abilities.

There is yet another question that these data address but do not resolve. Jakobson (1940) claimed that the child in its babbling stage produces the sounds of all human languages as well as the sounds of its linguistic environment. Although we have not found acoustic evidence that would support the hypothesis that the child is producing non-English vowels even when we take account of all the vowels that we can measure during a recording session (Figure 7.10), we still cannot rule out this hypothesis. The general trend of the data seems to be more consistent with the alternative hypothesis that the child, during the babbling stage, is attempting to imitate the sounds of his or her linguistic environment, producing many sounds that are, in fact, not satisfactory English vowels (when the linguistic environment is English) because of errors. A phonetician who had a wide linguistic background might interpret the child's errors as the sounds of another language because they, in fact, fit more closely into the acoustic template of the sound that occurs in another language (e.g., Swedish, where the acoustic vowel space is partitioned differently (Lieberman, 1976, 1977). When a child enters the phonologic stage, we can bring contextual cues to bear on the problem of assigning a child's error signal to the proper linguistic category of English if the child is attempting to speak English. The child's phonetic ability is also gradually improving, and fewer errors occur. The hypothetical abrupt change in behavior (Jakobson, 1940) that is supposed to occur between the babbling and phonologic stages of language acquisition thus may be a consequence of a different frame of interpretation that the phonetician brings to bear on the question of classifying the child's speech sounds: (a) Contextual cues are available to aid in the perception of speech; contextual cues play an important role in the classification of the sounds of adult speech in normal conversation (Lieberman, 1963, 1967); and (b) The child's phonetic ability also is continually improving. Gathering more data relevant to the transition between babbling and the phonologic stage, and studies of speech development of children raised in linguistic environments that have vowel systems that differ from English, will resolve this question.

We have not presented data that we are gathering on the development of children's control of the duration of vowels, or for that matter, other segmental phonetic elements. These data however, indicate that a gradual improvement involving better approximations to the temporal distinctions of adult speech occurs as children begin to produce meaningful words and proceed thereon. We intend to continue these studies, using computer-implemented procedures to derive formant frequencies, formant transitions, burst frequencies, burst intensities, VOT distinctions, and fundamental frequencies of childrens' speech. We hope that these data will provide some further insights into the development of speech in normal children in relation to the development of other aspects of linguistic ability and other behavioral skills. We already have some normative data on fundamental-frequency ranges (Keating and Buhr, 1978), stop consonant production, and the formant frequencies of vowels. It already is apparent that different children can behave quite differently and may acquire speech by means of different strategies. We, therefore, must continue to test the hypotheses that we have noted herein and keep an open mind to other alternatives.

Acknowledgments

The data that I have presented results from the dedicated activity of a number of people. I would especially like to note Robert Buhr's (Buhr, 1976) contributions, as well as those of Karen Landahl, Patricia Keating, and Katherine Kubaska. Our efforts have been made possible by Grant 5R01–HD–09197 from the National Institute of Child Health and Human Development.

References

Atal, B.S., and Hanauer S.C. (1971) "Speech Analysis and Synthesis by Linear Prediction of the Speech Wave," *Journal of the Acoustical Society of America* 50, 637–655.

Blumstein, S.E., Stevens, K.N., and Nigro, G.N. (1977) "Property Detectors for Bursts and Transitions in Speech Perception," *Journal of the Acoustical Society of America,* 61, 1301–1313.

Buhr, R.D. (1976) "The Emergence of Vowels in Infants: A Progress Report," M.A. Thesis, Brown University, Providence, R.I.

Fant, G. (1960) *Acoustic Theory of Speech Production,* Mouton, The Hague.

George, S.L. (1978) "The Relationship between Cranial Base Angle Morphology and Infant Vocalizations," Doctoral Dissertation, University of Connecticut, Storrs.

Irwin, O.C. (1948) "Infant Speech: Development of Vowel Sounds," *Journal of Speech and Hearing Disorders,* 13, 31–34.

Jakobson, R. (1940) "Kindersprache, Aphasie und Allgemeine Lautgesetze," in *Selected Writings* (1962) Mouton, The Hague.

Jakobson, R.C., Fant, G.M., and Halle, M. (1952) *Preliminaries to speech analysis,* MIT Press, Cambridge, Mass.

Keating, P., and Buhr, R. (1978) "Fundamental Frequency in the Speech of Infants and Children," *Journal of the Acoustical Society of America,* 63, 567–571.

Ladefoged, P., De Clerk, J., Lindau, M., and Papcun, G. (1972) "An Auditory-motor Theory of Speech Production," *UCLA Working Papers in Phonetics,* 22, 48–76.

Lieberman, P. (1963) "Some Effects of Semantic and Grammatical Context on the Production and Perception of Speech," *Language and Speech,* 6, 172–187.

Lieberman, P. (1967) *Intonation Perception and Language,* MIT Press, Cambridge, Mass.

Lieberman, P. (1976) "Phonetic Features and Physiology: A Reappraisal," *Journal of Phonetics,* 4, 91–112.

Lieberman, P. (1977) *Speech Physiology and Acoustic Phonetics,* Macmillan, New York.

Nearey, T. (1976) "Phonetic Features for Vowels," unpublished Doctoral Dissertation, University of Connecticut, Storrs.

Peterson, G.E., and Barney, H.L. (1952) "Control Methods Used in a Study of the Vowels," *Journal of the Acoustical Society of America,* 24, 175–184.

Russell, G.O. (1928) *The Vowel,* Ohio State University Press, Columbus, Ohio.

Stevens, K.N. (1972) "Quantal Nature of Speech," in E. E. David, Jr., and P.B. Denes, *Human Communication: A Unified View,* eds., McGraw-Hill, New York.

Stevens, K.N., and House, A.S. (1955) "Development of a Quantitative Description of Vowel Articulation," *Journal of the Acoustical Society of America* 27, 484–493.

Chapter 8

ASPECTS OF THE ACQUISITION OF STOP SYSTEMS: A CROSS-LINGUISTIC PERSPECTIVE

MARLYS A. MACKEN

Introduction

This chapter is concerned with child phonology universals in the acquisition of stop consonants, specifically with the characteristics of speech-sound production (not perception) during the age range that begins with the child's use of words (not babbling) and concludes with the age at which the child acquires an adult-like representation. The search for universals in child phonology is motivated both by the belief that there are invariant properties of cognition, language, and other phenomena that hold true across all groups of people, and by the need to determine the structure of such universals. Despite considerable research, particularly in the last 15 years, the search for universals of child phonology has not fared particularly well. In fact, recent studies have tended to show that there are remarkable differences between children acquiring even the same language. Some of these "differences" actually stem from differences between studies in methodology (e.g., the criterion used to identify "acquisition") and/or in the theoretical orientation adopted by the analyst (e.g., the status given syllable- or word-structure constraints); despite these factors, there nevertheless seem to be substantive differences between children. Two of the general themes in this chapter will, therefore, be the difficulty of defining unviersals of child phonology, and the extent to which language-specific features of phonological systems may affect the acquisition of stops and thus interfere with the "universality" of sound patterns.

Given the purpose of the chapter, it is appropriate to begin with the putative universals of stop acquisition put forth by Jakobson (1941/1968), specifically, universals on the order of acquisition and on the acquisition of voicing.

Evidence on order of acquisition is primarily taken from longitudinal, "diary" studies of individual children who were observed by one researcher (in nearly all cases, a parent), who kept written records but made no audio recordings. Although we will find, for example, that there are substantial differences in the order in which stops are acquired by children acquiring the same language, patterns of acquisition still emerge. To describe the occurrence of these patterns, we will deal with the term universal in the sense of a statistical probability rather than as an absolute prediction.

Evidence on the acquisition of voicing comes primarily from experimental data on English and Spanish. In contrast to the diary studies where all aspects of a child's phonological development were studied and where the child's speech was observed primarily in the home, the studies on voicing were designed to investigate only *one* aspect of the child's development, and the data were collected in a laboratory setting. The latter studies are similar to the diary studies in the emphasis on real words uttered in natural conversations; in addition, the voicing studies were designed to elicit words that *each* child knew and used at home. Here, we found substantial corroboration of Jakobson's prediction regarding the early, exclusive use of voiceless unaspirated stops; this "universal"—rather than being subject to individual child variation and language-particular variation—appears to be a "true" universal, one of absolute prediction. In these studies, a single unit of analysis was employed, and this unit was instrumentally examined (and thus was considerably less subject to conflicting interpretation by different analysts). To a certain extent, methodological controls and the use of a phonetically appropriate and instrumentally determined unit of analysis can be said to be partially responsible for the demonstration of this true universal. Because however, these data also provide evidence for the effect of language-particular features, the question of a truly universal sequence for stop acquisition remains open.

The purpose of the chapter is then to present data relevant to several Jakobsonian predictions for the acquisition of stops and to evaluate the universality of the various sound patterns that emerge in these data. The scope is restricted to the acquisition of stops as contrastive segments in production in initial, prevocalic position. Thus, several important aspects of stop acquisition will be omitted, as they were likewise omitted from Jakobson's theory, now widely recognized as an oversimplified model of acquisition partially because of such omissions. These other aspects include: (*a*) the acquisition of stops in positions other than initial (see, in particular, Menn, 1971; Smith, 1973; Stampe, 1972; Velten, 1943); (b) rules affecting stops in consonant clusters (see Greenlee, 1974; Hawkins, 1973; Menyuk and Klatt 1975); (c) the role of stops in phonological processes like assimilation, harmony, and metathesis (see Cruttenden, 1978; Drachman and Drachman, 1973; Ferguson, 1975b; Ingram, 1974; Macken, 1978, 1981; Smith, 1973; Vihman, 1978); and (d) the perception of stop contrasts (see Barton, 1976; Greenlee, 1978; Macken, 1980; Zlatin and Koenigsknecht, 1975, 1976). In each of these areas, some sound patterns appear to be very widespread and perhaps even universal, but individual differences between children are common and the issue of universals in these areas is likewise far from resolved.

Jakobson's Universals

Jakobson's theory, as found primarily in his 1941/1968 monograph *Child Language, Aphasia and Phonological Universals* (and slightly revised in Jakobson and Halle, 1956), is probably the best-known theory of phonological development. On the premises that every phonological system is stratified and that the same general structural principles that determine the universal and invariable hierarchy of layers in phonemic systems also determine the development of child language, Jakobson specified for the acquisition of sound classes an invariant chronological sequence, one that will be followed by all children regardless of the language being learned. The theory claims that the synchronic, phonemic stratification and phonological history of languages of the world, and the "fixed" developmental order of phonemic oppositions are explained by the basic principle of maximal contrast along two acoustic axes, sonority and tonality. Following the maximal contrasts, subsequent differentiations into finer and more complex distinctions will occur. The two axes of sonority (prosodic force and quantity features) and tonality (prosodic pitch features) yield twelve *inherent* distinctive feature oppositions. The second class of features, *prosodic,* contains three additional types of features—tone (pitch), force (loudness), and quantity (duration). In languages of the world and in language acquisition, these distinctive features will be structured as a system according to the general laws of implication: if Y occurs in a phonemic system, then X occurs also.

Mirroring these implicational relations, the child's successive acquisitions of phonemic oppositions thus proceed through the universal feature hierarchy from the most general contrast to the finest and rarest contrast, and although the rate of development may be variable for different children, the relative chronology is invariant. Moreover, the relative frequency, combinatorial capacity, and assimilatory powder of particular phonemes, once acquired, and the substitution patterns within each stage of the child's developing system also are affected by the priority relationships within the universal feature hierarchy. Although a complete analysis of Jakobson's theory is beyond the scope of this chapter (see Ferguson and Garnica, 1975, for a fuller analysis), I will summarize the predictions that are relevant to stop consonants.

The child first establishes an opposition between the optimal consonant /p/ and the optimal vowel /a/. With respect to consonants, the next step is the acquisition of the nasal/oral opposition /p:m/ and next the opposition labial/dental /p:t/. Elsewhere in the monograph, Jakobson's predictions take a more general shape: (a) stops are acquired before fricatives and serve as substitutes for fricatives in the early stages[1]; (b) front consonants are learned before back ones (e.g., the contrast /p:t/ before the contrast /p:k/); (c) voiceless consonants (i.e., "voiceless unaspirated" for stops) are acquired before voiced ones. The first two predictions (a,b), with the prediction that /p/ precedes /m/ and /t/, constitute Jakobson's predictions on "order of acquisition," and the third (c), his prediction regarding the "acquisition of voicing."

Order of Acquisition

Since 1941, a number of authors have presented evidence either supportive of or opposed to Jakobson's model—more precisely to his specific predictions, as the underlying theory has largely been ignored. Several studies of children have been analyzed as conforming to the general Jakobsonian "spirit" or outline of development (e.g., the English acquisition studies of Ferguson and Farwell, 1975; Leopold, 1947; Velten, 1943; the 1968 study of Czech acquisition done by Pačesová; Vanvik's 1971 study of a child acquiring Norwegian, the 1971 study by Contreras and Saporta of a child learning Spanish and English; and the 1976 study by Hinofotis of a child acquiring Greek). Since there is ample evidence from children acquiring even the same language that the predictions on order of acquisition are not true universals, the primary data in this section will be taken from diary studies of children acquiring English (see Table 8.1 for information on these children).

The first counter evidence to Jakobson's specific prediction regarding the order of acquisition of the first consonants probably came in Velten, 1943. Velten's daughter Joan first used /b/ and /s/ and then /d/.[2] Velten,

[1] This prediction will be treated in considerably less detail here, because extensive data on this issue can be found in the Ingram et al., Chapter 9 on fricatives in this volume (cf. also the references cited there).

[2] I will refer to the stops here as voiced, because Velten represents word-initial labial and dental stop phones with the corresponding voiced symbols. However, voicing was not distinctive: from 0:11 to 1:9, Joan had a realization rule that rendered both phonemically voiced and voiceless stops as phonetically "voiced" in initial position and "voiceless" in final position. Voicing was not distinctive in initial position until 2:1.

TABLE 8.1
Five English-learning Children Studied by Linguists Using the 'Diary' Method[a]

Source	Child's name	Ages during study	Data collection
Velten, 1943	Joan[b]	0:11–3:0 (from first two words)	No information given. Presumably frequent if not daily diary entries and no tape recording. Phonetic transcription.
Leopold, 1947	Hildegard[c]	0:1–2:0 (0:9, date of first words)	Usually daily entries (to 1:11;15). All written records; no tape recording. Phonetic transcription.
Menn, 1971	Daniel	1:4–2:1;15	Written notes supplemented with sporadic tape recording. Phonetic transcription.
Menn, 1976	Jacob	1:0–1:8 (from first word)	Author was care-taker of child in home 20 hrs/wk; 3 days/wk. Written notes were supplemented by 6–8 hrs/wk of tape recording and monthly audio videotape recording in a sound-treated booth. Phonetic transcription of tapes in addition to those made at time of utterance.
Labov and Labov, 1978	Jessie	1:3–1:8 (from first two words)	Nearly complete written record of *everything* child said, plus frequent tape recordings and occasional videotape recordings. Phonetic transcription of tapes in addition to those made at time of utterance.

[a] Every author but one is a parent of the child studied (the exception is Menn, 1976).

[b] Joan also knew and used a small number of French words.

[c] Hildegard was also acquiring German; Vihman (1978) determined that German words comprised about 13% of Hildegard's total vocabulary up to and including age two.

accordingly, restated Jakobson's prediction to be that the first consonantal opposition will be noncontinuant:continuant, and the continuant may be either a nasal or a fricative. Although this adjustment fits Velten's data, it does severe damage to the theoretical structure that underlies Jakobson's predictions, specifically the arguments based on tonality and sonority. Leopold (1947) also modified Jakobson's prediction and did so to account for his daughter's acquisition sequence. In Hildegard's speech, the opposition labial:dental among stops preceded rather than followed the oral:nasal opposition. However, Leopold (1947) concluded that although Jakobson's postulates needed correction in details, the model was basically sound (p. 200).

In both the Leopold and Velten data, the first stops to be acquired were the labial and alveolar stops, and in this early stage, both children substituted the alveolar stop for the velar stop.[3] In constrast, in Stage 1 from his first word at 1:4 to the age of 1:10;15, Daniel Menn had a stop set composed of /b/ and /g/. Although he had no alveolars, he also used no adult words that began with /d/ or /t/ that did not also have a labial or a velar stop in them. Thus, although Daniel produced adult /d,t/ as /b/ or /g/, we cannot establish that he had no contrast /b:d/, as there is no unambiguous evidence of a phonemic merger: His productions can be directly attributed to consonant harmony (Menn, 1971). Menn (1975) emphasizes that Jakobson does *not* predict that the phonetic order of appearance in stops will be labial before dental before velar but that no child will have a phonemic opposition of /b:g/ or /d:g/ before he or she has the opposition /b:d/. Thus before a child's data may be said to be counterevidence, there must be evidence that /b/ and /d/ are phonemically merged, in addition to evidence that the child has an opposition of /b:g/ or /d:g/. So, Daniel's data fail to meet the conditions for a rigorous test.

A few years later, Menn followed the phonological development of a child named Jacob who was also acquiring English, and for the first time we find not only differences in the order in which stops were acquired but also evidence of the requisite merger. Jacob's first stop was an alveolar one (cf. also the child in Pačesová, 1968). Later, both /d/ and /k/ were produced and /b/ was produced as [d]; thus, we found such words as 'down' → [dʌ] (1:2;7) and 'Jacob' → [geka] (1:2;7) and also 'bye-bye' → [dæ dæ] (1:3;24) (Menn, 1976). Keeping in mind the difficulty that we encounter when trying to determine phonemic oppositions in childrens' speech (as a result of the large amount of variation, virtual absence of good minimal pairs, etc., in the children's corpora), we can conclude that, to date, Jacob's data provide the clearest counterevidence to Jakobson's prediction, in that we found in his speech both a "phonemic opposition" of /d:k/ and also a "phonemic" merger /b/ → /d/.

Although early stops are indeed frequently labial and dental, some children like Daniel and Jacob acquire one of the two front stops and the velar stop before acquiring the second front stop. What we have yet to find is a child who starts out with a velar stop, but we have a child who comes close. Labov and Labov (1978) describe the "cat and mama" grammar of their daughter Jessie's first words. This 5-month period was dominated by two words 'cat' [ʔæʔ] and 'mama' [mama], both acquired at 1:3;15. Jessie's three phonemes for the first month were /a,ʔ,m/. 'Hi' with an initial /h/ appeared at 1:4;19 and 'dada' with an initial and medial /d/ at 1:4;27, but neither of these two words (nor any of the other six or so words that appeared in the

---

[3] A context-free substitution rule that replaces velar stops with alveolar stops is extremely widespread (Jakobson 1941/1968, p. 87; see, for example, on English: Albright and Albright, 1956; Cohen, 1952/1971; Cruttenden, 1978, on Spanish: Jespersen, 1929; Macken, 1978, 1981, on Czech: Ohnesorg, 1959; Pačesová, 1968, on French: Pupier, 1977).

same period) were used very often. Noting that other children do not use a glottal stop for /k/ and /t/ at such an early stage, the authors describe Jessie's phonetic form for 'cat' as language-specific. Although Jessie does not produce an actual velar stop (and in fact had some trouble learning how to use the back of her tongue [p. 60]), her use of the glottal stop is at least outside the range of Jakobson's prediction for phonemic acquisition.[4] The predominance of [ʔ] and [m] in Jessie's early speech is atypical and demonstrates once again the extent to which individual children may vary in the early stages. However, at the end of the cat and mama period, there was a dramatic loss of lexicon and phonology, and when words like *cat, open, hot* and *blow* eventually reappeared, "they had entirely different forms [p. 61]." For example, "when the word cat reentered her vocabulary many programs later, it was 'ao' [ao] [p. 59]." The authors allude to the fact that the phonology of the later period was considerably different from that of the cat and mama period, but they give no details.

At this point, we must say that Jakobson's invariant sequence for stops (/p/ > /p:t/ > /p:k/) is *not* followed by all children, that occasionally we find a child whose development runs counter to the prediction in important respects, but that nevertheless the general sequence "front before back" holds for most children. Our universal is now a more general statement, less predictive at the level of specific sounds but more accurate across a large number of children; the reformulated universal has become a statistical probability rather than an absolute prediction.

Similarly, for another of Jakobson's predictions, we find that although stops frequently do appear in place of fricatives in children's early productions (see Edwards, 1978; Ferguson, 1975a; Ingram, 1977), some children may not go through such a stage (see, in particular, the review in Edwards, 1978). Virve, a child requiring Estonian, acquired /s/ as her second consonant (after /t/) and produced it correctly in nearly all environments. Although /v/ was regularly deleted or assimilated during the earliest stages, Vivre produced it correctly in final position when no other consonants appeared in the word (Vihman 1976, 1978). For another example, we observe that in English, [d] or [t] is a common substitute for [ð].[5] However, in Spanish, [ð] frequently patterns with the liquids and is substituted for by [l] and in some cases [r] (Stoel, 1974); the use of [l] for [ð] is also seen in the data from children acquiring Greek (Hinofotis, 1976; and Drachman and Drachman, 1973), but is extremely rare in the acquisition of English (Edwards, 1978).

That there may be such interlanguage differences is a possibility that Jakobson explicitly excluded. As we have seen, however, there are differ-

---

[4] Jakobson does, however, note that velar stops may be replaced by glottal stops in child language (1941/1968, p. 81).

[5] Leopold (1947) noted that Hildegard rarely substituted stops for fricatives other than /ð/ and /Θ/, whereas Karla (Leopold's other daughter) did so much more frequently; however, both children regularly produced stops for word initial /ð/ and /Θ/.

ences between children, even acquiring the same language, and we have already been forced to make substantive modifications in Jakobson's theory. Our notion of a universal is already a probabilistic (rather than an absolute) one, and we have had to restate Jakobson's predictions on order in a much more general form. As we shall see in the next section also, language-particular properties do affect acquisition; this fact constitutes a crucial problem for a theory of child phonology universals. However, the final Jakobson prediction to be considered here appears to be a true universal (insofar as data from a small number of children from only two language groups can be considered a demonstration). This prediction states that voiceless stops (i.e., voiceless unaspirated stops) are acquired before voiced stops. Although the acquisition of the voicing contrast, because it is the acquisition of an opposition, falls completely within the Jakobsonian model, Jakobson did not specifically state when the voicing contrast is acquired relative to other oppositions, nor does he identify the place of articulation where the voicing contrast will appear first relative to other places.

Acquisition of Voicing

Phonologically contrastive stops produced at the same place of articulation are traditionally said to differ in voicing: A set of stops usually represented orthographically as *b, d,* and *g* are referred to as voiced and the set *p, t,* and *k* are labeled voiceless. Although these labels may be sufficient to identify the phonological contrast in particular languages, the voicing contrast is not the same at the phonetic level in all these languages, and in fact the voicing contrast may consist of any number of acoustic and articulatory components. For example, in Spanish, the voiced stops *b, d,* and *g* are truly voiced in that they are characterized by glottal pulsing during articulatory closure, whereas English voiced stops are usually not voiced at all and are more similar to Spanish voiceless stop phonemes than they are to the Spanish voiced stop phonemes.

To use, then, the phrase the "acquisition of the voicing contrast" is misleading in the same sense that reference to the terms voiced–voiceless or their corresponding orthographic symbols is misleading: We may speak of the acquisition of the voicing contrast in a particular language, but when we compare across languages that differ phonetically, different skills may actually be being acquired. In the child phonology literature, however, we frequently find reference to voiced–voiceless or to segments [b]–[p] implying that those terms or segments are equivalent in data from children acquiring languages that in fact have very different voicing systems both at the phonetic and phonological levels. For example, given the phonetic differences between voiced and voiceless stop phonemes in languages like English and Spanish, data would inevitably be found that would contradict a proposed universal such as voiceless stops are learned before voiced ones or, to take another, "initial consonants will be voiced in the early stages and final consonants will be voiceless."

Fortunately, Jakobson (1941/1968) was comparatively explicit as to what voiceless means: "so long as stops in child language are not split according to the behavior of the glottis, they are generally pronounced as voiceless and unaspirated [p. 14]." With this definition, we can now reconcile data that would otherwise appear contradictory. In Velten (1947), we find that Joan acquired the labial (0:11), and dental (1:1) "voiced" stops before the voiceless ones (2:1), whereas the child acquiring Spanish in Contreras and Saporta (1971) acquired the voiceless (1:0–1:2) before the voiced stops (1:6) (also see Cohen, 1952/1971, on French; Montes Giraldo, 1971, on Spanish). As English "voiced" stops are usually voiceless unaspirated stops as are the Spanish (and French) voiceless stops, it is probable that both children first produced stops that were phonetically similar. Thus, the first problem for describing child phonology universals is that of determining the appropriate units of analysis—units, that have empirically verifiable content and that can be described independently of particular language characteristics.

For our studies of the acquisition of the voicing contrast in (initial position) stops in English and Spanish, we needed a phonetic framework that would provide a language-independent means of comparing the acquisition process, since a simple two-way labeling paradigm, "voiced" versus "voiceless," would not distinguish between the voicing categories in these two languages. We selected voice onset time VOT as the unit of analysis primarily because of the Lisker and Abramson (1964) claim that VOT is the single, most reliable feature separating voiced–voiceless stop cognate pairs in languages of the world, regardless of the conventional feature designations used in descriptions of those languages. There are, of course, other features that are claimed to be relevant to the voicing contrast. The Chomsky and Halle (1968) system uses three features, voice, heightened subglottal pressure, and glottal constriction; this system has been replaced in Halle's more recent work by the features stiff versus slack vocal cords and spread versus constricted glottis (Halle, 1972). Ladefoged (1971, 1975) includes the Lisker and Abramson feature in his set: (a) glottal stricture; (b) voice onset; (c) fortis; and (d) glottality. Apart from the theoretical controversy over the status of these features, clearly not all are equally amenable to analysis particularly in the speech of children; thus, a second reason for selecting VOT as our voicing feature was that it is relatively easy to measure from spectrograms of recorded speech. Nevertheless, we also assumed that VOT is related significantly to the perception and production of the voicing contrast in the languages studied (cf. Abramson and Lisker, 1970, 1973; Lisker and Abramson, 1964; Williams, 1977), and that, moreover, it serves a primary, distinctive function.

Our predictions were, then, that voiceless unaspirated stops (or short-lag stops in the Lisker and Abramson framework) would be acquired first as Jakobson had predicted (cf. also Kewley-Port and Preston, 1974), and that as the children acquired productive control over voicing, VOT values would change concomitantly during this period. Thus, the English-speaking children would first acquire the English phonemes /bdg/ (the short-lag stops) and only later /ptk/ (the long-lag stops). In contrast, the Spanish-speaking children should first use the Spanish phonemes /ptk/ (i.e., the short-lag stops) and later acquire /bdg/ (the lead stops, where the onset of voicing *precedes* the burst).

Details about the children who served as subjects are found in Table 8.2. Data described in the "English data" and "Spanish data" sections are reported in greater detail in Macken and Barton (1980 and forthcoming, respectively). The English data are from a longitudinal study of English acquisition; for Spanish, results from both a longitudinal study and a cross-sectional study of 4-year-olds are summarized here. We have also investigated the voicing contrast in the speech of English-speaking 4-year-olds (see Barton and Macken, forthcoming) and the acquisition of the aspiration contrast in Cantonese (see Clumeck *et al.*, forthcoming).

English Data

There are four aspects of the English data that are relevant to our topics of universals of stop acquisition and language-specific factors:

1. Three of the children produce voiceless unaspirated stops (i.e., short-lag stops) for both the voiced and voiceless phonemes during the earliest stages.

2. The data provide evidence for three general stages in the acquisition process, but the age of acquisition varies considerably.

3. The vocabularies of all four children show asymmetries such that words that begin with /b/, /d/ and /k/ predominate in the earliest stages.

4. Two of the children acquire the voicing contrast first at the dental place of articulation, next at the labial, and finally at the velar place.

These findings apply to initial position only. Although children generally acquire the voicing contrast first in this position, occasionally there are children who produce voicing contrasts first in final position (see Menn, 1971; Smith 1973; Velten, 1943).

In general, the three stages in the acquisition of the English voicing contrast (as based on the data from this small number of children) are the following. Initially (Stage 1), the child does not produce a voicing contrast.

TABLE 8.2
Four English-learning and Seven Spanish-learning Children who Participated in Experiments Conducted by the Stanford Child Phonology Project

Subjects	Ages during study	Number of sessions	Data collection	Number of stop tokens analyzed	Data analysis
I. American–English			All sessions were conducted in a sound-isolated room. The children under I and II A were recorded at 2- to 3-week intervals for a 7-month period.		Tokens were from child productions of words that began with an initial singleton stop in the adult model and for which the child produced a stop of the correct place of articulation.
Tom	1:6;24–2:1;13	15		404	
Tessa	1:4;28–2:0;13	16		463	
Jane	1:6;19–2:1;16	16		396	
Jay	1:7;9–2:4;2	19		510	
II. Mexican–Spanish					
A. "2-year-olds"					
Manuel	1:7;9–2:2;0	15		267	
Fernando	1:7;3–2:1;20	15		236	Analysis included: phonetic transcription from tapes; spectrographic analysis; calculation of means, standard deviations, and ranges; and tests of significance.[a]
Beto	1:9;24–2:4;8	14		126	
B. "4-year-olds"					
José	3:6;22	1		80	
María	3:10;21	1		84	
Cecilia	3:10;5–3:10;16	2		57	
Beatriz	4:0;10–4:0;13	2		80	

[a] Complete descriptions of data collection and analysis procedures are found in Huntington *et al.* (1978) and in Macken and Barton (1980 and forthcoming).

He or she uses predominantly short-lag stops, and there is not a significant difference between the mean VOT values for the voiced and the voiceless stop phonemes. In Stage 2, the child still produces mainly short-lag tokens, but, for the first time, the mean VOT for the adult voiceless phoneme is consistently longer across several points in time than the mean VOT for the adult voiced stop. This difference between the means is consistently significant across several sessions or on some sessions but not on others. At the beginning of Stage 3, the child produces adult voiceless stop tokens with extremely long-lag voicing and the child's means for these phonemes are considerably longer than adult means. Later, the child begins to shorten the VOT values back toward the adult values. Beginning at Stage 2, we attribute to the child the acquisition of a voicing contrast.

The most interesting stage is Stage 2. The contrasts that the children are maintaining in this stage show up with instrumental analysis; the children's tokens were transcribed as voiceless unaspirated, and even on careful relistening, we were not able to detect the differences that showed up in the statistical analysis. During this stage, the children's mean VOT values for both the adult voiced and voiceless phonemes fall in the short-lag range characteristic of adult voiced phonemes, or, alternatively, within the adult perceptual boundaries for the adult voiced stop phonemes (cf. Lisker and Abramson, 1967; Pisoni and Lazarus, 1974; Zlatin, 1974; and others). Thus, adults will either fail to perceive or at least have considerable trouble consistently hearing the child's contrast. The categorical nature of adult perception is well established, and it is this aspect of our perceptual systems that, at least in this case, makes us less than adequate judges of the children's development; particularly in those areas where our perceptual system fails us, spectrographic analysis can be of great value.

The categorical nature of our perception has another effect: not only may we not "hear" an early contrast that a child is making, but we will tend to abruptly hear a change in the child's system. The across-the-board model for phonology acquisition may in fact be more a function of the nature of adult perception (i.e., when we notice or ascribe importance to some aspect of the child's production) than an adequate description of a child's development. For example, Tessa was gradually improving her voicing contrast throughout Stage 2 by producing her /ptk/ stops with gradually longer values. However, at some point, her tokens will appear to have been produced with long-lag VOT values for the "first" time, and adult listeners will say she "acquires" the voicing contrast at that time, when in actual fact she acquired it several weeks or months before.

In all the children's early sessions, we found an asymmetry in the distribution of word-initial stops: Words beginning with /bdk/ were more frequent than words beginning with /ptg/. For two children (Tessa and Jane), the number and frequency of /d/-initial words were only slightly higher than the number and frequency of /t/-initial words; thus, the asymmetry was more precisely that few /p/ and very few, if any, /g/ words occurred. Both of these children showed evidence of a voicing contrast on the first session at the dental place of articulation only. In Jane's data, the sessions on which she showed a voicing contrast for the first time at the labial and velar places of articulation were also sessions characterized by a substantial increase in the production of /p/ and /g/ words; particularly for this child, the disappearance of the asymmetry in word-initial stops appeared to correlate with her acquisition of the voicing contrast.

Tessa and Jane both acquired the voicing contrast in the following order: /d:t/ > /b:p/ > /g:k/. Tom had a significant difference between the means for all voiced-voiceless pairs from the beginning of the study. The fourth child, Jay, did not change during the study: He produced both adult voiced and voiceless phonemes as short-lag stops. However, his mean for /t/ was consistently longer than his mean for /d/, and the difference between the means was significant on two of the six "anchor points" selected for analysis and also in the combined data. Similarly, the mean for /k/ was longer than the mean for /g/ on five of the six anchor points, and the difference between the means was significant on two points and in the combined data. These results suggest that Jay was attempting to distinguish dental and velar voiced-voiceless cognate pairs. When Jay was 2:4;2, his parents moved to Massachusetts. When we visited him there when he was 2:6;19, he was producing an acceptably adult-like voicing contrast at all three places of articulation.

The range of individual differences in the age of acquisition is striking. Tom, Tessa, and Jane acquired a relatively adult-like voicing contrast at all three places of articulation by approximately 1:9; Jay did not do so until some time between the ages 2:4;2 and 2:6;19. The first evidence of a contrast can be found in Tessa's data from 1:5 and in Jane's data from 1:8. These early contrasts and the contrasts that Jay was making between /d:t/ and /g:k/ as early perhaps as 1:7 could not, however, be detected by adults; Tom's first contrasts, at 1:7, could not have unequivocally been identified by adults either.

Spanish Data

The English results confirmed our initial hypotheses, and the choice of VOT as the unit of analysis proved particularly valuable in that the VOT analysis provided evidence that the children were consistently maintaining contrasts between adult voiced and voiceless phonemes even at the stage in which all their stop productions would presumably have been labeled "voiced" by adult speakers of English. However, for the Spanish studies, only the first hypothesis was supported: The children did produce primarily voiceless unaspirated stops; an adult speaker of Spanish would, in contrast, have labeled the children's productions voiceless (cf. the discussion of the

Velten (1943), Contreras and Saporta (1971) accounts). With respect to the second hypothesis, the analysis of VOT did not prove to be completely useful. What did prove useful in determining the children's phonological knowledge and the acquisition process was a spirantization analysis.

In Spanish, the voicing contrast has a second phonetic characteristic that appears to be more important than the VOT dimension, namely the voiced phonemes have two allophones—a stop and a voiced spirant of the same place of articulation. According to conventional descriptions, the stops [bdg] occur in utterance-initial position and after nasals, and [d] also appears after /l/ (e.g., Harris, 1969). The spirant allophones for the voiced stop phonemes occur in all other positions. Although the spirants occur much more frequently than the stops (cf. Navarro's analysis of written corpora, 1968, and Delattre, 1965), most phonological descriptions of Spanish set up the stops /bdg/ as basic and derive the spirants from the stops by rule. Although this analysis is defensible on many grounds, the predictions concerning acquisition that can be extrapolated from such a description are not borne out by the data. The data from the children acquiring Spanish do not support the analysis of the stops as the underlying phonemes: The children acquire the spirant feature early; it is this feature that most reliably carries distinctive function; and the phonetic feature of VOT that is said to be distinctive is learned late.

The VOT and spirantization analyses were carried out for two studies. Study 1 is a longitudinal study of the productions of three children (referred to as the 2-year-olds) who were about 1:7 at the beginning of the study. Study 2 is a cross-sectional study in which four children aged about 3:10 (the 4-year-olds) served as subjects.

Five of the seven children produced no significant differences between the VOT means for any voiced and voiceless stop cognate pair at any place of articulation; the remaining two children, Beto and José, produced a significant difference between /b/ and /p/. Moreover, only José's /b/ and /p/ were remotely adult-like, in that only José produced at least some adult voiced stop phonemes with adult-like voicing lead. On the basis of this criterion alone, we would have to conclude that only Beto and José had a voicing contrast and that, moreover, voicing was contrastive in their systems only at the labial place of articulation. Two other VOT characteristics proved to show significance in some cases: The proportion of tokens produced with (some amount of) voicing lead, and the incidence of "continuous voicing" (i.e., voicing that continues uninterrupted from a previous voiced segment through the initial stop phone of the following word). Using all three criteria, we found evidence that suggested that all the children except María and Beatriz had a contrast between /b/ and /p/ and that Cecilia and José had some kind of contrast at three and two places of articulation, respectively. Nevertheless, the most striking feature of the results was the overwhelming absence of an adult-like VOT/voicing system: None of the children—not even the 4-year-olds—were producing adult voiced stops with lead voicing in contradistinction to short-lag productions for adult voiceless phonemes.

In the spirantization analysis, we were interested in those cases in which there was a statistically significant difference in the number of continuant phones produced for the voiced as opposed to the voiceless phonemes at each place of articulation. Since such differences would indicate that the children were treating voiced and voiceless phonemes different, we could assume that the children had acquired a phonemic contrast. In general, the voiceless stops were produced as continuants only 1.6% of the time by the 2-year-olds and only .8% of the time by the 4-year-olds. In contrast, the children produced 45.7% (2-year-olds) and 31.4% (4-year-olds) of /bdg/ tokens as continuants. Among the 2-year-olds, both Manuel and Fernando produced continuant phones more often for /bdg/ than for /ptk/. Beto's data also show different patterns for voiced as opposed to voiceless phonemes: The difference between /b–p/ is significant, but there were too few /d/ and /g/ tokens to be conclusive. Evidence for a voicing contrast at all three places of articulation can also be found in the data from José and Beatriz among the 4-year-olds. The differences between /b–p/ and /d–t/ are signficant in Cecilia's data. María's labial and velar data show that both /b/ and /g/ were produced as continuants more often than were /p/ and /k/, although only the difference between /g–k/ is significant.

It was during the spirantization analysis that the first developmental trend emerged in the 2-year-old data. All three children acquired a phonemic voicing contrast first at the labial place of articulation: Manuel by 1:7;16, Fernando by 1:10;26, and Beto by 2:0;7. For Fernando (by 2:0;6) and possibly also for Manuel (by 2:1;5 but maybe as early as 1:11;22), the next stage was one in which the velar contrast was acquired. Finally the dental voiced–voiceless contrast was acquired, by 2:1;5 for Manuel (but perhaps as early as 2:0;11) and by 2:1;4 for Fernando (but perhaps as early as 2:0;6). Manuel may have acquired the dental and velar contrasts at the same time. Beto was possibly in the process of acquiring a dental and velar voicing contrast at the end of the study when he was 2:4;8. On the basis of a spirantization analysis, a Spanish-speaking child in a previous study acquired the voicing contrast in an identical set of stages at the following ages: /b:p/ 1:11; /g:k/ 2:0; and /d:t/ at 2:1 (Macken, 1978).

Finally, we found a parallel between the order in which the children acquired the voicing contrast and the asymmetry in the distribution of stop phonemes in the children's corpora: The children acquired the voicing contrast first at the labial place of articulation, and the frequency of /b/ was substantially greater than that for /d/ and /g/ to the point when the dental and velar contrasts were acquired; the children generally did not produce any /d/- and /g/-initial words for several months after /b/-initial words were used and also after the voicing contrast between /b:p/ had been acquired.

Thus, the spirantization analysis proved most useful in determining the children's acquisition of the voicing contrast. On the basis of the strong VOT criterion (i.e., a statistical difference between the means), only two children could be said to have acquired a voicing contrast and at only one place of articulation. In contrast, on the basis of the spirantization criterion, we can conclude that four children had a voicing contrast at all three places of articulation, the fifth child at two places of articulation, and the sixth and seventh children at one place. However, neither analysis provided any evidence for a contrast at the labial and dental places in Maria's data.

A recurrent theme in the preceding results has been the difference between the voicing contrast at the labial place of articulation and the contrasts at the other two places.

1. In both the VOT and spirantization analyses, considerably more evidence was found for a contrast of /b:p/ in all the children's data.

2. The voicing contrast was first acquired at the labial place of articulation, and this contrast preceded by several months any contrast at the other two places.

3. Finally, /d/ and /g/ occurred significantly less often in the corpora from both the 2- and 4-year-olds. Table 8.3 contains the number of tokens produced for all word-initial stops by the 2-year-olds and the 4-year-olds.

A striking feature of the data provided in Table 8.3 is the degree of similarity in the distributions of word-initial phonemes in both groups of subjects. Differences in the distribution of stops appear in the data despite our elicitation goals to obtain equal proportions of all stop types. That this should be the case for both age groups suggests that this asymmetry in stop distribution is a property of Spanish, rather than merely a function of some aspect of children's speech; the latter interpretation would be more reasonable if the asymmetry occurred only in the 2-year-old data. These frequency figures also demonstrate the special status of the labial contrast.

TABLE 8.3
Number and Percentage of Tokens for
All Word-Initial Stops

	2-year-olds (%)	4-year-olds (%)
/p/	579 (24.2)	242 (24.8)
/t/	385 (16.1)	122 (12.5)
/k/	616 (25.8)	230 (23.5)
/b/	556 (23.2)	176 (18.0)
/d/	132 (5.5)	68 (7.0)
/g/	124 (5.2)	139 (14.2)
	(100.0)	(100.0)

"Universals" of Voicing

In the data on the acquisition of the voicing contrast, we found strong support for Jakobson's prediction that children will produce voiceless unaspirated stops during the early stages when they do not yet produce a phonemic contrast. In addition to the large number of English studies that provide confirmation for this universal, the early, exclusive use of voiceless unaspirated stops is reported for Garo (Burling, 1959), Taiwanese (Lin, 1971), Hindi (Srivastava, 1974), Quechua (Solberg, 1976) and Mandarin (Jeng, 1979). In addition, we found both wide individual differences in the age at which the voicing contrast is acquired and language-specific differences in the order in which the voicing contrast appears at the three places of articulation. That we should find individual differences in age of acquisition is not surprising (cf. Jakobson, 1941/1968). For example, the age at which English-speaking children acquire voicing in initial stops may vary from 1:3 and 1:4 for the children in Moslin (1976) to 2:8, the age at which Amahl established voicing in initial position (Smith, 1973). Hildegard was 2:0 and Joan Velten 2:1. Clearly, Jay is within the age range that can be considered normal. The data reported in Srivastava (1974) is of relevance to our Spanish data, in that Hindi also contains lead voicing as part of its voicing contrast. The child studied by Srivastava first used the voiceless unaspirated stops (at 1:1) and next acquired the prevoiced Hindi stops (1:4); not until 2:0 did the voiceless and voiced aspirates appear. If we were to argue that the Spanish-speaking children do not acquire the Spanish voiced stops until (evidently) after age 4:0 because the production of lead voicing is inherently difficult to learn, the data from this Hindi-learning child would be difficult to explain.

The first of our cross-language differences is the late acquisition of the phonetic, VOT component of the Spanish voicing contrast. Since the data suggested that all the children were maintaining the voicing contrast primarily in the stop-spirant feature rather than in the VOT feature, we reexamined the "allophonic, nondistinctive status" of the spirants in *adult* speech. To do this, we analyzed the distribution of stop and spirant phones for absolute utterance-initial /bdg/—an obligatory environment for stops—in the speech of our three adult experimenters. Two of the three experimenters were female, monolingual Spanish speakers; the third was a woman bilingual in Spanish and English who had learned Spanish as her first language. Eighty minutes of randomly selected tape recording per experimenter were transcribed. The tapes were from the longitudinal study where the experimenter was interacting with a single child. We found that these adults produced from 30–40% of all utterance-initial /bdg/ phonemes as spirants. Preliminary analysis of nonutterance-initial environments reveals that in the obligatory environment for spirants, spirant phones are produced at least

95% of the time. This surprisingly high proportion of spirants produced for /bdg/ in utterance-initial position and, moreover, in an overwhelmingly andante speech style suggests that spirants in this position are an acceptable pronunciation to adult speakers of the language. It could be argued that this use of spirants is a characteristic of the baby-talk register; however, other researchers have found a similar use of spirants in utterance-initial position in adult-to-adult speech for Cuban and Peruvian dialects of Spanish. The adult data in combination with the data from the children suggest that the systematic phonemes of Spanish should be analyzed as /ßðγ/ rather than /bdg/. The important point for the present discussion is that when we look carefully at the adult language, we find sound patterns that might *not* have been the predicted ones but that nonetheless correlate with those in the child data.

The second cross-language difference is that the voicing contrast is first acquired at the labial place of articulation in Spanish but at the dental place in English, and that the voicing contrast next appears at the velar place of articulation in Spanish but at the labial place in English. We might state our universal to be that "when children acquire productive control over the voicing contrast, they will first do so either at the labial or at the dental place of articulation." To verify this universal statement, we will, of course, need additional data from other children acquiring English and Spanish (as the data on order of acquisition is based on a small number of subjects in each of our languages) and additional data from children acquiring other languages.

However, we also found that in the vocabularies of the subjects in our English and Spanish studies, there were asymmetries in the distribution of words that begin with different stop consonants.[6] In the Spanish data from both the 2- and 4-year-olds, there were significantly fewer words that begin with /d/ and /g/; alternatively, there were considerably more words beginning with /b/ than /d/ and /g/. (Recall that Stoel, 1974, found that /d/ participates with the liquids in Spanish acquisition; this may account for the Spanish voicing order of /g:k/ > (d:t/). In the English data, we found pronounced "gaps" at the labial and velar places of articulation: Words beginning with /p/ and /g/ were considerably less frequent than words beginning with /b/ and /k/ (N.B., Leopold, 1947, also found /g/ to be rare). (Note that significantly fewer *g*-initial than *p*-initial words occurred in all corpora; this may account for the English voicing order of /b:p/ > /g:k/.) In addition, we also found fewer /t/-initial words than words beginning with /d/, but for two of the children (i.e., the two children for whom we see that complete acquisition process), the frequency of /d/ and /t/ is similar. It may be that these distributional

---

[6] Asymmetries in stop systems occasionally are mentioned in acquisition studies for other languages. See Hinofotis (1976) and Drachman and Drachman (1973) on the absence of /g/ (phonetically truly voiced) in the corpora from Greek children; Drachman and Drachman also found no words with /d/ in the adult model).

asymmetries are characteristic of the core vocabulary of English and Spanish, where *core* is that part of a language's lexicon that is sufficiently basic as to be first acquired by children, or these asymmetries may hold for each language as a whole. In either case, the asymmetries demonstrate that languages will differ in the ways in which phonological contrasts are utilized in the lexicon. This is an important point, because in child phonology research, investigators generally work with the assumption that if a language permits /ptkbdg/ in initial position, each phoneme should occur with approximately equal frequencies in the lexicon. That languages in fact do not treat all phonemes the same or utilize all contrast to the same degree has at least two important consequences. The first concerns our formulation of a voicing universal and the second involves the notion "avoidance."

With respect to our universal, we must first notice the similarity between the particular types of asymmetries in Spanish and in English and the order in which the voicing contrast is learned in each of those two languages. Spanish maximally utilizes the voicing contrast (in initial position) at the labial place of articulation, and children acquiring Spanish first acquire the voicing contrast at the labial place. Because the asymmetry is not as pronounced in English, we will say that it appears that English maximally utilizes the voicing contrast (in initial position) at the dental place of articulation, and children acquiring English first acquire the voicing contrast at this place also. We can handle both sets of data by simply stating our universal to include acquisition at either the labial or dental places, as pointed out earlier. Another solution would be to say that "if a language has a voicing contrast, and also shows symmetries in the utilization of the contrast at one or more places of articulation, children will first acquire the voicing contrast at that place where the voicing contrast is most fully productive." This solution involves two issues. The first is empirical: Additional research must be done to verify that languages do in fact have functional gaps as a characteristic of stop systems (and other systems); additional research must also be carried out to determine whether or not the acquisition of particular contrasts in those languages correlates with those asymmetrical distributions in ways similar to the correlation that we have found between distribution and acquisition in English and in Spanish. The second issue is theoretical: To what extent must we incorporate language-specific facts into the model of universals? The empirical issue needs to be resolved first.

It may be that a universal phonetic principle will "explain" both the acquisition data and the asymmetries in the utilization of a contrast in the adult language. For example, we can argue on aerodynamic grounds that the labial place of articulation is the most conducive to voicing of the three places of articulation (due to the large supraglottal cavity); thus, children may learn to correctly produce [b] before [d] or [g], and the b-initial lexicon of a language may expand more rapidly due to the stability of voicing at this place of articulation (cf. Gamkrelidze, 1975). Note, however, that the evidence for the early acquisition of /b:p/ by Spanish-learning children is based on the spirantization analysis and *not* on the voicing/VOT analysis. Clearly, frequency is an independently relevant factor in this particular case, although generally the relevance of frequency of occurrence (and facts regarding the distributional constraints on phonemes) to phonological development has been a controversial issue. For example, Moskowitz (1970) claims such characteristics play a minor role. Additional and striking evidence for the view that, on the contrary, such factors may play a major role comes from Itkonen's (1977) study of his son's acquisition of Finnish. The last consonant to be acquired by this child was /d/, a sound widely regarded as "easy" and certainly considerably easier than many other Finnish phones, such as, for example, the trilled /r/. Itkonen notes that Finnish children often acquire /d/ "very late," and he attributes this to the marginal status of /d/ in the standard Finnish phonemic system: /d/ "is the only voiced stop, with *b* and *g* occurring in foreign-learned words only; its frequency is very small (textually about .78% of all phonemes); and in most instances it is only a morphologically conditioned variant of *t* [Itkonen 1977, p. 306]."

Asymmetries in stop and other consonantal systems also pose a crucial problem for the notion "avoidance." Probably because we have assumed that words beginning with each stop should occur with approximately equal frequency in a corpus, we have, likewise, concluded that a child must be avoiding a particular sound if we find that in that child's vocabulary words of a certain type do not occur. The next step in inference is that if a child is avoiding words that begin with a particular sound, that child must "know" enough about the particular sound to know that he or she cannot say it or does not want to say it. Avoidance has been used, therefore, as a powerful device for the demonstration of phonetic or phonemic knowledge in the child (Ferguson and Farwell, 1975; cf. also Drachman, 1973; Engel, 1965; Vihman, 1976). For example, Menn (1976) states that Jacob avoided words that began with /p/ and /g/ and that Jacob "seemed to know that he could only say initial /b/ correctly" and not initial /p/. I reexamined Menn's data on Jacob's active vocabulary (i.e., those words that Jacob produced) and his passive vocabulary (i.e., those words for which proof could be found that Jacob understood). In Jacob's passive vocabulary, there are 16 /b/-initial words, 11 /p/-words, 13 /t/ words and 16 /k/ words, with only 8 words beginning with /d/ and just 3 that begin with /g/. The small number of /g/ words was expected, but the large number of /p/ words was not. However, a large number of /p/ words were verbs (6) and 2 other /p/ words were 3 syllables long, whereas in Jacob's active vocabulary, verbs and words of 3 or more syllables were rare. If we eliminate verbs and words of 3 or more syllables because he does not produce many such words in the first place, we find that Jacob produced 83% of 12 /b/ words that he knew, 83% of 6 /d/ words, 60% of 10 /t/ words, and 58% of 12 /k/ words. In contrast, he did not use the 1 /g/ word, and he did not use any of the 3 /p/ words. The absence of /g/ words in Jacob's active vocabulary is *not* due to avoidance, and it is at least debatable whether he was avoiding /p/ words. Clearly there are factors that enter into a child's choice of what to talk about and what words to use: Jacob did not use many verbs or long words, and he did use words beginning with dental consonants almost exclusively in the very earliest stages. The point is that we cannot infer solely from the absence of rarity of words beginning with particular stops that Jacob was avoiding these words and then conclude that he knew something about the difference between /b/ and /p/ or between /g/ and /k/.

The notion avoidance makes strong claims about a child's phonological-phonetic system. It is precisely because of the importance that the avoidance concept has for our model of phonological acquisition that it is so necessary that unequivocal evidence be found in those cases where we assume it to be a factor. If there already are biases in the distribution of particular sounds, these biases must first be ruled out before we can conclude that the absence of a particular sound is evidence that the child is avoiding this sound.

Conclusions

The data discussed here have provided evidence for one "true" universal: Children will, as Jakobson predicted, use voiceless unaspirated stops before acquiring the pattern of voicing types that is contrastive in their language. In contrast, there is no invariant sequence in which particular stops are acquired and no invariant order to the acquisition of the voicing contrast at particular places of articulation. However, we have also found there to be a high probability that children will acquire front stops before back ones and voicing in a front cognate pair sooner than in a back one, and that children will substitute dental stops for velar ones and will substitute stops for fricatives. Conversely, it will be rare that a child will first acquire a velar stop (or voicing first at the velar place of articulation), and it will be equally rare that a child will substitute fricatives for stops. Thus, it appears that, for the most part, our "universals" of stop acquisition must be defined as statistical probabilities; Ferguson (1975c) uses the expressions "universal tendencies" and "normal states" to describe such phenomena.

A striking aspect of the data presented on the acquisition of the voicing contrast is the extent to which language-specific factors appear to influence the acquisition sequence, and we have found several unexpected correlations. The children's acquisition of the voicing contrast in English and Spanish appears first at that place of articulation where we find maximal utilization of the contrast in the children's lexicons; they acquire the contrast last at those places that correspond to minimal utilization. In the Spanish study, both the children and adults frequently use spirants in utterance-initial position, which is—according to traditional phonological accounts—the obligatory environment for stops in Spanish and is hypothesized to be the favored environment for stop phones in child phonology in general (cf. Ferguson, 1975a). The first findings points to an area that has been ignored or neglected in most accounts of child phonology and, in some cases, also in recent phonological theories; this area is that of asymmetries in the utilization of phonological contrasts. Repeatedly, the data have demonstrated how important it is to closely examine (or, more appropriately, reexamine, in the case of Spanish spirantization) the sound patterns that occur in the language (specifically, the particular lexicon) being acquired by the child.

In conclusion, it could be argued that in these data and in child phonology in general, the determination of true universals (as opposed to statistical probability universals) depends on the prior completion of at least two tasks. First, we must determine what the appropriate phonetic units of analysis should be, a basic requirement being that such units not be subject to conflicting interpretation either within or across languages. It is of course clear that those contrasts that lie on more nearly continuous acoustic dimensions—such as voicing/VOT contrasts as opposed to place of articulation contrasts—are more vulnerable to differential identification by adult speakers of the same language and to different categorization in different languages. The identification of such units of analysis is, in effect, the determination of a universal phonetic and phonological theory. Second, we must agree on at least a single criterion of acquisition if not on a unified methodological framework for the investigation of child phonology. Here, in child phonology as in other branches of phonology, the absence of a universally accepted phonetic and phonological theory is a cause of at least some of the contradictions found in the literature. However, to argue completely along these lines is to ignore the considerable amount of data already amassed that demonstrate that there are wide-spread, nontrivial differences between children—in this age range, acquiring productive control over sounds in real words—who are acquiring both the same language and different languages. The challenge is to determine which aspects of the child's acquisition process are truly universal (and why), and which have a high probability of occurrence across different children—and, finally, what principles, if any, govern the, perhaps not insubstantial, residue.[7]

Acknowledgments

This paper was supported in part by NSF Grant BNS 76–08968 to C. A. Ferguson and D. A. Huntington, Departments of Linguistics and Hearing and Speech Sciences, Stanford University.

---

[7] See Ferguson and Macken (1980) for a theoretical discussion of the implications of individual differences for universalist models, followed by a presentation of an alternative model, one that incorporates linguistic universals yet places primary emphasis on the cognitive aspects of phonology acquisition.

References

Abramson, A. S., and Lisker, L. (1970) "Discriminability Along the Voicing Continuum: Cross-language Tests," in *Proceedings of the Sixth International Congress of Phonetic Sciences,* 1967, Academia, Prague, pp. 569–573.

Abramson, A., and Lisker, L. (1973) "Voice-timing Perception in Spanish Word-initial Stops," *Journal of Phonetics,* 1, 1–8.

Albright, R. W., and Albright, J. (1956) "The Phonology of a Two-year-old Child," *Word,* 12, 382–390.

Barton, D. (1976) "The Role of Perception in the Acquisition of Phonology," Doctoral Dissertation, University of London (reprinted by the Indiana Linguistics Club).

Barton, D., and Macken, M. A. (Forthcoming) "An Instrumental Analysis of the English Voicing Contrast in Four-Year-Olds," *Language and Speech.*

Burling, R. (1959) "Language Development of a Garo- and English-Speaking Child," *Word,* 15(1), 45–68.

Chomsky, N., and Halle, M. (1968) *The Sound Pattern of English,* Harper & Row, New York.

Clumeck, H., Barton, D., Macken, M. A., and Huntington, D. A. (Forthcoming) "The Acquisition of the 'Voicing' Contrast in Cantonese," *Journal of Chinese Linguistics.*

Cohen, M. (1952/1971) "Acquisition and Practice of Child Language," in A. Bar-Adon and W. F. Leopold, eds., *Child Language: A Book of Readings,* Prentice-Hall, Englewood Cliffs, N. J., pp. 130–133.

Contreras, H., and Saporta, S. (1971) "Phonological Development in the Speech of a Bilingual Child," in J. Akin, *et al.,* eds., *Language Behavior, a Book of Readings in Communication,* Mouton, The Hague, pp. 280–294.

Cruttenden, A. (1978) "Assimilation in Child Language and Elsewhere," *Journal of Child Language* 5(2), 373–378.

Delattre, P. (1965) *Comparing the Phonetic Features of English, French, German and Spanish,* Chilton Books, Philadelphia.

Drachman, G. (1973) "Some Strategies in the Acquisition of Phonology," in M. J. Kenstowicz and C. W. Kisseberth, eds., *Issues in Phonological Theory,* Mouton, The Hague, pp. 145–159.

Drachman, G., and Malkouti-Drachman, A. (1973) "Studies in the Acquisition of Greek as a Native Language: I. Some Preliminary Findings on Phonology," Ohio State University *Working Papers on Linguistics,* 15, 99–114.

Edwards, M. L. (1978) "Patterns and Processes in Fricative Acquisition: Longitudinal Evidence from Six English-learning Children," Doctoral Dissertation, Stanford University.

Engel, W. von R. (1965/1973) "An Example of Linguistic Consciousness in the Child," in C. A. Ferguson and D. I. Slobin, eds., *Studies of Child Language Development,* (trans. Yole Correa) Holt, Rinehart and Winston, New York, pp. 155–158.

Ferguson, C. A. (1975) "Fricatives in Child Language Acquisition," in L. Heilmann, ed., *Proceedings of the Eighth International Congress of Linguistics,* Società Editrice il Mulino, Bologna, pp. 647–664. (a)

Ferguson, C. A. (1975) " Sound Patterns in Language Acquisition, in D. P. Dato, ed., *Developmental Psycholinguistics: Theory and Application,* Georgetown University Round Table 1–16. (b)

Ferguson, C. A. (1975) "Universal Tendencies and 'Normal' Nasality," in C. A. Ferguson, L. M. Hyman, and J. J. Ohala, eds., *Nasálfest,* Stanford University Language Universals Project, Stanford, 175–196. (c)

Ferguson, C. A., and Farwell, C. B. (1975) "Words and Sounds in Early Language Acquisition," *Language,* 51(2), 419–439.

Ferguson, C. A., and Garnica, O. K. (1975) "Theories of Phonological Development," in E. H. Lenneberg and E. Lenneberg, eds., *Foundations of Language Development* (Vol. 2.) Academic Press, New York, pp. 153–180.

Ferguson, C. A., and Macken, M. A. (1980) Phonological Development in Children: Play and Cognition, *Papers and Reports on Child Language Development*, 18 (Linguistics, Stanford University).

Gamkrelidze, T. V. (1975) "On the Correlation of Stops and Fricatives in a Phonological System," *Lingua*, 35, 231–262.

Gilbert, John H. V. (1977) A Voice Onset Time Analysis of Apical Stop Production in Three-year-olds," *Journal of Child Language* 4, 103–110.

Greenlee, M. (1974) " Interacting Processes in the Child's Acquisition of Stop–liquid Clusters," *Papers and Reports on Child Language Development*, (Linguistics, Stanford University) 7, 85–100.

Greenlee, M. (1978) "Learning the Phonetic Cues to the Voiced–voiceless Distinction: an Exploration of Parallel Processes in Phonological Change," Doctoral Dissertation, University of California, Berkeley.

Halle, M. (1972) "Theoretical Issues in Phonology in the 1970s," in A. Rigault and R. Charbonneau, eds., *Proceedings of the Seventh International Congress of Phonetic Sciences*. Mouton, The Hague, pp. 179–205.

Harris, J. W. (1969) *Spanish Phonology*, The MIT Press, Cambridge, Mass.

Hawkins, S. (1973) "Temporal Coordination of Consonants in the Speech of Children: Preliminary Data," *Journal of Phonetics*, 1, 181–217.

Hinofotis, F. B. (1976) "An Initial Stage in a Child's Acquisition of Greek as his Native Language," *Workpapers in Teaching English as a Second Language*, (University of California, Los Angeles) 11, 85–96.

Huntington, D. A., Clumeck, H., Macken, M. A., and Ohsiek, D. (1978) "Some Methodological Considerations on the Study of VOT in Children, Unpublished manuscript, Stanford University: Hearing and Speech Sciences.

Ingram, D. (1974) "Phonological Rules in Young Children," *Journal of Child Language*, 1, 49–64.

Ingram, D. (1977) "The Production of Word-initial Fricatives and Affricates by Normal and Linguistically Deviant Children," in A. Caramazza and E. Zuriff, eds., *The Acquisition and Breakdown of Language*, Johns Hopkins Press, Baltimore, pp. 63–85.

Itkonen, T. (1977) "Notes on the Acquisition of Phonology," (English summary of Huomioita lapsen äänteistön kehityksestä), *Virittäjä*, 279–308.

Jakobson, R. (1941/1968) *Child Language, Aphasia and Phonological Universals* (Trans. A. Keiler, 1968), Mouton, The Hague.

Jakobson, R., and Halle, M. (1956) *Fundamentals of Language*, Mouton, The Hague.

Jeng, H. (1979) "The Acquisition of Chinese Phonology in Relation to Jakobson's Laws of Irreversible Solidarity," Paper presented at the International Congress of Phonetic Sciences, Copenhagen.

Jespersen, O. (1929) *Language: Its Nature, Development and Origin*, H. Holt, New York.

Kewley-Port, D., and Preston, M. S. (1974) "Early Apical Stop Production: A Voice Onset Time Analysis," *Journal of Phonetics*, 2, 195–210.

Labov, W., and Labov, T. (1978) "The Phonetics of *Cat* and *Mama*," *Language*, 54(4), 816–852.

Ladefoged, P. (1971) *Preliminaries to Linguistic Phonetics*, The University of Chicago Press, Chicago.

Ladefoged, P. (1975) *A Course in Phonetics*, Harcourt Brace Jovanovich, New York.

Leopold, W. F. (1947) *Speech Development of a Bilingual Child: A Linguist's Record*. (Vol.2): *Sound-Learning of the Two-Year-Old Child*, AMS Press, New York.

Lin, S. (1971) "Phonetic Development of Chinese Infants," *Acta Psychologica Taiwanica*, 13, 191–195.

Lisker, L., and Abramson, A. S. (1964) "A Cross-language Study of Voicing in Initial Stops: Acoustical Measurements," *Word*, 20, 384–422.

Lisker, L., and Abramson, A. S. (1967) "The Voicing Dimension: Some Experiments in Comparative Phonetics," *Proceedings of the Sixth International Congress of Phonetic Sciences*,

Academic Publishing House of the Czechoslovak Academy of Sciences, Prague, pp. 563–567.

Macken, M. A. (1978) "Permitted Complexity in Phonological Development: One Child's Acquisition of Spanish Consonants,'' Lingua, 44, 219–253.

Macken, M. A. (1980) "The Child's Lexical Representation: The 'Puzzle-puddle-pickle' Evidence,'' Journal of Linguistics.

Macken, M. A. (1981) "Long Domain Processes in Child Phonology,'' Papers and Reports on Child Language Development, (Linguistics, Stanford University).

Macken, M. A., and Barton, D. (1980) "A Longitudinal Study of the Acquisition of the Voicing Contrast in American-English Word-initial Stops, as Measured by Voice Onset Time, Journal of Child Language, 7, 41–74.

Macken, M. A., and Barton, D., (Forthcoming) "The Acquisition of the Voicing Contrast in Spanish: a Phonetic and Phonological Study of Word-initial Stop Consonants,'' Journal of Child Language.

Menn, L. (1971) "Phonotactic Rules in Beginning Speech,'' Lingua, 26, 225–251.

Menn, L. (1975) "Counter Example to 'Fronting' as a Universal of Child Phonology,'' Journal of Child Language 2, 293–296.

Menn, L. (1976) "Pattern, Control and Contrast in Beginning Speech, a Case Study in the Development of Word Form and Word Function,'' Doctoral Dissertation, University of Illinois.

Menyuk, P., and Klatt, M. (1975) "Voice Onset Time in Consonant Cluster Production by Children and Adults,'' Journal of Child Language 2, 223–231.

Montes Giraldo, J. J. (1971) "Acerca de la Apropriación por el Niño del Sistema Fonología Español,'' Thesaurus, 26, 322–346.

Moskowitz, A. B. (1970) "The Two-year-old Stage in the Acquisition of English Phonology,'' Language, 46, 426–441.

Moslin, B. J. (1976) "Development of the Voiced–Voiceless Contrast in English Stops: A VOT Analysis of Two Mother–Child Dyads,'' Paper presented to the seventh meeting of the Northeast Linguistic Society, 7.

Navarro Tomás, T. (1968) Studies in Spanish Phonology, Coral University of Miami Press, Gables.

Ohnesorg, K. (1959) Drůha Fonetička Studie o Dětske Reči, Bruno, Universita v Brně s podporou Ministerstva školství a kultury.

Pačesová, J. (1968) The Development of Vocabulary in the Child, Universita J. E. Purkyne, Bruno.

Pisoni, D. B., and Lazarus, J. H. (1974) "Categorical and Noncategorical Modes of Speech Perception along the Voicing Continuum,'' Journal of the Acoustical Society of America, 55(2), 328–333.

Pupier, P. (1977) "Quelques Observations sur L'acquisition de la Phonologie par des Enfants Montréalais de 2 Ans,'' Recherches Linguistiques à Montréal, 9.

Smith, N. V. (1973) The Acquisition of Phonology, A Case Study, Cambridge University Press, Cambridge.

Solberg, M. E. (1976) "Developing Phonological Systems; Nomogenesis or Individual Solutions?'' Paper presented at the summer Linguistic Society of America meeting, Oswego, New York.

Srivastava, G. P. (1974) "A Child's Acquisition of Hindi Consonants,'' Indian Linguistics, 35, 112–118.

Stampe, D. (1972) "A Dissertation on Natural Phonology,'' Doctoral Dissertation, Uinversity of Chicago.

Stoel, C. M. (1974) "The Acquisition of Liquids in Spanish,'' Doctoral Dissertation, Stanford University.

Vanvik, A. (1971) "The Phonetic–Phonemic Development of a Norwegian Child,'' in H. Vogt, ed., Norsk Tidsskrift for Sprogvidenskap, Bind XXIV, Universitetsforlaget, 269–325.

Velten, H. V. (1943) "The Growth of Phonemic and Lexical Patterns in Infant Language," *Language*, 19, 281–292.

Vihman, M. (1976) "From Pre-speech to Speech; on Early Phonology," *Papers and Reports on Child Language Development* (Linguistics, Stanford University), 12, 230–243.

Vihman, M. (1978) "Consonant Harmony: Its Scope and Function in Child Language," in J. H. Greenberg, C. A. Ferguson, and E. A. Moravcsik, eds., *Universals of Human Language*, Stanford University Press, Stanford, pp. 403–442.

Williams, L. (1977) "The Voicing Contrast in Spanish," *Journal of Phonetics*, 5, 169–184.

Zlatin, M. A. (1974) "Voicing Contrast: Perceptual and Productive Voice Onset Time Characteristics of Adults," *Journal of the Acoustical Society of America*, 56(3), 981–994.

Zlatin, M. A., and Koenigsknecht, R. A. (1975) "Development of the Voicing Contrast: Perception of Stop Consonants, *Journal of Speech and Hearing Research* 18, 541–553.

Zlatin, M. A., and Koenigstknecht, R. A. (1976) "Development of the Voicing Contrast: A Comparison of Voice Onset Time in Stop Perception and Production," *Journal of Speech and Hearing Research*, 19, 93–111.

Chapter 9

THE ACQUISITION OF WORD-INITIAL FRICATIVES AND AFFRICATES IN ENGLISH BY CHILDREN BETWEEN 2 AND 6 YEARS

DAVID INGRAM, LYNDA CHRISTENSEN, SHARON VEACH,
AND BRENDAN WEBSTER

Introduction

It has been known for some time that fricatives and affricates are the most difficult class of sounds for English-speaking children to acquire. They are avoided by very young children (Ferguson, 1973); they are the last sounds acquired by older normal children (Templin, 1957), and are the most difficult sounds for children with articulatory delay (Morley 1957; Morrison, 1914–15). Evidence to this effect comes from both diary studies of individual children as well as from large-sample studies of many children across several age ranges (cf. reviews in Ingram 1976; Winitz, 1969).

Despite this accepted finding, we still have only a very general picture of how these sounds are acquired by children. This is the result of the natural limitations of diary and large-sample studies that represent most of the research on phonological development. The studies have been concerned with two broad questions: "How do individual children acquire general sound patterns?" and "How do children in general acquire individual speech sounds?" They consequently provide limited information on specific sounds. The diary accounts deal only with individual children, so that variations across children are obscured, and the periods of observation are usually inadequate as fricative and affricate acquisition occurs across several years. The problem of time is overcome to a degree in large-sample studies, but

CHILD PHONOLOGY
VOLUME 1: PRODUCTION

there are other serious limitations. Each sound is usually elicited once, and consequently in just one word. This procedure does not take into account factors of variation, the influence of word length, neighboring sounds, nor the influence of imitation. Because studies vary in their methods of elicitation, ages of subjects, and criteria for acquisition, it becomes difficult to make comparisons and to explain discrepancies in results, and as they typically group data, little information is given about individual variation.

Recently, two studies have appeared attempting to review the results of a variety of research projects, to provide a better idea of how English fricatives and affricates are acquired (Ferguson, 1973; Ingram, 1978). From these reviews, the following picture emerges. Based on a comparison of results from Wellman *et al.* (1931) and Templin (1957), /f −/ is the earliest fricative to appear, and is usually acquired by 3 years of age. By 4 years /tʃ −/, /ʃ −/, and /dʒ −/ reach criterion, which in these studies was 75% correct production across all subjects at a particular age. The more difficult sounds are /Θ −/, /ð −/, /v −/, and /z −/, which are acquired between the ages of 5 and 6 years. The results for /s −/ are mixed and present a situation that deserves closer investigation. An /s −/ like sound is produced early in acquisition, but it may be bladed or otherwise distorted for several years before sounding like the adult sound (cf. discussion in Ingram, 1978).

At the earliest stages of acquisition, children avoid words that begin with fricatives. Once they attempt them, children acquire each sound individually rather than all at once. The patterns of substitution are either toward a more closed articulation (e.g., ð to d), a looser articulation (e.g., v to w), or to an acoustically similar fricative (e.g., Θ to f; cf. Ferguson, 1973). Based on these observations and a review of 15 diary studies, Ingram (1978) proposed five stages of acquisition of this class of sounds:

Stage 1. Nonuse or deletion of fricatives and affricates from adult models.

Stage 2. Predominant substitution of stops for fricatives and affricates. One or two continuants may occur.

Stage 3. Widespread appearance of continuants with glides and liquids possible early substitutions, followed by use of obstruents. Some stops may remain. First attempts at alveopalatals take place.

Stage 4. Most fricatives are acquired: /Θ −/, /ð −/, and perhaps /v −/ are still to be acquired. Occasional distortion of some fricatives, such as /s −/.

Stage 5. Acquisition is complete.

As most studies have been concerned with general trends of development, little work has been devoted to the topic of individual variation between children until recent years. Regarding the acquisition of fricatives and affricates, Ingram (1979) notes that individual children may have particular phonological preferences for certain fricatives over others (also see Farwell,

1976). There he reports on data from three French children who each had a unique preference pattern, these being labial, dental, and palatal preferences, respectively. The child with the palatal preference, for example, used [ʃ −] for adult words with [ʃ −], and also as a substitute for other French fricatives. There are no data on how varied the widespread particular preferences might be, although Farwell (1976) suggests that they may be quite extensive.

To pursue more detailed investigation into fricatives and affricates, certain methodological issues need to be addressed. As mentioned, most large-sample studies use only one test word for adult target sounds. Templin (1957) justified this practice as well as the use of imitation on the basis of an earlier study (Templin, 1947) indicating that neither affected production. The data from this study, however, are not conclusive. Both Faircloth and Faircloth (1970) and Olmsted (1971) have claimed that imitation results in improved production of speech sounds (cf. discussion in Ingram, 1976, pp. 81–83; Winitz, 1969). Diary studies typically have noted variations in production from word to word (e.g., Ferguson and Farwell, 1975; Velten, 1943). It is also apparent now that acquisition of speech sounds is gradual, so that a child may produce a particular sound only occasionally even within the same word. Consequently, detailed study of speech sounds requires multiple productions of target sounds that vary in both the method of elicitation (spontaneous versus imitation) and in the phonological structure of the test words.

The purpose of the present investigation was to provide more detailed information than currently exists on the acquisition of English fricatives and affricates. To narrow the topic for detailed study, only word-initial sounds were studied. We were concerned both with the acquisition of these sounds across subjects and within subjects as a system. The following questions were posed:

1. What is the order of acquisition of these sounds?
2. Is acquisition gradual or abrupt?
3. Does the phonological structure of the word affect the production of the test sound?
4. Does the method of elicitation affect production?
5. What are the main substitutions used by young children for individual fricatives and affricates?
6. Do data from a large sample of subjects confirm the five stages proposed by Ingram (1978)?
7. What are the kinds and extent of individual variations that children show in acquiring this particular class of sounds?

This was done by conducting a large-sample study with children between the ages of 2 and 6 years and, when possible, making comparisons with previous investigations.

Method

Subjects

The subjects were 73 children, ranging in age from 1:10;22 to 5:11;18. They were divided into the following nine age groups: 1:6–1:11 (2 subjects, 1 boy and 1 girl); 2:0–2:5 (6 subjects, 2 boys, 4 girls); 2:6–2:11 (12 subjects, 4 boys, 8 girls); 3:0–3:5 (11 subjects, 5 boys, 6 girls); 3:6–3:11 (8 subjects, 5 boys, 3 girls); 4:0–4:5 (9 subjects, 4 boys, 5 girls); 4:6–4:11 (8 subjects, 3 boys, 5 girls); 5:0–5:5 (10 subjects, 3 boys, 7 girls); 5:6–5:11 (8 subjects, 6 boys, 2 girls). They were all normal children living in the communities of Palo Alto, Menlo Park, and Mountain View, California.

Materials

The test sounds were eight English word-initial fricatives and affricates: /f–/, /v–/, /θ–/, /s–/, /z–/, /ʃ–/, /tʃ–/, /dʒ–/. /ð–/ was not tested because a picture task was selected for this particular study, and this sound occurs initially in English only in grammatical words (e.g., *this, the, those*). Four test words were selected for each sound that fell into the following sets: (*a*) monosyllabic word; (*b*) bisyllabic word with initial stress; (*c*) trisyllabic word with initial stress; and (*d*) multisyllabic word with medial stress. We had originally hoped to have all multisyllabic words in (*c*) consist of three syllables, but this proved to be impossible because we wanted words that either the children would know or could learn from the pictures used. Table 9.1 presents the 32 stimuli used.

The materials consisted of 34 line drawings that were colored, placed in protective plastic, and put into a 21.25 × 27.50 cm (8½ × 11 in.) loose-leaf binder. They were arranged so that only one picture was visible at a time. Of the 34 pictures, 32 represented objects named by the test items;

TABLE 9.1
Four Groups of Test Words Used for Eight Test Sounds

Test sound	Test words			
	I	II	III	IV
/f–/	fish	feather	photograph	farina
/v–/	vase	village	vegetables	volcano
/θ–/	thief	thermos	theatre	thermometer
/s–/	six	sailfish	saxophone	safari
/z–/	zees	zither	xylophone	zucchini
/tʃ–/	chief	chopsticks	chesterfield	chimpanzee
/ʃ–/	shelf	shovel	sheriff	shampoo
/dʒ–/	juice	gypsy	gingerale	giraffe

2 other pictures were pretest items, 1 consisting of a boy eating an ice cream cone, the other, a girl pointing to three balloons.

Elicitation

Three methods of elicitation were selected for study; they were sentence completion, sentence recall, and imitation. In sentence completion, the experimenter would show the child a picture that would have a predetermined description, such as "The man is catching the fish." The experimenter would then say "This is the man; this is the fish. The man is catching the___." The child was expected to complete the sentence. In sentence recall, which followed sentence completion, the child was asked "Now you tell me what is happening." In imitation, the child was given the target word and asked to repeat it. If imitation facilitates production, it was expected that children would do best on imitation, better on sentence completion, and least well on sentence recall. The 34 predetermined descriptions were as follows:

Pretest a. *The boy is eating the ice cream.*
b. *The girl is buying the balloon.*
Set I. 1. *The man is catching the fish.*
2. *The girl is holding the vase.*
3. *The policeman is chasing the thief.*
4. *The girl is drawing a six.*
5. *The girl is making zees.*
6. *The dog is watching the chief.*
7. *The boy is making a shelf.*
8. *The boy is selling juice.*
Set II. 9. *The woman is wearing the feather.*
10. *The man is going into the village.*
11. *The girl is opening the thermos.*
12. *The mouse is riding the sailfish.*
13. *The boy is playing the zither.*
14. *The girl is eating with chopsticks.*
15. *The boy is digging with the shovel.*
16. *The woman is watching the gypsy.*
Set III. 17. *The people are taking a photograph.*
18. *The lady is holding the vegetables.*
19. *The children are watching the theatre.*
20. *The cat is playing the saxophone.*
21. *The girl is drinking the gingerale.*
22. *The girl is sitting on the chesterfield.*
23. *The dog is watching the sheriff.*
24. *The boy is playing the xylophone.*

Set IV. 25. *The woman is eating the farina.*
       26. *The bird is flying over the volcano.*
       27. *The seal is looking at the thermometer.*
       28. *The people are on a safari.*
       29. *The girl is cutting zucchini.*
       30. *The boy is catching the chimpanzee.*
       31. *The dog is getting a shampoo.*
       32. *The children are watching the giraffe.*

Design

With 32 test items and three procedures, there were a total of 96 possible elicitations. This was considered too much to elicit from children in this age range without a high risk of not completing the test session. To compensate for this, two designs were established. For children under 4, subjects were given the sentence completion and sentence recall for Test Items I, II, and III. The items were given in the order of increasing phonological complexity, proceeding from Set I to II to III. For each item, the sentence completion and sentence recall were done together, beginning with sentence completion. This resulted in 24 words elicited for each of the two procedures. When completed, the subjects were then asked to imitate Groups II and III, or 16 words. The design differed for children over 4:0 in that they were given all four groups of test items. Like the younger children, these subjects only had to imitate Groups II and III. These designs are as follows:

	Sentence completion	Sentence recall	Imitation
Set I	all subjects	all subjects	
Set II	all subjects	all subjects	all subjects
Set III	all subjects	all subjects	all subjects
Set IV	4:0 and up	4:0 and up	

This meant that each test sound was to be elicited 8 times for children under 4:0, and 10 times for those over this age.

Procedures

Each subject was tested individually with the experimenter and an observer present, either in a selected room at the preschool being visited, or in the test room at the Stanford Child Phonology Project. Before the testing began, the experimenter and the observer would spend some time with the child in the play area. Younger subjects usually took from 10 to 25 min to become comfortable; older subjects took less than 5 min. After rapport was established, the subject was asked to look at a picture book with the experimenter. Three pieces of equipment were shown to the subject: the tape recorder, the microphone that was sewn into a jacket, and the cord that connected the microphone to the tape recorder. The subject donned the jacket and was given a pencil to hold so that the cord would remain undisturbed. If the subject refused to wear the jacket, it was rolled up and placed between the subject and the experimenter. Sentence completion and sentence recall were used with the two pretest pictures and then testing proceeded in the manner described. If the child did not respond, he was encouraged to name the test word. If neither procedure elicited a response, imitation was used. Most subjects caught on quickly, with older subjects showing some impatience at having to do the sentence recall. Each session took approximately 15 min. The observer kept written notes of the session, including free-field transcriptions noting visible indications of the sounds being produced (e.g., lip rounding, tongue protrusion).

Transcription

All responses were audiorecorded and transcribed with the use of earphones by two independent transcribers (L.C. and S.V.). All test words were transcribed using the symbols developed by the Stanford Child Phonology Project (cf. Bush et al., 1973). A third transcriber (B.W.) listened to all the tapes and resolved cases where the two transcribers differed on the quality of the sound. The transcriptions of the first two transcribers of the target sounds agreed 86% of the time, ranging from a low of 70% for the 2:0–2:5 group to 88% for the 5:6–5:11 one. The third transcriber was able to resolve 45% of the unresolved pairs. Items were marked as to whether they were produced as a sentence completion, sentence recall, or imitation. Transcriptions of each child's production were accepted as final when at least two of the three transcribers agreed on them. This procedure accounted for 92.4% of all utterances recorded.

Comparative Analysis

To place the present study into perspective, nine previously published large-sample studies were selected for comparison of results when possible: Bricker (1967), Cairns and Williams (1972), Olmsted (1971), Poole (1934), Snow (1963), Templin (1957), Tracy (1895), Wellman et al. (1931), Williams (1937). These studies varied from one to the other in ages and number of subjects, stimulus items, elicitation, and methods of analysis so that only general comparisons were undertaken.

TABLE 9.2
Selected Response Measures for Nine Groups

Response measures	1:6– 1:11	2:0– 2:5	2:6– 2:11	3:0– 3:5	3:6– 3:11	4:0– 4:5	4:6– 4:11	5:0– 5:5	5:6– 5:11	Total
Number of subjects	2	6	12	11	8	9	7	10	8	73
Subject identification number	1–2	3–8	9–20	21–31	32–39	40–48	49–55	56–65	66–73	1–73
Number of responses	70	156	511	630	480	701	560	797	655	4560
Range of responses	35	19–32	20–62	33–80	36–82	69–83	75–85	76–82	76–88	19–88
Mean number of responses per subject	35	26	42.6	57.3	60	77.9	80	79.7	81.9	62.5
Mean number of responses per test sound per subject	4.38	3.25	5.32	7.16	7.5	9.7	10	9.96	10.2	7.8

Results

Not all children were able to complete the task but performance improved in each age group (Table 9.2). Subjects were numbered from 1 to 73 in increasing order of age for purposes of individual analysis as shown in Table 9.2). By 2:6 to 2:11, subjects were producing an average of 5.32 responses for each test sound, which increased to over 7 responses for all older subjects. Percentages of correct production for each sound by each subject were then calculated to determine order of acquisition. A child had to attempt a sound at least four times to have performance on that sound included in the subsequent analysis. With 70% set as a criterion of correct production for a subject to "pass" a sound, Table 9.3 presents the percentages of subjects at each age group to pass each of the eight word-initial English fricatives and affricates. Table 9.4 compares these percentages to those found in studies conducted by Olmsted (1971), Templin (1957), and Wellman et al. (1931). For Olmsted, the percentages given are for those subjects who pass a sound, although pass in his case is correct production greater than 50%.

Setting a criterion of 70% for acquisition, it is possible to get an initial impression of acquisition from Table 9.4. Only /f − / is acquired by age 3:0. Between ages 3:6 and 4:2, /ʃ − /, /tʃ − /, and /dʒ − / begin to reach criterion. /v − / also does for Wellman et al., and the present study, but not for Templin.

TABLE 9.3
Percentage and Number of Subjects who Pass a Sound[a]

| | Age groups | | | | | | | | | |
Sound	1:11	2:2	2:10	3:2	3:10	4:2	4:8	5:2	5:8	Total
/f − /	50	60	73	100	88	89	100	100	100	87
	1/2	3/5	8/11	11/11	7/8	8/9	7/7	10/10	8/8	62/71
/v − /	0	0	10	40	50	78	71	80	88	53
	0/2	0/4	1/10	4/10	4/8	7/9	5/7	8/10	7/8	36/68
/θ − /	0	0	0	11	25	22	43	70	63	30
	0/2	0/2	0/11	1/9	2/8	2/9	3/7	7/10	5/8	20/66
/s − /	0	33	46	46	75	67	57	70	63	57
	0/2	1/3	5/11	5/11	6/8	6/9	4/7	7/10	5/8	39/69
/z − /	0	0	20	36	50	56	29	40	50	37
	0/1	0/3	2/10	4/11	4/8	5/9	2/7	4/10	4/8	25/68
/ʃ − /	0	33	50	27	63	100	86	90	100	68
	0/2	1/3	5/10	3/11	5/8	9/9	6/7	9/10	8/8	46/68
/tʃ − /	0	33	89	33	63	78	100	90	100	74
	0/2	1/3	8/9	3/10	5/8	7/9	7/7	9/10	8/8	48/65
/dʒ − /	0		75	36	29	78	100	90	100	69
	0/2	0/0	6/8	4/11	2/7	7/9	7/7	9/10	8/8	43/62

[a] To be included the subject had to attempt the sound four times. To pass, the subject had to produce it correctly 70% of the time.

178

TABLE 9.4

Percentages of Correct Production of Word-initial Fricatives by Subjects in this Study as Compared to Results Found in Olmsted (1971), and Templin (1957), Wellman et al. (1931).

Sound	study	1:8	2:0	2:2	2:8	2:10	3:0	3:2	3:6	3:10	4:0	4:2	4:6	4:8	5:0	5:2	5:8	6:0	7:0	8:0
/f-/	Olmsted	100ᵃ	78	78	78			83	100			100								
	Ingram			60		73ᵃ		100		88		89		100		100	100			
	Wellman		53				83ᵃ				92				100			100	100	100
	Templin						88ᵃ		90		93		97		92			100	100	100
/v-/	Olmsted																			
	Ingram		0	0		10		40		50		78ᵃ		71		80	88			
	Wellman						58		30		72ᵃ				84			70	88	98
	Templin						12		25		40		47		55			80ᵃ	88	98
/Θ-/	Olmsted	0						0												
	Ingram		20	9	40			11		25		22		43		70	63			
	Wellman						36		28		51				76ᵃ			89	88	98
	Templin						27		33		48		60		67			85ᵃ	90	97
/ð-/ᵇ	Olmsted	0	7	0	14			17												
	Wellman						39				49				79ᵃ			89	90	97
	Templin						23		32		57		60		62			83ᵃ	97	98

Ages

Sound	Study	1	2	3	4	5	6	7	8	9	10	11	12	13
/s-/	Olmsted	36	23	67	80ᵃ	75	67	57	70	63				
	Ingram		0	46	85	46	80							
	Wellman							7	51	64	77ᵃ	74	92	
	Templin								70	77ᵃ	78	77		97
/z-/	Olmsted	40	40	36	55	50	56	29	40	50				
	Ingram		0		60	20	72ᵃ							
	Wellman							14	61	73ᵃ	87	78	90	
	Templin								30	62	65	67		95
/ʃ-/	Olmsted	27	31	43	72	63	75ᵃ	86	90	100				
	Ingram		33	27		50	88	100ᵃ						
	Wellman							7	46	74ᵃ	88	96	95	
	Templin								53	75	87	87		98
/tʃ-/	Olmsted	0	40	33	60	63	78ᵃ	100	90	100				
	Ingram		33			89	75							
	Wellman							21	59	72ᵃ	88	92	98	
	Templin								50	72ᵃ	82	88		95
/dʒ-/	Olmsted	50	40	43	58	29	78ᵃ	100	90	100				
	Ingram			36		75	87							
	Wellman							29	74	81ᵃ	90	82	98	
	Templin								53	85ᵃ	92	95		97

ᵃ Percentages that meet the criterion of 70% and do not drop below that in older age groups.

ᵇ Sound not tested in Ingram et al.

An examination of Templin's procedure, however, shows that she used phonologically more complex words for this sound, *vacuum cleaner* and *valentine*, then did Wellman *et al.*, who used *vest* and *vase*. /s − / and /z − / are next, but showed mixed results. In the present study, narrow phonetic transcription was used that resulted in poorer performance on these than has been reported in the literature. The reasons for this discrepancy will be discussed shortly. /Θ − / and /ð − / are acquired last, between 5:0 and 6:0. Referring only to the present study, the order of acquisition based on correct production across all subjects was /f − / 87%; /tʃ − / 74%; /dʒ − / 69%; /ʃ − / 68%; /s − / 57%; /v − / 53%; /z − / 37%; /Θ − / 30%.

The comparison of percentages of correct production for the three methods of elicitation did not show any differences (Table 9.5). Success on imitation was low from 1:6 to 2:5, but most responses were imitations for these subjects. From 2:6 to 5:11, the mean proportion of correct responses across age groups were nearly identical: .73, .74, and .73 for sentence completion, sentence recall, and imitation respectively. For children beyond 2:6, there was no indication of improvement with imitation, which contradicted our hypothesis.

To examine whether or not the word in which a sound appears affects production, two analyses were done. Since only subjects from 4:0 to 5:11 received all four words for each test sound, data from these children were examined for the proportions of correct productions (Table 9.6). In most cases, performance was similar across words, but two words resulted in markedly poorer production: *thief* and *zucchini*. Next, performance on Set I (presumably the easiest words) was compared to that on Set IV, the hardest ones, in those subjects who had attempted both words. As can be seen in Table 9.7, the results suggest that some words may result in poorer performance, but not in all cases. For some pairs (e.g., /ʃ − /, and /dʒ − /), the results were the same. Others show the Set IV words to be more difficult (i.e., /v − / and /z − /), yet the reverse was true for /Θ − / where *thief* was

TABLE 9.5

Proportion and Number of Correct Responses to Three Methods of Elicitation by Subjects across Nine Age Groups

	Age groups									
Elicitation	1:6–1:11	2:0–2:5	2:6–2:11	3:0–3:5	3:6–3:11	4:0–4:5	4:6–4:11	5:0–5:5	5:6–5:11	Mean[a]
Sentence completion		.50	.60	.56	.63	.81	.79	.84	.87	.73
		6	62	79	70	114	89	133	111	
Sentence recall		.60	.63	.58	.66	.87	.76	.85	.82	.74
		3	48	77	63	120	84	135	105	
Imitation	.24	.39	.54	.53	.77	.84	.77	.82	.81	.73
	9	28	83	78	66	119	88	130	108	

[a] Mean of age groups 2:6–5:11.

TABLE 9.6

Proportion and Number of Correct Responses to 32 Test Words by Subjects Between 4:0 and 5:11

Test word	Proportion	Number	Test Word	Proportion	Number
fish	.97	64	zees	.77	46
feather	.99	101	zither	.66	71
photograph	.96	97	xylophone	.67	68
farina	.87	60	zucchini	.29	20
vase	.83	54	shelf	.84	57
village	.85	87	shovel	.93	95
vegetables	.83	85	sheriff	.86	87
volcano	.59	40	shampoo	.77	52
thief	.38	26	chief	.97	65
thermos	.64	67	chopsticks	.95	97
theatre	.68	68	chesterfield	.92	93
thermometer	.66	43	chimpanzee	.65	46
six	.79	52	juice	.89	63
sailfish	.77	80	gypsy	.80	82
saxophone	.69	68	gingerale	.90	87
safari	.70	49	giraffe	.85	57

more difficult than *thermometer.* The results showed performance to be similar between similar words, but that marked differences in phonological complexity may result in poorer performance.

The type and frequency of substitutions made by all subjects for the eight test sounds are shown in Table 9.8. Certain substitutions are quite dominant, such as [b] for /v − /, [f] for /Θ − /, and [Θ −] for /s − /. To compare these results to those in previous studies, data on substitutions from six large-sample studies were tabulated (Appendix). Table 9.8 contains our results and a summary of findings from these six previous studies. All studies show the same most frequent substitutions except for /z/. Our data indicated that [ð −] and [s] are equally frequent substitutes for /z − / whereas [s] is the

TABLE 9.7

Proportion and Number of Correct Productions on Set I and Set II word Pairs by Subjects between 3:0 and 5:11 who Produced Both Words

Test word	Proportion	Number	Test word	Proportion	Number
fish	1.00	39	zees	.65	24
farina	.85	33	zucchini	.35	12
vase	.84	32	shelf	.81	33
volcano	.55	21	shampoo	.81	33
thief	.33	13	juice	.78	32
thermometer	.63	25	giraffe	.78	32
six	.76	28	chief	.91	32
safari	.65	24	chimpanzee	.71	25

TABLE 9.8

Major Substitutions, Frequency, and Proportions from 73 Subjects, Compared with Findings of Previous Studies (Appendix)

Test sound	Frequency	Substitution–proportion		Substitutions from appendix listed in order of frequency
/f −/	47	[s]	.23	[s]
		[fᵛ]	.13	
		[p]	.11	
		[b]	.09	
/v −/	194	[b]	.57	[b]
		[f]	.14	[f]
		[vᵃ]	.10	
/θ −/	309	[f]	.62	[f]
		[s]	.16	[s]
		[θ]	.09	[t]
		[t]	.04	
/s −/	176	[θs]	.26	[θ]
		[θ]	.23	[ʃ]
		[f]	.14	[t]
/z −/	237	[ð]	.23	[s]
		[s]	.23	[θ]
		[zᵃ]	.18	[ð]
		[dz]	.08	[d]
/ʃ −/	138	[s]	.33	[s]
		[sj]	.23	[tʃ]
		[ʃᵃ]	.14	
		[tʃ]	.10	
/tʃ −/	114	[t]	.18	[t]
		[s]	.15	[ʃ]
		[ts]	.11	[s]
		[ʃ]	.10	
		[dʒ]	.08	
/dʒ −/	133	[d]	.30	[d]
		[ts]	.15	[tʃ]
[dz]			.14	
		[tʃ]	.05	
		[ʃ]	.05	

ᵃ Distorted.

most frequently reported one in the literature. Other less frequent substitutions do not match as well, although the procedure used in the Appendix is quite general and too much should not be argued from it.

Regarding the acquisition of these sounds as a class, Table 9.9 presents the number of the eight sounds that reached the 70% criterion for subjects in each age group. It was not until the 4:6 to 4:11 age group that one subject reached criterion on all sounds. Even at 5:6 to 5:11, only two of eight subjects

TABLE 9.9
Number of Subjects in each of Nine Age Groups to Acquire from None to Eight Fricatives and Affricates

Age group	No. of subjects	Number of sounds acquired									Mean no. of sounds acquired per subject
		0	1	2	3	4	5	6	7	8	
1:6–1:11	2	1	1								.50
2:0–2:5	6	2	2	2							1.00
2:6–2:11	12	1	4		1	3	2	1			2.92
3:0–3:5	11		2	2	3	2	1	1			3.09
3:6–3:11	8			1	2	2	1		2		4.38
4:0–4:5	9				1	1	1	3	3		5.67
4:6–4:11	7					2		3	1	1	5.86
5:0–5:5	10					1	2	3	1	3	6.30
5:6–5:11	8				1	1			4	1	6.38
Totals	73	4	9	5	8	12	7	11	11	6	

had acquired all eight sounds, although four subjects had acquired seven. These data show the gradual and late acquisition of these sounds as a class.

Data as presented so far usually give the impression of an invariant order of acquisition. The extent of individual variation is particularly evident when the data are broken down into patterns for individual subjects, and placed into one of the five stages described earlier. Those sounds that have reached 70% criterion are circled; the other symbols indicate the most frequent substitution pattern. These data show how extensive the individual variation can be within the stages. Regarding the stages themselves, the following distribution occurred among subjects with median ages: Stage 1: none; Stage 2: 4 subjects, 2:1;16; Stage 3: 17 subjects, 3:2;25; transition to Stage 4: 7 subjects, 4:2;4; Stage 4: 26 subjects, 4:1;8; and Stage 5: 16 subjects 4:11;14.

As is typical in language acquisition studies, age varied a great deal across stages. Tables 9.10–9.15 contain individual data reflecting patterns

TABLE 9.10
Stage 2. Predominant Substitution of Stops for Fricatives and Affricates

Subject		1	2	8	10
Age		1:10;22	1:11;20	2:3;10	2:7;22
	/f – /	(p)	f	f	(p,f)
	/v – /	(p)	(d)	(d)	b
	/θ – /	—	(f)	f	—
	/s – /	—	—	(sj,s)	t
Sound	/z – /	(d)	z	(d)	(dz)
	/ʃ – /	—	(s)	(ʃ,sj)	t
	/tʒ – /	t	(t)	(tʃ,d)	(tʃ)
	/dʒ – /	—	d	(dʒ,d)	—

TABLE 9.11
Stage 3. The Widespread Appearance of Continuants

Sound			Subject and age				
	6	7	14	21	25	29	31
	2:2;20	2:3;4	2:10;15	3:10;27	3:2;13	3:3;23	3:5;23
/f−/	○f	(f)	(f,fʷ)	○f	○f	○f	○f
/v−/	(v)	(b)	b	v(f)	b	○v	○v
/θ−/	f	—	(s)	f=s	(f)	s	f
/s−/	○s	(s)	(z)	○s	○s	○s	s.f
/z−/	(z)	(z)	(sz)	s	○z	○z	z
/ʃ−/	sj	(sj)	(sj)	ʃ	ʃ(s)	s(ʃ)	s,sj
/tʃ−/	—	(tʃ)	(ts)	(s)	tʃ(t)	tʃ(s)	tʃ,ts
/dʒ−/	(d)	(dʒ)	○dʒ	○dʒ	(z)	dʒ,z	dʒ,dz
	33	27	37	30	39	66	16
	3:7;12	3:2;25	3:10;15	3:5;5	3:11;28	5:6;2	2:10;28
/f−/	○f	○f	○f	○f	○f	○f	○f
/v−/	b	b,v	f,v(b)	(b)	v	v	b(v)
/θ−/	(f,ʃ)	f	f(s)	—	θ,f	θ	f,θ
/s−/	○s	f s	z(s)	(s,θ)	s	sθ	s f
/z−/	s	z	○z	(z)	z	zð	ð,z
/ʃ−/	○ʃ	(ʃ)	○ʃ	(θ)	s	s	○ʃ
/tʃ−/	(tʃ)	○tʃ	tʃ(t)	—	ts,(s)	tʃ	○tʃ
/dʒ−/	—	dʒ=d	dʒ	(d,z)	dz	dʒ,d	○dʒ
			48	18	32		
			4:5;15	2:11;14	3:6;16		
/f−/			○f	s,f	s		
/v−/			v,b	b	b		
/θ−/			f	sθ	s		
/s−/			s,θ	○s	○s		
/z−/			s,z	z(d)	s		
/ʃ−/			○ʃ	○ʃ	s		
/tʃ−/			○tʃ	○tʃ	○tʃ		
/dʒ−/			○dʒ	dʒ	d(dʒ)		

TABLE 9.12
Transition to Stage 4 (most Fricatives and Affricates are Acquired)

Sound			Subject and age				
	2:0;17	4:2;12	4:10;11	2:11;18	3:2;19	5:4;10	5:7;16
/f−/	○f	f,b	○f	○f	○f	○f	○f
/v−/	v	b=v	○v	○v	v(b)	v,b	v=b
/θ−/	(f)	(θ=f)	f	f,s	f,θ	○θ	θ
/s−/	−	s	s	○s	○s	s,sθ	sθ
/z−/	−	z	z	○z	z,s	z,sθ	s(l)
/ʃ−/	ʃ	○ʃ	s,sθ	s(ʃ)	ʃ	○ʃ	○ʃ
/tʃ−/	○tʃ	○tʃ	○tʃ	○tʃ	○tʃ	○tʃ	○tʃ
/dʒ−/	d	○dʒ	○dʒ	(dʒ,tʃ)	○dʒ	○dʒ	○dʒ

TABLE 9.13

Stage 4, Type /Θ/. Most Fricatives and Affricates are Acquired (except for /Θ/)

	Subject and age											
	41	54	23	11	24	13	73	64	46	43	49	59
Sound	4:1;5	4:11;5	3:2;6	2:8;6	3:2;9	2:9;24	5:11;18	5:5;16	4:4;11	4:1;10	4:7;19	5:2;10
/f−/	f⃝	f⃝	f⃝	f⃝	f⃝	f⃝	f⃝	f⃝	f⃝	f⃝	f⃝	f⃝
/v−/	v⃝	v⃝	v	(v)	v	v	v⃝	v⃝	v⃝	v⃝	v⃝	v⃝
/Θ−/	f	f	f	f	f	f(Θ)	f(Θ)	Θ,f	Θ,f	Θ,f	Θ,f	Θ,f
/s−/	s⃝	s⃝	s⃝	s	(s)	s⃝	s⃝	s⃝	s⃝	s	s⃝	s⃝
/z−/	z⃝	z⃝	z⃝	(z)	z⃝	z	z⃝	z	z⃝	z	z,s	z,s
/ʃ−/	ʃ⃝	ʃ⃝	ʃ⃝	ʃ	ʃ⃝	ʃ⃝	ʃ⃝	ʃ⃝	ʃ⃝	ʃ⃝	ʃ⃝	ʃ⃝
/tʃ−/	tʃ⃝	tʃ⃝	tʃ⃝	tʃ	tʃ⃝	tʃ⃝	tʃ⃝	tʃ⃝	tʃ⃝	tʃ⃝	tʃ⃝	tʃ⃝
/dʒ−/	dʒ⃝	dʒ⃝	dʒ⃝	dʒ	dʒ(tʃ)	dʒ⃝	dʒ⃝	dʒ⃝	dʒ⃝	dʒ⃝	dʒ⃝	dʒ⃝

TABLE 9.14

Stage 4, Type /Θ,v/. Most Fricatives and Affricates are Acquired (eacept for /Θ/ and /v/)

Sound	Subject and age							
	9 2:7;2	12 2:9;1	17 2:11;10	19 2:11;15	28 3:3;3	36 3:10;9	50 4:8;14	61 5:2;14
/f – /	f	ⓕ	ⓕ	ⓕ	ⓕ	ⓕ	ⓕ	ⓕ
/v – /	(f)	(f)	b	b	b = v	b	b(f)	b
/Θ – /	(f)	f	f	(s)	f = Θ	f	f,Θ(s)	f,Θ
/s – /	s	s	s(Θ)	ⓢ	s	ⓢ	s	ⓢ
/z – /	(z)	z	z	ⓩ	z	ⓩ	z	z,ð
/ʃ – /	–	ʃ	ⓙ	ⓙ	ⓙ	ʃ,sj	ⓙ	ⓙ
/tʃ – /	(tʃ)	ⓣʃ	ⓣʃ	ⓣʃ	tʃ	ⓣʃ	ⓣʃ	ⓣʃ
/dʒ – /	(dʒ)	ⓓʒ	ⓓʒ	ⓓʒ	dʒ	ⓓʒ	ⓓʒ	dʒ

of responses. These patterns are grouped into stages of development. The identification number and age of each subject are provided. Acquired sounds are circled. The sounds shown are those that occured at least three times; those that occured twice are placed in parentheses. If two sounds are listed together, the first was the most frequent of the two.

The fact that no subjects fell into Stage 1 was expected as this stage characterizes the period of the child's first 50 words and usually lasts from 1:0 to 1:6. Our youngest subject was 1:10;22. Stage 2, the use of predominant stops, is also an early stage (Table 9.10). Both subjects who were below 2:0 were in this stage. Most subjects fell into the next three stages and provided insight into their nature. Stage 3 showed widespread variation and development as expected (Table 9.11). It was characterized by each subject showing incomplete or varied production for at least four of the eight sounds

TABLE 9.15

Stage 4, type /s,z/. Most Fricatives and Affricates are Acquired (except for /s,z/, which tend to have dental substitutes)

Sound	Subject and age					
	22 3:1;2	58 5:1;28	62 5:4;8	55 4:11;12	34 3:9;14	70 5:8;23
/f – /	ⓕ	ⓕ	ⓕ	ⓕ	ⓕ	ⓕ
/v – /	ⓥ	ⓥ	ⓥ	ⓥ	ⓥ	ⓥ
/Θ – /	–	ⓞ	ⓞ	ⓞ	ⓞ	ⓞ
/s – /	(Θ)	Θ	s,Θ	s	ⓢ	ⓢ
/z – /	ð	ð	ð,z	ð	z,(Θ,ð)	z,ð
/ʃ – /	ʃ	ⓙ	ⓙ	ⓙ	ⓙ	ⓙ
/tʃ – /	(tʃ)	ⓣʃ	ⓣʃ	ⓣʃ	ⓣʃ	ⓣʃ
/dʒ – /	dʒ	ⓓʒ	ⓓʒ	ⓓʒ	ⓓʒ	ⓓʒ

observed. One difference from the stages as proposed here was that liquids or glides did not occur consistently for any subject. Seven subjects appeared to be between Stage 3 and Stage 4, see Transition to Stage 4, Table 9.12.

The data for Stage 4 fell into three very consistent patterns. Twelve subjects showed difficulty with /Θ − /, whereas all other sounds were being produced stably and, in most cases, to criterion (Table 9.13). In all cases, the substitution for /Θ − / was [f]. The difficulty with /Θ − / also appeared in the second pattern where errors occurred for /Θ − / and /v − /, a pattern that eight subjects had (Table 9.14). The last pattern was the "lisp" problem, where /s − / and/or /z − / were dentalized; six children showed this pattern (Table 9.15). These three patterns appeared to capture the three most persistent problems children have in acquiring this class of sounds. As mentioned in Ingram (1978), these subjects also showed occasional distortion of /s − / and /z − /.

Regarding Stage 5, two patterns emerged, which we labeled "complete" and "developmental." The complete pattern is the one in which the subject shows 70% correct production in all of the sounds. The developmental pattern represented those cases where subjects did not show 70% production on all sounds, but did show correct stable production of all sounds. In other words, there was no consistent substitution pattern that was interfering with production of the correct sounds. These subjects were capable of good production of all the sounds, although there was enough inconsistency on individual sounds that the 70% criterion was not met. Ten subjects fell into the developmental category.

The last aspect of the data to be analyzed was the use of specific phonological preferences for sounds. The data did not show widespread use of specific sounds except in a few cases such as subject 32 who used [s −] as a substitute for /f − /, /Θ − /, /z − /, and /ʃ − /. Given the existence of a developmental pattern as mentioned, it may be that only certain individual children use widespread and consistent substitution patterns. As concluded by Ferguson (1973), children were learning sounds on an individual basis and widespread patterns did not emerge. This is similar to the results in Farwell (1976) who states "Some children do not show any particular approach to fricatives as a class [p., 98]." Also, preferences of the sort discussed in Farwell (1976) and Ingram (1979) may be more noticeable in diary accounts that have a larger number of words for each sound than were available from these subjects.

Discussion

The data collected confirmed and provided more detail about previous findings on English word-initial fricatives and affricates, and demonstrated the need to look at data from individuals as well as grouped data to gain greater insights into the processes of phonological development. When the data were grouped and scored by percentages of correct production, they reflected the findings of earlier studies such as those by Templin (1957) and Wellman *et al.* (1931) that were based on fewer elicitations per subject of each test sounds. /f −/ was the earliest acquired sound by far, followed by the alveopalatals /ʃ −/, /tʃ −/, and /dʒ −/; /s −/ and /v −/ and /v −/ were next, with /z −/ and /Θ −/ being the most difficult. The acquisition of /s −/ and /z −/ was different than the others, however, in that these did not show the same gradual improvement as the others. For these sounds, children come to some approximation of them, especially for /s −/, and then take a while to achieve a production that is not distorted in some way. This suggests a need to separate phonological from phonetic production, the current study focusing only on the latter. Both /s −/ and /z −/ are probably acquired phonologically at an earlier age than this study indicates (cf. Menn, 1976; Moskowitz, 1975).

As found by Templin (1947), imitation did not result in improved production, contrary to our expectations. Because some studies have reported improvement, this notion deserves continued study. It may be that some children are better imitators than others, or that children younger than these studied are more likely to show improvement (cf. Leonard *et al.*, forthcoming). Also highly possible is that our decision to give imitations after the other procedures may have had an adverse effect on the results.

The results with individual words showed that production may vary, but the majority of cases had similar results across words. This indicates that articulation tests with just one word may be justified, although one would need to be careful about which words were selected. The selection of a monosyllabic familiar word will be more likely to show correct production than a multisyllabic unfamiliar one. More serious in this regard is the elicitation of only one production per test sound. One of the striking results here was the variant productions of sounds across several trials. To capture this, articulation tests will need to elicit each test sound several times.

The most striking results concerned the extent of individual variation that occurs in the acquisition of these sounds. When data were grouped, general patterns emerge, yet individual variations are extensive. Even though a general order of acquisition occurs, children show other orders that contradict it. Thus, even though children tend to acquire certain sounds before others, one should not be surprised to come across children who show an opposite order. The interchange between general patterns and individual variation was best observed in the examination of five stages of acquisition of these sounds. It was possible to define stages in terms of facility with certain numbers of sounds, but the choice of individual sounds varied tremendously. Results like these indicate that one should not be as concerned with comparing children against some norm as with studying their own individual patterns of acquisition.

The need to do qualitative analyses was evident in looking at the patterns of children who have acquired most of the English fricatives and affricates. Quantitative analyses showed /s−/, /z−/, /v−/, and /θ−/ to be the last sounds acquired. The results here show three distinct patterns and that not all possibilities occur. There are children who lisp, those with difficulties with /θ−/ and /v−/, and those who cannot produce /θ−/; there were also subjects who used a developmental pattern, indicating that they were not using widespread substitutions for any of these sounds. It has been noted that some children are more "interesting" in their development than others (e.g., Adam, in Brown, 1973). These children are usually the ones that make the most errors or mistakes or non-adult-like productions. It may be that many children do not do this, showing instead a rather cautious, gradual developmental process. These appear to be children who either speak clearly or tend to distort more than substitute.

The results indicate that young children do acquire fricatives and affricates in certain predictable orders and stages, along with certain substitutions that are more likely than some others; they show that individual differences are substantial, though within certain limits. These results can be used to ascertain an individual child's particular stage and acquisition of this particular subset of English sounds.

Summary

Extensive study of word-initial English fricatives was undertaken to determine detailed findings about this class of difficult sounds. Grouped and individual analysis of data from 73 subjects provided answers to seven questions asked:

1. When data are grouped, these sounds show an order of acquisition similar to that observed in other studies: /f−/ before /tʃ−/, /dʒ−/, /ʃ−/ before /s−/, /v−/, /z−/, /θ−/. Within subjects, however, this order is often contradicted when the sounds are not at the extremes of the general pattern.

2. Acquisition is gradual, and individual subjects will vary between correct and incorrect production of a sound; acquisition can be best observed by having several productions of the same sound.

3. Production of a sound may vary across words; the most variation occurs between words that are familiar and simple in structure and those that are unfamiliar and complex.

4. Production across subjects did not improve with imitation.

5. Consistent substitution patterns were noted for all sounds: for /f−/:

APPENDIX
Major Patterns of Substitution for Word-initial English Fricatives as Reported in Six Large-Sample Studies

Investigator(s)	Ages of subjects	Substitutions								
		/f-/	/v-/	/θ-/	/ð-/	/s-/	/z-/	/ʃ-/	/tʃ-/	/dʒ-/
Tracy (1895)[a]	1:6–2:5	p(6) s(5) k(2) t(2)	b(5) f(2)	f(10) t(4) s(3)	d(13)	t(8) h(8) f(3) b(3) d(3)		s(19) h(4)	s(7) t(4) ʃ(2)	d(4)
Williams (1937)[c]	2:6–6:6		b(17)	s(5) t(3)	d(18)	θ(6) t(3)	s(3)	s(14)	t(4) s(4)	d(6) tʃ(3)
Bricker (1967)[b]	3:0–3:9	s(49) θ(10)	b(50) m(48) f(31) ð(16)	s(125) f(103) ð(12)	v(74) z(37) f(29) b(20) l(19) s(18) θ(16) d(14)		s(45) ð(28) θ(18)	dʒ(16)	ʃ(47) t(17)	
Snow (1963)[b]	6:5–8:7		b(144)	f(145) s(16)	d(24)	ʃ(19) θ(17) ts(11)	dz(64) ʃ(48) d(11)	s(42) sʃ(30)	ts(28) ʃ(25)	dz(29)
Cairns and Williams (1972)[a]	6:0–12:0	b(6)	b(29)	f(21) t(5) s(4)	d(18)	s[d](8)	s(42)	tʃ(8) s(3)	t(6) ʃ(5)	tʃ(6) d(3)
Olmsted (1971)[a,b]	1:3–4:5		b(37) f(10)	f(36) s(21)	d(753) z(43)	θ(59) ʃ(50) f(28) t(19) z(18)	s(27) θ(25) ʃ(17) ð(15) d(13)	s(85) θ(12) tʃ(10)	t(38)	d(24)

[a] Substitutions are for all positions in word.
[b] Only those that occur 10 times or more are given.
[c] The figures here are for percent of total substitutions for all words in data.
[d] Distorted.

[s] or a stop [p] or [b]; for /v − /: [b]; for /Θ − /: [f]; for /s − /: [Θ]; for /z − /: [ð], [s] and a distorted form of [z]; for /ʃ − /: [s] or a form slightly palatalized; for /tʒ − /: [t], [s] and [ts]; for /dʒ − /: [d] (most frequently), [ts] and [dz].

6. Stages of development occurred, based on the major patterns children used for adult fricatives and affricates. When children were producing fewer than five of the eight sounds accurately, there was a great deal of individual variation. Children with consistent production of most of them showed three distinct types: errors with /Θ − /, errors with /Θ − / and /v − /, and errors with /s − / and /z − / (lisping). A developmental pattern was observed for children who showed no marked substitution pattern.

7. Despite general patterns, individual variations were quite considerable.

The findings suggest that one needs to look at each individual child's system to get a realistic picture of this class of sounds.

Acknowledgments

This research was supported in large part by the National Science Foundation Grant GS–03962. We would like to express our appreciation to the members of the Stanford Child Phonology Project who assisted us during the summer of 1975, especially Charles Ferguson and Marcy Macken.

References

Bricker, W. (1967) "Errors in the Echoic Behavior of Preschool Children," *Journal of Speech and Hearing Research*, 10, 67–76.

Brown, R. (1973) *A First Language*, Harvard University Press, Cambridge, Mass.

Bush, C. *et al.* (1973) Edwards, M.L., Luckau, J.M., Stoel, C.M., Macken, M.A., Petersen, J.D., "On Specifying a System for Transcribing Consonants in Child Language: A Working Paper with Examples from American English and Mexican Spanish," Unpublished paper, Child Language Project, Stanford University.

Cairns, H., and Williams, F. (1972) "An Analysis of the Substitution Errors of a Group of Standard English-speaking Children," *Journal of Speech and Hearing Research* 15, 807–810.

Faircloth, M., and Faircloth, S. (1970) "An Analysis of the Articulatory Speech Defective Child in Connected and Isolated Word Responses," *Journal of Speech and Hearing Disorders*, 35, 51–61.

Farwell, C. (1976) "Some Strategies in the Early Production of Fricatives," *Papers and Reports on Child Language Development*, (Linguistic, Stanford University) 12, 97–104.

Ferguson, C. (1973) "Fricatives in Child Language Acquisition," *Papers and Reports on Child Language Development* (Linguistics, Stanford University) 6, 61–85.

Ferguson, C., and Farwell, C. (1975) "Words and Sounds in Early Language Acquisition: English Initial Consonants in the First 50 Words," *Language*, 51, 419–439.

Ingram, D. (1976) *Phonological Disability in Children*, Edward Arnold, London.

Ingram, D. (1978) "The Production of Word-initial Fricatives and Affricates by Normal and Linguistically Deviant Children," in A. Caramazza and E. Zurif, eds., *The Acquisition and*

Breakdown of Language: Parallels and Divergences, Johns Hopkins University Press, Baltimore, Md.

Ingram, D. (1979) "Phonological Patterns in the Speech of Young Children," in P. Fletcher and M. Garman, eds., *Studies in Language Acquisition,* Cambridge University Press, Cambridge.

Leonard, L., Schwartz, R., Folger, K., and Wilcox, J. (n.d.) "Some Aspects of Child Phonology in Imitative and Spontaneous Speech."

Menn, L. (1976) "Evidence for an Interactionist-discovery Theory of Child Phonology," *Papers and Reports on Child Language Development,* (Linguistics, Stanford University) 12, 169–177.

Morley, M. (1957) *The Development and Disorders of Speech in Childhood,* Livingstone, London.

Morrison, C. "Speech Defects in Young Children," *The Psychological Clinic,* 8, 138–142.

Moskowitz, A. (1975) "The Acquisition of Fricatives: A Study in Phonetics and Phonology," *Journal of Phonetics,* 3, 141–150.

Olmsted, D. (1934) *Out of the Mouth of Babes,* Mouton, The Hague.

Poole, E. (1934) "Genetic Development of Articulation of Consonant Sounds in Speech," *Elementary English Review,* 11, 159–161.

Snow, K. (1963) "A Detailed Analysis of Articulation Responses of 'Normal' First Grade Children," *Journal of Speech and Hearing Research,* 6, 277–290.

Templin, M. (1947) "Spontaneous versus Imitated Verbalization in Testing Articulation in Preschool Children," *Journal of Speech and Hearing Disorders,* 12, 293–300.

Templin, M. (1957) *Certain Language Skills in Children: Their Development and Interrelationships,* Institute of Child Welfare Monograph 26, The University of Minnesota Press, Minneapolis.

Tracy, F. (1893) *The Psychology of Childhood,* Heath, Boston.

Veltan, H. (1943) "The Growth of Phonemic and Lexical Patterns in Infant Speech," *Language,* 19, 281–292.

Wellman, B.L., Case, I.M., Mengert, I.G., and Bradbury, D.E. (1931) "Speech Sounds of Young Children," *University of Iowa Studies in Child Welfare,* 5.

Williams, H. (1937) "Development of Language and Vocabulary in Young Children: Part 2. A Qualitative Analysis of the Erroneous Speech Sound Substitutions of Preschool Children," *University of Iowa Studies in Child Welfare,* 13,(2), 19–32.

Winitz, H. (1969) *Articulatory Acquisition and Behavior,* Appleton-Century-Crofts, New York.

Chapter 10

THE PREDICTION OF CHILD SPEECH ERRORS: IMPLICATIONS FOR A THEORY OF ACQUISITION

JOHN L. LOCKE

Recently, a theoretical review of child phonology (Ferguson and Garnica, 1975) found "the present state of theory construction . . . unsatisfactory [p. 174]" In an attempt to encourage more efficient theorizing in the future, Ferguson and Garnica suggested certain requirements for a theory of child phonology. One requirement was that the theory "must account for known facts of phonological development that are not included in the characterization of adult phonology [p. 155]." In this chapter, we will report an attempt to predict children's segmental substitutions and discuss the implications of this sort of endeavor for a theory of acquisition.

It is, of course, a clear violation of the zeitgeist in child phonology to limit one's self to speech segments. The more accepted approach subsumes individual substitutions under categories of change by phonetic feature or phonological process. It also is unusual to encounter attempts to explain, much less to predict, children's speech errors: More commonly they are described or labeled. Ohala (1974) comments that many phonologists notice that some

> sounds do one thing whereas another group does the opposite . . . rather than seek an explanation for this difference in behavior they simply tack on different labels to the two groups, X and not-X, and then 'explain' the behavior of a given sound or the whole group of sounds as being due to the fact that they are 'X' (or 'not-X') [pp. 251–253].

CHILD PHONOLOGY
VOLUME 1: PRODUCTION

In child phonology it might be productive to exhaust the range of phonetic explanations before accepting the need of higher-order constructs and
abstract principles. Were it possible with a phonetic model to predict that
children will say X in place of Y, an analysis of its component parts presumably could tell us something about what is and what is not important to
the child's acquisition of phonology.

In predicting the course of a child's development, one can think of
nothing more valuable than some knowledge of the child's recent history,
but, when it comes to child speech, one is often told that infant phonetic
experience is irrelevant. The basis for this misunderstanding is traceable to
some statements by Jakobson (1941/1968) who undoubtedly was influenced
by the earlier work, and conclusions, of Grégoire (1937, cited in Jakobson,
1941/1968). Grégoire had commented that the babbling infant "is capable
of producing all conceivable sounds." Somehow this was misconstrued to
mean that his capability, real or not, was randomly exercised. Since child
speech is highly patterned, this logically encouraged the rejection of infant
vocal play as linguistically irrelevant. Our claim is that babbling is importantly related to the child's acquisition of phonology; a categorical rejection
of infant sound preferences would, ipso facto, disallow much of the child's
early speech.

Let us consider the continuity of babbling and lexically based sound
production. Were there a period of silence from 10 to 12 months, after which
the first word dramatically emerged, one might wish to entertain the hypothesis that early speech is unrelated to late babbling. But according to
Ferguson (1978),

> at some point in the babbling period, the child typically begins to make active use
> of sound–meaning correspondences of his own, i.e., he produces a set of vocables
> which function communicatively much like the later 'first words' but are not based
> on words of the adult language. . . . The active lexicon of the child at around the
> end of the first year . . . typically consists of a dozen or so vocables of which
> only one or two are pretty clearly based on adult words [p. 28].

Of the other vocables, according to Ferguson, many involve novel
words *contrived* by the child. In creating new words, the child presumably
draws heavily upon whatever sounds were in his phonetic repertoire at that
time. This stage of the acquisition process is important because it serves to
bridge the phonetic play of the infant and the early phonological shapes of
the child.

The Child at 1 Year: A Working Model

For the last 6 months or so the child has been heard to produce many
different sounds. Some of the English consonants have been heard fre-

quently, others not at all. The child, then, approaches his first birthday with a phonetic repertoire that includes only a portion of the consonant inventory of his parents' language. Having been produced spontaneously, and without any·significant linguistic influence, this repertoire may be considered his biologically native sound system. The child reaches a stage in which it becomes interesting to use speech sounds in a meaningful way. He designates certain things with creative strings of sound similar to patterns he has produced before. In other cases, he makes a phonetic stab at replicating some of the sound patterns of his parents, siblings, and friends. When he does so, his utterances still sound pretty much like his earlier vocalization patterns. The reason is related to the way the child decides a particular cognitive question: whether the sounds he hears are enough unlike the ones he already is making to warrant some sort of special effort. In most cases, they will not be, because the child cannot be sure which features are crucial and which are trivial, and he cannot know how much phonetic precision is required to play this particular game. Anyway, it is not clear that he has a set of efficient motor–phonetic strategies for correcting any deviations he might notice in his speech. Consequently, the child borrows freely from the repertoire of sounds he developed as an infant and still has at his disposal. Our continuity model predicts that segmental substitutions will occur whenever the child attempts to represent a word in which the salient sounds are *not* in his repertoire, but are perceptually similar to sounds that *are* in his repertoire.

Let us, then, take a look at the probable contents of this phonetic repertoire and examine the perceptual similarity of consonant sounds. In doing so, perhaps we may determine if, with the two, one can predict child substitutions.

Infant Sound Production

If infant vocal play is not phonetically random, as we have said, what is the evidence that it is in some way patterned? Cruttenden (1970) recorded the babbling of his twin daughters from birth to 15 months. Prior to the emergence of "first words," at 14 and 15 months for the two girls, neither was heard to produce [Θ], [ð], [s], [z], [ʃ], [ʒ] and one never uttered [f] or [v]. Their babbling did contain at least one variant of all other English consonants, though Cruttenden does not give their relative frequencies. He does, however, comment that there was a "general drift" toward adult phonology even before the appearance of the first word. Somewhat earlier, Brown (1958) had referred to this phenomenon as "babbling drift."

The Cruttenden (1970) report makes it clear that infant babbling is phonetically selective, but to what degree and in what ways? Oller, Wieman, Doyle, and Ross (1976) transcribed the babbling of infants at 6–8 months and at 12–13 months. Their analysis showed that consonant sounds occurred with different frequencies; due to the frequency differences, certain featural trends emerged. For example, singletons were more common than consonant clusters. This, they reasoned, could account for cluster reduction in child speech. On similar grounds, Oller *et al.* also found support for final consonant deletion, deaspiration, final devoicing, stopping, gliding, and fronting. The authors asserted that with such data it should be possible to predict substitutions and deletions some months or years ahead of their appearance, adding that the accuracy of such projections might be enhanced by taking into account the "acoustic and/or articulatory similarities" of the sounds in question.[1]

In a series of studies in the 1940s, Irwin (1947) reported the sound productions of infants at different ages. He tabulated the frequency with which consonants and vowels were transcribed reliably by his team of listeners. Though the subjects ranged from 1 to 30 months, we selected the yearlings for analysis as they would have been at or near their first word.

Table 10.1 shows the English consonants in decreasing order of frequency of production by Irwin's infants. The segments were not tabulated by syllable position so the figures in the table represent a summing of their occurrence across various syllabic structures. By separating the first 12 from the second 12 sounds, one gets an idea of what the contents of the infants' phonetic repertoire might be. The upper half accounts for 92.3% of the infants' total consonant production, the 12 less frequent sounds for just 5%. There are other things to observe in this tabulation. Most of the sounds commonly replaced by children are in the lower half; many of the replacing sounds are in the upper half. All the stop consonants are among the top 12; so are the glides and two of the nasals. Six of the eight fricatives are in the bottom group. The voiced stops are more frequent than their voiceless cognates; among the fricatives the opposite is true in all but one case.

It is possible, of course, that the production frequencies of year-old infants reflect the corresponding statistics of the adult language. Indeed, an examination of several tabulations indicates that the more common infant sounds also are more frequent in the spontaneous speech of 1–4-year-olds (Olmsted, 1971, Table 31), children in the early elementary grades (Mader, 1954, Table 1) and adults (French, Carter, and Koenig, 1930, Table 8).

As mentioned earlier, Oller *et al.* (1976) were able to predict many patterns of child substitution purely from the statistical frequency of the various segmental "preferences" in the vocalization of infants. It also is true, based on the phoneme frequencies of *adults* (French *et al.*, 1930, Table 8), that one can predict that children will commit errors of cluster simplification (i.e., singletons are more frequent than clusters), final devoicing, deaffrication, stopping, and gliding. Could it be that children's errors *and*

---

[1] Elaborated somewhat in another paper (Oller and Warren, 1976).

TABLE 10.1

The Percentage of English Consonants Occurring in the Spontaneous Vocalizing of 11–12-month-old Infants (adapted from Irwin, 1947, p. 398)

Rank	Sound	Percentage	Rank	Sound	Percentage
1	h	31.77	13	v	1.03
2	d	20.58	14	l	.96
3	b	9.79	15	θ	.85
4	m	6.69	16	z	.56
5	t	4.34	17.5	f	.37
6	g	4.15	17.5	ʃ	.37
7	s	3.45	19	ð	.34
8	w	3.39[a]	20	ŋ	.33
9	n	2.65	21.5	ʒ	.10
10	k	2.12	21.5	r	.10
11	j	1.77	23.5	tʃ	.00
12	p	1.63	23.5	dʒ	.00
		$\Sigma\chi = 92.33$			$\Sigma\chi = 5.01$

[a] Sum of /w/ and /hw/; I have added the affricates which, according to Winitz (a student and collaborator of Irwin's), were not heard even at 30 months. The column totals are less than 100% because I deleted /ç/, /x/, and /ʔ/.

infant production frequencies simply mirror the segmental statistics of their linguistic environment?

There are several reasons for supposing that this is *not* so. First, there are the phonologies of other languages. Ruhlen (1976) inventoried 700 of the languages of the world. From these we selected the 135 languages having a million or more speakers. The consonants in Irwin's top 12 were found in an average of 100 languages, the sounds in the bottom 12 occurred in an average of 52 of the inventories. Consequently, we have our first indication that the infants may not simply have been imitating and preserving in their mimicry the relative frequencies of the sounds in their linguistic environment.

Second, we have a little-noticed study, some 25 years old, which reported the spontaneous sound productions of 48 deaf children (Carr, 1953). Though they were 5 years old, these deaf-born children had received no formal speech or language training at the time of the observations. Carr found that when she put three children in the same room they vocalized spontaneously, and she was able to obtain 90 samples per subject over a 4-week period. One can see from Table 10.2 that Carr's top 12 sounds constitute 92% of the deaf children's spontaneous utterances.[2] Eleven of the 12 also are among Irwin's high-frequency sounds, but there are also some interesting differences between the deaf children's sound-production frequen-

[2] One might speculate that if the infant frequencies were not influenced by the environment, languages must reflect the preferences of the organism that constructed them initially, and that continues to change them over time.

TABLE 10.2
*The Percentage of English Consonants Occurring in the Spontaneous Vocalizing of 5-Year-Old
Deaf-Born Children (adapted from Carr, 1953, p. 26)*

Rank	Sound	Percentage	Rank	Sound	Percentage
1	b	20.48	13	k	1.57
2	m	12.19	14	ʃ	.87
3	p	11.36	15	v	.82
4	h	10.47	16	g	.66
5	w	10.18[a]	17	θ	.61
6	f	8.35	18	r	.20
7	d	6.79	19	ð	.19
8	j	4.69	20	ʒ	.04
9	l	3.16	22.5	ŋ	.00
10	n	2.71	22.5	z	.00
11	t	2.64	22.5	tʃ	—
12	s	2.01	22.5	dʒ	—
		$\sum \chi = 95.03$			$\sum \chi = 4.96$

[a] The sum of /w/ and /hw/. The affricates were added on the assumption that they were listened for but
not heard to occur.

cies and those of the hearing infants. The main one is that labial sounds were
more frequent in the deaf. One might suppose that this was due to the greater
visibility of labial productions. However, /p b m w f v/, as a group, also are
more frequent in Ruhlen's (1976) cross-linguistic data than they were in
Irwin's infants. Consequently, there is no reason to believe the frequencies
of deaf children's productions are, for visual reasons, different from the
productions of hearing infants. But the deaf children were observed at 5
years, when articulatory maturation is nearly complete in normal children.
For this reason, it was assumed that their data would provide a more realistic
base for predicting the errors of hearing children at about that age.

According to our continuity model, the infant's repertoire provides the
raw material from which substitutions are created, with high-frequency
sounds replacing low-frequency ones. Beyond that, the specific substitutions
are determined initially by perceptual similarities between the items in the
two sets.

Perceptual Similarities

It would be nice to know what a child perceives when a particular speech
sound is heard, but that is not possible. Even a cooperative, normally articulating adult cannot indicate *what* is perceived. With young children,
whose articulatory capability is limited, about the best we can do is get a
discrimination or recognition response, and this is not satisfactory for a
number of reasons (cf. Locke, 1979, in press a). By default, we turn to the

misperceptions of adult listeners. Fortunately, a study by Wang and Bilger (1973) reports some valuable information on adult misperception. Their data are more appropriate to the child case than were the earlier findings of Miller and Nicely (1955), to which Olmsted (1966) turned in supporting his argument that children's acquisition of phonology was guided primarily by perceptual factors. Wang and Bilger's (1973) data, unlike those of most other studies, include the misperceptions of all English consonants, and in CV and VC syllables. The syllable-position comparison is important as there are several sound changes that are strongly position-sensitive. Another feature of the Wang and Bilger study is that some of the data come from a control condition in which misperceptions were encouraged merely by turning down the intensity of the signal. For several reasons, these kinds of errors are preferable to those achieved with filtering or competing noise.

Wang and Bilger's listeners found it somewhat difficult to identify weak signals in quiet, and they produced a nicely analyzable corpus of errors. Syllable position proved to be a powerful determinant of misperception, and it is apparent that many child substitutions could be predicted *solely* on the basis of adult misperceptions. The main difficulty in doing that is a problem of directionality. Some misperceptions are unidirectional, and in the same way that children's substitutions are (e.g., f/Θ = 321; Θ/f = 63 in Wang and Bilger, Table 6). Other confusions are skewed in the opposite direction (e.g., w/r = 8; r/w = 19). But /f/ is more common than /Θ/, and /w/ more frequent than /r/, in the utterances of Carr's deaf children. Therefore, there was reason to be optimistic that the two sets of data would converge upon the errors children commonly make.

Although readers are encouraged to consult the data reported in Wang and Bilger (particularly Tables 6–9), Table 10.3 reports the figures we used to generate substitutions. The CV data represent a blending of two Wang and Bilger tables, as do the VC data. This was necessitated by the fact that they used two stimulus sets for each syllable shape. We also have violated the Wang and Bilger matrices in a very major way: the stimuli were selected from Carr's second 12 sounds, and only her first 12 sounds were treated as possible responses. This is because the continuity model predicts that no high-frequency sound will be replaced, and no low-frequency sound will intrude, in a segmental substitution.

Because all predictions of child errors were generated from the data in Table 10.3, it now is appropriate to consider the child substitutions to be predicted.

Children's Substitutions: The Explicanda

There have been many surveys (cf. Prather, Hedrick, and Kern, 1975; Templin, 1957) that report what children *did not say* correctly, but there are

TABLE 10.3
Adult Misperceptions of Low-Intensity CV and VC Syllables in Quiet[a]

CV responses

CV stimuli	b	m	p	h	w	f	d	j	l	n	t	s
k	11		71			14	14				89	4
ʃ	3		5	3	7	0	5	15	21	12	4	{7}
v	128	26	7			23	11				10	6
g	27		4			3	41				4	5
θ	64	22	22			321	11				15	{34}
r	7	7	6	7	8	6		3	27	2	6	6
ð	88		11			21	24				1	18
z	15	2	7	5	5	10	9	13	5	5	8	20
tʃ	7	5	3	6	3	9	5	2	4	5	17	13
dʒ	2	4	3	0	2	3	8	14	10	6	6	8

VC responses

VC stimuli	n	m	p	f	d	n	t	s
k	2		66	18	7		{36}	4
ʃ	7	3	9	6	9	6	17	18
v	38	5	5	41	22	14	5	11
g	22		16	18	7		10	4
θ	9	2	11	73	42	9	14	{28}
ð	38	3	8	10	77	57	7	6
ʒ	1	5	9	4	13	13	3	15
ŋ	4	44	9	6		41		4
z	4	4	4	8	12	10	8	42
tʃ	5	4	10	2	2	3	17	5
dʒ	2	7	16	4	25	5	20	11

[a] The holes in these matrices are due to the fact that /l w j h m n/ in the CV set, and /m n/ in the VC set, were tested with a different set of response alternatives than the other CV and VC syllables. Neither subset had as stimuli the sounds for which there are no entries here. Figures enclosed by { } were ignored in the rankings for prediction because the sounds in question were involved in bidirectional substitutions (see text).

[b] Adapted from Tables 6–9 in Wang and Bilger, 1973. Stimuli and responses are limited to the low-frequency (rank 13–24) and high-frequency (rank 1–12) items, respectively, from our Table 10.2.

few investigations that tell what a large group of children *did say*. In one, Olmsted (1971) tabulated the substitutions committed by 100 children, from 1:3 to 4:6 years of age, in their spontaneous speech. As the children were free to select their own targets, Olmsted's data may reflect avoidances of the type described by Ferguson and Farwell (1975). Unfortunately, Olmsted did not report his subjects' substitutions by syllable position, which severely limits their usefulness here.

The children in Snow's (1963) study, regrettably, were older, all 438 enrolled in the first grade (median age was 7:2). Their speech was elicited mostly by picture naming, with two different words at each of three word positions. All English consonants were tested in their allowable word positions.

Before Snow's data could be used here, it was necessary to make several adjustments. One modification involved the phoneme /ʒ/. There were 374 /dʒ/ substitutions in the word *garage*. Since many adults pronounce garage with a /dʒ/, this was not treated as an error. As the other word-final /ʒ/ was in the word *mirage*, which would have to be elicited echoically, this case was likewise ignored.

There were numerous w/hw substitutions in *wheel* and *whistle*, and there is reason to doubt that these changes were errors in that "the distinction between /w/ and /wh/ is dying in English (Williams, 1970)." In *swimming*, there were 146 cases in which /n/ replaced /ŋ/ but only five n/ŋ substitutions in *swing*. Since "swimmin' " is a common morphologically based change in the speech of midwestern adults, and /ŋ/ was not otherwise replaced, that "error" was similarly dropped.

We made one major modification in Snow's tabulation; bidirectional errors were discarded. This was because it seemed that no simple theory could predict both the substitution of X/Y and the converse, Y/X. There were six cases in which the more common substitution occupied less than 75% of the sum of both directions of change. In the word-initial position, there were three ($s - \int$, $t\int - \int$, $s - \Theta$) and there were three word-final ($z - ʒ$, $s - \Theta$, $t - k$). All others were from 87 to 100% unidirectional, and they were retained.

Table 10.4 shows the 15 most frequent substitutions in word-initial and word-final positions. To the right of each substitution is the number of Snow's 438 children who made the error. The total possible is 876 as there were two elicitation words per phoneme at each of the two word positions. Because the frequencies fell off very rapidly after the first few errors, we expected to find our predictions similarly reducing in accuracy as we went down the two lists.

To the immediate right of the initial and final errors, in Columns 2 and 4 of the table, are the substitutions predicted from the figures in Table 10.3. The ordering of these predictions reflects a procedure in which each prospective substitution was ranked on two bases. Consider the example of

TABLE 10.4

The More Common Word-Initial and Word-Final Substitutions of Children (from Snow, 1963, Table 1) and Substitutions Generated by the Continuity Model

Word-initial				Word-final			
Observed		Generated		Observed		Generated	
f/Θ	145[a]	f/Θ	1–1[a]	v/ð	212[b]	d/ð	1–1[a]
b/v	144[a]	b/v	1–1[a]	f/Θ	130[a]	f/Θ	1–1[a]
w/r	76[a]	t/k	1–1[a]	s/ʃ	98[a]	p/k	1–1
s/z	48[a]	d/g	1–1[a]	s/z	81[a]	m/ŋ	1–1
d/ð	24[a]	l/r	1–1	Θ/ð	53[b]	s/z	1–1[a]
w/l	24[b]	s/z	1–1[a]	f/v	50[a]	f/v	2–1[a]
d/g	21[a]	b/ð	2–1	d/ð	37[a]	s/ʃ	2–1[a]
dʒ/z	15[b]	t/tʃ	2–1	tʃ/dʒ	35[b]	t/tʃ	2.5–1
t/k	13[a]	j/dʒ	2–1	b/v	32[a]	d/dʒ	3–1
d/z	11	w/r	1–2[a]	d/g	15	b/g	3–1
ð/z	9[b]	p/k	1–2	t/Θ	13	s/ʒ	3–1
s/tʃ	7	m/v	1–2	f/ð	11	n/ð	1–2
t/Θ	6	t/dʒ	1–2	p/f	7[b]	b/v	1.5–2[a]
n/ð	6	d/ð	2–2[a]	k/g	5[b]	d/Θ	2–2
f/v	5[a]	f/v	3–2[a]	d/v	5	t/ʃ	2.5–2

[a] Successful predictions.

[b] Substitutions in which both sounds belong to the same high- or low-frequency category in Table 10.2.

[c] Observed substitutions are followed by their raw frequencies; generated substitutions by the ranks used in their selection and ordering (see text).

syllable-initial /f/ for /Θ/, which Table 10.3 shows to have occurred 321 times. In our rankings, the first number shown for f/Θ is a 1 because there were more /f/s for /Θ/ than for any other sound (in second place is /f/ for /v/, at 23). The second number in the f/Θ ranking also is a 1 because /Θ/ was replaced by /f/ more frequently than it was replaced by any other sound (/b/ for /Θ/ is in second place with 64). Predicted errors are listed in decreasing order, with priority assigned somewhat arbitrarily to the second rank.

Errors marked by [b] are those that the theory could not predict because the two sounds belonged to the same upper 12 or lower 12 category. There were eight such cases, though in six of them the intruder still was more frequent in deaf children's vocalization. One other error, initial n/ð, could not be predicted because there were no perceptual data for it in Table 10.3. Of the remaining 20 errors, 14 were predicted, 8 in the word-initial position and 6 word-finally. This amounts to a 47% accuracy rate overall.[3]

The errors predicted by the model were committed by Snow's subjects an average of 65 times; the unpredicted substitutions occurred with a mean frequency of 28. In other words, the model predicted the more common substitutions better than the less common ones. The top 7 errors in each list

[3] When Irwin's data were substituted for Carr's, there were 10 correct predictions, 5 in each syllable position.

(i.e., $N = 14$) were predicted with 71% accuracy, the bottom 8 in initial and final lists with just 25% accuracy.

Of the 14 successfully predicted substitutions, 11 also were among the top 15 substitutions committed by Olmsted's subjects. Of the 16 missed predictions, just one was among the list compiled from Olmsted's data. Consequently, of the 12 substitutions common both to Snow and Olmsted, 11, or 92%, were predicted by the model (based, though, on the original list of 30 predictions).

Perhaps we might also learn something by looking at the false positives in the second and fourth columns of Table 10.4 (those not followed by ^{a}). Some, such as t/tʃ and d/dʒ were not all that illogical. A reexamination of Snow's data shows that for final /tʃ/ there were 106 intrusions of [ts]; for final /dʒ/ there were 53 substitutions of [dz]. The generation of l/r is logical featurally, and it was the most common segmental error of normal adults in slips of the tongue (Shattuck-Hufnagel and Klatt, 1979, Table 2). The substitution of l/r also was a common short term memory error (following veridical input) in Wickelgren's (1966, table 12) subjects. Many of the other false positives would be eliminated, making room for additional correct predictions, by the imposition of nonselective linguistic rules. For example, none of the observed substitutions involved as many place-of-articulation changes as some of our false positives (e.g., p/k; b/g) or as many features as certain others (e.g., b/ð). Simple constraints on the featural range of a substitution would produce even better predictions.

Discussion

Speech substitutions undoubtedly are sensitive to the child's developmental stage. In the early stages of acquisition, it is probable that errors are more straightforwardly perceptual. As the child recognizes his failures at perfect mimicry, and learns that certain previously ignored features are linguistically important, he will invoke articulatory strategies for closing the gap between his own and adult forms. Since Snow's subjects were 7 years old, it is likely that, in some cases, we put our model to an unrealistic test: accounting for motor errors with perceptual data. Consider, for example, word-initial d/z, which our model did not predict. Shattuck's (1975) data show that /d/ was the most common replacer of /z/ in misspeaking adults. Our model could not predict Θ/ð, but Wickelgren's (1966) data show that, when /ð/ is forgotten, it is replaced most frequently by /Θ/, and loss from short term memory usually follows a period in which the material is motorically rehearsed (cf. Locke and Kutz, 1975).

Moskowitz (1975) has a nice observation on this point. In one part of her article, she refers to f/Θ as a child's "best temporary solution," distinguishing it from ''[d] for /ð/ [which] is not an expedient, temporary solution. When imitating /ð/, the child does resort to the parallel expedient phone [v]. Otherwise he is busily at work, attempting to approach [ð] in an articulatory way, via [d] [p. 49].'' Unfortunately, we assume most of Snow's subjects had long since abandoned ''temporary solutions'' in favor of those produced by articulatory strategy, to which our predictions would have been less sensitive.[4]

Innateness and Suppression

Stampe (1969) has said that certain processes are innate and require suppression if the adult forms are to be realized. We disagree that processes need to be suppressed. If anything, it would be the overextension of segments that would need to be inhibited. And it probably is fortunate that the child has some segments available to him when he begins to utter words and wordlike forms. Since the child appears to use them *judiciously*, putting repertorial units in place of missing segments of similar sound, much of his early speech is intelligible. And, indeed, the most common sounds in the adult inventory are already in his repertoire. Consequently, he is better off— for communication purposes—suppressing nothing until he is capable of applying suppression selectively. From this perspective, his infant repertoire gives him the opportunity to speak with fair intelligibility while he acquires additional articulatory skill and learns enough about the linguistic system to effect the appropriate distributional constraints.

That the child is marginally intelligible during this period is a function not just of the perceptual similarity between targets and intrusions, and the high frequency of his producible units, though these factors are not to be underestimated. His intelligibility also is a function of certain characteristics of his listeners, most importantly, the fact that they are accustomed to hearing children speak in particular ways, and as they, themselves, once spoke. Consequently, the adult listener has heard this sort of speech before, and he possesses a set of transforming rules[5] that permit him to recover—or, more accurately—to hypothesize many of the ''intended'' phonemes.

Although it may be a bit unfashionable these days to appeal to language ''habits,'' this is precisely what our model requires, for we suppose that a certain amount of phonological inertia is a property of the system. Though not completely like the problems of second-language learners, there are certain similarities; one can anticipate specific sound changes from a knowledge

---

[4] Not only were we forced to use the data of too-old subjects, the lack of really appropriate data made it necessary to reconstruct a dynamic process from group data, and from three separate populations at that. What is needed to test our model adequately—or, as far as we can see, any model—is an investigation that tracks the speech production and perception of individual children from infancy into early childhood. Indeed, without such a study, it is unlikely that the critical issues of phonological acquisition will ever be resolved or fully understood.

[5] I base this on the fact that most adults can, to some extent, generate ''baby talk.''

of infant vocalization patterns as one may predict—with some success—the adult learner's prospective difficulties with L_2 from an awareness of the structure of L_1. In that sense, one might suggest that all first-language learning is to a degree "second," with interference and projection from so-called "prelinguistic" periods.

What Is Learned?

Any theory of acquisition that invokes or depends upon innate processes—if not innate segments—needs to deal with the question of how much of the "stuff" of phonology must be learned. Should the child get as much credit for a correct /b/, which was babbled often, as he does for an identifiable /z/, when no [z]-like sounds were heard in his prelexical vocalizations? The concept of phonological *error* appears not to be of much theoretical use. To be sure, there are degrees and types of *mismatch*, but even they could be viewed as casualties of the misalignment between infant production preferences and adult surface requirements. It is too bad for the child that his parents' language has an /r/, but he is lucky it has a /w/.

It should be possible to construct a developmentally optimal phonology in which the primary consonants were /b/, /m/, /p/, /h/, and /w/. If this reduced "phonological" errors—because the child's phonetic proclivities just happened to map conveniently onto the target language—then it could be said that phonology has a very large phonetic component indeed! Left to be learned, discovered, and hypothesized would be the structure of the system, the contextual dependencies, and the rest. But in this artificial sound system could the phonological *units* more or less emerge?[6]

Phonetic and Cognitive Accounts

What if phonological rules had a basis in phonetic fact? Is there any reason to think of linguistic patterns and phonetic processes as incompatible? It would seem more harmonious, and ultimately more productive, to think of patterns of sound change simply as that, patterns. They exist in the mind of the analyst. Whether there is any physiologic or perceptual motivation for them, whether the child is aware of them, and so forth, would be useful information in the linguistic analysis, just as the linguistic analysis identifies the phenomena for which a phonetic explanation may be sought.

Ferguson (1977) has said that "It is all very well to hypothesize and speculate about the nature of phonological systems, but we can no longer afford to do so in as much ignorance as we have often shown about human anatomy and physiology [p. 296]." In other words, phonological *explanation*

---

[6] Elsewhere (Locke, in press, b) I have elaborated upon the mechanisms that seem to operate in children's phonological development; one of them, maintenance, is like what I am suggesting here for this "artificial" case.

is more likely to succeed if the pertinent physiological phonetics are pursued. Let us consider an example. In language change, the final devoicing of obstruents has been a frequent effect (cf. Hock, 1975). Final devoicing also is common in children (cf. Ingram, 1976). Were one to seek a phonetic basis for this change, one could imagine the following logic. Subglottal pressure is a function of the relaxation pressure generated by the passive forces of exhalation; relaxation pressure primarily is a function of the volume of air in the lungs. Thus, during the course of an utterance, as the volume of air in the lungs decreases, subglottal pressure also decreases unless expiratory muscle activity is increased (cf. Ladefoged, 1967). This, by itself, would predict more devoicing finally than initially, and this is the characteristic child pattern. And there is a conspiracy afoot: A perceptual theory would make the same prediction. Of the devoicing in misperceptions, 69% comes from syllable-final forms (Wang and Bilger, 1973, Tables 6, 8).

One can be even more specific. Subglottal pressure must exceed supraglottal pressure (by 2–3 cm aq; Ladefoged, 1967) if voicing is to occur, and voiced fricatives are measurably higher in intraoral pressure than are voiced stops (Prosek and House, 1975). Consequently, an aerodynamic model would predict more devoicing of fricatives than of stops. This prediction also would be correct. According to Snow (1963, Table 1; controlling for the unequal number of stops and fricatives), 93% of children's final devoicing occurs in the fricatives. And, again, perceptual data permit the same prediction; 58% of all devoicing misperceptions (Wang and Bilger, 1973, Tables 6, 8) is due to the fricatives.

Not all linguistic rules presently have such tidy phonetic explanations. But with additional research it may ultimately develop that most patterns of sound change can be accounted for in articulatory or perceptual terms. To do so, I believe, also might suggest to the speech clinician some specific ways to manipulate articulation and more directly induce phonological change.

There is evidence that "voiced" and "voiceless" sounds may be identified by VOT (Lisker and Abramson, 1964), vowel length (Raphael, 1972), duration of the stop closure (Lisker, 1957), fundamental-frequency contour (Hombert, Ohala, and Ewan, 1979) or aspiration (Winitz, LaRiviere, and Herriman, 1975). The perceiver, of course, is not consciously aware of the cues; he only knows that a child was expected to say /b/ and that instead /p/ was perceived. If there are enough cases of this, a pattern is seen to emerge and the child is said to "devoice." But what happened to all that good phonetics research? It is understood that, to be manageable, children's utterances may require some type and degree of reduction in their analysis. However, it is not clear that we know enough of the articulatory dynamics to select the phonetic basis for their reduction.

To categorize by feature or phonological process—given our present state of knowledge—sometimes may be prematurely committal, and it may even mask the relevant phonetic effects. First, far from being a "physical" process, as Stampe (1973) classifies it, perception is very much constrained by one's sense of phonological structure (cf. Locke, in press, b) and lexical expectation (Oller and Eilers, 1975; Olney and Scholnick, 1977). As perception and organization also are influenced by speech-production capabilities, it may be difficult to prove that any sound change is motivated *purely* by a single component of the total process. Second, a sound change could be due to an articulatory process in one phonetic environment that diffused to other contexts. The motivation for its present use might not, then, be *traceably* phonetic (cf. Hyman, 1976). Third, as we pointed out earlier, there is nothing in the concept of rule that makes it incompatible with phonetic motivation. Designations such as fronting, gliding, and the like simply are taxonomic categories. It is not even clear that they in any behavioral sense are descriptive, and clinically their use may be counterproductive. When the prefix de- is used, it suggests that a phonetic feature has been removed from a segment with the rest of the bundle left intact. In the case of [t] for /tʃ/, is there deaffrication, fronting, stopping, depalatalization or all of these? To the child, it just could be that it is none, if he has had lots of experience producing [t]-like sounds, little experience saying [tʃ]-like sounds, and thinks them not different enough to warrant the articulatory exploration or work necessary to their distinctive production.

Acknowledgments

This work was supported, in part, by NICHD Grant HD–05951 and by NIMH Grant MH 31965–01. I am grateful to Lee Becker for his helpful comments on a preliminary draft.

References

Brown, R. (1958) *Words and Things*, Free Press, Glencoe, Ill.

Carr, J. (1953) "An Investigation of the Spontaneous Speech Sounds of Five-year-old Deaf-born Children," *Journal of Speech and Hearing Disorders*, 18, 22–29.

Cruttenden, A. (1970) "A Phonetic Study of Babbling," *British Journal of Disorders of Communication*, 5, 110–117.

Ferguson, C.A. (1977) "New Directions in Phonological Theory: Language Acquisition and Universals Research," in R.W. Cole, *Current Issues in Linguistic Theory*, Indiana University Press, Bloomington.

Ferguson, C.A. (1978) "Learning to Pronounce: The Earliest Stages of Phonological Development in the Child," in F.D. Minifie and L.L. Lloyd, eds., *Communicative and Cognitive Abilities, Early Behavioral Assessment*, University Park Press, Baltimore, Md.

Ferguson, C.A. and Farwell, C.B. (1975) "Words and Sounds in Early Language Acquisition: English Initial Consonants in the First Fifty Words," *Language*, 51, 419–439.

Ferguson, C.A., and Garnica, O. (1975) "Theories of Phonological Development," in E. and E. Lenneberg, eds., *Foundations of Language Development* (Vol. 1), Academic Press, New York.

French, N.R., Carter, C.W., and Koenig, W. (1930) "The Words and Sounds of Telephone Conversations," *Bell System Technical Journal*, 9, 290–324.

Hock, H.H. (1975) "Final Weakening and Related Phenomena," paper read at the 1975 Mid-America Linguistics Conference, Lawrence, Kansas.

Hombert, J-M., Ohala, J.J., and Ewan, W.G. (1979) "Phonetic Explanations for the Development of Tones," *Language*, 55, 37–58.

Hyman, L.M. (1976) "On the Nature of Linguistic Stress," in L. Hyman, ed., *Southern California Occasional Papers in Linguistics No. 4*, University of Southern California, Los Angeles, 37–81.

Ingram, D. (1976) *Phonological Disability in Children*, Elsevier, New York.

Irwin, O.C. (1947) "Infant Speech: Consonantal Sounds According to Place of Articulation," *Journal of Speech Disorders*, 12, 397–401.

Jakobson, R. (1968) *Child Language, Aphasia and Phonological Universals*, Mouton, The Hague.

Ladefoged, P. (1967) *Three Areas of Experimental Phonetics*, Oxford University Press, London.

Lisker, L. (1957) "Closure Duration and the Intervocalic Voiced-voiceless Distinction in English," *Language*, 33, 42–49.

Lisker, L., and Abramson, A.S. (1964) "A Cross-language Study of Voicing in Initial Stops: Acoustical Measurements," *Word*, 20, 384–422.

Locke, J.L. (in press) "Levels of Speech Perception Analysis," in W.D. Wolfe and D.J. Goulding, eds., *Articulation and Learning* (2nd ed.), Charles C Thomas, Springfield, Ill. (a)

Locke, J.L. (in press) "Mechanisms of Phonological Development in Children: Maintenance, Learning and Loss," *Papers from the Sixteenth Regional Meeting of the Chicago Linguistic Society*. (b)

Locke, J.L. (1979) "The Child's Processing of Phonology," in W.A. Collins, ed., *The Minnesota Symposia on Child Psychology* (Vol. 12), Lawrence Erlbaum, Hillsdale, N.J.

Locke, J.L., and Kutz, K.J. (1975) "Memory for Speech and Speech for Memory," *Journal of Speech and Hearing Research*, 18, 176–191.

Mader, J.B. (1954) "The Relative Frequency of Occurrence of English Consonant Sounds in Words in the Speech of Children in Grades One, Two, and Three," *Speech Monographs*, 21, 394–300.

Miller, G.A., and Nicely, P.E. (1955) "An Analysis of Perceptual Confusions among some English Consonants," *Journal of the Acoustical Society of America*, 27, 338–352.

Moskowitz, B.A. (1975) "The Acquisition of Fricatives: A Study in Phonetics and Phonology," *Journal of Phonetics*, 3, 141–150.

Ohala, J.J. (1974) "Phonetic Explanation in Phonology," in *Papers from the Parasession on Natural Phonology*, 251–274, Chicago Linguistic Society.

Oller, D.K., Wieman, L.A., Doyle, W.J., and Ross, C. (1976) "Infant Babbling and Speech," *Journal of Child Language*, 3, 1–11.

Oller, D.K., and Eilers, R.E. (1975) "Phonetic Expectation and Transcription Validity," *Phonetica*, 31, 288–304.

Oller, D.K., and Warren, L. (1976) "On the Nature of the Phonological Capacity," *Lingua*. 39, 183–199.

Olney, R.L., and Scholnick, E.K. (1977) "An Experimental Investigation of Adult Perception of One-word Utterances," *Journal of Child Language*, 15, 131–142.

Olmsted, D.L. (1966) "A Theory of the Child's Learning of Phonology," *Language*, 42, 531–535.

Olmsted, D.L. (1971) *Out of the Mouth of Babes*, Mouton, The Hague.

Prather, E.M., Hedrick, D.L., and Kern, C.A. (1975) "Articulation Development in Children Aged Two to Four Years," *Journal of Speech and Hearing Disorders*, 40, 179–191.

Prosek, R.A., and House, A.S. (1975) "Intraoral Air Pressure as a Feedback Cue in Consonant Production," *Journal of Speech and Hearing Research*, 18, 133–147.

Raphael, L.J. (1972) "Preceding Vowel Duration as a Cue to the Perception of the Voicing Characteristic of Word-final Consonants in American English, *Journal of the Acoustical Society of America*, 51,1296–1303.

Ruhlen, M. (1976) *A Guide to the Languages of the World*, Language Universals Project, Stanford University.

Shattuck-Hufnagel, S., and Klatt, D.H. (1979) "The Limited Use of Distinctive Features and Markedness in Speech Production: Evidence from Speech Error Data," *Journal of Verbal Learning and Verbal Behavior*, 18, 41–56.

Snow, K. (1963) "A Detailed Analysis of Articulation Responses of 'Normal' First Grade Children," *Journal of Speech and Hearing Research*, 6, 277–290.

Stampe, D. (1973) "A Dissertation on Natural Phonology," Doctoral Dissertation, University of Chicago.

Stampe, D. (1969) "The Acquisition of Phonetic Representation," *Papers from the Fifth Regional Meeting of the Chicago Linguistic Society*, 443–454.

Templin, M.C. (1957) *Certain Language Skills in Children*, University of Minnesota Press, Minneapolis.

Wang, M.D., and Bilger, R.C. (1973) "Consonant Confusions in Noise: A Study of Perceptual Features," *Journal of the Acoustical Society of America*, 54, 1248–1266.

Wickelgren, W.A. (1966) "Distinctive Features and Errors in Short-term Memory. *Journal of Speech and Hearing Research*, 18, 176–191.

Williams, F., ed. (1970) "Analysis of Production Errors in the Phonetic Performance of School-age Standard-English-speaking Children," Office of Education, United States Department of Health, Education, and Welfare.

Winitz, H., LaRiviere, C., and Herriman, E. (1975) "Variations in VOT for English Initial Stops," *Journal of Phonetics*, 3, 41–52.

Chapter 11

THE ROLE OF CONTEXT IN MISARTICULATIONS

PAULA MENYUK

Introduction

The assessment tools that have been used and are still being used by speech clinicians to determine the articulation problems of language-disordered children provide good evidence of how phonological production in these children and in normally developing children has been viewed. These tools are primarily designed to elicit from the children isolated words containing "target" phonemes in various positions (initial, medial, and final) in these words. It was assumed for a very long time, not only by speech clinicians but by students of child development, that the acquisition of phonology could best be described as a process of mastering the articulation of speech sounds in the language (McCarthy, 1954). Thus, early studies of phonological acquisition describe the *sequence* of acquisition of speech sounds in the three positions of words just described.

The data obtained from these assessments were used by speech clinicians to determine three things. First, the clinician could presumably determine whether or not the child was performing in a manner comparable to that of normally developing peers as these tools provide age norms for speech-sound mastery. Second, the child's degree of deviance from normal phonological development could presumably be determined by the number

CHILD PHONOLOGY
VOLUME 1: PRODUCTION

and types of errors in production, and the child then, was classified as having a moderate, mild, or severe articulation problem. This second piece of information could be used to determine whether or not therapeutic intervention should proceed immediately or if it could be postponed to allow for maturation. Third, and very important, a therapeutic program of intervention could presumably be designed based on the particular problems of each child. Therapy could be concentrated on bringing about articulation mastery of the particular phonemes in the particular positions that a child had difficulty with.

The conclusions drawn from these data are based on several false assumptions. First, it is clearly not the case that production of isolated words provides an accurate picture of the phonological development of either normally developing or language-disordered children. Second, a single sampling of production of a speech sound in an isolated word and the number of errors do not indicate the degree of deviance of a child's phonological development. Such issues as consistency of error and conditions of error or nonerror are not addressed in such assessments nor is the issue of type of error addressed as error is grossly categorized as omission, substitution, or distortion. Furthermore, the relation between perception and production of speech-sound differences is also not examined because the stimulus materials ordinarily used to assess speech-sound discrimination are not those used to assess articulation. Finally, therapeutic programs based on the notion that practice and mastery of speech sounds in isolated words will bring about desired change are questionable given the myriad facts that have been obtained on coarticulation effects in connected speech (Ohman, 1966). Indeed, the literature is filled with discussions of the problems of "carry over." That is, children appear to master a sound during therapeutic sessions and then maintain their original realizations of a sound in connected speech.

An awareness of the problems associated with such types of assessment led to the application of Jakobson's theory of phonological development (Jakobson, 1968) to the study of articulation problems in children. This theory postulates that the process of phonological acquisition is one of differentiating the distinctive features of speech sounds in a *fixed sequence*. Thus it was hypothesized that the difference between children who were acquiring phonology normally and those who were not was either one of delay (i.e., these children were going through the same fixed sequence of distinctive feature development but at a much slower rate) or that these children were having difficulty with particular distinctive features (Menyuk, 1968).

Assessment instruments were designed to contrast certain features in both perception and production of words. In some instances, these words were embedded in sentences and children were asked to perceive differences and articulate differences between words within sentences. It followed that suggestions were made that therapy be based on teaching these children a feature distinction with one set of speech-sound contrasts since, theoretically, once a feature distinction was acquired, it would be supplied to all germane contexts. For example, if a child did not preserve the + voice distinction with initial stops, teaching them the difference between /p/ and /b/ should lead to their differentiation of all other stops on the basis of voicing (i.e., the /t/–/d/ and /k/–/g/ distinctions, (Compton, 1975).

The view of these children as having particular difficulties in feature distinctions appeared to provide better insights into their articulation problems than did simple assessment of speech-sound mastery because errors with clusters of speech sounds could be explained. However, there are clearly false assumptions in this position as well. Speech-sound feature distinctions are not acquired by normally developing children in an all-or-none manner as theorized by Jakobson (1968) for productive acquisition as shown by Moskowitz (1970), or as theorized by Schvachkin (1973) for perceptual acquisition as shown by Garnica (1973). Indeed it is not clear that either single features or segments play a critical role in the initial acquisition of phonological categories and rules (Menyuk and Menn, 1979). If this is the case with normally developing children, there is no reason to assume that children with articulation problems are more sophisticated in their strategies of phonological acquisition than are normally developing children.

Neither approach to the study of articulation problems in children provides several important pieces of information. One missing piece of information is how speech is generated by these children when conversing with others. Another is how it is generated in particular sentence structures, and in particular phonological sequences that play a particular role in these structures. Data concerning the relation between speech perception and production in these children under similar conditions are also missing; that is, when the children are perceiving and producing the same sounds in the same contexts. Still another piece of missing information is whether or not there are generalizations that can be made about the phonological processing of children within particular diagnostic groups; that is, groups of children that presumably share the same cause of difficulty. In this chapter, bits of this missing information will be examined.

The population to be described consists of only those children with suspected central nervous system (CNS) abnormalities; thus the population is limited. The effect of context on the speech-sound realizations and perceptual distinctions of these children will be examined. However, not all aspects of processing within the same contexts were examined with all children. Therefore, the information is limited. Finally, context in this discussion is defined as the conditions under which speech behavior was sampled (i.e., the task conditions) and the linguistic structure in which speech was contained (i.e., nonsense syllables, words, sentences, and discourse). Although contexts were also clearly limited, the results of these studies will be discussed in terms of possible approaches to the study of speech-sound use by children who misarticulate.

The Effect of Linguistic Context

In all the studies to be described the children were without any of the detectable abnormalities of the peripheral or central processing systems that can affect speech development such as hearing loss, mental retardation, or cerebral palsy. These children were of average or above average intelligence as measured by performance scales of standard intelligence tests. Their development, as recorded in their medical histories, was quite normal except for two children who gave some evidence of motor difficulties. These difficulties did not involve their peripheral speech mechanisms.

The purpose of the initial study to be described (Menyuk and Looney, 1972) was to examine the effect of meaningfulness and particular linguistic structure on the speech-sound reproduction of both language-disordered and normally developing children. The mean age of the normally developing children was 4:6 years and the mean age of the language-disordered children was 6:2. The children were given two types of tasks. One was a sentence repetition task in which the sentences varied across a narrow range of sentence types (primarily active–declarative, imperative, negative, and question sentences). Every American-English consonant in initial, medial, and final position was represented several times. In addition, a fairly large number of initial and final consonant clusters was represented. The final clusters were in some instances part of the word stem and in other instances part of a grammatical morpheme. A few weeks later these same children were asked to repeat strings of three nonsense syllables.

The list of nonsense-syllable strings represented initial, final, and medial singleton consonants in American-English and there were two lists of such strings. In one list, a triad of syllables held the consonant constant and varied the vowel (for example, /mi/, /ma/, /mu/). In the other list, syllables in a triad varied in terms of either place of articulation (for example /pa/, /ta/, /ka/) or in manner (for example /pa/, /ba/, /ma/). All reproductions were both transcribed immediately and retranscribed from tape recordings to test for scorer reliability.

The results of this study indicated that meaningfulness of the material (i.e., nonsense versus words) and morphemic and/or syllabic context (initial, medial, and final) played a role in accuracy of recall for both groups of children. It was found that words were more accurately reproduced at a significant level than nonsense syllables by the language-disordered children. The difference for the normally developing children only approached significance because, in general, they made very few errors with either type of material. In the repetition of words, the position of the consonant in the word caused no significant difference in percentage of errors within a group, but the trends varied for the two groups. The normally developing children had proportionately less difficulty with both initial and final consonants than did the language-disordered children, and the type of error observed in each position with a consonant varied for both groups. With nonsense syllables, where the consonant was held constant over a syllable, the effect of position played a significant role in accuracy of recall (initial consonants were recalled more accurately than either medial or final consonants) by language-disordered children but not by normally developing children. Repetition of nonsense syllables that contained consonants in a triad that varied, either in place or manner, caused much greater difficulty for both groups of children than did the first type of nonsense syllable.

In addition to these general findings on the effect of meaningfulness and position of consonant in accuracy of recall for both groups, it was also found that the grammatical role of a segment or a morpheme had a marked effect on the accuracy of reproduction for both groups but especially so for the language-disordered group. For example, there was a marked tendency for the language-disordered children to omit final consonants when they were grammatical morphemes and to either omit or substitute auxiliaries and modals. This latter behavior was more frequent in negative and question sentences as compared to active–declarative sentences. There was an obvious relation between the syntactic categories and rules available to the children and their ability to reproduce phonological segments and sequences.

There was marked variation in the performance of the children in the language-disordered population. This was not the case with the children who had no language problem. To illustrate the variation between the children in this presumably homogenous group and to examine the effect of context on how phonological segments were recalled in this group, two children's performance on the different tasks with ± voice stops, two ± voice stridents (/s/ and /z/) and two liquids (/l/ and /r/) will be described. Both of the children were the same age (6 years) and both were boys. One of the children (V. S.) was described as having a moderate to severe articulation problem and the other (K. M.) as having a moderate problem. The data presented in Table 11.1 indicate the kinds of errors each of the children made with the set of sounds in varying positions when repeating words in sentences.

These data indicate that the primary distinction between the children is what they do with sounds in the final position in words, and what they do when repeating words in general. V. S. makes proportionately more errors with the sounds when they are in final position in a word then when they are initial or medial. Furthermore, almost all his errors are ones of omission; either of the sound (especially if it is a syntactic marker) or of the entire word in which the sound appears (especially if it is a functor). K. M., on the other hand, not only makes fewer errors, but most of his few errors are substitution errors (the exception is final /z/) and his errors are quite consistent (i.e., /d/ for /g/, /t/ for /k/, /w/ for /r/). Thus the nature of V. S.'s problem, at least in repetition of sentences, seems to be primarily omission of sounds in final position. If only the number of sounds with which each

TABLE 11.1
Errors in Repetition of Certain Sounds within Sentences by Two Subjects

Sound	No.[a]	Initial		No.	Final		No.	Medial	
		K. M.	V. S.		K. M.	V. S.		K. M.	V. S.
/b/	(7)			(1)				(3)	
/d/	(6)	1,0[b]	1,∅[c]	(6)				(3)	1,w
/g/	(5)	4,d		(2)	1,dz			(2)	1,k
/p/	(5)			(2)				(2)	
/t/	(7)		1,∅	(11)	1,∅		3,∅	(3)	2,0
/k/	(13)	4,t;ld	3,∅	(14)			1,∅	(2)	
/s/	(6)		1,∅	(5)			3,0	(1)	
/z/	(1)			(17)	1,∅		8,0;7∅	(3)	1,0;ld
/r/	(4)	2,w		(15)	6,w		15,0	(4)	
/l/	(6)			(11)			3,∅	(4)	

[a] Number of instances when sound appeared in position.

[b] 0 = omission of sound.

[c] ∅ = omission of word in which sound appears.

child had difficulty were calculated to determine degree of severity of the problem, then K. M. and V. S. would be similar as 12 and 11 sounds are "misarticulated" respectively. Clearly, both the nature and severity of the problem differ for the two children.

It is not the case that omission is the strategy most frequently employed by children with more marked articulation problems. T. H., another child in the population, who was also described as having a moderate to severe articulation problem, as was V. S., did not primarily omit words. His problem appeared to be inconsistency in realization of segments. For example, in the five instances in which /p/ appeared initially, he realized it as /f/ in one instance, /b/ in one instance, and correctly in the three remaining instances. In the seven instances in which /t/ appeared initially, it was realized correctly in four instances, and as /k/ in three instances. In the four instances in which /š/ appeared initially, it was correct once, realized as /r/ twice, and omitted once.

A comparison was made of the phonological reproduction in nonsense syllables of the same sounds examined in word repetition by the two children K. M. and V. S. Table 11.2 presents the data on their reproduction of sounds with the first set of nonsense syllables; that is, the set in which the consonant is held constant across the triad. In this set, each sound was presented three times in three positions.

As can be seen in Table 11.2, phonological reproduction by both children when repeating nonsense syllables is, on the whole, markedly different from their reproduction of the same segments when repeating words. For K. M., the + anterior stops (/p/ and /t/) are repeated as their + voice cognates in both initial and medial positions. This is never observed in this child's repetition of words. In final position, two of the + voice stops are reproduced as their + nasal cognates. This also never happens in the reproduction of words. V. S. also performs in a very different manner in this task. Although final sounds are, again, very frequently omitted, substitions occur much more frequently in this task and, in general, appear to be quite random.

Different strategies are used by different children in this population when the task is reproduction of phonological sequences. Each child uses a different strategy to reproduce meaningful material and to reproduce meaningless material. Thus behavior varies across children and across linguistic contexts. One might logically presume, given a reasonable model of language processing, that, in repetition of sentences, higher-order semantactic categories are being used for reproduction of morphemes within sentences. Apparently this allows V. S. to perform fairly well with the initial portion of morphemes. He cannot, however, preserve final portions, especially when the final portions are grammatical markers. His performance with nonsense syllables indicates that he is not a very accurate tracker of the segmental aspects of phonological sequences per se, even initial portions. In this context, his behavior becomes not only less accurate but also more random. V. S. appears to be relying on higher-order categorizations to make "good guesses" about the principal morphemes in the sentences. K. M., in general, pronounces phonological sequences much more accurately. His phonological realization rules in both linguistic contexts are much more predictable. In both contexts, some rules remain constant. For example, in both contexts the sequence C + stop, − anterior, − coronal + V is realized as C + stop, + anterior, + coronal + V. However, he, like V. S., appears to be relying

TABLE 11.2
Errors in Repetition of Certain Sounds within Nonsense Syllables by Two Subjects

	Initial		Final		Medial	
Sound	K. M.	V. S.	K. M.	V. S.	K. M.	V. S.
/b/			1,m;1∅	2,∅		2,∅
/d/		3,k	[a]	3,∅		2,∅
/g/	3,d		1,n,2∅ 2,h,1∅		2,d	1,d;2∅
/p/	3,b			1,k;1∅	3,b	1b;1d
/t/	2,d			1,∅;1k	2,d	1k;1,g;1d
/k/	3,t		1,t;1p	2,∅	2,d	3,∅
/s/		1,z		2,∅	3,z	2,g
/z/		1,s;1d	1,∅	3,∅	1,y	1,w;1∅
/r/	3,w	1,∅			3,w	3,w
/l/			2,∅	1,y;1∅	1,y	2y;1∅

[a] ∅ sound or syllable omitted.

on higher-order categories for reproduction of morphemes, as his performance is quite different in sentence repetition than in nonsense-syllable repetition and, for example, voicing distinctions in stops are better preserved in the former linguistic context than in the latter.

These data not only highlight the importance of linguistic context in determining the phonological knowledge of the children but, also, the fact that the children within this population differ quite markedly from each other. One can say that this distinction was initially noted since K. M. was labeled as having a moderate articulation problem and V. S. a moderate-to-severe problem. However, these labels do not lead to a better understanding of each child's particular problem nor to an understanding of where the problems lie. For example, such labels would not indicate that K. M. is a much more accurate processor of phonological segments than is V. S., or that V. S. relies much more heavily on higher-order categories for good approximate guesses than does K. M., and that he is attending primarily to the beginning of sequences. It is this latter type of information, it seems to me, that can be quite helpful in understanding the particular problems of particular children. To obtain this information, phonological processing within both meaningful and meaningless contexts needs to be examined.

The Effect of Task Context

As was stated in the introduction to this chapter, it is rarely the case that phonological production and perception in these children are assessed using the same stimulus materials and with the same task requirements. There is very good evidence that the results of speech-sound discrimination tests or experiments and word-generation tests and experiments can be seriously affected by the familiarity of the stimulus materials (Barton, 1976; Langdon, 1977). We have already discussed the effect of familiarity on reproduction. What might appear to be a difficulty in discrimination between sounds or in producing or reproducing sounds may, in reality, be a function of what particular lexical items are available to the child. Furthermore, it is often the case that, when children's speech-sound discrimination is being assessed, they are asked to make minimal-pair distinctions. This is never the case when production or reproduction is being assessed.

There were several questions that were pursued in the study to be described. One was concerned with the relation between perception and production of the *same speech-sound* stimuli when the task requirements were also the same; that is, when each task required selection of an appropriate response from a small set in which members differ minimally. A second question was concerned with the similarities or differences in the relation of speech-sound discrimination and production in children with articulation problems and in those without such problems. A third question was concerned with whether or not within-population differences existed in patterns of relation between speech-sound production and discrimination in children with articulation problems. The findings of the previous study described indicated that this might be the case.

In this study, a group of children with articulation problems and a group of children without such problems were given the same four sets of lexical items for assessment of speech-sound discrimination and speech-sound reproduction. Each set contained items contrasting with each other in terms of the initial segment of the word, and the contrast was in terms of place of articulation. Sounds that are often presumably confused with one another both in normal development and in problematic development were selected. One set contrasted /p/, /t/, /k/, another /b/, /d/, /g/, another /f/, /š/, /s/, and another /w/, /r/, /l/. To test discrimination and reproduction, an adult female speaker recorded words with these sounds in initial position. The words used were *pot, tot, cot* in Set 1, *beer, deer, gear* in Set 2, *feet, seat, sheet* in Set 3 and *white, right, light* in Set 4. There were 36 stimulus words in each set with each word appearing 12 times in a random arrangement. A practice period preceded the presentation of each set. The children were asked to identify and to name pictures representing the stimuli in each set. They were asked to point to the appropriate picture when they heard "Show me *X*" and to reproduce the word when they heard "Say *X*." No set was presented until the experimenter was confident that the children understood the task and could identify and name the pictures.

The population of children without articulation problems had a mean age of 4:2 and the population of children with articulation problems had a mean age of 6:3. Overall, the children without articulation problems did significantly better in both tasks than did children with articulation problems. However, three distinctly different patterns of phonological processing could be observed in the population of language-disordered children (Groups A, B, and C). These distinct patterns of performance were based on differences among language-disordered groups in how each performed in the two processing tasks (discrimination versus reproduction) and also on distinctions among them as to which speech-sound sets the children had greater or lesser difficulty with. Table 11.3 indicates the overall percentage of errors of the language-disordered and normally developing children, the overall percentage of errors of each group of children with articulation problems (Groups A, B, and C) and percentage of errors in each task with particular sets of sounds.

As can be seen in Table 11.3, the Group A children are markedly different in their perceptual performance as compared to their reproductive performance with the speech sounds. They do much better in the former as compared to the latter. Group B also has greater difficulty in reproduction than in perception. Both Group C and the children without articulation prob-

TABLE 11.3
Percentage of Errors in Discriminating Between Members of Certain Speech-Sound Sets

| | Perception | | | Production | | |
	Articulation problem		No problem	Articulation problem	No problem	
OVERALL ‰	14.6		12.6	20.3	6.6	
Within set %						
p/t/k/	19.6		21.6	9.5	4.1	
b/d/g	16.9		11.7	27.6	9.5	
s/f/š	7.6		2.3	33.6	3.8	
w/r/l	14.8		14.9	27.5	10.9	
Between groups	A	B	C	A	B	C
Overall	9.2	16.5	18.2	20.1	24.3	16.7
Within set						
p/t/k	12.4	19.4	26.9	16.5	12.8	9.3
b/d/g	10.0	20.8	19.9	12.9	22.2	18.1
s/f/š	5.1	13.9	3.7	29.0	42.4	9.7
w/r/l	9.3	11.0	24.1	23.0	30.0	29.6

lems show a tendency to have fewer difficulties in reproduction than in perception. Besides this distinction between groups, Group A's pattern of errors in perception is fairly similar to that of Group C and the No Problem group, with some differences. The latter groups have greater difficulty in perceiving differences among the members of the /w/, /r/, /l/ set than the /b/, /d/, /g/ set, whereas the inverse is true of Group A. However, these are only tendencies. Where they and Group B differ markedly from Groups C and children with no problems is in reproduction of members of the fricative set (/f/, /s/, /š/). Although there are differences in percentage of errors for the Group C children and the children with no problem, they, nevertheless, tend to show the same pattern of errors in terms of direction of differences between perception and production and, also, in terms of which sets of sounds in which task they are having greater or lesser difficulty with.

Not only are percentages of errors different for the groups depending on the task (perception versus production) and on the particular speech sound set but, also, patterns of types of errors varied among the groups. The most frequent type of error in each task with each sound and the number of differing errors that were observed in the reproduction task for each sound in all four groups is presented in Table 11.4.

For the children with no problem, none of the reproduction errors are outside of the speech-sound set being presented; that is, confusions are always among the members of the speech-sound set. Furthermore, no response is an extremely rare occurrrence in both tasks for these children (a

.004% occurrence). With Group A, errors outside the speech-sound sets can be observed in the reproduction task and, also, errors of omission are more frequent in this task than in the perception task. Furthermore, Group A children are very inconsistent in their substitution of sounds. For example, substitutions for /s/ include /Θ/, /d/, /š/, /t/ and /f/ as well as omission. Omission of response is also a relatively frequent occurrence for Group B in both the perception and reproduction of words, but much more frequent in reproduction than in perception and much more frequent in this group as compared to Groups A and C. There is a tendency in this group to be inconsistent in their reproduction substitutions, although it is not as marked as with Group A children. They also, like the other groups of children, indicate confusion among the stops, but, unlike the other children, they omit these sounds in reproduction rather than substituting them. All three groups of children with articulation problems have particular difficulty in realizing the fricative sounds and either omit them, as with Group B, or replace them with + voice stops as in Groups A and C. Finally, there is much greater consistency between the most frequent types of errors in perception and production for the nonproblem group as compared to any of the other groups; their perceptual and productive confusions matched for the most part. This was not the case with children with articulation problems.

It has often been stated that there is no correlation between the perceptual problems and the productive problems of children with articulation

TABLE 11.4

Most Frequent Types of Errors in Perception and Production and Number of Differing Errors for Each Group in Production

	Groups											
	A			B			C			No problem		
Sounds	Per	Pro[a]	No.	Per	Pro	No.	Per	Pro	No.	Per	Pro	No.
/p/	t	k	4	t	∅	1	t	k	2	k	k	2
/t/	p/k	d	4	k	∅	1	p	k	2	k	k	2
/k/	t	t	4	p	p	2	t	p	2	t	p	1
/b/	d	d	1	g	∅	1	g	d	2	d	0[d]	
/d/	g	g	3	g	th[+vb]	1	g	b	2	g	0	
/g/	d	d	3	d	d	4	d	d	3	d	d	2
/f/	s	d	4	s	∅	2	š	b	2	š	š	2
/s/	f	d	6	š	∅	2	š	b	3	š	š	1
/š/	s	th[−vb]	7	s	f	3	s	s	4	s	s	1
/w/	l	∅[a]	3	r	r	3	l	r	2	l	r	2
/l/	e	∅	4	w	∅	3	w	∅	3	w	w	2
/r/	w	w	3	w	w	3	w	w	3	w	w	2

[a]   Per. = perception, Pro. = production

[b] $^{-v}$ = − voice + voice = + v

[c]   ∅ = no response

[d]   = no error

problems. Indeed, it has been suggested that children with so-called "functional" articulation problems may have no perceptual problems at all (Powers, 1957). The findings of this study indicate the possibility that there are marked differences between the perceptual categorizations of phonological segments and the productive realization of those same segments by children with articulation problems. This appears to be so even when the same stimulus materials are being used and the task requirements are the same; that is, to differentiate between members of a set that vary in only one parameter. However, these data do not indicate that these children are without perceptual problems. Instead, they indicate that such problems exist within the population, and that it is important to assess both aspects of speech-sound processing with the same stimulus materials. Processing of synthetic speech materials would provide more information about the parameters used to perceive differences, and spectrographic analysis of production would provide more information about the parameters used to produce differences. There is evidence that the latter type of analysis can reveal differences that the ear alone cannot perceive, and that these differences differentiate between productions that sound alike (Chaney, 1978; Menyuk and Klatt, 1968).

These data as well as the data obtained in the previous study indicate that there are marked differences between children in this population. However, whereas the previous study only described differences in phonological realization rules among children, the present study indicates that there are also marked differences among these children in their ability to perceive segmental speech differences. The question that remains unanswered is: In what way are segmental perceptual problems related to the perception and production of connected speech? That this is an important question is attested to by the fact that the previous study also indicated that there were marked differences in the phonological realizations of the same child when the linguistic contexts of the stimulus materials were altered. In assessing children with articulation problems, this is a crucial question.

The Effect of Conversation

The last study to be discussed is a study of very young children who were observed while they participated in a play group for language-disordered children. The purpose of the study was to examine the communicative competence and linguistic behavior of these children. It is clear that the ability to communicate effectively is not only dependent on what has been termed "pragmatic" rules or rules of conversation but, also, on the ability to understand what is being said and the ability to be intelligible. Watson (1977), in a study of the conversation participation of a group of language-disordered children and a group of normally developing children found that the former group much more frequently took the "back-channel" in conversation than did the latter group. The question that remained was whether the language-disordered children's behavior was a function of avoidance, developmental delay, or a difficulty in both understanding the language put to them and a difficulty in retrieving appropriate responses.

At the beginning of this study, the children ranged in age from 2:8 to 3:7. There were three girls and two boys in the population. The children were followed for a period of 4 months. During this time, weekly half-hour samples of their language were collected. In general, the same amount of data was collected for each child and in the same activities so that the conditions for language generation were quite similar for all the children. The children varied in their level of language performance. Two of the children were generating multiword utterances. All the children had articulation problems, but the nature of their misarticulations varied in conjunction with the structure of the utterances they produced. To oversimplify, the two children with more sophisticated sentence structures were also more intelligible than the two children who were producing primarily one-word utterances, and the child who alternated single and multiple word utterances was between the two groups in terms of intelligibility. All of the children except one made some progress in both their speech-sound production and in the structure of utterances produced over the 4 month period.

For this discussion, only the question of whether phonological production was affected by the communicative intent of the child in conversation with others was examined. For each child, such an effect was observed. This was so even for one child who showed little progress over the 4-month period. To illustrate the effect of communicative intent on phonological realizations, we will provide some examples for each child. In each instance the change that occurred in the production of a segment or segments took place within an observational session. The following are the examples:

1. M. omits final /s/ and /z/ as a rule even when it is part of a morpheme. M., in requesting information initially, says "Weh di wun go? (Where this one go)" gets no response and says "Weh dis wun go?" and when requesting action says "Pud dis hi! (Put this here)."

2. R. usually omits all final consonants, but in an exchange with another child begins by saying "Deh wan my." and then changes it to "Deh wan mine (That one mine)." When providing information about what he likes to eat he says "Me lay tuna fish (Me like tuna fish)" and "Me lay melo dus (Me like tomato juice)."

3. Am. has difficulty with vowels as well as consonants and produces primarily single-syllable utterances. When requesting that a particular story be reread to him, he starts by saying "gi,gi (gppse)" and then changes it to "maw gu (more goose)." When demanding the right to some toy doctor equipment, he says "Eymuh daktuh (His name, doctor)" and produces one of his rare multisyllabic utterances.

4. J. uses place markers for most functor words (primarily "uh"). She

is trying to convince the teacher that it's juice and crackers time. She begins by saying "I time uh eat" then changes to "It time tuh eat (It time to eat)." She frequently reduces medial clusters. When demanding an object, she begins by saying "Beybaw" and changes it to "Beytbaw (baseball)" and, when requesting an action, begins by saying "I wan you do sopin" and then changes it to "I want you do sompfin." (I want you do something)."

5. Al.'s language is, in general, the most impoverished of the group. Most of her utterances are single syllables and her lexicon is very limited. Final consonants are eliminated and initial consonants often substituted. When she wished to leave the room (a frequent wish) she began by saying "Waw, waw (walk)" changes it to "wawk, wawk" and finally "Dawya, wawk, wawk (Teacher's name, walk, walk)."

The finding that general rules of phonological realization are modified when the child is attempting to communicate important (to them) information is hardly a new finding. There are instances of this kind of behavior that have been observed in normally developing children (Chao, 1973). The point being made here is that children with articulation problems also can and do alter their phonological realization when they are motivated to communicate "more intelligibly." The conclusion that might be reached from these data is that assessment of these children's phonological performance that does not take into account what they can do under appropriate circumstances provides a too narrow picture of their phonological abilities.

Some Conclusions and Suggestions

It has been argued in this chapter that phonological perception and production by children can vary depending on the context, linguistic and situational, in which this behavior is sampled. Implicit in this argument is a model of language processing that is hardly innovative. It is that processing on the phonological level is dependent on higher-level categories and relations; pragmatic and semantic and syntactic. These higher-level categories and relations will affect both perception and production of phonological sequences. One distinction between children with articulation problems and those without such problems may be their differing abilities to process at different levels of the language, (semantic, syntactic, morphophonological, and phonetic) when the task requires it. This appears to be the distinction between the mature and the immature child phonologist. (Menyuk, 1977). Children with articulation problems may have problems at all these levels or only at some of them. A further distinction may be in the relation between perceptual and productive phonological processing in these children. Relations between these processes may be much more distant in children with articulation problems than in those without such problems. It is clear, however, that the nature of the problem may vary from child to child in this population. Indeed, the degree of variability among these children may be another mark of distinction between them and children without language problems.

What was suggested in the introduction to this chapter was that present methods of assessment of these children's phonological behaviors provide us with very limited data and, furthermore, that these limited data are not very helpful in understanding their behavior or in planning therapeutic interventions. These approaches, although limited, are not, however, incorrect. The alternative of collecting language samples and analyzing these data would also be limited. A better alternative, it seems to me, would be to examine these children's phonological processing under varying conditions of context; both linguistic and situational. Information about how a child categorizes synthetic speech stimuli along a continuum, how a child discriminates between and produces isolated nonsense syllables and words, how a child deals with phonological sequences in certain sentence structures, and how a child communicates in conversational interaction are all needed to understand the nature of his or her problem and to determine what should be done about it. Therapeutic planning needs to be based on in-depth studies of the phonological processing of these children and not simply on screening devices. Given that phonological processing in these children can vary depending on context and that we can define contexts, the problem for us now is to devise generic situations that will provide us with information about each child's phonological abilities in each domain or context. It is, admittedly, not a small problem but, nevertheless, a solvable one.

References

Barton, D.P. (1976) "The Role of Perception in the Acquisition of Speech," Unpublished Doctoral Dissertation, University of London.

Chaney, C.F. (1978) "Production and Identification of /y,w,r,l/ in Normal and Articulation Impaired Children," Unpublished Doctoral Dissertation, Boston Univeristy.

Chao, Y.R. (1973) "The Cantian Idiolect: An Analysis of the Chinese Spoken by a Twenty-eight-month-old Child," in C.A. Ferguson and D.I. Slobin, eds., *Studies of Child Language Development*, Holt, Rinehart and Winston, New York, pp. 13–33.

Compton, A.J. (1975) "Generative Studies of Children's Phonological Disorders: A Strategy of Therapy," in S. Singh, ed., *Measurement Procedures in Speech, Hearing and Language*, University Park Press, Baltimore, pp. 55–90.

Garnica O.K. (1973) "The Development of Phonemic Speech Perception," in T.E. Moore, ed., *Cognitive Development and the Acquisition of Language*, Academic Press, New York, pp. 215–222.

Jakobson, R. (1968) *Child Language, Aphasia and Phonological Universals*, Mouton, The Hague.

Langdon, H.W. (1977) "Determining a Language Disorder in a Bi-lingual Spanish-English Population," unpublished Doctoral Dissertation, Boston University.

McCarthy, D. (1954) "Language Development in Children," in L. Carmichael, ed., *Manual of Child Psychology* (2nd ed.), John Wiley and Sons, New York, pp. 492–630.

Menyuk, P. (1977) *Language and Maturation*, MIT Press, Cambridge, Mass.

Menyuk, P. (1968) "The Role of Distinctive Features in Children's Acquisition of Phonology," *Journal of Speech and Hearing Research*, 11, 138–146.

Menyuk, P. and Klatt, D. (1968) "Children's Production of Initial Consonant Clusters," *Quarterly Progress Reports of the MIT Research Laboratory of Electronics*, 91, 205–213.

Menyuk, P., and Looney, P. (1972) "Relationships among Components of the Grammer in Language Disorder," *Journal of Speech and Hearing Research*, 15, 395–406.

Menyuk, P., and Menn, L. (1979) "Early Strategies for the Perception and Production of Words and Sounds," in P. Fletcher, and M. Garman, eds., *Studies in Language Acquisition*, Cambridge University Press, Cambridge. pp. 49–70.

Moskowitz, A. (1970) "The Two-year-old Stage in the Acquisition of English Phonology," *Language*, 46, 426–441.

Ohman, S.E.G. (1966) "Coarticulation in VCV Alterances: Spectrographic Measurements," *Journal of the Acoustical Society of America*, 39, 151–168.

Powers, M.H. (1957) "Functional Disorders of Articulation: Symptomatology and Etiology," in L.E. Travis, ed., *Handbook of Speech Pathology*, Appleton-Century-Crofts, New York, pp. 707–768.

Schvachkin, N.Kh. (1973) "The Development of Phonemic Speech Perception in Early Childhood," in C.A. Ferguson and D.I. Slobin, eds., *Studies of Child Language Development*, Holt, Rinehart and Winston, New York, pp. 91–127.

Watson, L. (1977) "Conversational Participation by Language Deviant and Normal Children," Paper presented at the annual meeting of the American Speech and Hearing Association.

Chapter 12

PHONOLOGICAL RHYTHM: DEFINITION AND DEVELOPMENT

GEORGE D. ALLEN AND SARAH HAWKINS

One of the persistent problems faced in research on phonological rhythm is the difficulty of conveying to others what is meant by this term. Much of the blame may be laid at history's door: So little attention has been given by linguists to this important topic that there is no conventional wisdom upon which we may draw. Consequently, most people rely on a traditional definition of rhythm as the pattern of beats within a strict metric scheme, a definition that is too restricted for understanding the rhythm of speech. To establish a context for this chapter, therefore, we shall first describe in some detail our broader conceptualization of phonological rhythm and then review published material relevant to the topic as thus defined and to the goals of this research.

A Definition of Phonological Rhythm

One may define rhythm most broadly as "the structure of a sequence" (cf. Allen, 1975). This definition has two very important implications. First, it establishes rhythm as a *structure,* which can therefore be understood only as a relationship or set of relationships among the units making up that structure. Second, it deliberately leaves open what those units are; they can

CHILD PHONOLOGY
VOLUME 1: PRODUCTION

be features, segments, syllables, words, phrases, or paragraphs, or even sneezes or total eclipses of the moon—all that is important is that they occur in a sequence. Even the role of time is deemphasized in this definition of rhythm, for although time is necessary for both the production and perception of a sequence, it is the *structure* of the sequence that for us defines its rhythm, and time is only one of several possible components of that structure.

It is obvious from this definition of rhythm as a form of structure that it plays an organizing role in speech. But then so do syntax, semantics, and anything else of interest in linguistics, and sometimes their organization may properly be called rhythmic, too. As Hrushovsky (1960) writes on the subject of poetic rhythm, for example:

> We can observe many rhythmic factors: metrical sequences and deviations from their ideal norms; word boundaries and their relations to feet boundaries; syntactic groups and pauses and their relation to metrical groups (line, caesura); syntagmatic relations, word order, syntactic tensions; repetitions and juxtapositions of sound, meaning, elements, etc. Practically everything in the written poem can contribute to the shaping of the rhythm.

One can similarly argue that the organizing rhythm of the *spoken utterance* can be influenced by virtually any element of speech that is subject to sequential patterning.

Despite this all-inclusiveness of potential rhythmic sources in speech, some processes play a more dominant role than others in defining what is commonly felt to be the rhythm of a phrase. Speech communication is a motor–perceptual process, and thus the rhythmic structures typically found in it are of the sort that are reasonable for speakers to produce and for listeners to perceive. In our motor actions, including the production of speech, we cannot move randomly but are constrained in both rate and pattern (Allen, 1975; Michon, 1967; Miles, 1937; Miyake, 1902). Furthermore, listeners have such strong biases as to the rhythmic structures they perceive in auditory sequences, again including speech, that they impose structure which is not physically there (Allen, 1975; Coleman, 1974; Fraisse, 1963; Woodrow, 1951). Because prosodic (or suprasegmental) phonology deals explicitly with temporal–sequential constraints that fall within the domain of these motor–perceptual rhythmic biases, speech rhythm is perhaps best understood within the framework of this linguistic level.

This phonologically related rhythm greatly facilitates speech communication by contributing temporal predictability to the spoken sequence. For example, experiments using stylized synthetic intonation contours (Collier and t'Hart, 1975) or cross-spliced sentences pitting prosody against syntax (e.g., Darwin, 1975; Wingfield and Klein, 1971) have demonstrated the role of prosody in helping listeners to locate syntactic boundaries. Durational factors alone can also be crucial to speech intelligibility, as has been shown for both phonemes and larger units in real and synthetic speech (cf., Huggins, 1978; Klatt, 1976; Lehiste, 1970; Nooteboom, Brokx and de Rooij, 1976).

Listeners appear to be particularly sensitive to the rhythmic onset of stressed syllables, both when listening to speech (e.g., Cutler, 1976; Cutler and Foss, 1973, 1977; Huggins, 1972; Shields, McHugh, and Martin, 1974) and when tapping to the rhythm of their own speech (Allen, 1972). The listener appears to anticipate when stresses will occur and focuses attention at these times. As Martin (1972) argues, if speech sounds were only concatenated, with no temporal redundancy, the listener would have to attend continuously to the speech input to locate the message-bearing elements. However, "since rhythmically patterned sounds have a time trajectory that can be tracked without continuous monitoring, perception of initial elements in a pattern allows later elements to be anticipated, [facilitating] efficient perceptual strategies (e.g., attention cycling between input and processing. . .) [p. 488]." Rhythmic structure thus produces useful perceptual redundancy in speech by constraining the time when (important) articulatory events may occur.

Let us now examine this rhythmic time trajectory more precisely. Consider a simple sequential structure in which the metric beats are all similar in phonological form and equally spaced in time. The term "isochrony" has been appropriately applied to this simple meter, with the further differentiation between "syllable-timed" and "stress-timed" isochrony (Pike, 1945) depending upon whether all syllables or just stressed syllables are equally spaced. It is conceptually easy to see how such a simple metric form as isochrony might constrain the spoken phrase so strictly as to make it possible for the listener to anticipate when to look for syllables or stresses, information that would be helpful in the decoding process. Unfortunately, isochrony does not in fact characterize the rhythm of English speech, nor that of any other language; the measured time intervals between syllables and stresses have been found to vary considerably (Abe, 1967; Allen, 1972; Shen and Peterson, 1962). Thus any strictly metrical view of speech rhythm, for example, Pike's (1945) isochronic model or Martin's (1972) hierarchial model, is inadequate. This is *not* to say that the temporal configuration of the utterance is unimportant to its rhythm; to the contrary, the timing of the phrase may well be the *most* important rhythmic factor. Rather, we are arguing that this temporal configuration is not easy to describe in traditional metrical terms; phonological rhythm is the combined result of a number of concurrent sequential phonological processes, involving not just the time intervals between syllables and stresses but also the very nature of those syllables and stresses as well as a host of other phenomena (cf. Hrushovsky (1960) quote, cited earlier).

Probably the most complex aspect of phonological rhythm, from both theoretical and experimental points of view, is that the dimensions underlying it are often simultaneously involved in various other phonological contrasts as well. For example, greater phonetic duration not only signals the end of a spoken English phrase (cf. Oller, 1973) but also serves to differentiate phonologically long from short vowels, voiced from voiceless postvocalic consonants, and stressed from unstressed syllables; similarly, changes in the fundamental frequency of voicing not only mark many of the metrically accented syllables within the rhythmic phrase but also define the overall intonation contour; and the degree of stress-accent a syllable receives is determined partly by the rhythm of the phrase and partly by lexical, syntactic, and stylistic constraints. In investigating phonological rhythm, therefore, we are examining a set of interrelated phenomena, each of which aids in some way the sequential integration of the utterance while, at the same time, playing a number of other nonrhythmic phonological roles. As a result of this plurality of roles, both the rhythmic structure of the utterance and the pattern of correspondence between that rhythmic structure and its measurable physical and physiological correlates can become quite complex.

In attempting to understand better the nature of speech rhythm, we have had to make some assumptions concerning a profitable beginning point. For example, we have already mentioned that duration, intonation, and stress play important roles in defining the overall meter underlying the rhythmic structure of an English phrase. As Pike (1959) has made abundantly clear in elaborating his "particle–wave–field" concept of language, however, there are many other phenomena, both linguistic and nonlinguistic, that are of potential interest in studies of speech rhythm. For example, long-term rhythmic constraints, such as subtle changes in tempo or tessitura, allow the participants in a conversation to keep track of how their interaction is progressing. Likewise, there are many nonverbal events, such as changes in posture or facial expression, that accompany the spoken message and help to convey its organization. As interesting and important as those phenomena may be, however, we have chosen to restrict our attention largely, though not entirely, to (a) utterances the size of breath groups or less and (b) phonological processes influencing the potential metric weight of syllables.

The breath group, defined roughly as the speech output between two successive inspirations, has long been recognized as important in discussions of speech rhythm (cf., Pike, 1945). We shall not belabor this point here but just indicate briefly why we have chosen to focus on sequential structures within breath groups in our studies of phonological rhythm. Previous studies of adults' and children's abilities to control the time programs of their utterances (Cooper and Allen, 1977; Tingley and Allen, 1975) have indicated quite clearly that these programs do not extend beyond the limits of the breath group; that is, pairs of articulations within breath groups show a temporal coherence, as measured by our technique of statistical modeling, that similar pairs of articulations separated by a respiratory pause do not. We thus believe that motor preprogramming of speech is limited to phrases the size of breath groups or less and that the observable effects of specific constraints on these motor programs by phonological rhythm should be most clearly evident within those limits as well. (We have discussed this argument in more detail elsewhere; Allen, 1975.) It is also relevant to this point of view that normal auditory echoic memory (or "precategorical acoustic storage (PAS)," Crowder and Morton, 1969) has a temporal capacity of about 2–3 sec, sufficient to contain the greater part of a breath group, but not more than one at a time. It is true that there is not yet any evidence showing PAS to be directly involved with either the storage or decoding of prosodic features of speech; nor is there yet any evidence showing that listeners have particular perceptual difficulty with phrases longer in duration than PAS capacity. Nevertheless, this auditory memory does have the right characteristics to allow a listener to appreciate the rhythmic figure of a breath group in its entirety, and further research on PAS may show it to have such a role. Although we realize that many phenomena of interest in studies of sequential phonological structure do cross breath group boundaries, considerations of fluent articulatory and perceptual processing lead us to believe that a majority of the most powerful sequential constraints, and the most important linguistically and developmentally, derive from the strong interrelationships within and among the syllables uttered on a single breath. This choice of the breath group in studies of phonological rhythm is entirely analogous to the choice of the sentence as the basic unit in generative syntactic tree diagrams: There are many important syntactic processes that extend beyond the sentence, but most of the important ones do not.

The second major focus of our research so far has been phonological processes influencing the metric weights of syllables. Syllables with primary stress-accent are, to a good first approximation, the downbeats (in the musical sense) that a listener uses to divide an utterance into subphrases, also traditionally called "feet"; furthermore, the last accented syllable in the phrase is the point of origin of the so-called "terminal" intonation contour, which divides that phrase from the succeeding one. In between these rhythmic accents usually lie one or more metrically lighter unaccented syllables, some of which are very weak (the so-called "reduced" syllables) and are therefore always part of the offbeat portion of the rhythmic figure. Although most young children appear to express their terminal intonation contours acceptably from an early age, their ability to reduce weak syllables adequately develops much later. Two-year-olds tend to use far fewer reduced syllables than do adults, so that their speech rhythm has fewer syllables per foot, or more beats per utterance; in short, it sounds more syllable timed. Acquisition by the child of control over the full range of syllabic weight is thus an important step in the development of proper phrase rhythm.

It is important to note in passing the substantial role that speaking rate plays in defining the relative weights of syllables and thereby the overall phrase rhythm. Previous research on the perceptual psychophysics of time (cf. Fraisse, 1963; Woodrow, 1951) suggests that at fast rates of speech the listener will hear fewer rhythmic feet per phrase, with more syllables per foot. This apparently universal perceptual bias is reinforced by English speakers, who, according to Bailey (1978), tend to group intervocalic consonants more closely with the heavier of two neighboring syllable nuclei, this grouping becoming more pronounced as speech rate increases. Thus, with increasing rate, the relative salience of the stressed syllables increases, and the phrase sounds more and more stress timed. For reasons involving both perception and production, therefore, young children's speech should sound less stress timed than adults' simply because it is slower. In agreement with these constraints, we have observed a pair of utterances, one by a child and the other an immediate repetition by the child's mother, for which the rates differ by nearly two-to-one but for which the syllable durations, relative to total utterance duration, are nearly identical: The child's utterance sounds syllable timed and the mother's stress timed.

In this first section of the chapter, our conceptualization of phonological rhythm as "temporal–sequential structure within the breath group" has been very broad. Although in our research we have focused primarily on the length, pitch, and stress accent of children's and adults' syllables, other phonological units, both smaller than syllables (e.g., consonants and consonant clusters) and larger (e.g., words, phrases, and whole breath groups) should also be investigated. At least for the immediate future, syllables will probably dominate our own horizon; nevertheless we must be on our guard not to overlook the seemingly tangential or irrelevant. The review section that follows is thus rather all-inclusive, embracing much literature on segmental and prosodic processes whose relationship to speech rhythm is that they directly influence the sequential structure of the phrase. Only after a longer period of study will we be able to define our field of focus more narrowly.

Review of Past Research on the Development of Phonological Rhythm

Studies of English-Speaking Children

Although every researcher into the development of phonology in children makes at least some mention of the prosodies, by far the majority of the actual published data concerns segmental phenomena, and much of what remains lacks sufficient attention to phonetic detail. We shall nevertheless review here what little appears to be known about the development of rhythm in children's speech, involving linguistic and psycholinguistic studies of stress and segment timing. Additional helpful information may be found in recent reviews by Crystal (1973, 1975).

Weir (1962) suggests that some language specific prosodic changes occur within the first year of life, but this claim must be balanced by findings of Tervoort (1967) and Atkinson, MacWhinney, and Stoel (1969) that adult subjects could not reliably differentiate the sociolinguistic background of 1-year-olds using this information. Atkinson-King (1973) cites a variety of studies similar to Weir's (Chao, 1951; Lewis, 1936; Murai, 1960, 1963–1964; Nakazima, 1962; Pike, 1939), all of which share two defects: First, the presence of a small number of examples of "correct" prosody constituted evidence that the child controlled the distinction, regardless of how many incorrect uses also occurred; second, the decision as to whether or not the child used a prosodic distinction was based on one adult's perceptions, which were biased by their own adult phonological system. There are no published studies indicating the *degree* of prosodic control in a child's phonology, verified by multiple listener and acoustic–phonetic analysis of the utterances studied.

Production and Perception of Stress-Accent

One aspect of prosody that is relevant to our subject and has been studied with some care is stress-accent. For example, Risley and Reynolds (1970) showed that their 4- and 5-year-old subjects were more likely to imitate words that had been stressed (by pitch raising), so long as not too many other words in the sentence were stressed. Blasdell and Jensen (1970), using acoustically defined levels of stress, showed a similar effect for strings of nonsense monosyllables with 28- to 39-month-old children. This selective attention by children to stressed syllables, if it is in fact widespread, meshes nicely with our knowledge of the form of early reduplicated words (Ingram, 1974; Moskowitz, 1970; Smith, 1973; Waterson, 1970, 1971) and with our observations of when children learn to produce "reduced" syllable nuclei (discussed later in the chapter). All of these data suggest that the rhythm of very young children's speech will be syllable timed, since early polysyllabic utterances are composed largely of reduplicated or partially reduplicated forms that are themselves short sequences of phonologically similar, unreduced monosyllables (though usually differing in pitch accent). By the age of 4 or 5, the rhythm becomes more adult like, with increased rate and greater numbers of reduced nuclei. These data also fit well with presently emerging views of the relationship between stress, rhythm, and perceptual processing of speech (Darwin, 1975; Martin 1972, 1975).

That young children may not, in fact, be attending to stress-accent has been suggested by Eilers (1975), who showed that, when suprasegmental cues (pitch, intensity, and duration) were pitted against lexicogrammatical features (meaningfulness and word order) in a sentence imitation task for 18- to 36-month-olds, only the lexicogrammatical alterations produced statistically different performance. This apparent contradiction of the previous studies should be qualified in two ways (cf. Eilers, 1975, Table III). First, the sentences lacking suprasegmental cues were in fact imitated more poorly than the normal control sentences (Treatment II: 136 versus 152 correct for content words, and 48 versus 75 correct for function words, a substantial though nonsignificant trend). Second, and most interesting from the point of view of this discussion, there was *no* decrement in performance at all for those items whose pitch and intensity were altered but whose syllable durations were normal (Treatment III: 155 versus 152, and 74 versus 75 correct). The observed difference goes beyond mere numbers here, moreover, since Eilers writes that the trends toward poorer imitation when the pitch, intensity, and duration had been altered versus the normal imitation when pitch and intensity were altered, but duration remained normal, "were reflected by the difficulty the experimenter had in obtaining imitations in treatment II and the relative ease of persuading children to imitate treatment III type sentences [p. 236]." The presence of normal syllabic durations, and therefore more normal sentence rhythms, apparently was a very strong determinant of the children's reactions to these stimuli as sentences in their language. These data suggest that children's syllables will change in their relative durations as accent-related rhythmic patterns mature, since durational differences are both perceptible and important to the young speaker.

Although children thus may be sensitive to some differences in prosodic contour as early as 18 months, their ability to produce consistent differences in stress-accent develops much later. Atkinson-King (1973) showed, for example, that 5-year-olds are very inconsistent in their differentiation of noun phrases from compound nouns on the basis of stress placement alone, and that only by age 12 were her subjects perceiving and producing stress in a fully adult manner. She suggested that one major problem impeding children's progress in this area is interference between rules for stressing noun compounds and phrases, with which she was particularly interested, and the earlier learned rules for contrastive stressing.

Another rhythmically related stress process that has been noted by many observers of children learning English is the following: Initial weak syllables are usually omitted in children's productions of words that are polysyllabic in their adult form, whereas postnuclear weak syllables may or may not be omitted (Ingram, 1974; Moskowitz, 1970; Smith, 1973). The following items appeared, for example, in Amahl's Stage 1 (age 2:2) vocabulary (Smith, 1973): 'away' → /we:, wei/; 'banana' → /'banə/; 'escape' → /gep/. Such a process, though still in its descriptive state, gives some validation of our feeling that English is a "trochaic" language (i.e., characterized metrically by falling accent; Allen, 1975; Allen and Hawkins, 1979; Chomsky and Halle, 1968; Martin, 1972). The exact process involved here needs careful study, however, as the rule applies in different degrees for different children, and some of the attested forms contain segmental traces of the supposedly omitted initial weak syllable (e.g., Amahl's /'banə/). In other words, although the rhythmic form of children's early polysyllabic utterances may be described by a few simple rules, the process by which an individual child adapts any given adult word to his or her own system may be more complex, involving not only the word's stress pattern but also such features as the relative salience of its consonants (Waterson, 1970, 1971).

In summary, then, children appear to become sensitive to the stress patterns of phrases at about the age of 2 years, but although they may begin to signal some accentual distinctions in their own speech soon after, both their perception and their production of the full system of stress distinctions may remain inaccurate in some respects until the age of 12. Children's early polysyllabic utterances typically show a high frequency of unreduced syllables, in agreement with their apparent perceptual biases, and one of the first rhythmically important skills the child apparently must learn in order to produce fluent English phrases is that of reducing weak syllables in acceptable ways.

Production and Perception of Segment Duration

Several investigators have studied the development of durations within the syllable, involving individual vowel and consonant segments, consonant clusters, consonants within clusters, and subfeatures of both vowels and consonants. Naeser (1970) examined the vowels /i,IʌΘ/, as produced by 2- to 3-year-old children, and found that they used longer vowels before voiced as opposed to voiceless stops and fricatives. She proposed that they did so for different reasons at different ages: The youngest children appeared to mimic adult vowel durations, without control over final consonant voicing; later, as control of voicing became established, the vowels before voiced consonants became longer "by association"; finally, the association was reversed, and, as in adult English, the length of the vowel became a sufficient cue for the voicing of the consonant. More recently, Oller and Smith (1977) and Smith (1978) have shown that, although there is very little difference in the relative durations of the first and second syllables of a babbled two-syllable "word," by age 2 the differences take on nearly adult values, both absolutely and relatively. Keating and Kubaska (1978), on the other hand, found much smaller durational differences between first and second syllables in the words spoken by their single subject during a comparable age span (15 to 28 months), and they furthermore argue that infants' so-called "failure to lengthen" the final (second) syllable of a word should really be viewed as a "failure to shorten" the initial (first) syllable. This issue cannot be resolved without recourse to as yet unknown speech rate factors that influence overall syllable durations; furthermore, more subjects would be needed to support Keating and Kubaska's (1978) observations, since Oller and Smith's (1977) and Smith's (1978) sample outnumbers theirs 16 to 1. Finally, all these investigations involved only heavy syllables, but as pointed out in the previous section, mature syllable reduction occurs about 1 to 2 years later.

Hawkins (1979) investigated the duration on singleton and clustered consonants produced by children aged 4 to 7 years and found variability within and between consonant types and contexts in the maturity of their timing, and within and between children at any one time. Developmental trends were evident overall when the same children were studied 14 months later, however, and the factors influencing maturity of speech timing control appeared to differ between older and younger children. Substantially similar findings are reported by Gilbert and Purves (1977), who suggested that 5- and 7-year-olds can be roughly separated from 9- and 11-year-olds and adults on the basis of the absolute duration of their consonants. Similarly, there are large differences between children in the age at which the VOT distinction begins to be produced and is finally achieved. The pattern of production progresses from no distinctions, at around 18 months, through a series of stages that probably change fastest up to about 3 or 4 years, but are still not fully like the adults' until about 9 to 11 years (Eguchi and Hirsh, 1969; Gilbert, 1977; Kewley-Port and Preston, 1974; Macken and Barton, 1977; Menyuk and Klatt, 1975; Zlatin and Koenigsknecht, 1976). Again, manner of articulation is important in that the VOT for voiced stops is controlled earlier than for voiceless stops in English.

Within-subjects variability in VOT has been observed by Eguchi and Hirsh (1969) and others to decrease to adult norms by the age of 10 or 11 years. These trends agree, both in magnitude and in the age of total convergence, with Gilbert and Purves' (1977) findings mentioned earlier, and with Tingley and Allen's (1975) data on the durational variability of larger stretches of children's speech. Thus, control of intrasyllabic segment duration is rudimentary in the youngest speaker, and develops only slowly to its full adult form. It appears to be very sensitive to contextual influences, such as manner of articulation, and although developmental trends are evident from cross-sectional groups or longitudinal data, there are large age differences in the time when distinctions are achieved by individual children within age groups.

Summarizing these studies of the development of segment timing in English, then, children appear to produce durational differences associated with segmental phonology as early as 18 months, with vowels and consonants showing different patterns of convergence to adult norms. Vowels show mature patterns of relative and absolute duration quite early, by around 3 years for heavy syllable nuclei and by 4 or 5 years for light nuclei. Consonant durations show a much longer developmental pattern, characterized by great variability within and between children and among consonant types and contexts. Target consonant duration and variability around that target do not stabilize for the average child until about age 10 or later.

Cross-Linguistic Comparisons

English is but one language, with its own rhythmic patterns, and the comparison of data from all languages, English included, can help to differentiate between language-universal and language-specific constraints. Some of the literature already reviewed involved data from children learning to speak languages other than English, especially German (Ingram, 1974;

Moskowitz, 1970). One major finding of that research concerned the overall rhythmic form of children's early words and phrases, with a great deal of evidence pointing to a preference for a falling accent contour in English speaking children's early words. That is, although the second syllable of a two syllable word may be longer than the first, the first is usually higher in pitch, louder, and often produced with a tenser vowel quality in some sense (e.g., more peripheral, for English); in addition, adult listeners hear the first syllable as more stressed. In agreement with these data, Kroeber (1916) and Fónagy (1972) have noted the same pattern in early Zuñi and Hungarian speech, respectively, both of which also have predominantly initial stress (Hyman, 1975). However, the pattern is apparently reversed for French (personal observation), which has predominantly final accent. In addition, a more complicated pattern is found in Comanche, such that reduplicated forms have the second syllable accented (Casagrande, 1948), in contrast to the initial syllable accent of the adult language (Hyman, 1975). Thus, the pattern of falling accent noted for English apparently is language dependent, related to the fact that English nouns, which are more frequent in the early lexicon, have predominantly falling accent. Although different investigators employ different definitions of stress-accent (few of the cited studies corroborate their intuitions with acoustic measurements), these data nevertheless suggest that the accentual agreement between children's and adults' words will vary across languages and may in some cases be incomplete.

With respect to how children actually produce accented versus unaccented syllables in their early phrases, Fónagy (1972) studied the acoustic phonetic correlates of one- and two-word phrases spoken by his children as they learned Hungarian. He found that their very earliest two-word phrases were linked by parallel pitch movements, giving the whole an "unité musicale." This kind of intonational repetition is characteristic of babbling as well and may be one of the earliest correlates of phrase rhythm. In the children's later utterances, the predominant acoustic characteristic of phrase-final accented syllables was greater duration, whereas in nonfinal position the primary acoustic correlate was a pitch obtrusion, usually upwards. These results are similar to our own for English (discussed later), and the pattern agrees with both psychophysical universals of rhythmic accentuation (Allen, 1975) and prosodic features of adult English (Oller, 1973). Further research is therefore needed to determine the relative importance of universal versus language specific constraints on accentuation.

There appears to be very little additional literature on the development of rhythm in different languages, but occasional hints can be found here and there. For example, the prevalence of the reduplicated form of early words (both children's words and mothers' words to children) has been noted by Kroeber (1916) for Zuñi, Casagrande (1948) for Comanche, Voegelin, and Robinett (1954) for Hidatsa, Austerlitz (1956) for Gilyak, Ferguson (1956) for Arabic, Ferguson (1964) for Spanish, Kelkar (1964) for Marathi, Fónagy

(1972) for Hungarian, Drachman (1976) for Greek, and Stoel-Gammon (1976) for Brazilian Portuguese, reinforcing our notion that this form is somehow universal in child language. In addition, the deletion of unstressed syllables is described by Ferguson (1972) and Stoel-Gammon (1976), though they fail to note that their examples all involve pretonic position. Like most of the literature on phonological development, however, these studies make only passing reference, if any, to rhythm, and they do not treat rhythm as a distinct dimension of linguistic constraint.

The only studies of child language we have found that address phonological rhythm directly are by Burling (1966), Kirk (1973), Drachman and Malikouti-Drachman (1973), and Malikouti-Drachman and Drachman (1975). Burling's study demonstrates a cross-linguistic similarity in the accentual form of nursery rhymes, such that there are generally four accents to a line and four lines to a stanza. His data, drawn primarily from English, Chinese (Peking dialect) and Bengkulu, but containing some Cairo Arabic, Yoruba, Serrano, Trukese, and Ponapean examples as well, are very suggestive of a universal rhythmic organization within early phrases. They are *only* suggestive, however, as they were transmitted by adult native speakers and we therefore do not know how children in those cultures would in fact speak the rhymes.

Kirk (1973) is apparently the only investigator to test directly the relative strength of rhythmic versus tonal versus segmental constraints in children's speech. Her study, involving four children between the ages of 2 and 3 years who were learning to speak Gã (a tone language), examined the relative frequence with which the rhythm, tone, and segments were distorted when the children spontaneously repeated words and phrases that they heard around them. Her results, based on impressionistic transcriptions of 108 repeated sentence fragments found in 25 hours of tape recorded speech, show that tone was repeated by the children most accurately, segments least accurately, with rhythmic accuracy, measured here as the correct number of syllables and degrees of vowel length, lying intermediate. She corrected her observed error frequencies by the total number of chances for error (tone and rhythm are properties of the syllable, which are fewer in number than segments), demonstrating that the segmental error rate remains highest even when thus corrected. Kirk's (1973) work therefore presents, for the first time, a clearly supported developmental sequence for these three important phonological processes: Tonal contrasts are controlled earliest, rhythmic (here durational and syllabic together) next, and segmental last. This is not to say, of course, that the child does not *notice* contrasts of one sort or another earlier or later in the sequence, but only that, generally speaking, the child is further along toward adult control with tone and intonation than with rhythm and the full system of segmental contrasts. Some additional support for this order of acquisition comes from Kroeber (1916), who observed that a Zuñi child at age 2 had falling accent on his words, in agreement with the adult rhythmic pattern, but showed no evidence of either vowel or consonant length contrasts (p. 532).

It is not hard to find a physiological correlate for this difference in developmental schedule between tone, quantity, and segmental phonology: Tonal contrasts are signaled largely by changes in fundamental frequency, which originates in the larynx; quantity contrasts correlate primarily with durational differences, which are controlled by some presumed timing control mechanism in the CNS (Allen, 1973); and segmental contrasts involve a wide array of articulatory processes using both glottal, supraglottal, and durational mechanisms. The rates of maturation of these different physiological systems are presumably different, so that there is ample possibility for differences in phonological acquisition to result directly from differences in the rates of maturation for the relevant structures. More important, however, the systems of contrasts involve different degrees and kinds of coordination between structures (e.g., temporal coordination between larynx and articulators for VOT distinctions); thus, the complexity of the rules to be learned may influence their time of acquisition. This may be why, even though speech timing control matures rather slowly (Gilbert and Purves, 1977; Hawkins, 1976, 1979; Tingley and Allen, 1975), quantity contrasts that involve only two degrees (long versus short) are controlled far earlier than other, more complex segmental processes (such as external sandhi in Greek, to be discussed).

This hypothesis concerning the developmental sequence of different phonological systems clearly must be used only as a starting point for further research. Although there is considerable support in the literature for early acquisition of tonal and intonational processes (cf. Crystal, 1973, 1975, for a comprehensive review), we must be careful to distinguish between lexical tone, whose scope is often limited to a single vocalic nucleus, and the more prosodic uses of tone, as in contrastive accent or intonation. Furthermore, as Li and Thompson (1977) point out, there is both tremendous variation among children in their rate of acquisition of tonal contrasts and, more importantly, a huge range of linguistic complexity within the entire tonal system. Thus, although most children learn very early the major affirmative–negative intonational contrast found in many languages as a falling versus rising phrase-final contour, only very much later will such tonal delicacies as external sandhi be acquired.

Drachman and Malikouti-Drachman (1973) and Malikouti-Drachman and Drachman (1975) have accumulated probably the greatest amount of phonologically relevant information published in English on the development of a language other than English. Their studies of Greek children's speech have encompassed both the segmental and suprasegmental levels, with results that imply a great deal of interaction between linguistic systems. They show, for example, that the acquisition of accentuation depends not only on the basic "trisyllabic" rule (accent must fall on one of the last three syllables of a word) but also the underlying lexical stress pattern, its syntactic form class (principally noun versus verb), optional and obligatory enclitic stress adjustment rules, and the rhythmic pattern of the phrase, which in turn depends on rate and style.

It is especially interesting, from our rhythmic point of view, to contrast Drachman and Malikouti-Drachman's (1973) findings on the acquisition of segment-based external sandhi by Greek children with Li and Thompson's (1977) and Clumek's data (Chapter 13, this volume) for tone sandhi acquisition by Mandarin-speaking children. In agreement with the hypothesis suggested by Kirk's (1973) data, the Chinese children control the tonal productions "with very little error as soon as propositional utterances begin to be created" (presumably in the age range 2–3 years for their subjects), whereas some of the Greek children continue to show segmental sandhi errors at 9 years. These data do not represent a fair test of the hypothesis, however, since Mandarin tone sandhi involves a far simpler set of constraints than the very complex Greek segment sandhi (M. Macken, personal communication). A more complete answer will await the investigation of a range of both types of sandhi, including for example the more complex tonal system of Taiwanese and the simpler segmental system of French.

Finally, we must make some mention of an important aspect of this research mentioned by virtually every investigator: variability within and between children. Some children may begin to modify their speech rhythm in their second year, others not until their fourth. Drachman and Malikouti-Drachman (1971), for example, point to the different prosodic abilities of two Greek children, one a 33-month-old with "near perfect preservation of intonation and syllabification," the other a 42-month-old with good articulation and syntax but "serious trouble in her control of breath-groups and intonation." We have observed similar variability among our own subjects and are therefore well advised not to draw too firm conclusions from what must still be considered rather scanty data.

This section comparing the development of various aspects of phonological rhythm between languages is only a tantalizing suggestion of the work that lies ahead. As Crystal (1975) has pointed out, greatly needed in the more general area of developmental psycholinguistics is a "comparative analysis of the progressive differentiation of vocalization in different languages." Our review certainly shows this to be the case for our specific area where, to begin with, we have only widely scattered data generated by different investigators attacking different questions with different methods, and, as a result, we know with certainty only what appear to be some of the best problems to approach first. One of these, for example, would be a direct comparison of French and English children's biases in learning trochaic versus iambic disyllables (discussed later). The "preferred" accent contour of words in these two languages is directly opposite, and we should be able to observe the differential effects of this bias in the young children's speech.

We are presently beginning just such a study, along with other cross-linguistic investigations involving the detailed phonetic form of children's first disyllables in various languages and a comparison of slightly older children's use of suprasegmental cues for signaling accentual distinctions in their polysyllabic utterances. These studies have been designed to shed light both on the cross-linguistic questions suggested by the literature reviewed earlier and on some of the specific questions concerning the development of phonological rhythm in English.

Research in Progress

We would like now to summarize briefly some of our ongoing work on the development of rhythmic structure in English-speaking children's phonology. More detailed descriptions appear elsewhere (Allen and Hawkins, 1978; Allen and Hawkins, 1979; Allen, Hawkins, and Morris, 1979a,b).

Development of Light (Reduced) Syllables

As noted earlier, stressed syllables are very important contributors to the rhythm of the phrase within which they appear, and so we have tried to focus on how and where young children produce stressed and unstressed syllables in their polysyllabic utterances. In our initial view of this process, moreover, we have restricted our conception of syllabic stress to a three-level system, following Vanderslice and Ladefoged (1972). In this system, a syllable can be "heavy" versus "light" depending upon whether it is produced with "full articulation" versus "reduced timing" (1972, Table 1). If a heavy syllable, in addition to full articulation, shows a "pitch obtrusion" (upward or downward), it is then "accented"; "unaccented" syllables show no such obtrusion. Light syllables cannot be accented in English, so that the resulting three levels of stress are "light" (redundantly "unaccented"), "heavy unaccented," and "accented" (redundantly "heavy"). In the citation form of the word *telephone* (['tɛlə,foʊn]), for example, the first syllable is accented ('), the second is light (no mark), and the third is heavy unaccented (,).

Children's very earliest utterances often have only heavy syllables (some accented, some not), partly because many of these phrases consist of a single syllable, but partly because children apparently cannot reduce their articulatory timing sufficiently (Hawkins, 1979; Keating and Kubaska, 1978). For example, the ubiquitous reduplicated disyllable discussed earlier usually consists of an accented syllable followed by a heavy unaccented one. The child's task in developing correct syllable stress may therefore be primarily that of learning to produce light syllables, thereby extending the accentual dimension downwards, so to speak. By doing this, he can make his accented syllables begin to stand out more sharply from the other syllables in the phrase.

We tape recorded conversations with five children, aged 2:2–3:9, to determine the degree to which they used light syllables appropriately (i.e., in agreement with adult English) in their utterances. Our resulting tabulations showed that the children differed widely in this ability, ranging from about 65% of the time for the child who used light syllables most frequently to about 35% for the one who used them the least. We did not obtain longitudinal samples for these children, so that we cannot determine how this tendency develops with age; within our present sample, however, we did find that age and light syllable reduction were only weakly correlated, suggesting that, as with other developing phonological processes, there is substantial variation from child to child.

Besides assessing any overall tendency toward reduction of light syllables, we were also interested in their pattern of occurrence (i.e., specifically which light syllables in the adult language children do tend to reduce, which ones they do not, and how they reduce the ones they do). Although our data showed no particular differences in frequency of reduction for different syntactic classes of words, such as content versus function words or nouns versus verbs, there did emerge a *phonologically* interesting pattern. When we distinguished between two levels of syllable reduction, namely between (appropriate) partial reduction to either a central vowel (e.g., schwa) or to a syllabic consonant versus total reduction, or deletion of the syllable entirely, we then observed that syllables were totally reduced (deleted) in either of two environments: (*a*) word initial (e.g., [weɪ] for 'away'; or (*b*) next to another light syllable (e.g., ['sʌmbəɪ] for 'somebody'). Furthermore, words with either of these two phonological environments, which are relatively infrequent in adult English, are especially rare in the child's early vocabulary, suggesting additional selective pressures against these forms.

Although several possible reasons can be found for these observed patterns in the reduction of light syllables, for example that children cannot perceive them accurately, we propose an explanation based on an overall rhythmic constraint for English speaking children, specifically that their speech tends to be trochaic. (This explanation also suggests why fricatives are often acquired first in word final position, namely that fricatives are physiologically and acoustically very like weak syllables, Allen and Hawkins, 1979.) As noted previously, the earliest reduplicated disyllables have a falling accent contour (i.e., the first syllable is accented and the second unaccented, at least for English speaking children). This trochaic constraint thus appears to define an environment within which weak syllables may first develop. As to why sequences of two or more light syllables are infrequent we are less certain. There is a general constraint in English against such sequences (cf. "alternating stress rule," Chomsky and Halle, 1968), and the more general perceptual strategy of keeping the full range of any accentual dimension in view as much of the time as possible would also favor an alternation between heavy and light syllables as often as possible (cf. Allen, 1975; Bolinger, 1965). More research is needed, however, to decide this issue.

Development of Accented Syllables

A second syllabic feature of great importance to phrase rhythm, and another focus of our present work that we shall describe here, concerns the "accented" syllables (i.e., those syllables that we described earlier as being produced by adult speakers with a pitch obtrusion). Because stressed syllables in English are marked by a number of correlated acoustic phonetic cues, typically greater duration, greater intensity, and more precise vowel quality, along with the pitch movement already alluded to, we wanted to determine how children sort out this complex interaction. In addition, phrase accentuation in English obeys the rule that the so-called "nuclear" accented syllable is the last accented syllable in the phrase. Crystal (1969, p. 208) writes that the syllables following the nuclear syllable "usually" continue the pitch movement smoothly to the end of the phrase, suggesting that some accent-like pitch movement may under some circumstances occur on post-nuclear syllables, but other authorities (e.g., Vanderslice, 1977) argue to the contrary. This argument may be the result of dialectal differences between British and American English, but in any case the constraint against post-nuclear accentuation is very strong, perhaps absolute, and we wish to observe the degree to which children obey it in their spoken phrases.

One of the difficulties with this study, one that made problematic the comparison of nuclear and nonnuclear accented syllables, involved circularity in assigning accentuation to syllables. Since we were of course led by our adult language perceptions to hear as accented those syllables that had the appropriate phonetic features, our judgements as to the meaning of a phrase were thereby influenced by those features as well. Hence the circularity: We hear the syllable as accented; therefore the child intended it to be accented. Fortunately, however, there were contextual cues that corroborated our guess as to what the child meant and thus reduced the viciousness of the circle. The problem nevertheless remains, as with all studies of children's language, since we can never be absolutely certain of young speakers' intentions.

We have analyzed the acoustic properties of three types of syllables, namely nuclear accented, nonnuclear accented, and heavy unaccented syllables, in the speech of three children aged 36 ± 4 months. Recordings were made of each child playing in its home with its mother present, on two occasions two weeks apart. A high quality stereo tape recorder was used, with the child and its mother each wearing a lavalier microphone. From each session, 50 utterances were chosen, each consisting of two or more words, spoken at an adequate level in a normal voice register, and containing an identifiable nuclear syllable. (The first 25 utterances from the first session and the first 15 from the second were ignored, to allow the child to settle down with the tape recorder.) One person transcribed the segments, a second person assigned stress to each syllable using the system of Vanderslice and Ladefoged (1972), and both segments and stress assignment were checked by a third person. Differences were resolved by discussion or by exclusion of the utterance from the sample if no agreement was reached.

The duration and fundamental frequency of each heavy and accented syllable in the 50 utterances from each of the two sessions for each child were measured spectrographically and, in some cases, oscillographically also. In cases where the child had said two or more breath groups in quick succession, or had coalesced two phrases into one breath group, only syllables from the last breath group or phrase were used for this analysis. Measurements all refer to the vocalic nucleus of the syllable: that is, to the vowel and to any preceding or following nasals or approximants, but excluding stops, fricatives, and affricates. This decision was made partly on theoretical grounds (Allen, 1972; Huggins, 1972; Lehiste, 1972) and partly because 3-year-olds often use *only* the vowel *or* the approximant or nasal to mark a sequence of both, with some randomness as to which is used at a given time. Duration was measured to the nearest 5 msec, and changes in fundamental frequency to the nearest 5 Hz, with changes of less than 5 Hz assigned a value of zero.

In agreement with other studies (e.g., Oller, 1973), Table 12.1 shows that, to a large extent, the position of a syllable in the phrase influenced its length, with final and postnuclear stressed syllables tending to be longer than earlier ones. Subordinate to this position restriction, accented syllables tended to be longer than heavy syllables, with most of the effect being due to the extra length of *nuclear* accented syllables, final and nonfinal. (A nuclear syllable is defined as final if it is the last in the phrase, as in *There's a DOG*. If the nuclear syllable is followed by any other syllable, heavy or

TABLE 12.1
Mean Durations of Syllabic Nuclei by Syllable Type

	Syllable type						
	Nuclear accented			Non-nuclear accented	Heavy		
	Nonfinal	Final	Mean		Pre-nuclear	Post-nuclear	Mean
Duration (msec)	235	387	307	199	177	244	202
N	160	147	307	358	279	169	445

TABLE 12.2
Direction of Change in Fundamental Frequency, within each Syllable Type

Syllable type	Direction of change (%)				
	Rising	Falling	Complex	Steady	N
Nuclear-nonfinal	29	30	24	17	158
Nuclear-final	17	51	29	3	145
Non-nuclear accented	39	31	18	12	348
Heavy-prenuclear	14	52	13	20	270
Heavy-postnuclear	16	55	15	13	152
Total percentage	23	44	20	13	
Total N	271	453	201	148	1073

weak, it is defined as nonfinal, as in *There's a DOGgie.*) The type of stress (heavy, accented, or nuclear) associated with a syllable and the position of the syllable in the phrase also influenced the direction in which the pitch changed within that syllable. As Table 12.2 shows, fundamental frequencies were predominantly falling, but nonfinal accented syllables showed a high proportion of rising contours, particularly if the syllables were not nuclear. Additionally, nuclear syllables had a relatively high proportion of complex contours, in which the fundamental moved in more than one direction. The total amount of within-syllable pitch change, regardless of its direction, was likewise affected by the type of stress attached to the syllable, as well as by its position within the phrase. Non-nuclear syllables changed most (in Hz/msec), whereas nonfinal nuclear syllables changed least (Table 12.3). Our impressionistic transcriptions of the children's utterances are confirmed by these data and provide one further observation that we have not as yet checked in the acoustic records, namely that the change in pitch between a nonfinal accented syllable and the preceding syllable was the most common attribute of stress accent in the children's speech, with extra length being a secondary attribute.

In most respects, the acoustic patterning associated with stress accent and position of a syllable in the phrase in these 3-year-olds' speech closely resembled the patterns found in adult speech and indicated that the children had internalized the basic rules of accent in English. That is, pitch change

TABLE 12.3
Change in Fundamental Frequency (Hz/msec) within Syllables

	Nuclear accented			Non-nuclear accented	Heavy		
	Nonfinal	Final	Mean		Pre-nuclear	Post-nuclear	Mean
Hz/msec	.20	.28	.24	.34	.23	.21	.23
N	158	145	303	349	270	153	423

and accent are closely associated, with duration affecting phrase-final syllables and to a lesser extent nuclear syllables, whether final or nonfinal. There were some details, however, in which the children's syllables did not follow adult patterns, or in which they exaggerated processes that may sometimes occur in adult speech. A case in point is the changes that vowels sometimes underwent in phrase-final nuclear syllables. Thus, for example, in the sentence *He's a dog,* the word *dog,* if accented in phrase-final position might be produced as ['dɔ:g], ['dɔəg], or ['dɔwəg]. Furthermore, perhaps because the terminal intonation contour involves enough pitch change to signal accentuation, the pitch jump at the beginning of these phrase-final nuclear accented syllables was often rather small. Apparently the children recognized that no additional phonetic cues were required for distinguishing these syllables beyond their great length and associated intonation contour.

Although the children we have studied appeared to obey the constraint against postnuclear accents, there were occasional illuminating violations. In the so-called "unmarked" or noncontrastive meaning of an English sentence, the nuclear accent falls on the last accentable syllable, which in most cases is the last heavy syllable. It is usually the case, then, that the nuclear accent falls fairly near the end of the phrase, in which case children will most likely produce the terminal contour correctly, beginning on the nuclear syllable and continuing smoothly to the end of the phrase. Sometimes, however, when the nuclear syllable is followed by sufficiently many heavy syllables, the child produces a small pitch obtrusion on one of the noncontrastive postnuclear heavy syllables. We have observed, for example, a slight pitch obtrusion on the syllable *mat-* in one child's sentence *Now what's the matter,* even though the context indicated that *now* was the nuclear syllable. The conditions for this incorrect accentuation of a postnuclear syllable are not yet clear to us, but we suspect that either complex syntax or the presence of an idiomatic phrase, such as *what's the matter,* may contribute to the process. Such examples may eventually give us considerable insight into the extent of motor preprogramming and the roles of feedback and short-term memory in children's productions of long utterances.

Testing the Trochaic Hypothesis

We conclude by describing some pilot data from an experiment aimed at exploring a possible rhythmic constraint on children's speech that we have discussed earlier, namely that words with "falling accent" (e.g., with initial stress) are easier for children to produce and/or perceive than segmentally similar words with "rising accent" (e.g., with final stress). As noted earlier, there is much indirect evidence for such a bias, such as the abundance of trochaic words in children's early vocabulary in many but not all languages. In this experiment, we are trying to address the question directly.

Our experimental procedure, briefly, is as follows. Three pairs of "nonsense" toys (one pair of knitted worms with eyes, one pair of yarn balls, and one pair of stuffed "wug" like creatures [Berko, 1958]) are assigned the three pairs of names /'ta,ki/ − /,ta'ki/, /'smIp,fo/ − /,smIp'fo/, and /'gwa,vi,stru/ − /,gwa,vi'stru/. The two members of each pair are similar in segmental structure but differ in having falling versus rising accent. Of each pair of toys, one is red and the other blue, and for a given child the same color is always associated with the same accent pattern (i.e., red = falling and blue = rising, or vice versa). To introduce the children to the stress contour difference and the discrimination task, they are first shown a picture of a 'hot,dog (in a bun) and a ,hot'dog (a dog sweltering in the sun), the stress difference is pointed out to them, "This one is loud on the hot, 'HOT,dog, and this one is loud on the dog, ,hot'DOG," and they are asked to point to the correct picture when it is named. The first pair of toys is then introduced and named "This is a /taki/," in an ABBA or an AABB sequence. (ABAB sequences are not used because they always alternate; ABBA and AABB sequences contain both alternations and repetitions.) Order of presentation and association of color with accent contour are fully crossed and counterbalanced across subjects. After the names have been given twice each by the experimenter, the child is asked to point to each of the toys as they are named, "Show me," again in an ABBA or AABB sequence. The criterion for association of names with toys is four correct responses in succession. After the child has successfully completed the association task, the experimenter says, "Now I'm going to ask you to tell me their names," and then points to the two toys, in an ABBA or AABB sequence, and the child must say the toy's name. The criterion for this name production task is four utterances, each of which must appear to be the child's best approximation to the name; that is, completely correct segmental composition is not required, and the accent contour is ignored. After successfully completing the association and production tasks for the first pair of toys, the second pair (/smIpfo/) is introduced and tested. Then the first pair is retested for production only. If the child cannot remember the names, the experimenter names the toys twice each and then elicits the names from the child. Then the third pair (/gwavistru/) is introduced and fully tested, followed by production tests for the second pair, the first pair, and finally the third pair. Thus each pair is tested at least twice for production of the names, with the first pair (/taki/) being tested three times. The entire experimental session is recorded on a high quality stereo tape recorder, with one lavalier microphone on the child and another on the experimenter. The resulting tape recordings are of high enough quality to support a variety of acoustic analyses.

The results to date are based on full orthographic transcriptions of the experimental sessions plus close auditory phonetic analysis of the test names, by two trained phoneticians, for six pilot subjects aged 3:7 to 6:7.

Data from a seventh subject (aged 5:0) were unusable because the child often whispered, especially on the final syllable of the name. The responses of two additional children (aged 3:5 and 5:2), tested using a slightly different protocol, will also be discussed.

On the basis of the trochaic hypothesis (that trochees are preferred to iambs), we expect children to favor responses with falling accent. Although Julie (6:7) made no accentual errors and thus provided us with no data of immediate interest here, such a bias was clearly evident in data from Jessica (6:6) who substituted falling for rising forms two or possibly three times, but never the reverse. In addition, Jessica used level accent for rising forms, by accenting *both* syllables, in seven or eight responses, whereas all of her falling responses were truly falling. Her pattern of substituting falling for rising forms was not random: She was tested using a FRRF sequence (F = falling), and her errors were always in the third position, giving FRFF; that is, she switched to a falling response immediately after having said it correctly.

David (5:8) also showed a bias toward the falling form, but since he was tested using the RFFR sequence, his errors were in the fourth position, giving RFFF. This pattern, which might be termed "perseverative," is easier to understand than Jessica's. David's responses were not as reliable as Jessica's, however, since he sometimes substituted in the opposite direction. This was also the case with Jennifer (4:5), who showed a slight bias toward falling responses but with no clear pattern of substitution by position in the sequence.

The younger children, Erin (3:7) and Cara (3:9), showed a completely different pattern of responses, both preferring the *rising* accent form. This apparent contradiction of the trochaic hypothesis is softened, however, by the extreme response form used by these children. Erin produced a stronger degree of accent than necessary on the last syllable, by using extra vowel length, high pitch, and extra force, often to the point that the syllable was transcribed as emphatically stressed, and Cara *always* produced the names with (ear-splitting) emphasis. These two children thus behaved in a qualitatively different way from the ones, essentially using only one name for both toys in a pair, choosing the theoretically "marked" number of the pair and underlining this markedness with emphatic stress.

Two other children, Eric (3:5) and Laura (5:2), were tested using a different protocol, so that their response patterns cannot be compared directly with those of the other six children. Their data nevertheless show a strong bias in favor of the trochaic hypothesis, in that they produced many correct tokens of falling forms but almost no correct rising forms. Their substitutions for rising forms could involve major rhythmic changes, such as deletion of the initial unstressed syllable (e.g., [foU] for /ˌsmɪpˈfo/ or accentual strengthening of the first syllable, yielding level accent (e.g., [ˈtaːˈkiː] for /ˌtaˈki/). Many of the other children's responses, including those of Erin and Cara, also had this latter type of level accent. In addition to the major rhythmic alterations, Eric and Laura often produced rising forms with minor changes, such as devoicing of the initial syllable.

It is clear to us from these pilot data that children can hear the accentual differences between the stimuli easily, and thus far we have seen no obvious bias toward or away form either from during the association part of the task. It is possible that association training using a "rising first" sequence (i.e., RFFR or RRFF) results in more trials to criterion, but the data are not yet clear on this point. In their production, however, the children have often shown that the rising accent form is unusual for them. They sometimes hesitate before saying the rising form, and what they do say for the rising forms is seldom like the experimenter's model. There does seem to be a trochaic bias in these children's productions; the variety of their responses makes it difficult to say in detail yet, however, what the exact nature of this bias is.

Summary of Research in Progress

In the initial part of this chapter we presented a view of phonological rhythm in which syllabic weight and accentuation play an important role. In agreement with that view, the research described in this section of the chapter has focused on the development of syllabic weight and accentuation in the speech of 3- to 5-year-old children. With respect to syllabic weight, the major consideration for children appears to be learning to reduce some syllables, from the full form typically used in their earliest polysyllabic words, to the shortened, weak forms found in mature, fluent phrases. We found that children differ greatly in their tendency to use reduced syllables appropriately, these differences being a function of both idiosyncratic style between children and maturation of the individual child. Just as has been found in other studies of language acquisition, children differ somewhat as to the exact age at which they acquire this ability to reduce syllables, relative to their progress both in other aspects of phonology and in more general linguistic and cognitive areas. It is obvious, however, that the older the child, the more he or she will use weak syllables correctly, and the more mature will the resulting phrase rhythm sound.

With respect to accentuation of syllables, we have been particularly interested in the phonetic features used by children to distinguish accented from unaccented syllables as a function of their position in the phrase. Adult speakers of English typically use changes in fundamental frequency of voicing to indicate that a given syllable is accented; if the syllable is the last one in the phrase, however, they may lengthen the syllable in addition to or instead of changing the pitch. Our young speakers showed this same differential pattern of phonetic features, although perhaps in a more stereotyped fashion (that is, the children did not yet have the full adult range or repertoire of accentuation skills). In addition, the children's use of accentuation generally obeyed the constraint against postnuclear accents in English. We concluded overall, then, that the basic idea of accentuation was well understood by even our 3-year-old speakers and that maturation in this area of phonology primarily involves learning a variety of phonetic means for expressing the accentual features.

In reviewing the literature and in reporting our research on the development of reduced syllables, we discussed evidence supporting the hypothesis that English in general, and children's English in particular, has a trochaic pattern of accentuation. We also noted that, although this idea is by no means new, there is no published evidence directly supporting the developmental aspect of this hypothesis. To this end, we have reported pilot data from an experiment in which we have begun to examine this question directly, By asking children to learn to discriminate and say pairs of nonsense words differing primarily in their rhythmic form, we have found a number of ways in which children perform better on items with falling accent (e.g., trochees) than on items with rising accent (e.g., iambs). For example, some children show a strong bias toward saying the falling accent form in place of the rising accent form. Most children also say the falling forms more accurately than the rising forms. Furthermore, many of the children, the younger ones especially, react to producing the rising forms as if they are somehow unusual. We have so far found no particular rhythmic bias in the discrimination learning part of this experiment; hence our conclusions from these pilot data are limited to speech production. Within that limitation, however, it appears that there is indeed a bias in young children's speech away from words with rising accent and/or toward words with falling accent.

Summary and Significance

One problem with linguistic theories of speech rhythm is that they have been either oversimplified or unjustifiably complicated. On the one hand, we have made do with the very simple distinction of "stress timed" versus "syllable timed" for describing the rhythmic character of widely varying languages; on the other hand, we have seen some very complex metric and intonational systems applied to the rhythm of spoken English with far from satisfactory results. It has been difficult to find a descriptive system that really "fits" the rhythm of our language, partly because we know so little about the specific characteristics of speech rhythm in general. In this chapter, we have touched on a number of issues which, by being germane specifically to this area, may add structure to our previous inadequately focused theory.

We began by defining speech rhythm, both broadly and narrowly, not so as to exclude other definitions, but rather to indicate what we believe to be the most important dimensions of this complex subject. We also indicated our reasons for choosing to examine syllabic weight and accentuation within the breath group as a starting point for our research, namely that these syllabic features appear to be the most important determinants of rhythmic structure and that they are most strongly organized within the breath group. That section of the chapter was thus presented to stimulate further discussion of speech rhythm, a topic that we feel is too important to remain so neglected.

The literature review, presented next, draws together a wide variety of studies bearing on the acquisition of phonological rhythm. From our viewpoint, few of these studies deal directly with the issue at hand, and none does so extensively; as a result, some readers will doubtless form impressions from the material that are different from the ones we have presented. Those interested in pursuing this topic further, however, should read Crystal's (1973, 1975) extensive reviews of prosodic development. The completeness and care with which the literature is assembled make those sources an important addition to the present chapter.

Finally, the studies we have presented show the way we have tried to investigate what we believe to be some of the more important questions in this area. Many of the details of these studies have been or will be presented more fully elsewhere; we have tried here primarily to indicate what we did, why we did it, and what our major findings were. As with most exploratory research, our results have generated more questions than answers. Nevertheless, we feel satisfied that we have begun to lay a solid foundation for our own and others' future work in this area.

The study of phonological rhythm in children's speech is for us interesting in itself, but it also has implications for a number of related areas that considerably magnify its importance. Within phonology, for example, there has recently occurred a substantial increased in interest in syllabic and prosodic processes (cf., e.g., Bell and Hooper, 1978; Hyman, 1975). In addition, even the more segmentally oriented studies of developmental phonology make both implicit and explicit use of such suprasegmental notions as position of the segment within the syllable or word and degree of stress on the syllable. Perhaps more important than these linguistic considerations, however, are the implications of language-universal features of speech rhythm for our understanding of other aspects of children's perceptuomotor and cognitive development. As has often been pointed out (e.g., Allen, 1975), any language universal suggests an underlying neuropsychological tendency as a possible cause. Rhythmic constraints found in English and other languages may thus be tied to more general sequential processing abilities of children and adults. Such links have already been demonstrated for children with reading disabilities (Bakker, 1972) and certain forms of mental retardation. The wide generality of rhythmic structure as a unifying element in human behavior leads us to expect to find speech rhythm a challenging and valuable subject for continued research.

Acknowledgments

We gratefully acknowledge the support of the National Science Foundation, the National Institutes of Health, and the University of North Carolina Faculty Research Council in the preparation of this report.

References

Abe, I. (1967) "English Sentence Rhythm and Synchronism," *Bulletin of the Phonetic Society of Japan*, 125, 9–11.

Allen, G.D. (1972) "The Location of Rhythmic Stress Beats in English: An Experimental Study," (Part 1) *Language and Speech*, 15, 72–100; (Part 2) *Language and Speech*, 15, 170–195.

Allen, G.D. (1973) "Segmental Timing Control in Speech Production," *Journal of Phonetics* 1, 219–237.

Allen, G.D. (1975) "Speech Rhythm: Its Relation to Performance Universals and Articulatory Timing," *Journal of Phonetics*, 3, 75–86.

Allen, G.D., and Hawkins, S. (1978) "The Development of Phonological Rhythm," in A. Bell and J. B. Hooper, eds., *Syllables and Segments*, North Holland, Amsterdam, pp. 173–185.

Allen, G.D., and Hawkins, S. (1979) "Trochaic Rhythm in Children's Speech," in H. Hollien and P. Hollien, eds., *Current Issues in the Phonetic Sciences*, pp. 927–933.

Allen, G.D., Hawkins, S., and Morris, M. (1979a) "Development of 'Nuclear Accent' Marking in Children's Phrases," in H. Hollien and P. Hollien, eds., *Current Issues in the Phonetic Sciences*, pp. 919–926.

Allen, G.D., Hawkins, S., and Morris, M. (1979b) "Rhythmic Constraints in Children's Speech: Data for 3–6-Year-Olds," *Journal of the Acoustical Society of America*, 65, Supplement 1.

Atkinson, K., MacWhinney, B., and Stoel, C. (1969) "An Experiment on the Recognition of Babbling," *Working Paper*, 15, Language Behavior Research Laboratory, University of California, Berkeley.

Atkinson-King, K. (1973) "Children's Acquisition of Phonological Stress Contrasts," *Working Papers in Phonetics*, 25, University of California, Los Angeles, Phonetics Laboratory.

Austerlitz, R. (1956) "Gilyak Nursery Words," *Word*, 12, 260–279.

Bailey, C-J. N. (1978) "Gradience in English Syllabization and a Revised Concept of Unmarked Syllabization," Indiana University Lingustics Club Publications, Bloomington.

Bakker, D.J. (1972) *Temporal Order in Disturbed Reading*, Rotterdam University Press, Rotterdam.

Bell, A. (1975) "If Speakers Can't Count Syllables, What Can They Do?" Indiana University Linguistics Club Publications, Bloomington.

Bell, A., and Hooper, J.B., eds., (1978) *Syllables and Segments*, North Holland Company, Amsterdam.

Berko, J. (1958) "The Child's Learning of English Morphology," *Word*, 14, 150–177.

Blasdell, R., and Jensen, P. (1970) "Stress and Word Position as Determinants of Imitation in First-Language Learners," *Journal of Speech and Hearing Research*, 13, 193–202.

Bolinger, D.L. (1965) "Pitch Accent and Sentence Rhythm," in I. Abe and T. Kanekiyo, eds., *Forms of English: Accent, Morpheme, Order*, Harvard University Press, Cambridge, Mass.

Burling, R. (1966) "The Metrics of Children's Verse: A Cross-Linguistic Study," *American Anthropologist*, 68, 1418–1441.

Casagrande, J.B. (1948) "Comanche Baby Language," *International Journal of American Linguistics*, 14, 11–14.

Chao, Y.-R. (1951) "The Cantian Idiolect: An Analysis of the Chinese Spoken by a Twenty-Eight-Months-Old Child," *University of California Publications in Semitic Philology*, 11, 27–44.

Chomsky, A.N., and Halle, M. (1968) *The Sound Pattern of English*, Harper & Row, New York.

Coleman, C. (1974) "A Study of Acoustical and Perceptual Attributes of Isochrony in Spoken English," Unpublished Doctoral Dissertation, Department of Speech, University of Washington, Seattle.

Collier, R., and 't Hart, J. (1975) "The Role of Intonation in Speech Perception," in A. Cohen and S.G. Nooteboom, eds., *Structure and Process in Speech Perception*, Springer Verlag, Berlin, pp. 107–123.

Cooper, M.H., and Allen, G.D. (1977) "Timing control accuracy in normal speakers and stutterers," *Journal of Speech and Hearing Research*, 20, 55–71.

Crowder, R.G., and Morton, J. (1969) "Precategorical Acoustic Storage (PAS)," *Perception & Psychophysics*, 5, 365–373.

Crystal, D. (1969) *Prosodic Systems and Intonation in English*, Cambridge University. Press, Cambridge.

Crystal, D. (1973) "Non-segmental Phonology in Language Acquisition: A Review of the Issues," *Lingua*, 32, 1–45.

Crystal, D. (1975) *The English Tone of Voice*, Edward Arnold, London.

Cutler, A. (1976) "Phoneme Monitoring Reaction Time as a Function of Preceding Intonation Contour," *Perception & Psychophysics*, 20, 55–60.

Cutler, A., and Foss, D.J. (1973) "The Importance of Lexical Item Stress for Lexical Access," Paper presented at the 44th Annual Meeting of the Midwestern Psychological Association, Chicago.

Cutler, A., and Foss, D.J. (1977) "On the Role of Sentence Stress Processing," *Language and Speech*, 20, 1–10.

Darwin, C.J. (1975) "On the Dynamic Use of Prosody in Speech Perception," in A. Cohen and S.G. Nooteboom, eds., *Structure and Process in Speech Perception*, Springer-Verlag, Berlin, pp. 178–194.

Drachman, G. (1976) "Baby Talk in Greek," in H.D. Pohl and N. Salnikow, eds., *Opuscula Slavica et Linguistica: Festschrift fur Alexander Issatschenko*, Verlag Johannes Heyn, Klagenfurt.

Drachman, G., and Malikouti-Drachman, A. (1972) "Studies in the Acquisition of Greek as a Native Language: I. Some Preliminary Findings on Phonology," Prepublication mimeograph, Ohio State University.

Drachman, G., and Malikouti-Drachman, A. (1973) "Studies in the Acquisition of Greek as a Native Language: I. Some preliminary findings," *Working Papers in Linguistics*, 15, Ohio State University, 99–114.

Eguchi, S., and Hirsh, I.J. (1969) "Development of Speech Sounds in Children," *Acta Oto-Laryngologica*, Supplement 257.

Eilers, R.E. (1975) "Suprasegmentals and Grammatical Control over Telegraphic Speech in Young Children," *Journal of Psycholinguistic Research*, 4, 227–239.

Ferguson, C.A. (1956) "Arabic Baby Talk," In M. Halle *et al.* eds., *For Roman Jakobson*, Mouton, The Hague, pp. 121–128.

Ferguson, C.A. (1964) "Baby Talk in Six Languages," *American Anthropologist*, 66, 103–114.

Ferguson, C.A. (1972) "Fricatives in Child Language Acquisition," in L. Heilman, ed., *Proceedings of the Eleventh International Congress of Linguists*, Societa Editrice il Mulino Bologna, Bologna, pp. 647–664.

Fónagy, I. (1972) "A propos de la Genèse de la Phrase Enfantine," *Lingua*, 30, 31–71.

Fraisse, P. (1963) *The Psychology of Time*, Harper and Row, New York.

Gilbert, J.H.V. (1977) "A Voice Onset Time Analysis of Apical Stop Production in Three Year Olds," *Journal of Child Language*, 4, 103–110.

Gilbert, J.H.V., and Purves, B.A. (1977) "Temporal Constraints on Consonant Clusters in Child Speech Production," *Journal of Child Language*, 4, 417–432.

Hawkins, S. (1976) "The Developing Organisation of Speech Production in Children: Evidence from Consonant Clusters," Unpublished Doctoral Dissertation, University of Cambridge.

Hawkins (1979) "Temporal Coordination of Consonants in the Speech of Children: Further Data," *Journal of Phonetics*, 7, 235–267

Hrushovsky, B. (1960) "On Free Rhythms in Modern Poetry," in T. Sebeok, ed., *Style in Language*, MIT Press, Cambridge, Mass., pp. 173–190.

Huggins, A.W.F. (1972) "On the Perception of Temporal Phenomena in Speech," *Journal of the Acoustical Society of America*, 51, 1279–1290.

Huggins, A.W.F. (1978) "Speech Timing and Intelligibility," in J. Requin, ed., *Attention and Performance VII*, Lawrence Erlbaum, Hillsdale, N.J., pp. 279–297.

Hyman, L.M. (1975) "On the Nature of Linguistic Stress," in L.M. Hyman, ed., *Studies in Stress and Accent*, Linguistics Department, University of Southern California, Los Angeles, pp. 37–82.

Ingram, D. (1974) "Phonological Rules in Young Children," *Journal of Child Language*, 1, 49–64.

Keating, P., and Kubaska, C. (1978) "Variation in the Duration of words," *Journal of the Acoustical Society of America*, 63, Supplement 1, 56 (A).

Kelkar, A.R. (1964) "Marathi Baby Talk," *Word*, 20, 40–54.

Kewley-Port, D., and Preston, M.S. (1974) "Early Apical Stop Production: A Voice Onset Time Analysis," *Journal of Phonetics*, 2, 195–210.

Kirk, L. (1973) "An Analysis of Speech Imitations by Gã Children," *Anthropological Linguistics*, 15, 267–275.

Klatt, D.H. (1973) "Durational Characteristics of Prestressed Word-Initial Consonant Clusters in English," *Quarterly Progress Report of the M.I.T. Research Laboratory of Electronics*, 108, 253–260.

Klatt, D.H. (1976) "Linguistic Uses of Segmental Duration in English: Acoustic and Perceptual Evidence," *Journal of the Acoustical Society of America*, 59, 1208–1221.

Kroeber, A.L. (1916) "The Speech of a Zuñi Child," *American Anthropologist*, 18, 529–534.

Lehiste, I. (1970) *Suprasegmentals*, MIT Press, Cambridge, Mass.

Lewis, M.M. (1936) *Infant Speech: A Study of the Beginning of Language*, Kegan Paul, Trench, Trubner, London.

Li, C.N., and Thompson, S.A. (1977) "The Acquisition of Tone in Mandarin-Speaking Children," *Journal of Child Language*, 4, 185–199.

Macken, M.A., and Barton, D. (1977) "A Longitudinal Study of the Acquisition of the Voicing Contrast in American-English Word-Initial Stops, as Measured by VOT," *Papers and Reports on Child Language Development*, 14, Stanford University, 1–47.

Malikouti-Drachman, A., and Drachman, G. (1975) "The Acquisition of Stress in Modern Greek," in G. Drachman, ed., *Salzburger Beiträge zur Linguistik*, 2, Verlag Gunter Narr, Tübingen.

Martin, J.G. (1972) "Rhythmic (Hierarchical) versus Serial Structure in Speech and Other Behavior," *Psychological Review*, 79, 487–509.

Martin, J.G. (1975) "Rhythmic Expectancy in Continuous Speech Perception," in A. Cohen and S.G. Nooteboom, eds., *Dynamic Aspects of Speech Perception*, Springer-Verlag, Berlin, pp. 161–177.

Menyuk, P., and Klatt, M.M. (1975) "Voice Onset Time in Consonant Cluster Production by Children and Adults," *Journal of Child Language*, 2, 223–231.

Michon, J.A. (1967) *Timing in Temporal Tracking*, Institute of Perception, RVO–TNO. Soesterberg, The Netherlands.

Miles, D.W. (1937) "Preferred Rates in Rhythmic Responses," *Journal of Genetic Psychology*, 16, 427–469.

Miyake, I. (1902) "Researches on Rhythmic Action," in E.W. Scripture, ed., *Studies from the Yale Psychological Laboratory*, 10, 1–48.

Moskowitz, A.I. (1970) "The Two-Year-Old Stage in the Acquisition of English Phonology," *Language*, 46, 426–441.

Murai, J-I. (1960) "Speech Development of Infants," *Psychologia*, 3, 27–35.

Murai, J-I. (1963–1964) "The Sounds of Infants," *Studia Phonologica*, 3, 21–24.

Naeser, M.A. (1970) "The American Child's Acquisition of Differential Vowel Duration," Technical Report No. 144 (2 parts), Wisconsin Research and Development Center for Cognitive Learning, University of Wisconsin, Madison.

Nakazima, S. (1962) "A Comparative Study of Speech Developments of Japanese and American English in Childhood" *Studia Phonologica*, 2, 27–39.

Nooteboom, S.G., Brokx, J.P.L., and de Rooij, J.J. (1976) "Contributions of Prosody to Speech Perception," Eindhoven, Holland: *IPO Annual Progress Report*, 11, 34–54.

Oller, D.K. (1973) "The Effect of Position in Utterance on Speech Segment Duration in English," *Journal of the Acoustical Society of America*, 54, 1235–1237.

Oller, D.K., and Smith, B.L. (1977) "The Effect of Final-Syllable Position on Vowel Duration in Infant Babbling," *Journal of the Acoustical Society of America*, 62, 994–997.

Pike, E.V. (1939) "Controlled Infant Intonation," *Language Learning*, 1, 21–24.

Pike, K.L. (1945) *The Intonation of American English*, University of Michigan Press, Ann Arbor.

Pike, K.L. (1959) "Language as Particle, Wave, and Field," *The Texas Quarterly*, 2, 37–54.

Risley, T.R., and Reynolds, N.J. (1970) "Emphasis as a Prompt for Verbal Imitation," *Journal of Applied Behavior Analysis*, 3, 185–190.

Shen, Y., and Peterson, G. (1962) "Isochronism in English," *Studies in Linguistics*, Occasional Papers 9, Buffalo, New York.

Shields, J.L., McHugh, A., and Martin, J.G. (1974) "Reaction Time to Phoneme Targets as a Function of Rhythmic Cues in Continuous Speech," *Journal of Experimental Psychology*, 102, 250–255.

Smith, B.L. (1978) "Temporal Aspects of English Speech Production: A Developmental Perspective," *Journal of Phonetics*, 6, 37–67.

Smith, N.V. (1973) *The Acquisition of Phonology: A Case Study*, Cambridge University Press, Cambridge.

Stoel-Gammon, C. (1976) "Baby Talk in Brazilian Portuguese," *Papers and Reports on Child Language Development*, 11, Stanford University, 83–88.

Tingley, B.M., and Allen, G.D. (1975) "Development of Speech Timing Control in Children," *Child Development*, 46, 186–194.

Tervoort, B.T.M. (1967) "Language Development of Deaf Children: Some Results of an 8-Year Project," *Het Gehoorgestoorde Kind*, 8, 214–227. (Cited in J.H.V. Gilbert, "Speech Perception in Children," in A. Cohen and S.G. Nooteboom, eds., *Dynamic Aspects of Speech Perception*, Springer-Verlag, Berlin, 1975).

Vanderslice, R. (1977) "I Don't WANT to See her Grease Gun Fittings"—Do Post-nuclear Accents Occur in English?" *Journal of the Acoustical Society of America*, 61, Supplement 1, 90 (Abstract).

Vanderslice, R., and Ladefoged, P. (1972) "Binary Suprasegmental Features and Transformational Word-Accentuation Rules," *Language*, 48, 819–838.

Voegelin, C.F., and Robinett, F.M. (1954) " 'Mother Language' in Hidatsa," *International Journal of American Linguistics*, 20, 65–70.

Waterson, N. (1970) "Some Speech Forms of an English Child—A Phonological Study," *Transactions of the Philological Society*, 1–24.

Waterson, N. (1971) "Child Phonology: A Prosodic View," *Journal of Linguistics*, 7, 179–211.

Weir, R. (1962) *Language in the Crib*, Mouton, The Hague.

Wingfield, A., and Klein, J.F. (1971) "Syntactic Structure and Acoustic Pattern in Speech Perception," *Perception & Psychophysics, 9,* 23–25.

Woodrow, H. (1951) "Time Perception," in S.S. Stevens, ed., *Handbook of Experimental Psychology,* Wiley, New York, pp. 1224–1236.

Zlatin, M.A., and Koenigsknecht, R.A. (1976) "Development of the Voicing Contrast: A Comparison of Voice Onset Time in Stop Perception and Production," *Journal of Speech and Hearing Research,* 19, 93–111.

Chapter 13

THE ACQUISITION OF TONE

HAROLD CLUMECK

Introduction

In the field of child phonology, study of the ways in which children acquire tone in tonal languages has barely begun. This is of course not surprising as the study of child language, in general, is relatively new, and most investigations deal with children acquiring Indo-European languages. Yet the very widespread use of tone in the world's languages, as evidenced by the enormous number of tone-language speakers in many parts of Asia, Africa, Central and South America, is indicative of the significance of this aspect of phonology.

More importantly, perhaps, the study of tonal development in children promises to provide insight into the acquisition process as tone is similar to other features such as intonation and stress in being suprasegmental, and yet its linguistic status is lexical (i.e., by serving to contrast meanings, it functions like segments). This raises a number of questions:

1. Is the acquisition of tones similar to the acquisition of segments?
2. When do children acquire tones? Specifically, when do children begin to use pitch in a lexically contrastive way? When is the process of acquiring tones complete in comparison to the development of segmental phonology?

CHILD PHONOLOGY
VOLUME 1: PRODUCTION

3. Is there an order, or sequence, in the acquisition of tones? Just as certain segments, such as fricatives and liquids, are generally more difficult than stops and nasals for children to produce consistently, are there any tones that children find harder than others to master in production?

This chapter will deal with all these questions and will try to provide answers to them where possible by reference to data available in the literature.

First, it is necessary to point out that the term "acquisition of tone" can have different meanings. The meaning it has throughout much of the literature is a basically phonetic one, having to do with the accuracy of tone production by children relative to the adult model: If a child produces tone A, then tone A is said to have been acquired; if a child fails to produce tone B (or at least does not produce it correctly), than that tone is not yet acquired. A second way of looking at the acquisition of tone is to consider the child's underlying knowledge of tones and of the adult tonal system. For example, if a child produces the tone of a given word correctly, is that accuracy due to good mimicry, or does the child have a deeper awareness of the lexical use of pitch and of which pitches are contrastive in the mother tongue? If a child has discovered by a given age that pitch is contrastive in the adult language, which contrasts have been acquired (i.e., what distinctions might the child recognize phonemically, whether or not they are consistently produced?).

Discussion of tone acquisition in this chapter will include both the phonetic and the phonological, or "underlying," development of tone, but these two aspects will be kept distinct.

The chapter is divided into two main sections, each dealing with a major issue in the acquisition of tone. The first section deals with the age at which children acquire tone, both phonetically and phonologically, in comparison to their acquisition of segmental phonology. The second section is a discussion of findings concerning the sequence of tone acquisition, focusing again on both phonetic and phonological aspects.

The Time of Tone Acquisition

The Phonetic Accuracy of Children's Tone Production

Studies addressing the question of the accuracy of children's production of tones compared to their segmental production are unanimous in the finding that articulatory control over tone production is mastered before the completion of segments. In most of the cases reported, the kinds of segments that children still find difficult, at the time they finish acquiring all the tones, are affricates, some fricatives, and the liquid /l/.

In a study of the speech of his Mandarin-speaking granddaughter at the age of 28 months, Chao reports only a few errors in tonal production, whereas there was more difficulty with some of the segments. Specifically, the child regularly substituted plain stops for the affricates, produced /j/ for the adult initial /l/, and had two main allophones for the adult retroflex fricative /ʃ/: before the full vowel /u/ or a labial medial, the child produced a voiceless bilabial fricative; in other environments, she produced a voiceless fricative articulated in the palato–alveolar region. Li and Thompson (1977) collected longitudinal data from 17 children between the ages of 18 and 36 months who were acquiring Mandarin and found that the children's accurate production of tones was far more frequent than accurate production of segments. As in Chao's data, many of their examples of segmental inaccuracy involved fricatives, affricates, and the liquid.

Similar data exist for a child acquiring Cantonese. Tse (1978) reports that his subject seldom made errors in tone production at the time he was 22 months old, but that a number of segments were still difficult for him: Of the three final unreleased stops in Cantonese, / − p/, / − t/, and / − k/, he produced only final / − k/.[1] Like Chao's subject Canta, this child substituted /j/, or occasionally /n/, for initial /l/, and for the adult low rounded front vowel /œ/, the child produced /ɔ/.

Tuaycharoen (1977), who investigated the very early phonetic and phonological development of a child acquiring Thai, makes the statement that the tones were all mastered by the twenty-third month, whereas complex segments and segment sequences, such as diphthongs, triphthongs, and initial consonant clusters, had not yet been acquired.[2]

Further data comparing tonal with segmental acquisition come from a study by Westermeyer and Westermeyer (1977) on 43 Lao children ranging in age between 3 and 15 years. Speech production was elicited by presenting each child with pictures and asking the child what the objects in the pictures were, how many of them there were, and requesting them to count from 1 to 10. The children's taped responses were then analyzed for errors in the articulation of vowels, consonants, and tones. It was found that the children aged 9 years and older made no errors in either segments or tones, whereas segmental errors occurred in the data collected from the younger groups: Of a total of 438 responses from the younger children, there were five segmental errors and no tonal errors. The authors conclude that this finding supports the hypothesis that correct tonal production is acquired before cor-

[1] If Cantonese children experience difficulty in learning to distinguish the three final stops in their production, this may be due to an acoustic reason: The final stops are unreleased, and, as a result, there is very little information on point of articulation. My own informal observations of one Cantonese child from 1:7;20 to 2:6;11 indicate that the child produced stopped syllables with no problem, but he may have been producing many of these with final glottal stop.

[2] No specific data are presented in support of this observation as the child's twenty-third month was beyond the age range of the study.

rect segmental production. This is not really justified, however. Despite the fact that no tonal errors were made, the number of segmental errors was so small that a conclusion about tonal versus segmental acquisition is not warranted. To collect data on this question, a study on children younger than 3 years would have been more appropriate.

The studies cited so far deal either with spontaneous speech alone or include both spontaneous and imitated speech. One study examining imitations exclusively is by Kirk (1973), who investigated phonetic accuracy of tones, rhythm, and segments as produced by children acquiring Gã, a language of southern Ghana. Data were collected from four children, aged 2–3 years, and the imitations appear to have been produced freely by the children while interacting with adults and older children (i.e., they were not purposefully elicited by a single experimenter). Results show the largest proportion of errors to be segmental, and the smallest proportion to be tonal, with errors in rhythm being intermediate.

In summary, data from Chinese, southeast Asian languages, and a West African language all indicate that children experience relative ease in approximating the phonetic values of tones in the adult language, and that tonal production in young childen is more adultlike than segmental production.

Tone Production in Non-Final Position

With regard to the phonetic accuracy of children's tones, I would like to discuss, as a side issue, some differences in the phonetic realization of tones depending upon whether or not they occur in utterance-final or non-final position. Clumeck (1977) reports data from two Mandarin-speaking children between the ages of 2 and 3 years, who exhibited certain alternations among pitches in non-final position but not in utterance-final position or in isolation. It seems likely that these alternations are effected entirely by the pitch of a following syllable and are therefore low-level phonetic processes.

The alternations that occur are the following:

1. High-falling tone in the adult model is sometimes produced by the child as high-level before a low pitch.[3]
2. Rising tone in the adult model is sometimes produced by the child as high-level pitch before a low pitch.
3. Rising tone in the adult model is sometimes produced as a low-level pitch before high-level or falling tones.

These alternations are formalized and illustrated in Table 13.1.

In the adult model of the first alternation, the pitch of the initial syllable begins high, then falls low, and remains low during the next syllable. In the

---

[3] The three tones mentioned in these rules, high-level, rising, and falling, are all phonemically distinctive from each other in Mandarin.

TABLE 13.1
Pitch Alternations in the Speech of Mandarin-Speaking Children[a]

Alternation		Adult			Child
		Meaning	Pinyin[b]	Phonetic form	
1. Falling – – → low high-level ⟋⟋ pitch		a. 'this'	*zhèige*	[cèikə]	[tīkə]
		b. 'here'	*zhèli*	[cəlī]	[tīlī]
2. Rising – – –→ low high-level ⟋⟋ pitch		'rope'	*shéngzi*	[sə́ŋcɨ]	[sə̄ncɨ]
3. Rising – – → low level ⟋ {high-level / falling}		a. 'towel'	*máojīn*	[máutçīn]	[māutçī̠]
		b. 'soap'	*féizào*	[féicàu]	[fēicàu]

[a] Phonetic symbols used in the table include: c = unaspirated dental affricate; tç = unaspirated alveo–palatal affricate; ɨ = apical vowel; and a small circle above a vowel = neutral tone.

[b] The term 'pinyin' refers to a standard romanization system used in the People's Republic of China.

child's form, the pitch begins high in the first syllable and is low during the following one, just as in the adult model; the difference, however, being in the point in time at which the pitch is lowered: in the adult model, the pitch is lowered during the first syllable, and in the child's form, the pitch lowers abruptly in going from the first to the second syllable.

In the second alternation, the adult model presents a rising-contour tone in the first syllable which is high contrasted with the low pitch of the next syllable. This contrast between high and low is preserved in the child's form except that the pitch of the first syllable lacks a contour.

Whereas in the second alternation, the rising tone of the adult model is realized as a high pitch, it is realized by the child as a low-level pitch in the third alternation where the low initial component of the adult rising tone contrasts with the high component of the high-level or high-falling tone of the following syllable. Here again, a contrast is preserved between low and high pitch in the first and second syllables, respectively, but the point in time at which the pitch goes from low to high differs in the adult and child forms.

It seems likely that these pitch alternations are due to the child's mistiming of the raising and lowering of pitch in going from syllable to syllable. It has been pointed out (John Ohala, personal communication) that syllables in non-final position are shorter in duration than those that occur finally, so that the pitch alternations observed in these children's speech, rather than being alternations among *tones*, may simply be a result of the children's inability to consistently produce contour pitch in non-final syllables.

The Beginnings of Tone Perception

Whereas many studies examine children's production of tones, the question of when children first perceive pitch as having a lexical function has been neglected. The one paper with some data on this issue is a longitudinal diary study by Tse (1978) whose subject was acquiring Cantonese. Before the child was 10 months old, the author often called his attention to a ceiling light by pointing to the light and saying the word [təŋ təŋ ⌐⌐] 'light.'[4] During the child's tenth month, the author produced the word for light out of context, and the child looked in the direction of the room where the light was located, with nothing else happening that might have distracted his attention in that direction. Tse claims that the child was associating the sound of the Cantonese word with the object and then concludes that this event marked the beginning of the child's perception of linguistic tone contrasts. This is a questionable conclusion, however: The child might well have been demonstrating a mental association between an acoustic signal and a specific object, but he might have been associating the entire word, both segments and pitch together, with the light on the ceiling. In addition, there is no evidence that the child can contrast the high level pitch of the word with any other pitch since only a single word is involved in this event. (For that matter, the child does not have to contrast the segments of this word with any other segments.)

Subsequent to this, the author conducted a series of experiments to see whether the tone of a word was more salient to the child than segments. In the first experiment, he produced four different utterances to the child: (a) the word for "light" with both correct segments and tone; (b) the high pitch of light with different segments; (c) the correct segments of light but with different pitches; (d) different segments and different pitches. In the first situation, the child looked at the ceiling light, and in the fourth situation, where both segmental and tonal information were missing, he gave no response at all. In the second situation, where segmental information alone was lacking, the child looked at the ceiling light, whereas when tonal information alone was lacking (in the third situation), the author says that the child looked at the ceiling light with "hesitation." This finding would seem to indicate that the tone is more salient to the child since his response was

---

[4] In discussing the data from Cantonese, I shall use a convention for representing the tones also used by Tse (1978) and first proposed by Chao (1930). This is a tone scale in which a high-level tone is represented by a horizontal line that touches the top of the vertical line. Mid and low-level tones are represented, similarly, by horizontal lines touching the mid and low points, respectively, of the vertical lines. Falling and rising tones are represented by sloping lines. The tone scale will be used in this article for Cantonese since that is the system of tone representation used by Tse (1978), from whom the Cantonese data are taken. For other tone languages, however, a system of tone representation will be used in which tones are marked above vowels. Both tone marks, and their corresponding representation on tone scales, are provided for Mandarin in Table 13.2.

less "sure" when the correct tone was not provided. Such results should probably be treated with caution, however, since the distinction between simply looking at something and looking at something with hesitation might be quite fine for a 10-month-old child.

The next experiments are more revealing. When the child was 11 months old, he understood more words, specifically the ones below:

Adult form	Meaning
1. təŋ təŋ ⌐ ⌐	'lamp, light'
2. fuŋ sin ⌐ ⊣	'electric fan'
3. pu pu ⌐ ⌐	'Teddy bear'
4. tim tsʰuŋ tsʰuŋ ⟋ ⌐ ⟋	first sentence in nursery rhyme in which the index fingers are brought together

When Tse produced each of these words for the child with correct segments and tones, the child responded by looking at the appropriate object, and, in the fourth case, brought his index fingers together. Next, the author produced the vowel /a/ with the tonal patterns of each of the four words above. In the last case, the child failed to respond, but in the other three cases, he looked at the appropriate object.

Finally, the author uttered the correct segments of these four words but used different tones. When he produced the segments for light, the child looked at the light, but in the remaining cases, made no response. It is reported that these experiments were conducted many times over a 2-month period, and the same results were obtained each time. Since the child responded more often when correct tonal information was provided without the correct segments than in the converse situation, Tse concludes that tones are probably more salient than segments.

More details of the experimental settings would have been desirable; it would have been useful, for example, if, at each session, the objects were all in front of the child and roughly equidistant so as to present the child with a choice of responses. The tests were informal, and the author accepts this. (It is difficult for very rigorous experiments to be conducted with 10–11-month-old children.) Nevertheless, the results are suggestive, and similar experiments need to be done with many more children of this age before a solid conclusion can be reached.

The Beginnings of Tone Production

This section will deal with the very first productions of tone by children and will examine the question not so much from the point of view of children's phonetic accuracy but with a focus on when children's speech production first exhibits the use of pitch in a lexically contrastive way, that is, when pitch first begins to be used as tone, approximating its function in the adult language. Two diary studies are available, one of a Thai child (Tuaycharoen, 1977) and one of a child acquiring Mandarin (Clumeck, 1977), which cover the period of transition between the children's use of non-adultlike vocalizations with communicative function and their subsequent adoption of words based on adult models.

Thai

Tuaycharoen studied the phonetic and phonological development of her nephew between the ages of 3 and 18 months, collecting data from babbling right through to the earliest utterances that used adult models. She reports that at about the age of 8 months, the child had a "proto-language," in which vowels and a variety of pitches served to express different communicative intents. When the child asked what something was, demanded, or requested something, or wanted to point out objects or people who were unusual to him, he used a high or high-and-slightly-rising pitch. When acknowledging people's responses to his demands or questions, or when indicating an object or person whom he knew, he used a mid or lower-mid pitch. The vowel qualities of these utterances varied somewhat so that different communicative functions were contrasted principally by different pitches, similar to what has been reported by Halliday (1975) for an English-speaking child.

At the age of 0:11;15, the child began using words based on adult models. Most of these words were ones with mid-level or low-level pitch, and he produced these correctly and consistently. In addition, the use of pitch was now different in that it appeared to be a feature of specific words: for example, he produced the low-level pitch of the baby-talk word for "food" even when he was requesting food, a communicative function that had been expressed by high pitch in the proto-language.

In using pitch as a lexical feature of words, and not so much as a means for contrasting communicative intent, the child is producing pitch in a way that approximates more closely its use as tone in the adult language. Moreover, there is no evidence that pitch served to contrast lexical meanings before the child began to use words modeled on items in the adult language. The acquisition of tone therefore began no earlier than the acquisition of segmental phonology, whereas the use of pitch as an expression of emotional or affective state (i.e., as an intonation) began before either of these.

Mandarin

The case study reported in Clumeck (1977) is of a boy, M., acquiring Mandarin from the age of 1:2 until he was 2:8;2. Compared to the language development of many children reported in the literature, M.'s was different in that he spoke very little, and, during the first few years of his life, met his communicative needs through gestures, vocalizations not based on adult models, and, after the age of about 18 months, single-word utterances. He did not begin to use words based on adult models until he was about 22 months old.

From 1:2 to 1:5;2, M. had a proto-language very similar to the one described by Tuaycharoen for her nephew: A number of vowels were used with different pitches, and these pitches seemed to correlate with the child's emotional state: if M. wanted something or called on someone to do something for him, he used rising, high-level, high-and-slightly-rising, high-and-slightly-falling, or mid-level pitch. He used falling pitches, going either from high to low or from mid to low, to indicate something he had found, to accompany an action he was performing, or if he was simply content.

During the next few months, M. had a small repertoire of "early vocables," (Ferguson 1978) that were phonetically consistent sound-meaning correspondences having communicative functions but not based on words from the adult language. One of these was the form [mumu] with falling pitch on the second or on both syllables. It was used to refer to animals, birds (or pictures of these), and some nonsense objects that were small wooden blocks with faces painted on them. A second, and similar, vocable was [jojo] also with falling pitch, and used to refer to plants, flowers, and trees. M. produced one of these vocables when he had the object referred to in his hand, was looking at it, showing it to someone, or reaching for it. In addition to these, M. used another word of his own invention to express a request, anxiety, or concern about something. Its form was [ini] or [nēⁱni] with high level pitch.

The two vocables making reference to animals and plants, on the one hand, and the other "requesting" vocable, on the other, had mutually exclusive segments, pitch, and communicative function. For instance, M. would say [ini] to ask that someone give him a toy animal, but, once he had the animal in his hand, might then say [mumu].

At about the age of 1:10, M. abandoned these vocables and began using words based on adult models. These are bisyllabic reduplications that referred to various animals and familiar objects such as fruit and cakes. He produced all these words with rising pitch, which was essentially the correct tone his parents used with these words. (Although a number of the words he spoke have citation tones which are not rising tone, M.'s parents used rising tone most frequently in their baby-talk to him so that frequency may account for his early use of this pitch.)

M.'s use of pitch in his proto-language was very similar to that of Tuaycharoen's Thai subject when he was at the corresponding stage. Pitch was used by both children as a reflection of their emotional or affective states and served to mark different communicative intents, but there is no evidence that either child used pitch to mark contrasts in lexical meaning. The two case studies therefore indicate that the onset of tonal acquisition does not begin prior to the beginning of the acquisition of segmental phonology. The use of pitch for intonational purposes, however, begins earlier. In this respect, the acquisition of tones is much more like the acquisition of segments and less like intonation.

Lexical versus Phonological Contrastivity

When M. began producing words based on adult models, he generally produced the rising tone as this was the most frequent in the reduplicated baby-talk nouns spoken to him. Words with high-level tone, however, were produced with that pitch by his parents, so that a few items in his vocabulary had this other tone. On occasion, M. produced high-level tone words with rising pitch: it would appear that, although he had discovered that words have pitch as a lexical feature, he began with a fairly strong "hypothesis" that words have rising tone. Nevertheless, his consistent use of rising tone with rising-tone words and fluctuation between rising tone and high-level tone for high-level-tone words suggests that he was beginning to make some distinction among different tones.

A problem to be considered at this point concerns the status of tone in the child's speech. Ferguson and Farwell (1975) have pointed out the difficulty in deciding whether or not a child has a phonological distinction between two given sounds if his speech does not actually contain minimal pairs in which the sounds are directly contrasted. In the case of tone, if the child has a contrast between two words that differ both in segments and tone, and if the tones are produced consistently and correctly, they certainly contrast *lexically* even though there is no direct evidence for a purely *phonological* contrast, which would be one where pitch alone is the distinctive feature.

In M.'s vocabulary, there were no minimal pairs, although there was one that came very close: the word for "melon," [kᵘa kᵘā] and the word for "fruit," [kᵘɔ kᵘɔ] (these are the adult forms). For about 4 months after he adopted words based on adult models, M. produced fruit most often as [kōkᵘái] in spontaneous or elicited (non-imitated) speech; as for melon, he produced it with high-level tone in imitation, but two instances of this word in elicited speech are phonetically similar to his rendition of fruit: [kɔ̄ᵘkᵘi] and [kᵘɔkᵘái].

There were two minimal pairs in the speech of Tuaycharoen's Thai subject. The adult forms were (a) [má:] 'dog,' and [mā:], 'horse'; and (b) [mɔ́ʔ], 'name of district', and [mɔ́], literally 'doctor' in the adult language but used by the child to refer to the place where his mother worked. Tuaycharoen reports that there was no difference for the child between the forms of the first pair, and, similarly, that the tones of the items in the second were interchangable in his speech (pp. 141, 148).

It is hardly surprising that the children would have difficulty mastering the phonological differences between these forms since the two items of each pair are so alike semantically. We thus would expect that these forms would not be distinct in the children's production until they begin to classify the members of each pair into separate semantic categories. Shvachkin (1973) touched on this issue when he wrote that "the basic determining factor underlying the phonemic development of child language, is the semantics of the language. The semantic development of child language determines the phonemic development, [p. 92]." Certainly the child's classification of two objects into separate semantic categories and the child's production of a phonological contrast between these two objects are very closely related; exactly what determines what, or which one precedes the other, is a more difficult question to settle.

At any rate, it seems clear that the children's consistent and, in many cases, correct use of pitch with various lexical items from the adult language suggests that they are realizing pitch as a feature of words, and as such, different pitches in their vocabulary are contrastive, at least at the lexical level. What is still unknown at this point is when children are able to contrast tones phonologically as well.

The Completion of Tone Acquisition

If the acquisition of tones begins at about the same time as that of segments; if children's production of tones is on the whole more accurate phonetically than their production of many segments, and as tones are fewer in number than segments, it would be expected that the process of acquiring the tonal system would be accomplished relatively quickly and easily. Complete acquisition of the tonal system can be complicated, however, by rules of tone sandhi, or tone alternation, within the system. Although a child may be able to produce all the tones along with their allophones from the point of view of phonetic accuracy, underlying knowledge of all the tonal contrasts, and consistent and correct use of tone allophones in different environments may take a longer time to achieve. Two case studies involving children acquiring Mandarin are described in Clumeck (1977).

The Mandarin Tonal System

Before going into the details of these children's tonal production, it would be useful to describe the Mandarin tonal system. There are four contrastive tones, as listed in Table 13.2: high-level, rising, low-dipping, and

TABLE 13.2
Mandarin Tones

Tones	Romanization	Tone scale
High-level	mā	⌐ 55
Rising	má	⌐ 35
Low-dipping	mǎ	⌐ 214
Falling	mà	⌐ 51

falling. The middle column in the table shows how the tones are represented by tone marks above the vowel, and the right-hand column shows how they are represented by the 1–5 tone scale provided by Chao (1930). The rest of the chapter will use the system of marking tones above the vowel.

There are two principal tone sandhi rules operating on non-final syllables:

1. The low-dipping tone becomes low-level when it occurs before the high-level, rising, or falling tones (i.e., any tone but itself).

2. The low-dipping tone becomes a rising tone when it occurs before another word with low-dipping tone.

Chao (1968) has called the first of these rules "allophonic" because the low-level tone is an allophone of the low-dipping tone and is not similar phonetically to any other tone in the system, whereas he has referred to the second rule as "morphophonemic," since the rising tone produced by the rule is identical to the rising tone which is phonemically distinct from the low-dipping tone (p. 27).[5] Both of these tone-changing rules are illustrated in Table 13.3.

The Children's Tone Production

The two children of this study came from monolingual Mandarin-speaking families in the San Francisco Bay Area; the parents in both families were natives of China. The older child, a boy referred to as P., was 2:3 at the beginning of the study and 3:5 at the end. The other was a girl, J., who was observed between the ages of 1:10 and 2:10. These children were visited approximately once every two weeks in their homes, and tape recorded samples of their speech contain spontaneous, elicited, and imitated speech.

Analysis of the children's tone production includes only those words that were uttered either in isolation or in utterance-final position.[6] Results for each child have been pooled from the whole period during which the data were obtained, and the percentages of accuracy for each tone are presented in Table 13.4. It is immediately clear that both children had almost complete mastery of the high-level and falling tones, and that they had considerably more difficulty with the rising and low-dipping tones. Alternation between the two latter tones was more frequent than that between any other

[5] This fact has been confirmed by the perceptual experiment of Wang and Li (1967), in which native Mandarin listeners could not correctly and consistently identify rising tones originating from underlying low-dipping tones versus rising tones originating from rising tones.

[6] Only tones in isolation or utterance-final position were analyzed, as the purpose was to investigate the children's accuracy and consistency of tone production in environments that are free of possible contextual effect on pitch. As was seen earlier, the children's production of a tone in any given syllable, in non-final position, can be affected by the tone of the following syllable.

TABLE 13.3
Tone Sandhi Rules of Mandarin

1. Allophonic rule:

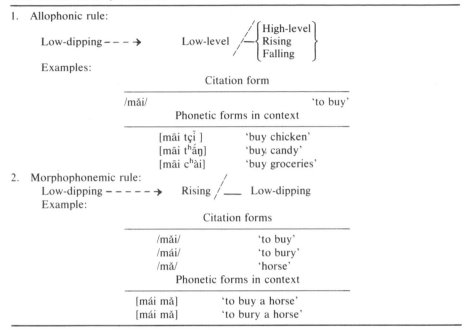

Low-dipping – – – → Low-level $\Big/$ $\begin{Bmatrix} \text{High-level} \\ \text{Rising} \\ \text{Falling} \end{Bmatrix}$

Examples:

Citation form	
/măi/	'to buy'
Phonetic forms in context	
[māi tçi̅]	'buy chicken'
[māi tʰǎŋ]	'buy candy'
[māi cʰài]	'buy groceries'

2. Morphophonemic rule:
   Low-dipping – – – – – → Rising $\big/$ ___ Low-dipping
   Example:

Citation forms	
/măi/	'to buy'
/mái/	'to bury'
/mă/	'horse'
Phonetic forms in context	
[mái mă]	'to buy a horse'
[mái mă]	'to bury a horse'

pair of tones, for example, where P. exhibited 83% accuracy for the rising tone, the overwhelming majority of tokens of the remaining 17% were low-dipping tones, and vice versa for the low-dipping tone category. For J., rising and low-dipping pitches were almost allophones of each other.

The children differed in the extent to which they had mastered the contrast between the rising and low-dipping tones: P. had much greater control over the distinction, and, in fact, his speech underwent a change during the latter half of the period of study to where production of the rising and low-dipping tones almost reached the level of accuracy of the other two tones. The percentages presented for J., on the other hand, remained roughly the same throughout the year that she was observed. Even at the age of 2:10, she did not exhibit control over the contrast between rising and low-dipping tones.

Two reasons can be suggested to account for the children's greater difficulty in mastering the rising versus low-dipping tone distinction: (*a*) the tones are phonetically alike in that each has a rising component; and (*b*) they alternate with each other morphophonemically in a specific environment, such that rising-tone words are always heard with rising tone, whereas low-dipping-tone words are heard sometimes with the low-dipping tone and sometimes with the rising tone. This may lead the children to overgeneralize and to treat the tones as phonologically equivalent. As a result, it may take

TABLE 13.4
Percentages of Accuracy in Tone Production of Two Mandarin-speaking children

Tone production by P.		
Tone type	Percentage	Number of tokens
1. High-level tone	97.0	(231)
2. Falling tone	94.3	(283)
3. Rising tone	83.3	(269)
4. Low-dipping tone	87.4	(334)
Tone production by J.		
1. High-level tone	97.2	(213)
2. Falling tone	95.8	(264)
3. Rising tone	61.3	(194)
4. Low-dipping tone	73.9	(341)

some time for them to discover that the tones are phonologically contrastive, but that they do alternate in one environment.

It should be emphasized that the children were able to produce all of the tones of Mandarin accurately throughout the period of study. From this point of view, the process of acquiring tones was completed well in advance of segmental acquisition. On the other hand, it took the children a longer time to acquire all the phonemic tonal distinctions in the sense of having an underlying knowledge of which tones are in contrast and which are simply allophones of others. It would be most interesting to have data on the acquisition of tones by children learning one of the Southern Min dialects of Chinese, such as Taiwanese, in which there is not simply one morphophonemic tone sandhi rule as in Mandarin, but where all the tones alternate with each other according to a number of sandhi rules.

The Sequence of Tone Acquisition

Production

This section will deal with two questions:

1. What is the order of tone acquisition in the particular languages that have been studied?

2. Are there certain kinds of tones that are consistently acquired in children's production before other kinds? In other words, is there any basis for making universal statements or hypotheses about the order in which children learn to produce tones?

Some of the literature on tone acquisition in Chinese suggests that the high-level and falling tones are acquired before rising tones. Li and Thompson (1977) collected data from 17 Mandarin-speaking children ranging in age from 1:6 to 3 years. The two youngest children produced no rising or low-dipping tones. In fact, one of these children produced no contour tones at all, but substituted level tones of different heights for the rising, low-dipping, and falling tones; the high-level tone, on the other hand, was produced correctly. The second of these children produced only high-level and falling tones and appeared to avoid all adult words with either rising or low-dipping tone, with the exception of the rising-tone word for 'fish', which she consistently produced with falling tone. On the basis of the data from these two children, Li and Thompson propose a hierarchy of "ease of learning" for the four tones, according to which the high-level and falling tones are easier for children to learn to produce than the rising and low-dipping tones.

In his study of Cantonese, Tse (1978) reports that the high-level and low-level tones were the first to be acquired by his subject (there are no falling tones, but two rising tones: one goes from low to mid, and the other rises from low to high). The high-rising tone and the mid-level tone were acquired subsequently, and, finally, the low-rising tone and another level tone intermediate between the mid-level and low-level tones. Tse suggests that, regardless of the number of tones in a language, the first ones that children seem to acquire are the highest-level tone (if there is more than one level tone) and either the lowest-level tone or a falling tone.

Li and Thompson hypothesize that the high-level and falling tones are acquired earlier because rising tones are more difficult to produce. They cite experimental phonetic studies from the literature on adults (Ohala and Ewan, 1973; Sundberg, 1973) indicating that falling pitch is produced more quickly than rising pitch, reflecting, perhaps, greater physiological effort in the production of a rising pitch.

If it is true that physiological ease, or difficulty, accounts for the data from the studies by Li and Thompson and by Tse, then it would be expected that other studies would show similar results. This is not the case, however. The Thai-speaking child of Tuaycharoen's (1977) study first acquired the mid-level and low-level tones at the age of about one year, and the rising tone was acquired soon after (Thai has three level tones: high, mid and low, a rising tone, and a falling tone). This disconfirms Tse's suggestion that the highest-level tone will be the first of the level tones to be acquired, if the language has more than one level tone. It was not until nearly 4 months after the appearance of the first three tones that the child began to produce the high-level and falling tones. Those tones that this child acquired last in his production were therefore the first tones to appear in the speech of the two Mandarin-speaking subjects of Li and Thompson.

Second, the Mandarin child M. (whose speech development was discussed earlier) first produced the rising tone when he began to use words based on adult models at about the age of 1:10. As was suggested, he probably acquired this tone first because of its frequency in the reduplicated nouns which his parents addressed to him: low-dipping-tone words, a large number of falling-tone words, and, of course, rising-tone words were all reduplicated in their baby-talk speech with the rising tone. High-level-tone words were reduplicated with the high-level tone, and, in M.'s speech, these words were variously produced with the rising or the high-level tones.

These data conflict with Li and Thompson's finding that the rising tone is learned later than other tones and disconfirms their hypothesis that the rising tone is more difficult for children to learn to produce for physiological reasons. It is perhaps true, as suggested by the phonetic literature on adults, that rising pitch is more difficult and takes longer to execute than falling pitch. On the basis of adult behavior it is perfectly reasonable to hypothesize that children also find rising pitch more difficult than falling. What is unknown, however, is to what degree a rising pitch may be harder (i.e., how much difference does it really make to a child?). It appears from the data of all the studies taken together that we cannot yet determine which tones are "harder" than others for children to learn, if indeed any are more difficult.

Because there is no way to determine an order of acquisition of tones for any single language at this point, there is no basis for making statements of a universal nature about the sequence of tone acquisition. Many more case studies are needed, especially of the earliest stages of language development when children first begin to use words based on adult models.

Recognition

By the term "recognition," we are not concerned with the child's ability to discriminate phonetic differences between pitches; rather, we are referring to the child's perception of a phonemic distinction between two given pitches (i.e., the child's ability to recognize and match tonal categories). With regard to the question of the order of acquisition of tonal contrasts, some data are available on Mandarin in Clumeck (1977), and these are only relevant to the later stages of acquisition. No data at all exist on the earliest contrasts recognized by children.

Two Mandarin-speaking children participated in a series of phonemic recognition tasks conducted longitudinally. These are the children P. and J., whose tone production has been discussed, and whose ages during the study were 2:3–3:5 and 1:10–2:10, respectively. The purpose of the tasks was to determine which phonemic contrasts the children could perceive, and the methodology was similar to that used by earlier studies of Russian- and English-speaking children (Barton, 1976; Edwards, 1974; Garnica, 1971; Shvachkin, 1973).

At each testing session, the child was presented with two objects, or pictures of objects, whose names were identical except for the tone, and, in addition, a third object, a "distractor," whose name was entirely different from those of the other two. The experimenter (myself) pronounced the name of each object as it was presented to the child. Afterwards, there followed a series of trials, at each of which the child was asked to give one of the three objects to the experimenter. Each of the three objects was asked for five times, for a total of 15 trials, and the order in which the objects were asked for was random. The two test objects were therefore asked for a total of 10 times.

It was decided that the child had to make a minimum of eight correct responses out of the 10 trials in which one of the test objects was asked for; the binomial probabilities distribution was used to determine whether or not the probability of the observed number of correct responses was less than .05.

Throughout the study, the attempt was made to find minimal pairs of real Mandarin words that the children already knew. However, it was difficult to find an appropriate word with the rising tone that could be contrasted with the low-dipping and falling tones. As a result, a nonsense object was used in testing the children's perception of these two contrasts: rising versus low-dipping and rising versus falling. The object was a small wooden block with a face and ears painted on it; it was given a name with a rising tone and was contrasted with the word for "mouse," which has a low-dipping tone and the word for "tree," which has a falling tone. The children played with this nonsense object during the home visits over a period of several months before being tested with it.

Both children were tested first on the distinction between rising and falling tones, and both exhibited recognition of the contrast. Within a month after this, they were tested for the second distinction, between rising and low-dipping tones, but failed to recognize the contrast. It can therefore be concluded that, when the children were taught a new word with the rising tone, they found it more difficult to contrast this word with one having the low-dipping tone than one having the falling tone. Consequently, the children might have acquired the distinction between rising and falling tones earlier than that between rising and low-dipping tones.

On being tested for the other contrasts, where both members of the minimal pair were familiar words, the children consistently exhibited ability to recognize the contrast. The results from these tests cannot be compared to those that made use of the nonsense object, because it is known that children's performance on phonemic recognition tasks is affected by the degree of their familiarity with the test words (Barton, 1976). However, results for the two contrasts that were tested with the nonsense object can at least be compared to each other as testing conditions were the same for both.

Results for the phonemic recognition tasks correspond with the data from the children's production described earlier, where it was reported that the high-level and falling tones were stable in their speech but that there was some amount of variation between rising and low-dipping tones. As was suggested, it is proposed that the greater difficulty experienced in learning to recognize the distinction between rising and low-dipping tones is due to the phonetic similarity of the two tones, in that they both have a rising end-component, and also to the fact that they alternate with each other mor-phophonemically in one environment, which might lead the children to treat both tones as phonologically equivalent.

On the basis of the recognition and production data from the Mandarin-speaking children, it is hypothesized for other tone languages that contrasts acquired relatively late are ones in which both members of the pair are either phonetically similar, alternate with each other in accordance with a tone sandhi rule, or both.

References

Barton, D. (1976) "The Role of Perception in the Acquisition of Phonology," Doctoral Dissertation, University of London. (Indiana University Linguistics Club)

Chao, Y. R. (1930) "A System of Tone Letters," *Le Maitre Phonétique*, 45, 24–27.

Chao, Y. R. (1973) "The Cantian Idiolect: an Analysis of the Chinese Spoken by a Twenty-eight-month-old Child," in C. A. Ferguson and D. I. Slobin, eds., *Studies of Child Language Development*, Holt, Rinehart and Winston.

Clumeck, H. (1977) "Studies in the Acquisition of Mandarin Phonology," Doctoral Dissertation, University of California, Berkeley.

Edwards, M. L. (1974) "Perception and Production in Child Phonology: The Testing of Four Hypotheses," *Journal of Child Language*, 1, 205–219.

Ferguson, C. A. (1978) "Learning to Pronounce: The Earliest Stages of Phonological Development in the Child," in F. D. Minifie and L. L. Lloyd, eds., *Communicative and Cognitive Abilities—Early Behavioral Assessment*, University Park Press: Baltimore, pp. 273–297.

Ferguson, C. A., and Farwell, C. B. (1975) "Words and Sounds in Early Language Acquisition," *Language*, 51, 419–439.

Garnica, O. K. (1971) "The Development of the Perception of Phonemic Differences in Initial Consonants by English-speaking Children: A Pilot Study" *Papers and Reports on Child Language Development* (Linguistics, Stanford University), 3–29.

Halliday, M. A. K. (1975) *Learning How to Mean: Explorations in the Development of Language*, Edward Arnold, London.

Kirk, L. (1973) "An Analysis of Speech Imitations by Gā Children," *Anthropological Linguistics*, 15, 267–275.

Li, C. N., and Thompson, S. A. (1977) "The Acquisition of Tone in Mandarin-speaking Children," *Journal of Child Language*, 4, 185–199.

Ohala, J. J., and Ewan, W. (1973) "Speed of Pitch Change," (Abstract) *Journal of the Acoustical Society of America*, 53, 345.

Shvachkin, N. K. (1973) "The Development of Phonemic Speech Perception in Early Childhood," in C. A. Ferguson and D. I. Slobin, eds., *Studies of Child Language Development*, Holt, Rinehart and Winston.

Sundberg, J. (1973) "Data on Maximum Speed of Pitch Changes," Royal Institute of Technology, Stockholm, Speech Transmission Laboratory, *Quarterly Progress and Status Report*, 4, 39–47.

Tse, J. K. P. (1978) "Tone Acquisition in Cantonese: A Longitudinal Case Study," *Journal of Child Language*, 5, 191–204.

Tuaycharoen, P. (1977) "The Phonetic and Phonological Development of a Thai Baby: From Early Communicative Interaction to Speech, Doctoral Dissertation, University of London.

Wang, W. S-Y., and Li, K. P. (1967) "Tone 3 in Pekinese," *Journal of Speech and Hearing Research*, 10, 629–636.

Westermeyer, R., and Westermeyer, J. (1977) "Tonal Language Acquisition among Lao Children," *Anthropological Linguistics*, 19, 260–264.

GLOSSARY

KAY ATKINSON-KING

Acoustic—Refers to the physical properties of a sound (cf. auditory).

Affricate—A consonant sound beginning as a stop but ending as a fricative with approximately the same place of articulation (e.g., /tʃ/ as in *church*, which begins with /t/ as in *tie* and is followed by /ʃ/ as in *shy*). It may be specified as a stop with delayed release.

Allophone—A nondistinctive or noncontrastive phonetic realization of a phoneme in a given language (e.g., the aspirated and unaspirated versions of the bilabial voiceless stop in *pot* [pʰ] and *spot* [p] in English are classified as allophones of the phoneme [p]; cf. phoneme).

Alveolar—A consonant sound articulated with the tip or blade of the tongue against the alveolar ridge (e.g., /d/).

Alveolar ridge—The bony ridge located behind the upper teeth.

Alveo–palatal—A consonant sound articulated with the blade of the tongue against the alveolar ridge and the main body of the tongue raised toward the palate (e.g., /ʃ/ in *ship*).

Amplitude—The magnitude of maximum displacement of air molecules in response to a vibratory force. In speech production, amplitude may be considered a function of the energy with which the vocal cords vibrate (cf. loudness, intensity).

Analysis-by-synthesis—A theory of speech perception in which the

CHILD PHONOLOGY
VOLUME I: PRODUCTION

hearer internally generates speech signals to find the best match to an incoming signal.

Antiformants—Resonant qualities of the nasal cavity that obscure formants (cf. formants).

Aphasia—A language disorder resulting from brain injury or disease in the areas of the brain associated with linguistic ability.

Assimilation—A phonetic process in which one sound affects another sound in such a way that the sounds become more like each other. Children acquiring language may simplify through the process of assimilation (e.g., /gɔgi/ for *doggy*, /næm/ for *lamb*).

Audiometry—The systematic measurement of auditory acuity by means of a calibrated instrument known as an audiometer.

Auditory—Refers to the perception of a sound (cf. acoustic).

Autonomous phonemic level—A type of analysis used by structuralists in which phonology is entirely independent of syntax and morphology (cf. systematic phonemic level).

Behaviorism—A theoretical inductivist view that attempts to explain behavior only by reference to directly observable events rather than to underlying mental processes (cf. mentalism).

Bilabial—A consonant sound articulated with a combined movement of both lips (e.g., /p,b,m/).

Blade of tongue—Part of the narrow extremity of the tongue that is immediately behind the tongue tip and in front of the middle of the tongue.

Canonical form—The most basic or simplest form of a word or morpheme.

Categorical perception—Refers to the inability of listeners to hear the acoustic differences among sounds that they identify as belonging to the same phonemic category and their ability to discriminate among stimuli that fall at phoneme category boundaries. Thus, categorical perception occurs when there is a close relationship between identification and discrimination (cf. continuous perception).

Cinefluorography—See cineradiography.

Cineradiography—X-ray motion picutres. In speech research they are used to study the movements of the articulatory organs during speech activity (syn.: cinefluorography).

Coarticulation—An overlap in the production of gestures in successive and in some cases nonsuccessive segments of a speech utterance. The effects of coarticulation may be anticipatory or perseveratory.

Communicative competence—The ideal speaker–hearer's tacit knowledge underlying communicative behavior, including not only the language itself, but the rules for using it appropriately in the social world (cf. competence, performance).

Competence—The ideal speaker–hearer's tacit knowledge of his or her native language (he/she grammar) that allows the production and comprehension of an infinite number of grammatical sentences, among other things (cf. communicative competence, performance).

Consonant—A speech sound produced with partial or complete constriction of the vocal tract at one or more points.

Content words; contentive—A noun, verb, adjective, or adverb that carries lexical meaning (cf. function words).

Continuant—A speech sound produced with incomplete closure of the vocal tract, allowing the airflow from the lungs to continue to pass through the mouth relatively unimpeded. All speech sounds are classified as continuants except stops, where the airstream from the oral cavity is completely obstructed (cf. stops).

Continuous perception—Refers to the ability of listeners, when presented with continuously varied acoustic stimuli, to make fine discriminations among stimuli of the same or of different categories while they are unable reliably to identify stimuli as belonging to a small set of categories. Thus, there is no one-to-one relationship between discrimination and identification (cf. categorical perception).

Cross-sectional study—A method of investigation in which a number of individuals are tested and/or observed for a short period of time (cf. longitudinal study).

Decibel—A unit representing 10 times the logarithm of the ratio of the intensity of the given sound to the intensity of a referent sound.

Deep structure—In the standard theory of transformational grammar, the abstract underlying form of a sentence generated by the phrase-structure rules. The deep structures interpreted by the semantic rules provide the meanings of sentences. Transformational rules apply to deep structures to produce the surface structures (cf. surface structure).

Degemination—The process of depriving a sound of its geminated (doubled or lengthened) quality (i.e., shortening of contact; cf. gemination).

Dental—A consonant sound articulated with the tip of the tongue against the upper teeth (e.g., /θ/ in *thin*).

Diachronic—Refers to the changes in a language occuring over time (i.e., historical change; cf. synchronic).

Dichotic listening tests—A task in which two different auditory signals of equal intensity and duration are simultaneously presented to a listener, one to each ear. The subject is asked to report on what is heard in one or both ears.

Diphthong—A vowel sound whose quality changes from its beginning to its end within one syllable. Phonetically, it is analyzed and transcribed as a sequence of two vowels, or vowel plus glide within one syllable combining to form a single unit (e.g., [aɪ] (or [ay]) in *kite*; [aʊ] (or [aw]) in *cow*; and [ɔɪ] (or [ɔy]) in *coy*).

Distinctive feature—A phonetic feature or property of a language that distinguishes one phonological segment from another (e.g., /p/ and /b/ are distinguished by a different value of the voicing feature with /p/ being [– voice] and /b/ being [+ voice], or both may be distinguished from /m/ by the value [– nasal] from [+ nasal]. Distinctive feature theory postulates that there is a finite set of phonetic features from which all languages draw their phonological oppositions. Although as yet there is no universally accepted set of features, the most commonly used today is the binary system suggested by Chomsky and Halle (1968). Ladefoged (1971) has proposed an n-ary set of features that is also used.

Dorsum—The upper surface of the back portion of the tongue. It lies below the palate and the velum.

Electromyography (EMG)—A technique for measuring electrical voltages produced by muscles as they contract. It is used in speech-production research to study the action of speech muscles.

Empiricist theory of language acquisition—A theory that language is learned through experience by such factors as reinforcement and generalization of verbal behavior (syn.: learning theory; cf. nativist theory).

Feature detector—A hypothesized genetically determined perceptual mechanism that functions to discover and analyze just those acoustic cues serving as distinctive features. Whether the perception is at a peripheral acoustic (auditory) level or higher phonetic level is an open question.

Flap—A sound resulting from an articulator, most commonly the tip or blade of the tongue, making rapid contact with the articulating region, usually with the alveolar ridge, and then immediately releasing; the approach and release together are made by one ballistic movement. In American English, alveolar stops are generally produced as flaps (or taps) when they occur intervocally after stressed vowels (e.g., *writer–rider, latter–ladder*).

Formant—A frequency region for vowels and resonant consonants in which a relatively high degree of acoustic energy is concentrated. Formants are characterized by dark horizontal bands on a spectrogram. Three formants (F_1, F_2, and F_3) are generally considered of primary importance in the analysis (and perception) of speech sounds.

Fourier analysis—The analysis of a complex wave as the sum of a number of simple sine waves of different amplitudes, frequencies, and phases. This was first done by the French mathematician Joseph Fourier.

Free variation—Different versions of a sound that can occur in the same environment without changing meaning (e.g., the final consonant in *hat* may optionally be released with or without aspiration, the allophones [tʰ] and [t] in free variation. Also the phonemes /Θ/ and /ð/ in *with* vary freely with some speakers; (cf. phoneme, allophone).

Fricative—A consonant produced with partial closure in the vocal tract such as to cause audible friction as the air is expelled from the lungs (e.g., /f/ as in *fig*; syn.: spirant).

Function words; functors—A small, closed class or morphemes or words expressing grammatical or syntactic relationships and having little or no lexical meaning. This class includes pronouns, prepositions, conjunctions, articles, and modal and auxiliary verbs (cf. content word).

Fundamental frequency (F_0)—The lowest frequency component and principal component of a sound wave that generates a series of harmonics. Auditorily, it corresponds to the pitch of a speaker's voice and thus to the intonation of an utterance. The fundamental frequency is produced by vibrations of the voice cords; the faster the rate of vibration, the higher the pitch.

Gemination—Doubling that is often indicated in written form by a doubled consonant or vowel letter, and in speech by lengthening of a sound or of the period of closure before a stop consonant is released (cf. degemination).

Generative phonology—The theory of phonology related to transformational grammar. It is best exemplified by the model proposed in Chomsky and Halle (1968). The "standard theory" has been modified and revised in the last few years (see, e.g., Anderson, 1974).

Generative Syntax—A theory of syntax, usually used to refer to transformational (generative) grammar. "Generative" refers to the requirement that the theory be explicit and automatically account for all and only the well-formed sentences and syntactic structures of a language.

Glide—A speech sound characterized primarily by the shifting of the vocal organs from the articulation of one sound to another. Glides also are sometimes called semivowels, as they may function like vowels or like consonants (e.g., /y/ in *yellow* and /w/ in *win* precede vowels occurring in syllable-initial position like consonants). In many languages, vowels become glides intervocalically, or glides may become vowels. In distinctive feature terms, glides are specified as [− syllabic, − consonantal] differing only in one feature value from vowels that are [+ syllabic, − consonantal].

Glottal—Pertaining to the glottis (see glottis).

Glottal stop—A sound produced by the vocal cords closing tightly, creating a complete closure of the airstream at the glottis (e.g., a glottal stop occurs between the two vowels in the negative expression *uh uh*).

Glottis—The space between the vocal cords.

Grammatical morpheme—A morpheme that expresses a grammatical relationship or a category (e.g., plurality, possession, verb tense, negation; cf. morpheme, function words).

Harmony—In language, phonetic constraints on the types of vowels (or consonants) that may cooccur within a word (e.g., only front vowels or only back vowels may occur together, or vowels within a word must be all [+ round] or [− round].

Hertz (Hz)—The number of cycles completed in 1 second (formerly cps), the rate of oscillation of a periodic sound wave. Hz is a measure of frequency.

Historical linguistics—The branch of linguistics that studies how and why languages change over time (cf. diachronic).

Homophone; homonym—A word that is pronounced the same as another word but has a different meaning (and sometimes a different spelling) (e.g., *bear*—"to give birth to" or "to tolerate;" and *pair–pear*).

Homorganic consonants—Consonants with the same place of articulation, but differing in one or more features (e.g., /p,b,m/ are all bilabial but differ with respect to voicing and/or nasality).

Innateness hypothesis—See nativist theory.

Intensity—In the measurement of sound, the flow of energy or power, transmitted along the wave. The level of sound intensity is usually measured in decibels (cf. loudness, amplitude).

Intonation—The linguistic pitch pattern of the voice, rising and falling, over the sentence or phrase. In many languages, the intonation pattern may be grammatically distinctive. For example, in English "He's here" produced with a falling pitch reflects neutral, declarative status, whereas when it is produced with a rising intonation ("He's here?") it is interpreted as a question (cf. suprasegmental; pitch).

Labio–dental—A consonant sound articulated with the upper teeth against the lower lip (e.g., /f/).

Larynx—The cartilaginous structure located below the hyoid bone and tongue roots and at the top of the trachea. It houses the vocal cords and is the primary organ of phonation.

Lateral—A consonant sound produced with the tip of the tongue touching the alveolar ridge and one or both sides of the tongue down so that the airstream passes laterally around it.

Laws of irreversible solidarity—One of the fundamental factors governing Jakobson's (1941) postulated universal order of acquisition of phonemic feature contrasts by children. Such laws state that there are universal asymmetries in the phonemic systems of all languages, which Jakobson claims affect the order of acquisition (e.g., no language has back consonants without also having front consonants, though the converse is not true; therefore, front consonants are acquired first).

Lax vowels—See tense vowels.

Liquid—A frictionless sonorant sound produced with only partial obstruction of the airstream in the mouth (e.g., English /l/ and /r/). Like vowels, liquids have formant structure. They are distinguished from vowels in distinctive feature terms by being [+consonantal, +vocalic] with vowels being [−consonantal].

Long vowels—Vowels in some languages are distinguished solely by length or duration (e.g., /a/ versus /aa/). In other languages, vowel length is completely predictable from the phonetic environment or from other feature specifications (e.g., in many languages, like English, tense vowels are longer than lax vowels; cf. tense vowels).

Longitudinal study—A study in which the same individual or individuals are observed and/or tested over a period of time, generally to assess development (cf. cross-sectional study).

Loudness—The subjective counterpart to the intensity of sound. An attribute of auditory sensation that enables a listener to order sound on a perceptual continuum from soft to loud. The unit of loudness is the sone.

Mean length of utterance (MLU)—The average number of morphemes in a child's utterance, computed by dividing the total number of morphemes in a speech sample by the total number of utterances in that sample. It is frequently used to indicate the stage of a child's linguistic development.

Mentalism—The theoretical point of view that postulates underlying mental processes and internalized cognitive systems (cf. behaviorism).

Metathesis—Transpositions of the order of sounds in a word or between two words (e.g., some dialects of English pronounce *ask* as /æks/.

Minimal pair—Two words that have the same set of phonemes in the same sequence with the exception of one phoneme (e.g., /pɪt/ versus /bɪt/ are minimal pairs, whereas /pɪt/ versus /tɪp/ and /pɪt/ versus /pad/ are not).

Morpheme—The smallest meaningful unit of language (e.g., the word *writer* consists of two morphemes, *write* and *er*).

Morpheme structure rules (or conditions)—See redundancy rules.

Morphology—The study of the structure of words (i.e., the rules for the combination of morphemes; cf. morpheme).

Morphophoneme—The unit by means of which morphemes are phonologically represented. In structural linguistics, the morphophonemic representation of a morpheme differed from the phonemic representation. This distinction no longer holds in the standard theory of generative phonology.

Morphophonological level—See morphophoneme.

Motor theory of speech perception—A model of speech perception in which segmental phonemes are mainly perceived by reference to their articulation or production.

Myographic analysis—See electromyography.

Narrow band—See spectrograph.

Nasal—A consonant sound produced with the velum lowered to permit the airstream to pass through the nasal cavity.

Nativist theory of language acquisition—Refers to the proposal that there exists an innate language acquisition device or system (LAD or LAS) that biologically predisposes a child to acquire language as natural maturation proceeds. Experience serves to trigger the innate mechanism rather than to account directly for language learning (syn.: rationalist theory; Cf. empiricist theory).

Natural class—A set of sounds grouped together by virtue of their sharing one or more phonetic features or properties (e.g., sounds specified as [+nasal] [m, n, ŋ] form a natural class of "nasals"). Such classes are frequently referred to in the phonological rules of the world's languages).

Neutralization—The suspension of the opposition between the values of a distinctive feature, or of the opposition between phonemes in specific environments. For example, the [+ voice] / [− voice] distinction is "neutralized" in syllable-final position in German, as all voiced obstruents are "devoiced" in that position.

Obligatory environment—A linguistic context in which a given linguistic form or segment is required by the rules of that language (e.g., in English, the third person singular present tense verb form requires an − *s*: "He sings;" also, a voiceless stop consonant is aspirated in word-initial position; such as /p/ in *pig*, [pʰIg]).

Obstruent—A sound in which the airstream is obstructed before it is released (e.g., fricatives, affricates, nonasal stops; syn.: nonsonorant; cf. sonorant).

Oral stereognosis—The ability to use lip and tongue sensations to discriminate and identify different types of objects and their locations.

Oscillograph—An instrument that registers oscillations of electric current and records the variations. In phonetic research, it is used to convert sound waves into electric impulses that can be registered and recorded to permit the analysis of peak amplitude of waves and differences between pure and complex tones.

Output constraint—A term used in generative grammar for a set of constraints or conditions on the surface structure of sentences. These constraints reject sentences generated by the grammar that do not meet these conditions.

Palatal—A consonant sound articulated with the front portion of the tongue against or near the hard palate (e.g., *ich* in German).

Palate—The roof of the mouth; the long anterior portion is referred to as the "hard palate," whereas the posterior portion is called the "soft palate" or "velum."

Paralinguistic features—Features that are not part of the formal linguistic system but may carry information about the speaker's emotional state, sex, size, etc. (e.g., variations in loudness, pitch, duration, and facial gestures).

Performance—The actual production or comprehension of speech. It may be affected by grammatically irrelevant factors such as fatigue, memory limitations, nervousness, etc. (cf. competence).

Pharynx—A tube composed of muscle and mucous membrane situated behind the larynx, mouth, and nose. It acts as a resonating chamber for the voicing produced by the vocal cords in the larynx; it also provides a passageway for air into the larynx.

Phone—A single phonetic segment or speech sound, specified by the phonetic properties, articulatory or acoustic, that distinguish it from all other phonetic units.

Phoneme—An abstract contrastive phonological unit in a language; two sounds are separate phonemes when the phonetic difference between them contrasts meaning (e.g., in English /f/ versus /v/ distinguishes *fan* and *van*; cf. allophone, phone, distinctive feature).

Phonetics—The study, analysis, and cassification of the production and perception of speech sounds (see the table of phonetic symbols; cf. phonology).

Phonological rules—In generative phonology, rules operating on the underlying representation of words (systematic phonemic level) to yield the pronunciation (systematic phonetic level; cf. redundancy rules, realization rules).

Phonology—That part of a grammar accounting for speakers' knowledge of the sounds and sound patterns of their language. Also refers to the study or science of sound systems (cf. phonetics, phonological rules).

Phonotactics—Limitations on the phonological sequences and structure of words or syllables occurring within a given language (e.g., in English, nonlow lax vowels, like /ɛ/ in *bet,* never occur word finally; also initial clusters like /bn/ do not occur; (cf. redundancy rule).

Pitch—The subjective counterpart to the frequency of sound. An attribute of auditory sensation that enables a listener to order sound on a perceptual continuum from low to high. Pitch is related to the acoustic property known as the fundamental frequency of that sound (cf. fundamental frequency).

Plosive—See stop.

Pragmatics—The study of the rules underlying an individual's functional use of language in its social context, an ability that is part of that speaker's communicative competence.

Prosody; prosodic features—See suprasegmental features.

Psychoacoustics—A branch of psychophysics dealing with the relationship between acoustic stimuli and accompanying psychological sensations. The concern of psychoacoustics is the quantification of behavioral responses to a variety of auditory stimulus configurations.

Psychological reality—The goal set for linguistic theory by those concerned that models of grammar reflect the actual (though idealized) competence of native speakers. What constitutes a test of psychological reality is under discussion and is being debated widely by linguists and psycholinguists.

Psychophysics—The study of the relation between stimulus and response, wherein the measurement and specification of the stimulus are encompased by the science of physics, and the measurement and specification of the response are encompassed by the field of psychology.

Quantity—In phonology, quantity refers to length or duration. Speech sounds are labeled "long" or "short" when their relative duration is phonologically important in a language.

TABLE
Phonetic Symbols

Consonants

Stops			Affricates		
p	pig	[pɪg]	5ʃ (tš, č)	choke	[tʃ ok]
b	big	[bɪg]	dʒ (dž, ǰ)	joke	[dʒ ok]
t	tip	[tɪp]			
d	dip	[dɪp]			
k	cap	[kæp]			
g	gap	[gæp]			

Nasals			Liquids		
m	sum	[sʌm]	l	led	[lɛd]
n	sun	[sʌn]	r	red	[rɛd]
ŋ	sung	[sʌŋ]			

Fricatives			Glides		
f	fan	[fæn]	w	wet	[wɛt]
v	van	[væn]	y (j)	yet	[yɛt]
θ	thigh	[θaɪ]			
ð	thy	[ðəɪ]			
s	sip	[sɪp]			
z	zip	[zɪp]			
ʃ (š)	shun	[ʃʌn]			
ʒ (ž)	vision	[vɪʒən]			
h	hat	[hæt]			

Vowels

Front			Central		
i	beet	[bit]	ə	above	[ˌəˈbʌv]
ɪ	bit	[bɪt]	ʌ	but	[bʌt]
e	bait	[bet]			
ɛ	bet	[bɛt]			
æ	bat	[bæt]			

Back			Diphthong		
u	boot	[but]	aɪ (ay)	bite	[baɪt]
ʊ	put	[pʊt]	aʊ (aw)	bout	[baʊt]
o	boat	[bot]	ɔɪ (oy)	boy	[bɔɪ]
ɔ	bought	[bɔt]			
a	pot	[pat]			

Various phonetic markings

:   indicates preceding sound is lengthened (e.g., [e:])

h   indicates preceding sound is aspirated (e.g., [tʰ])

~   indicates a nasalized vowel (e.g., [æ̃])

ʔ   indicates a glottal stop (e.g., *oh oh!* [oʔo])

ˈ   indicates the following syllable has primary stress (e.g., the first syllable of *eggplant* [ˈɛgˌplænt])

ˌ   indicates the following syllable has secondary stress (e.g., the second syllable of eggplant [ˈɛgˌplænt])

Rationalist theory—See nativist theory.

Realization rules—In phonology, rules that convert abstract, underlying phonological forms of a grammar into actual phonetic form are called realization rules (e.g., one such rule may specify that an underlying bilabial stop is pronounced as voiced in word-initial position and voiceless in word-final position; cf. phonological rules).

Redundancy rules—In phonology, language-specific rules accounting for the predictable, general, nonidiosyncratic phonemic representations of words in that language. Redundancy rules (also called morpheme structure rules or conditions) may be segmental or sequential (e.g., in English, the rule that all nasal phonemes are voiced is a segmental redundancy rule; the rule that the first segment of a word-initial obstruent cluster must be /s/ is a sequential redundancy rule). Phonological redundancy rules distinguish "accidental gaps" (e.g., in English /blIk/ is permissible although not in the lexicon) from "Systematic gaps" (e.g., in English /bnIk/ cannot occur) by defining admissible sequences (cf. phonological rules).

Reduplication—Either the repetition of syllables in a word (e.g., in the English *mama*), or a rule or process in a language using this kind of repetition to derive morphologically complex words.

Retroflex—Sounds that are produced by curling the tip of the tongue back behind the alveolar ridge (e.g., English /r/).

Rewrite rules—In generative grammar, a formal mathematical rule in which an arrow acts as an instruction to replace the symbol on the left of the arrow with the symbol or string of symbols on its right (e.g., $X \rightarrow Y + Z$; noun phrase $\rightarrow$ article + noun). Rewrite rules are used formally to express linguistic operations such as deletion (e.g., deletion of a final nasal would be shown by the rule $/n/ \rightarrow \emptyset$ / ___#, where $\emptyset$ indicates deletion, / indicates "in the environment of," and ___# indicates final position).

Sandhi—Adaptive changes in speech sounds occurring at the boundaries of words as the result of their mutual influence on each other.

Semantic features—A set of general elements or components of meaning that are used to analyze word meaning (e.g., *man* is analyzed as having such features as "human," "animate," "male," and "adult").

Semivowel—See glide.

Sensorimotor—Piaget's first stage in the development of intelligence in which the form of knowledge is linked with the content of specific sensory input or motor actions.

Short vowel—See long vowel.

Sibilant—A hissing fricative sound like [s], [z], [ʃ], and [ʒ]; or the affricates [tʃ] and [dʒ].

Sociolinguistics—The study of language in society, variations and dialect differences existing between social classes, groups or regions. These differences may be phonological, syntactic, semantic, or pragmatic.

Sonorant—A sound produced with a relatively unobstructed airstream.

Sounds in this category are vowels, liquids, glides, and nasals. Although there is an obstruction in the oral cavity with nasals, the open nasal passage permits the air to resonate (cf. obstruents).

Sonority—One of the two classes of inherent features defined by Jakobson and Halle (1956). Sonority features deal with the amount and concentration of energy in the spectrum and in time (e.g., consonantal versus nonconsonantal are sonority features that acoustically show low, as opposed to high, total energy).

Spectrogram—The visual representation of an acoustic speech signal produced by a spectrograph.

Spectrograph—An instrument used to analyze sound signals and to produce a visual display of frequency and intensity as a function of time. The spectrograms produced may be the result of analysis with a narrow band filter (usually at 45 Hz) or a wide band filter (usually at 300 Hz).

Spectrum—A graph or diagram displaying the relative amplitudes of the frequency components of a complex acoustic signal.

Spirant—See fricative.

Steady state—The relatively nonchanging portion of a speech sound (e.g., time midsection of a vowel with onset and offset transitions not included.

Stop—A consonant sound produced with complete closure of the articulators in the mouth, thus totally blocking the airstream (e.g., /p,g/; syn.: plosive).

Stress—Emphasis or accent on a syllable that is produced by increased duration, pitch, and/or intensity on some syllables as compared with others (cf. suprasegmental).

Structuralism—A theoretical approach in the social sciences that is usually associated, in linguistics, with De Saussure and his followers. It views "facts" or data in terms of their functions in a system, and sharply separates historical (diachronic) phonomena from the linguistic system at any one point in time (synchronic). Units in the system are viewed both paradigmatically (e.g., the phonemes /t/ and /d/, which, when substituted for each other, change meaning, as in *tip* and *dip*) and syntagmatically, (e.g., the phonemes /t/, /I/, /p/ concatenate to form a larger unit, the morpheme *tip*).

Subglottal—The parts of the speech mechanism that are below the glottal opening between the vocal cords (i.e., the lungs, trachae, etc.).

Supraglottal—The parts of the vocal tract that are above the glottal opening between the vocal cords (i.e., oral, pharyngeal, nasal, and buccal cavities).

Suprasegmental—Nonsegmental, prosodic features of speech that may be superimposed over one or more speech segments (i.e., over consonants and vowels) and that function linguistically. These nonsegmentals may include stress, tone, rhythm, intonation, and duration.

Surface structure—The phrase marker (or tree structure) of a sentence that is derived from its underlying deep structure by the application of transformational rules. Phonological rules apply to surface structures to produce the systematic phonetic representations of sentences (cf. deep structure).

Synchronic—Refers to language at a specific point in time, or at a given stage of linguistic development, divorced from the historical developments that produced that system (cf. diachronic).

Systematic phonemic level—The lexical (phonological) representation of formatives and sentences prior to the application of phonological rules (cf. autonomous phonemic level; morphophoneme).

Systematic phonetic level—A level of representation used in generative phonology, that is the surface-structure phonetic output of the phonological component.

Taxonomic—Refers to categorization and classification. In linguistics it is the approach transformational grammarians attribute to American structuralists such as Bloomfield.

Tense vowels—A class of vowels distinguished from those specified as "lax." For example, in English, /i, u, e, and o/ are in some descriptions specified as [+ tense] whereas their counterparts /I, ʊ, ɛ, ɲ/ are marked as [– tense]. The tense vowels in English are longer in duration, diphthongized, and sometimes produced with a slightly higher tongue position and a narrower glottis.

Token—An instance of a general type or category (e.g., when one repeats a word five times, each production is a token of the word; cf. type).

Tonality—One of the two classes of inherent features defined by Jakobson and Halle (1956). Acoustically, tonality features deal with the ends of the frequency spectrum (e.g., grave versus acute are tonality features that acoustically show a concentration of energy in the lower, versus upper, frequencies of the spectrum; cf. sonority).

Tone language—A language in which relative pitch is used to distinguish lexical units.

Transcription—The written symbolic representation of utterances. "Broad" or "phonemic" transcription is enclosed within slashes (e.g., /pIt/); "narrow," "fine," or "phonetic" transcription is indicated by brackets (e.g., [pʰIt].

Trill—One articulator (e.g., tongue tip or uvula) vibrating against another, such as the roof of the mouth or the velum.

Triphthong—A sequence of three adjacent vowels or glides within a single syllable (e.g., /auər/ in *hour*; /faIər/ in *fire*. Note the *rs* may be syllabic in these words.)

Type—Refers to a general category (e.g., all the vowel segments in *bee, neat,* and *eel* are tokens of the vowel type /i/; cf. token).

Underlying form—Usually refers to the lexical representation of morphemes. Thus, two words that differ phonetically but contain the same morphemes may be represented by the same underlying form of the morpheme (e.g., *telegraph, telegraph-ic, telegraph-y*).

Uvula—The small cone-shaped appendage that hangs down at the end of the velum.

Uvular—A consonant sound articulated by raising the back portion of the tongue near the uvula.

Velar—A consonant sound articulated with the back portion of the tongue against or near the soft palate (e.g., /k/).

Velum—The soft palate (cf. palate).

Vocal folds—Folds of ligaments located on each side of the larynx and extending from the arytenoid cartilages at the back of the larynx to the Adam's apple at the front (syn.: vocal cords). There is a superior pair referred to as the ventricular or false folds and the inferior pair called the true vocal folds.

Vocal fry—A series of low-frequency oscillations of the vocal cords in which the closed phase is longer than the open phase, creating a series of relatively sharp acoustic impulses and a "crackling" type of phonation (syns.: laryngealization; glottal fry; "fry" register; pulsated voice).

Voice onset time (VOT)—The interval between the release of closure (burst) and the onset of vibration of the vocal cords in the production of stop consonants. It is used as an acoustic measure to distinguish voiced and voiceless stops in most languages (cf. voicing lag, voicing lead).

Voiced—A sound produced with vibrating vocal cords (cf. voiceless).

Voiceless—A sound produced with the glottis open, as in breathing, without any vibration of the vocal cords (cf. voiced).

Voicing lag—A category of voice onset time in which the onset of glottal vibration (voicing) follows the burst release. The onset of voicing may coincide with or immediately follow the consonantal burst (short lag), or it may be somewhat delayed (long lag; cf. voice onset time).

Voicing lead—A category of voice onset time in which the onset of glottal vibration (voicing) precedes the burst release (cf. voice onset time).

Volume—In speech, the loudness of a sound, determined by frequency and intensity (cf. frequency; intensity).

Vowel—A speech sound produced by the unobstructed passage of air through the oral cavity; the most prominent portion of a syllable.

Vowel nucleus—The portion of a vowel cluster (e.g., dipthong) that is loudest and most resonant.

Vowel quality—The characteristic that distinguishes one vowel from another, determined mainly by the resonance of the vocal tract in production.

Vowel shift rules—Phonological rules that account for modern English vowel alternations reflecting the phonological changes of the middle-English vowel system (e.g., the pronunciation of the second vowel in *serene–serenity*).

Vowel space—When the vowel frequencies of Formants 1 and 2 are plotted against each other, the resulting diagram provides a picture of how the vowels relate to each other in what is called the "vowel space." In perception experiments using multidimensional scaling methods, it is also common to refer to the results as representing perceptual vowel space.

Wave form—A visual representation of a sound wave displaying its amplitude as a function of time; time analysis of an acoustic signal (syn.: wave shape).

Wide band—See spectrograph.

References

Anderson, S. (1974) *The Organization of Phonology*, Academic Press, New York.

Chomsky, N., and Halle, M. (1968) *The Sound Pattern of English*, Harper & Row, New York.

Jakobson, R., and Halle, M. (1956) *Fundamentals of Language*, Mouton, The Hague.

Ladefoged, P. (1971) *Preliminaries to Linguistic Phonetics*, The University of Chicago Press, Chicago.

SUBJECT INDEX

PERSPECTIVES IN
NEUROLINGUISTICS, NEUROPSYCHOLOGY, AND PSYCHO-
LINGUISTICS: A Series of Monographs and Treatises

Harry A. Whitaker, Series Editor
DEPARTMENT OF PSYCHOLOGY
THE UNIVERSITY OF ROCHESTER
ROCHESTER, NEW YORK

HAIGANOOSH WHITAKER and HARRY A. WHITAKER (Eds.).
Studies in Neurolinguistics, Volumes 1, 2, 3 and 4

NORMAN J. LASS (Ed.). Contemporary Issues in Experimental Phonetics

JASON W. BROWN. Mind, Brain, and Consciousness: The Neuropsychology
of Cognition

SIDNEY J. SEGALOWITZ and FREDERIC A. GRUBER (Eds.). Language Development and Neurological Theory

SUSAN CURTISS. Genie: A Psycholinguistic Study of a Modern-Day "Wild
Child"

JOHN MACNAMARA (Ed.). Language Learning and Thought

I. M. SCHLESINGER and LILA NAMIR (Eds.). Sign Language of the Deaf:
Psychological, Linguistic, and Sociological Perspectives

WILLIAM C. RITCHIE (Ed.). Second Language Acquisition Research: Issues
and Implications

PATRICIA SIPLE (Ed.). Understanding Language through Sign Language
Research

MARTIN L. ALBERT and LORAINE K. OBLER. The Bilingual Brain: Neuro-
psychiological and Neurolinguistic Aspects of Bilingualism

TALMY GIVÓN. On Understanding Grammar

CHARLES J. FILLMORE, DANIEL KEMPLER and WILLIAM S-Y. WANG (Eds.).
Individual Differences in Language Ability and Language Behavior

JEANNINE HERRON (Ed.). Neuropsychology of Left-Handedness

FRANÇOIS BOLLER and MAUREEN DENNIS (Eds.). Auditory Comprehension: Clinical and Experimental Studies with the Token Test

R. W. RIEBER (Ed.). Language Development and Aphasia in Children:
New Essays and a Translation of "Kindersprache und Aphasie" by
Emil Fröschels

GRACE H. YENI-KOMSHIAN, JAMES F. KAVANAGH and CHARLES A.
FERGUSON (Eds.). Child Phonology, Volume 1: Production and Volume
2: Perception

In preparation

FRANCIS J. PIROZZOLO and MERLIN C. WITTROCK (Eds.). Neuropsychological and Cognitive Processes in Reading

JASON W. BROWN (Ed.). Jargonaphasia